D0214490

Public Key Infrastructure

OTHER INFORMATION SECURITY BOOKS FROM AUERBACH

Asset Protection and Security Management Handbook
POA Publishing
ISBN: 0-8493-1603-0

Building a Global Information Assurance Program
Raymond J. Curts and Douglas E. Campbell
ISBN: 0-8493-1368-6

Building an Information Security Awareness Program
Mark B. Desman
ISBN: 0-8493-0116-5

Critical Incident Management
Alan B. Sterneckert
ISBN: 0-8493-0010-X

Cyber Crime Investigator's Field Guide
Bruce Middleton
ISBN: 0-8493-1192-6

Cyber Forensics: A Field Manual for Collecting, Examining, and Preserving Evidence of Computer Crimes
Albert J. Marcella, Jr. and Robert S. Greenfield
ISBN: 0-8493-0955-7

The Ethical Hack: A Framework for Business Value Penetration Testing
James S. Tiller
ISBN: 0-8493-1609-X

The Hacker's Handbook: The Strategy Behind Breaking into and Defending Networks
Susan Young and Dave Aitel
ISBN: 0-8493-0888-7

Information Security Architecture: An Integrated Approach to Security in the Organization
Jan Killmeyer Tudor
ISBN: 0-8493-9988-2

Information Security Fundamentals
Thomas R. Peltier
ISBN: 0-8493-1957-9

Information Security Management Handbook, 5th Edition
Harold F. Tipton and Micki Krause
ISBN: 0-8493-1997-8

Information Security Policies, Procedures, and Standards: Guidelines for Effective Information Security Management
Thomas R. Peltier
ISBN: 0-8493-1137-3

Information Security Risk Analysis
Thomas R. Peltier
ISBN: 0-8493-0880-1

Information Technology Control and Audit
Fredrick Gallegos, Daniel Manson, and Sandra Allen-Senft
ISBN: 0-8493-9994-7

Investigator's Guide to Steganography
Gregory Kipper
0-8493-2433-5

Managing a Network Vulnerability Assessment
Thomas Peltier, Justin Peltier, and John A. Blackley
ISBN: 0-8493-1270-1

Network Perimeter Security: Building Defense In-Depth
Cliff Riggs
ISBN: 0-8493-1628-6

The Practical Guide to HIPAA Privacy and Security Compliance
Kevin Beaver and Rebecca Herold
ISBN: 0-8493-1953-6

A Practical Guide to Security Engineering and Information Assurance
Debra S. Herrmann
ISBN: 0-8493-1163-2

The Privacy Papers: Managing Technology, Consumer, Employee and Legislative Actions
Rebecca Herold
ISBN: 0-8493-1248-5

Public Key Infrastructure: Building Trusted Applications and Web Services
John R. Vacca
ISBN: 0-8493-0822-4

Securing and Controlling Cisco Routers
Peter T. Davis
ISBN: 0-8493-1290-6

Strategic Information Security
John Wylder
ISBN: 0-8493-2041-0

Surviving Security: How to Integrate People, Process, and Technology, Second Edition
Amanda Andress
ISBN: 0-8493-2042-9

A Technical Guide to IPSec Virtual Private Networks
James S. Tiller
ISBN: 0-8493-0876-3

Using the Common Criteria for IT Security Evaluation
Debra S. Herrmann
ISBN: 0-8493-1404-6

AUERBACH PUBLICATIONS

www.auerbach-publications.com
To Order Call: 1-800-272-7737 • Fax: 1-800-374-3401
E-mail: orders@crcpress.com

Public Key Infrastructure

Building Trusted Applications and Web Services

John R. Vacca

AUERBACH PUBLICATIONS

A CRC Press Company

Boca Raton   London   New York   Washington, D.C.

Library of Congress Cataloging-in-Publication Data

Public key infrastructure : building trusted applications and Web services / edited by John
R. Vacca.
　　p. cm.
　Includes bibliographical references and index.
　ISBN 0-8493-0822-4 (alk. paper)
　　1. Computer security. 2. Computer networks--Security measures. 3. Public key
infrastructure (Computer security) 4. Web services. I. Vacca, John R.

QA76.9.A25P85 2004
005.8--dc22

2003070898

This book contains information obtained from authentic and highly regarded sources. Reprinted material
is quoted with permission, and sources are indicated. A wide variety of references are listed. Reasonable
efforts have been made to publish reliable data and information, but the author and the publisher cannot
assume responsibility for the validity of all materials or for the consequences of their use.

Neither this book nor any part may be reproduced or transmitted in any form or by any means, electronic
or mechanical, including photocopying, microfilming, and recording, or by any information storage or
retrieval system, without prior permission in writing from the publisher.

All rights reserved. Authorization to photocopy items for internal or personal use, or the personal or
internal use of specific clients, may be granted by CRC Press LLC, provided that $1.50 per page
photocopied is paid directly to Copyright Clearance Center, 222 Rosewood Drive, Danvers, MA 01923
USA. The fee code for users of the Transactional Reporting Service is ISBN 0-8493-0822-
4/04/$0.00+$1.50. The fee is subject to change without notice. For organizations that have been granted
a photocopy license by the CCC, a separate system of payment has been arranged.

The consent of CRC Press LLC does not extend to copying for general distribution, for promotion, for
creating new works, or for resale. Specific permission must be obtained in writing from CRC Press LLC
for such copying.

Direct all inquiries to CRC Press LLC, 2000 N.W. Corporate Blvd., Boca Raton, Florida 33431.

Trademark Notice: Product or corporate names may be trademarks or registered trademarks, and are
used only for identification and explanation, without intent to infringe.

Visit the Auerbach Web site at www.auerbach-publications.com

© 2004 by CRC Press LLC
Auerbach is an imprint of CRC Press LLC

No claim to original U.S. Government works
International Standard Book Number 0-8493-0822-4
Library of Congress Card Number 2003070898
Printed in the United States of America 1 2 3 4 5 6 7 8 9 0
Printed on acid-free paper

Chapter 2, "Growing a Tree of Trust" by Mark Merkow, © Jupitermedia Corporation

Chapter 3, "In PKI We Trust?" by Mike Fratto, © CMP Media LLC

Chapter 6, "Understanding Digital Certificates and Secure Sockets Layer (SSL)" by Peter Robinson, © Entrust

Chapter 7, "CA System Attacks" by Deloitte Touche Tohmatsu, © Deloitte Touche Tohmatsu

Chapter 8, "Key Escrow versus Key Recovery" by Bob Walder, © The NSS Group

Chapter 10, "Managed Public-Key Infrastructure: Securing Your Business Applications" © VeriSign, Inc.

Chapter 12, "PKI Design Issues" by Douglas P. Barton, Anthony S. Moran, and Luke O'Connor, © Queensland University of Technology, DSTC Pty Ltd.

Chapter 13, "PKI Return on Investment" by Derek Brink, © RSA Security Inc.

Chapter 15, "Architecture for Public-Key Infrastructure (APKI)" by The Open Group, © The Open Group

Chapter 17, "VeriSign's Foundation in Managed Security Services" by Allan Cary and Paul Johnson, © IDC

Chapter 18, "Implementation and Deployment" by June Leung, Amir Jafri, and Andrew Farmer, © FundSERV, Inc.

Chapter 23, "Ten Risks of PKI: What You're Not Being Told about Public Key Infrastructure" by Carl Ellison and Bruce Schneier, © Counterpane Internet Security, Inc.

Chapter 22, "Obtaining a Certificate," Office of Information Technologies, University of Virginia, reprinted with permission.

Chapter 25, "Certificate Revocation with VeriSign Managed PKI: Flexible, Open Revocation Solutions for Today's Enterprise PKI Needs" by VeriSign, © VeriSign, Inc.

Chapter 26, "Summary, Conclusions, and Recommendations" by M. Benantar, © IBM

DEDICATION

To my wife, Bee Vacca, for her love, her help,
and her understanding of my long work hours.

John R. Vacca

CONTENTS

ix

SECTION II: Analyzing and Designing Public Key Infrastructures

SECTION III: Implementing PKI

SECTION IV: Managing PKI

26   Summary, Conclusions, and Recommendations 321
M. Benantar

SECTION V: Appendices

Appendix A: Contributors of PKI Software Solutions 351

FOREWORD

Public Key Infrastructures (PKIs) are one of the key building blocks of the digital future. Without security, electronic communications hold little value in a competitive arena of business management and operations. The need for security has also permeated government and law enforcement operations. This has become even more true since the September 11, 2001 terrorist attacks on the United States. PKIs will play a key role in the efforts of The Department of Homeland Security (DHS) in implementing *The National Strategy for the Physical Protection of Critical Infrastructures and Key Assets* and *The National Strategy to Secure Cyberspace.*

Security professionals and application developers, along with IT and network staff in all types of organizations, will eventually need to work with PKIs. This book provides an extensive analysis of PKI standards and the type of certificate authorities (CAs) services available. Design issues and architectures are also expertly covered. But, this book goes beyond theory and analysis to explain numerous implementation issues including schedules, costs, and performance.

To move through an IT career, and especially to move into management positions, IT professionals need a well-rounded knowledge of secure computing and communications technology. It is essential for IT professionals to keep up with a quickly changing world; this book provides the knowledge that is necessary to achieve professional growth and development.

This book is written for people that need to cut through the confusion about PKIs and get down to adoption and deployment. The book starts with the basic concepts and takes readers through all of the necessary learning steps to enable them to effectively use PKIs.

Michael Erbschloe
Vice President of Research, Computer Economics
Carlsbad, California

ACKNOWLEDGMENTS

There are many people whose efforts on this book have contributed to its successful completion. I owe each a debt of gratitude and want to take this opportunity to offer my sincere thanks.

A very special thanks to my publisher, Rich O'Hanley, without whose continued interest and support this book would not have been possible. I also thank managing editor and art director, Claire Miller, who provided staunch support and encouragement when it was most needed, as well as my project editor, Andrea Demby, whose fine editorial work has been invaluable. Thanks also to my marketing manager, Michelle Reyes, whose efforts on this book have been greatly appreciated. And, a special thanks to Michael Erbschloe who wrote the foreword for this book.

Thanks to my wife, Bee Vacca, for her love, her help, and her understanding of my long work hours. I wish to thank the organizations and individuals who granted me permission to use the research material and information necessary for the completion of this book.

Finally, thanks to all the other people at Auerbach Publications whose many talents and skills are essential to a finished book.

INTRODUCTION

Traditionally, information technology (IT) systems have been largely centralized, with administration under the control of a single management domain, and with a fixed set of relationships between components. Not surprisingly, security mechanisms to support these systems tend to reflect this structure. This has led to the deployment of inflexible and non-scalable mechanisms, which are administered under a single, monolithic security policy. However, the rise of E-commerce and the trend toward decentralization is beginning to change the way you think about security. Users now have a situation in which entities in multiple domains may need to communicate with each other securely, and where relationships between these entities may appear and disappear dynamically. With the move toward disintermediation, users may sometimes need to establish trusted paths between systems that previously had no awareness of each other's existence. In addition, mobile staff need to be able to securely and remotely access resources as though they are simply sitting in their office attached to their local area network, and enterprises need to reach out to the Internet as though it were an extension of their own enterprise network.

All these challenges are leading to the emergence of new and more flexible security models. In the past, when two entities wished to communicate with each other securely, they needed to establish a shared secret such as a secret password or a one-time pad. This meant having to first establish some trusted means by which to agree on this shared secret (e.g., registered mail or a trusted key distribution service). Not only was this time-consuming and non-scalable, it also made it difficult for two parties with no preestablished relationship to undertake secure communications. However, all that changed when, in 1976, Whitfield Diffie and Martin Hellman published their landmark paper entitled "New Directions in Cryptography." This paper described a mechanism that would enable two parties to establish a secret key for secure communications without the need for a separate trusted channel. This system used two asymmetric keys: one that was kept private and one that was made publicly available. By exchanging their public values and combining them with their private keys, both parties could agree on a symmetric secret key, without an eavesdropper being able to deduce the same key by observing the communication channel. This mechanism became known as *public key cryptography*. This was an important discovery, as now parties could establish secure communications with each other dynamically, and without the need to form a prior relationship. Subsequent advances in public key cryptography led to other systems that used the same idea of a public and private key. Systems such as RSA (named for its creators Rivest, Shamir, and Adelman) were developed that enabled not only the secure exchange of secret keys, but also the creation of digital signatures. A digital signature is a mechanism for adding unique data to a document in such a way that only the holder of a given private key could have generated it, but anyone with the corresponding public key can verify the signature's authenticity. Digital signatures are extremely important for E-commerce, as they enable us to take the well-established and legally recognized practice of signing contracts and other agreements in the physical paper-based work and apply it to electronic documents. Indeed, it has been the adoption of digital signature technologies more than any other advance that has enabled the promise of a system for global secure electronic commerce to come one step closer to reality.

However, it is now more than 20 years since these technologies emerged into the spotlight, and you are only now beginning to see public key cryptography and digital signatures emerge as a ubiquitous part of the IT landscape. The problem lies not in the technology itself, but in the difficulty of managing one of human nature's most elusive qualities — trust. Supposing that Melanie has a digital signed document from Bert and that using Bert's public key she is able to verify that the signature is valid. The question is: how can Melanie be sure that she has Bert's public key, and not merely the key of some malicious person pretending to be Bert? To solve the problem of secure distribution of public keys, the concept of a digital certificate was introduced. A certificate is a structured document that binds some information (such as Bert's name) to a public key, and is digitally signed by a trusted third party called a certification authority (CA). To verify a certificate, the user of the public key (sometimes called the relying party) must first obtain the public key of the CA by some other trusted means. Although it seems that you are now back to square one, the difference is that you now only have to get one key out-of-band in order to communicate with any entity that has a certificate issued by that trusted CA. In addition, if the CA is able to certify the public key of other CAs, which can in turn certify other CAs and so on, you will be able to securely communicate with any entity, provided that you can find a chain of certificates between the CA that you trust and the CA that certified the key of the entity with whom you wish to communicate. In deciding whether to trust a given CA, it is important to know the particular policy that a CA uses to establish the identity of its subscribers. For example, you may be willing to accept a policy in which identification is done by doing a mail-back to the subscriber's e-mail address for some applications, but for others you might want to be assured that the person in the CERTIFICATE has been identified by some stronger means, such as by presenting a driver's license or passport to the CA or some authorized notary. Naturally, the management of these public key certificates on a global scale takes a considerable amount of effort. Not only do you need to ensure that you have a sufficiently interlinked network of CAs to ensure that any relying party can verify any given certificate, but you need systems to issue and store certificates, to determine their authenticity, and to revoke certificates if keys become compromised. In addition, to effectively utilize public key cryptography and digital signatures, you may need other services such as a non-repudiation service, digital notary or digital timestamping service. You need all these services to work together and to have a common understanding of the formats and protocols necessary to achieve their aims. You have come to know the collection of these components as a public key infrastructure (PKI).

Today, Web services adoption is gaining speed and some Web services security specifications are growing into a new phase of maturity. While not yet standards, some specifications are leading the pack and present opportunities for connecting Web services to a *trust infrastructure.*

A trust infrastructure built on Web services and public key infrastructure (PKI) can serve several enterprise purposes as an integral part of applications. First of all, Web services are now being widely deployed. Enterprises are now looking for some trust mechanism to authenticate their Web services transactions as providers or consumers of a service. Although a directory scheme such as Universal Description, Discovery, and Integration (UDDI) can connect Web services providers and users, the UDDI specification has yet to finalize an authentication mechanism. So, if you use UDDI and find a new Web service to suit your enterprise needs, you will still need to make a phone call or a visit to the Web service provider to verify that the vendor offering the Web service is who they say they are. Although this extra level of personal authentication makes sense for long-term enterprise relationships, it undermines the practicality of Web services and UDDI for smaller transactions and one-time or infrequent enterprise relationships. To be valuable to enterprises, Web services must reflect the often subtle, complex, and, above all, contractual relationships of trust among enterprises. That is where a trust infrastructure built on digital certificates and PKI can help. And, because you would be using Web services already, a trust infrastructure built on Web services is a good fit for Web services authentication.

A Web services trust infrastructure also has broader enterprise applications. You can streamline authentication in applications and transactions using PKI and certificates. So, providing a trust infrastructure as a Web service enables your enterprise to implement trusted transactions without investing in the development and maintenance of your own trust infrastructure. Providing this as a Web service offers the same benefits as the general promise of Web services — you can focus on your enterprise and customer expertise and plug into a Web service without gaining that expertise yourself.

The value of a PKI is proportional to the number of users on the network; it is very valuable if you can authenticate messages sent from anyone inside your enterprise. It becomes exponentially more valuable if you can authenticate anyone in any enterprise, such as all your partners and suppliers. Now, the Web services architecture provides an effective way to manage data in large distributed enterprises. So, would it not be nice to leverage the emerging Web services framework to make PKIs more efficient?

PKI's ability to manage digital certificates and cryptographic keys is one of its critical features. A number of protocols have been specified for certificate management, such as Certificate Request Syntax (CRS), CMC (Certificate Management using CRS), and Online Certificate Status Protocol (OCSP). Each of these protocols presents an onerous set of requirements for those tasked with implementing them. For example, because certificates are typically shipped in Abstract Symbolic Notation (ASN.1), a binary format, certificate manipulation software is difficult to implement, extraordinarily complicated to debug, and frequently dependent on baroque, high-priced proprietary toolkits to process ASN.1 structures. Furthermore, once implemented, your homegrown PKI is unlikely to interface with other PKIs. Although you might be able to exchange secured messages within your enterprise, you might not be able to exchange secured electronic messages with your partners and suppliers without considerable further development. If you are considering implementing applications secured using client certificates, these are some of the challenges you will face for each client application that will depend on PKI.

Despite these apparent shortcomings, PKI provides a promising mechanism for introducing trust into the anonymous, machine-to-machine world of Web services. In the same way that Secure Sockets Layer (SSL) server certificates provide proven security to users performing transactions over the Internet, digital certificates will enable Web services to authenticate one another and to provide secure, high-value automated transactions, without requiring extensive PKI infrastructure built into a client application. The current proposal for Web services security (WS-Security) provides for digital signatures within SOAP headers, and concretely points toward Web services transactions that are secured using digital certificates.

The preceding all came about back in 2001, when an industry group led by Microsoft, VeriSign, and webMethods announced support for a specification, known as the XML Key Management Specification (XKMS), to deliver the PKI-based trust through the Web services framework.

XKMS combines the interoperability of XML with the security of PKI. XKMS promises to meet today's requirements for interoperability, reduced integration costs, and higher levels of trust. Using the principles of the Web services architecture, XKMS provides a way for applications to maintain and exchange data about public keys. The XML Signature specification defines XML formats for describing public keys and digital certificates. XKMS uses data formats defined in XML Signature to enable applications to exchange and manage those public keys. In short, XKMS makes it easier and less expensive for applications to interface with PKIs.

In addition, XKMS can also streamline the process of certificate enrollment. If you have an enterprise messaging application that enables users to send digitally signed purchase orders, the first time a user starts the application, he or she must enroll for a digital certificate by going to the Web site of a certificate provider. With XKMS, however, the user does not have to leave the application to obtain a certificate. Rather, the XKMS-enabled application generates a key-pair, then registers the public key with a CA. The XKMS-enabled CA can be anyone from an internal PKI solution to an outsourced PKI provider such as VeriSign. If required, the CA can, in turn, generate X.509 certificate data. XKMS also specifies server-generated key-pairs, although as of this writing, this feature remains unimplemented by major vendors pending resolution of issues surrounding service-managed private keys. Public key revocation and renewal, also supported by XKMS, further simplify the integration of PKI functionality with enterprise administrative and account management systems. You can see how this is critical for Web services, which must be able to dynamically enroll for certificates without human intervention.

XML Signature defines a syntax for representing X.509 certificates. Depending on implementation choices made by the XKMS service provider, X.509 data may or may not be accepted or returned by the XKMS service. In general, however, enough applications use X.509 certificates that you can safely expect to get that data wherever you might need it. But one goal of XKMS is to focus applications that use PKI on the use of public keys as opposed to certificates. In an XKMS world, certificate data is managed transparently — all your application requires is the public key or the knowledge that a given public key is valid.

Therefore, with the preceding in mind, a public key infrastructure (PKI) consists of protocols, services, and standards supporting applications of public key cryptography. The term "PKI," which is relatively recent, is defined variously in current literature. PKI sometimes refers simply to a trust hierarchy based on public key certificates, and in other contexts embraces encryption-end digital signature services provided to end-user applications as well. A middle view is that a PKI includes services and protocols for managing public keys, often through the use of certification authority (CA) and registration authority (RA) components, but not necessarily for performing cryptographic operations with the keys. Among the services likely to be found in a PKI are the following:

- *Key registration:* issuing a new certificate for a public key.
- *Certificate revocation:* canceling a previously issued certificate.
- *Key selection:* obtaining a party's public key.
- *Trust evaluation:* determining whether a certificate is valid and what operations it authorizes.
- *Key recovery* has also been suggested as a possible aspect of a PKI.

There is no single pervasive public key infrastructure today, although efforts to define a PKI generally presume there will eventually be one, or, increasingly, that multiple independent PKIs will evolve with varying degrees of coexistence and interoperability. In this sense, the PKI today can be viewed akin to local and wide area networks in the 1980s, before there was widespread connectivity via the Internet. As a result of this view toward a global PKI, certificate formats and trust mechanisms are defined in an open and scalable manner, but with usage profiles corresponding to trust and policy requirements of particular customer and application environments. For example, it is usually accepted that there will be multiple "root" or "top-level" certificate authorities in a global PKI, not just one "root," although in a local PKI there may be only one root. Accordingly, protocols are defined with provision for specifying which roots are trusted by a given application or user.

Efforts to define a PKI today are underway in several governments as well as standards organizations. The U.S. Department of the Treasury and NIST both have PKI programs, as do Canada and the United Kingdom. NIST has published an interoperability profile for PKI components; it specifies algorithms and certificate formats that certification authorities should support. Some standards bodies that have worked on PKI aspects have included tile IETF's PKIX and SPKI Working Groups and The Open Group.

Most PKI definitions are based on X.509 certificates, with the notable exception of the IETF's SPKI. In other words, the purpose of PKI is to provide an environment that addresses today's enterprise, legal, network, and security demands for trust and confidentiality in data transmission and storage. PKI accomplishes these goals for an enterprise through embedded policy and technology components. These components determine and identify the roles, responsibilities, constraints, range of use, and services available.

Furthermore, PKI is a system for supporting digital signatures and document encryption for an enterprise. It is fast becoming essential for effective, secure E-commerce and to fulfill general security and authentication requirements over nonsecure networks (like the Net). The banking services are the most popular usage of this technology, which is quickly spreading over all the applications that need security to be fully operational.

As previously explained, the public key infrastructure provides for digital certificates that can identify individuals or enterprises and directory services that can store and, when necessary, revoke them. PKI is the underlying embedded technology that provides security for the Secure Sockets Layer (SSL) and Hypertext Transfer Protocol Secure Sockets (HTTPS) protocols, which are used extensively to conduct secure E-business over the Internet.

Using PKI, messaging systems can digitally sign messages, encrypt messages, or both, providing the authentication, integrity, and confidentiality that enterprises need in an asynchronous world. To enable these functions, however, enterprises must first enable basic PKI functions, such as issuing and managing key-pairs and digital certificates. That has many enterprises considering how they will support PKI, either internally or through outsourced services.

Finally, managed PKI embedded Web services remove much of the burden of securing and maintaining a PKI by hosting the server hardware and software in secure, monitored, and well-maintained facilities. Procedures are in place for every process the service provider performs, from adding new administrators to generating audit logs, and how these processes are audited.

PURPOSE

The purpose of this book is to show globally how public key infrastructures (PKIs) are paving the way for secure communications and Web services within organizations and on the public Internet. It will also show how, with the appropriate layers of security throughout the network, a PKI can put to rest the concerns of how to protect assets, freeing you to concentrate on adding value to your employees, your customers, and your enterprise partners. The book will also take a close look at what constitutes effective public key infrastructures, why their protection is crucial to success, and some thoughts for your consideration prior to implementing your own PKI.

In addition, the book will walk you through the steps of certificate management: requesting a certificate, obtaining a certificate, storing a certificate within the browser, using a certificate, and revoking a certificate. It also aims to remove much of the mystery surrounding requesting, obtaining, storing, using, and removing digital certificates via browsers.

Also, this book looks into expectations for a certificate authority (CA) and what a CA will expect of you. It will also show you how to use a CA as a template to look at some commercial CA outsourcing solutions to help you focus your search for a custom PKI.

Finally, this book details how public key infrastructures address the technological challenges presented by electronic commerce, and how the work of worldwide governments and other bodies are helping to provide a framework for deploying this technology. It describes an approach to the integration of a Kerberos or DCE infrastructure with a PKI, using interface standards that are consistent with the architecture for public key infrastructure (APKI).

SCOPE

Public key infrastructures (PKIs) are paving the way for secure communications within organizations and on the public Internet. This book also discusses how digital certificates allow end entities to use encryption and/or digital signatures to secure information between users and applications. All IT organizations should have a plan to implement this technology in their future digital certificate-aware applications. In addition to commercial organizations and governments, this book addresses, but is not limited to, the following line items as part of a PKI transition path:

- *PKI technology overview/technology transfer.* To fully benefit from the public key technology in a large-scale environment, an understanding of the current and future PKI technology and uses is required. The security goals provided by the technology are entity authentication (authorization) and end-to-end cryptographic services (single sign-on, mutual authentication, message privacy and integrity, and fine grain authorization).
- *PKI components.* A PKI relies on many existing enterprise services (Directory and Authentication servers). A certification authority (CA) server is responsible for the issuing and revoking of digital certificates. A digital certificate is binding (notarization) between an end entity and a public key. Most enterprises are deciding to manage

their own CA instead of outsourcing it to a third party (e.g., VeriSign, GTE, CyberTrust, etc.).

■ *PKI security policy, standards, and guidelines.* All PKI security policy, standards, and guidelines must be consistent with the overall enterprise security foundation.

■ *PKI tactical and strategic planning and transitions.* Time to market is a constraint for tactical planning that involves assisting an enterprise planning to integrate this technology into existing applications and/or plan for a long-term solution.

■ *Timeframe.* The time necessary for PKI transition planning depends on the size of the enterprise and its security awareness, as well as resources.

This book leaves little doubt that a new-world infrastructure in the area of PKI is about to be constructed. There is no question that it will benefit both enterprises and governments, as well as their advanced citizens. For the disadvantaged regions of the world, however, the coming PKI revolution could be one of those rare technological events that enable traditional societies to leap ahead and long-dormant economies to flourish in security.

INTENDED AUDIENCE

This book is primarily targeted toward domestic and international system administrators, government computer security officials, network administrators, senior managers, engineers, sales representatives, marketing staff, World Wide Web developers, military senior top brass, and other PKI users. Basically, the book is targeted at all types of people and organizations around the world that have Internet, extranet, and intranet security concerns. In addition, the targeted audience also includes:

■ Scientists
■ Engineers
■ Educators
■ Top-level executives
■ Information technology (IT) and department managers
■ Programmers and technical staff
■ The massive target market of more than 100 million Internet users

Finally, this book is written for anyone who wants to understand computer security. This author anticipates that most readers will use the information in this book to assess the applicability of specific technologies for their environments.

PLAN OF THE BOOK

This book is organized into five sections and 26 chapters — including the appendices (which include a glossary of PKI terms and acronyms).

Section I: Overview of PKI Technology

The first section of this book identifies public key infrastructures (PKIs) as the highest layer of application security that sits atop a secure computer operating environment. It also introduces the concepts of a certificate authority (CA), public key cryptographic standards (PKCSs), certificate revocation lists (CRLs), and certificate practices statements (CPSs), and offers some reasons for wanting to migrate to a PKI.

Chapter 1, "Public Key Infrastructures (PKIs): What Are They?," provides an overview of how to use applied cryptography and how PKIs govern the distribution and management of cryptographic keys and digital certificates. In addition, the chapter describes the use of effective PKIs that are based on the public key cryptographic standards (PKCSs).

Chapter 2, "Growing a Tree of Trust," takes a close look at what constitutes effective public key infrastructures, why their protection is crucial to success, and some thoughts for your consideration prior to implementing your own PKI.

Chapter 3, "In PKI We Trust," discusses the cost and complexity of rolling out a PKI.

Chapter 4, "PKI Standards," provides guidance on PKI standards and specifications with regard to information security.

Chapter 5, "Types of Vendor and Third-Party CA Systems," takes a close look at some of the vendor and third-party CA and PKI systems. It also discusses in detail RSA's Keon Certificate Server — the new public key infrastructure (PKI) that helps organizations worldwide move their businesses to the Internet and take advantage of E-commerce.

Chapter 6, "Understanding Digital Certificates and Secure Sockets Layer (SSL)," covers digital certificates and Secure Sockets Layers (SSLs).

Chapter 7, "CA System Attacks," addresses why CA systems may be the subject of attacks through several different ways. It also discusses why, in addition to hacker attacks from the outside, CA operations are vulnerable to collusion, sabotage, disgruntlement, or outright theft by employees from within.

Chapter 8, "Key Escrow versus Key Recovery," discusses key escrow versus key recovery.

Chapter 9, "An Approach to Formally Compare and Query Certification Practice Statements," compares and queries certificate practice statements (CPSs).

Chapter 10, "Managed Public Key Infrastructure: Securing Your Business Applications," discusses how to secure your business applications.

Chapter 11, "PKI Readiness," addresses why you might be ready to embark down the PKI path if several of the following conditions are true: you have migrated your application interfaces to Web browser technology, including the access to mainframe and midrange system applications; you have migrated to browser based e-mail systems that support S/MIME and digital signing of messages; you have migrated to application software that can deal with signed documents and messages to eliminate the routing of paperwork for authority determination purposes; and you have prepared for logical access controls via smart cards or token devices that store private keys and digital certificates.

Section II: Analyzing and Designing Public Key Infrastructures

Section II describes PKI design issues, cost justification, standards design issues, and architectural design.

Chapter 12, "PKI Design Issues," concentrates on a small but interesting area of software security based on public key cryptographic technology with regard to PKI design.

Chapter 13, "PKI Return on Investment," is not about PKI technology; rather, it is about time and money.

Chapter 14, "PKI Standards Design Issues," provides a brief overview of signature design technology standards, discusses existing and proposed digital signature design legislation in a range of jurisdictions around the world, and draws conclusions on the need for specific electronic signature design legislation.

Chapter 15, "Architecture for Public Key Infrastructure (APKI)," discusses PKI architectural design considerations. The first part of the chapter describes the requirements on a public key infrastructure. Next, the second part of the chapter presents the high-level structure of the PKI architecture by grouping the architecture's design components into broad functional categories. The third part of the chapter enumerates the design components in each of the architecture's functional categories, describes the functionality of each design component, lists existing specifications that could serve as candidate standards for each design component's interfaces and protocols, identifies where negotiation facilities are required to deal with the probable existence of a multiplicity of security mechanisms, enumerates important public-key-related protocols, and discusses the need for environment-specific profiles. Finally, the chapter discusses the use of hardware security devices in the architecture.

Section III: Implementing PKI

This section of the book covers development, implementation, and management of advanced PKI options and strategies that will forever change how organizations do business now and in the foreseeable future.

Chapter 16, "Implementing Secure Web Services Requirements Using PKI," begins this section with a discussion of how to implement secure Web services requirements using PKI.

Chapter 17, "VeriSign's Foundation in Managed Security Services," covers managed security services.

Chapter 18, "PKI Deployment — Business Issues," provides readers with information that may help enterprises prepare for their pilot project or testing phase of implementing PKI.

Chapter 19, "Implementation Costs," analyzes costs for the following: key-pairs, smart cards and infrastructure, key management and directory, and applications upgrade and support.

Chapter 20, "PKI Performance," covers what you should expect from a certificate authority (CA), and what a CA can expect of you.

Section IV: Managing PKI

Section IV walks through the process of certificate requests, issuance, usage, and revocation — giving you a better understanding of what work you will need to do behind the scenes to assure user convenience, flexibility, and most important — security.

Chapter 21, "Requesting a Certificate," focuses within the PKI, where the definition of the CA is well-defined, operating in conjunction with a registration authority (RA). It also discusses why the RA role or function makes the actual decisions of who may receive certificates and who may not. The RA *owns* the records that dictate the proof of identity and the rights of certificate users. Usually, the RA function is performed in one of two basic ways.

Chapter 22, "Obtaining a Certificate," presents a framework for dealing with the issuance of a certificate. Once the CA verifies the requester's information, the CA wrap the requester's public key (half the key-pair from the generation step) in a digital certificate, sign it using the CA private key, and return the certificate to the browser. The completed certificate and various optional steps for storing it are also discussed.

Chapter 23, "Ten Risks of PKI: What You Are Not Being Told about Public Key Infrastructure," covers the ten risks of PKI.

Chapter 24, "Using a Certificate," discusses why when you visit a Web site that requires a digital certificate for authentication, a message is sent to your browser to open the certificate store and ask for permission to send the appropriate certificate. Examples of certificate selection forms are also examined.

Chapter 25, "Certificate Revocation with VeriSign Managed PKI," discusses how to revoke a certificate.

Chapter 26, "Summary, Conclusions, and Recommendations," details how public key infrastructures address the technological challenges presented by electronic commerce, and how the work of worldwide governments and other bodies is helping to provide a framework for deploying this technology on a global scale. It also describes an approach to the integration of a Kerberos or DCE infrastructure with a PKI, using interface standards that are consistent with the architecture for public key infrastructure (APKI). The motivation for such integration is to allow Kerberos and DCE to take advantage of the authentication services provided by an existing public key infrastructure. This final chapter also discusses why PKI is one of the most misunderstood and troubling forms of security ever inspired. Finally, because Internet messaging is now a reality, this chapter discusses what is needed for secure messaging. In other words, what remains is to add the strong authentication, confidentiality, and integrity services to produce secure messaging. The S/MIME standard for secure messaging, which has been adopted by all the major vendors, is rapidly making its way onto the desktops of the world. However, to complete the picture of global, unbounded secure messaging, organizations must also put in place a global, unbounded public key infrastructure that can, with adequate assurance of authentication, deliver public keys of corresponding parties to each other.

Section V: Appendices

Six appendices and a glossary provide additional resources that are available for PKI. Appendix A is a list of contributors of PKI software. Appendix B is a list of PKI products: implementations, toolkits, and vendors. Appendix C is a comprehensive list of CAs. Appendix D is a list of information security management issue standards. Appendix E is a list of information security technical elements standards. Appendix F discusses basic certificates for Web administration. Finally, there is a glossary of PKI technology terms and acronyms.

CONVENTIONS

This book has several conventions to help you find your way around and to help you find important facts, notes, cautions, and warnings:

- *Sidebars.* We use sidebars to highlight related information, give an example, discuss an item in greater detail, or help you make sense of the swirl of terms, acronyms, and abbreviations so abundant to this subject. The sidebars are meant to supplement each chapter's topic. If you are in a hurry, on a cover-to-cover read, skip the sidebars. If you are quickly flipping through the book looking for juicy information, read only the sidebars.
- *Notes.* A note highlights a special point of interest about the PKI topic.
- *Caution.* A caution tells you to watch your step to avoid any PKI-related problems (security, etc.).
- *Warning.* A warning alerts you to the fact that a PKI-related problem is imminent or will probably occur (security, etc.).

John R. Vacca
Pomeroy, Ohio

1

OVERVIEW OF PKI TECHNOLOGY

Protecting the private keys that are tied to a digital certificate's public key, especially those keys that are used to sign lower-level digital certificates, is very serious business under any PKI uses. Without this protection, the notion of any trust goes out the window and the infrastructure will inevitably fail.

Stolen (copied) private keys from any end entity could be used to transact or communicate without any cause for suspicion. It is the same as a stolen identity, where a thief masquerades as the legitimate key holder without any reason to suspect wrongdoing. Similarly, if the keys for a certificate authority (CA) are compromised, the repercussions could be severe. With a stolen (copied) CA key in hand, a would-be forger could issue bogus certificates without any way to detect the forgery. Protection of all CA keys is absolutely critical to maintain the PKI's level of trust.

The more a private key is used to sign messages, the more instances a would-be attacker can obtain for cryptanalysis. If these keys are changed often and regularly, stored under North American Air Defense Command (NORAD)-like conditions, and managed well, they will remain safe from all forms of attack.

PKI cryptographic keys are extremely sophisticated in deterring would-be cryptosystem attackers. Because of its robustness, it is not really worth the effort to try breaking the cryptography. Even with all the computers on the planet working in tandem, an attacker would have a tough time trying to reverse-engineer or attempting brute-force methods (trying all possible combinations of a key) to determine the key. CAs will normally guard against such attacks anyway by using extremely long keys. They will also change their keys regularly and re-issue new certificates whenever they do. Rather than try to discover the key, thieves are better off trying to steal the actual key from where it is stored, so extra precautions must be taken to ensure that this cannot happen. Because CAs clearly understand the value of the keys in their possession, they go out of their way to keep them safe from all possible attacks, both physical and logical.

Every end entity under a PKI is responsible for the safety of its own keys and certificates. This is a central theme and cannot be over-emphasized. A PKI's ability to guarantee assurances of authentication, message integrity, privacy, and security cannot be realized once keys get into the wrong hands. Private keys are valuable. Although some are considered more valuable than others, that does not lessen the degree of care required for all keys at all times.

It is extremely important that the private keys of certifying authorities be stored securely. The compromise of this information would allow the generation of certificates for fraudulent public keys. One way to achieve the desired security is to store the key in a tamper-resistant device. This device should preferably destroy its contents if ever opened, and be shielded against attacks using electromagnetic radiation. Not even employees of the certifying authority should have access to the private key itself, but only the ability to use the private key in the process of issuing certificates.

If your private key is compromised — that is, if you suspect an attacker may have obtained your private key — then you should assume that the attacker can read any encrypted messages sent to you under the corresponding public key, and forge your signature on documents as long as others continue to accept that public key as yours. The seriousness of these consequences underscores the importance of protecting your private key with extremely strong mechanisms.

Digital IDs make use of a technology called public key cryptography. During the initial enrollment process for obtaining a digital ID, your computer creates two keys: one public, which is published within your certificate and posted within VeriSign's (http://www.verisign.com) repository, for example; and, one private, which is stored on your computer. VeriSign does not have access to your private key. It is generated locally on your computer and is never transmitted to VeriSign. The integrity of your certificate (your "digital identification") depends on your private key being controlled exclusively by you.

Caution: It is your responsibility to protect your private key. Anyone who obtains your private key can forge your digital signature and take actions in your name!

Digital certificates were created to overcome the general anonymity afforded by unsecured networks like the Internet, by providing a reliable and trustworthy proof of identity in much the same way as passports and driver's licenses. Used in conjunction with modern Web browsers, e-mail software, and other applications, digital certificates (and the public key technology they are based on) offer the potential for ensuring secure electronic commerce and transactions over these networks. Like a passport without a photograph attached, a digital certificate stored in the usual manner on a PC hard drive is susceptible to compromise and fraudulent use; and before they can be widely accepted as proof of identity, a way must be found to protect them.

Consequently, protecting the private key is the single most important aspect of using digital certificates because if the private key becomes known to others, it is possible for them to assume that identity and engage in fraudulent use of the certificate. Most digital certificates today — and more importantly, their associated private keys — are simply encrypted with a password and stored on the owner's PC hard disk drive where they may be vulnerable to attack either directly or through the network. The private key is vulnerable to many of the same password-related problems mentioned earlier, and several programs are available to either divert PC files or attack password mechanisms. Therefore, with the preceding in mind, you should:

- Secure your private key.
- Make sure your private key file is protected.
- Store the key file in a directory that only you or authorized administrators have access to.

It is also important to know whether the file is stored on backup tapes or is otherwise available for someone to intercept. If so, you must protect your backups as much as you protect your server.

The private key protection solution works in concert with other PKI components to provide strong authentication for your Web-based content and applications. Users are issued a software-only smart card. The smart card contains the user's credentials (the private key and the digital certificate) and is protected by a personal identification number (PIN). This technique is called cryptographic camouflage, and is used to protect a user's private key. With this technique, the user's private key is stored in the smart card and is camouflaged with the user's PIN. To use the card, the user simply enters his PIN, which reveals the private key. However, when a hacker attempts to decrypt the key by entering an invalid PIN, he or she also gets back a plausible key. Unlike other password-protected key containers, the hacker has no way of detecting that the key he or she has decrypted is a decoy, because it looks structurally similar to a valid key.

The public key can be freely distributed without compromising the private key, which must be kept secret by its owner. Because these keys only work as a pair, an operation (e.g., encryption) done with the public key can only be undone (decrypted) with the corresponding private key, and vice versa. A digital certificate securely binds your identity, as verified by a trusted third party (a CA), with your public key.

Now, in cryptography, a private or secret key is an encryption/decryption key known only to the party or parties that exchange secret messages. In traditional secret key cryptography, a key is shared by the communicators so that each can encrypt and decrypt messages. The risk in this system is that if either party loses the key or it is stolen, the system is broken. A more recent alternative is to use a combination of public and private keys. In this system, a public key is used together with a private key.

In the unlikely event of a private key compromise, the effects differ, depending on which keys were stolen, who performed the theft, and what their motivation was. A user's private key theft could occur if the user's PC was stolen or was used by someone else. Although some form of an electronic wallet will store the keys and certificates (which are usually protected by a password), if a correct guess does open the e-wallet, the thief instantly assumes the identity of the authorized key holder. If the theft is not reported, message and transaction recipients are left with no other choice but to believe that they were performed in earnest. At certificate issuance time, users must be made aware of these consequences when they agree to the use policies before accepting their certificates.

The theft of a CA private key is a whole other matter. With the proper systems, a CA key thief could establish himself as a CA, ready to issue certificates. These forged certificates would be undetectable as forgeries and could be used without question.

When it comes to maliciously poking around a system or a network, finding encrypted data, and decrypting it, the movies make it look easy. However, according to cryptography experts, a massive grid of interconnected and powerful systems would be required to break today's encryption algorithms in a timely fashion. Most bad guys do not have those kinds of resources. Even if they did, what sort of ciphertext would be important enough to warrant allocating such resources?

The answer is private keys — one half of the private/public key-pair is used to encrypt the data. If the bad guys get a hold of a private key, the integrity of the data is one huge step closer to being compromised.

Today, most private keys are stored on resources that are easy to penetrate, such as personal and network storage devices. Even so, the keys themselves are usually encrypted. Currently, there is not much that the bad guys can do to compromise their integrity. However, the future will bring the increasingly powerful systems that bad guys need to execute a successful system intrusion.

According to vendors such as Intel, HP, IBM, and Sun, it is not difficult to imagine the bad guys soon having access to the sort of computing power they would need to crack the encryption algorithms. For example, 64-bit symmetric multiprocessor systems based on Intel and HP's Explicitly Parallel Instruction-Set Computing are in place today. Moore's law says that those systems will be astronomically more powerful (and cheaper) by 2005. It is not difficult to imagine the bad guys having all the tools they need.

In other words, the last place a private key should be is on the easily compromised sectors of a storage device. Instead, keys should be hard-coded into special hardware that lives on the client device. Locating the key on special hardware on the client side is what is called "trust at the edge."

The solution protects keys in two ways. First, because the key is embedded in hardware and not on a storage device, there is no way for an intruder to get at it. Second, it is different from centrally administered key management solutions because the private key is never transmitted across a network. It is embedded in the hardware that should be in every client device, especially PCs.

Finally, the preceding solution is an interesting approach to a problem that is not an immediate threat, but may be just around the corner. The more systems and client devices that have the technology built-in, the fewer the systems that will have to be retrofitted when the threat reaches a more realistic level.

Beyond the limits of physical and logical protection of keys used to sign certificates, CA policies and procedures are clearly spelled out in Certificate Practice Statements (CPSs). These cover the human factors. CPSs consist of detailed descriptions of what certificate policies are and how they are implemented by a particular CA.

Note: A CPS is a statement of the practices that a certification authority employs in issuing certificates.

When CAs negotiate cross-certification services, they will examine and compare each other's CPSs. The liability that certificate issuers and end entities assume plays a role in the degrees of trust.

For example, the X.509 certificates contain certificate policies that allow certificate holders to decide how much trust to place in their certificates. According to the X.509, a CPS is "a named set of rules that indicates the applicability of a certificate to a particular community or class of application with common security requirements."

Keeping all of the preceding information in mind, this section begins with Chapter 1, which identifies the key concepts and issues surrounding the technologies and policies required to implement and support an enterprise PKI. Next, Chapter 2 takes a close look at what constitutes effective public key infrastructures, why their protection is crucial to success, and some thoughts for your consideration prior to implementing your own PKI. Then, Chapter 3 discusses the cost and complexity of rolling out a PKI. Chapter 4 explores issues related to the standards community and from the vendor community, as well as a discussion of why PKI standards are changing. Next, Chapter 5 provides several types of PKI solutions, including outsourced solutions in which the vendor manages the infrastructure and issues the certificates, in-house solutions in which the customer issues the certificates, and merchant certificates used mainly for business-to-consumer (B2C) transactions. Then, Chapter 6 covers digital certificates and Secure Sockets Layers (SSLs). Chapter 7 takes a detailed look at how to protect CAs from internal and external attacks. Next, Chapter 8 discusses key escrow versus key recovery. Then, Chapter 9 compares and queries certificate practice statements (CPSs). Chapter 10 discusses how to secure your business applications. Finally, Chapter 11 looks at whether you should build or buy your PKI readiness solution.

1

PUBLIC KEY INFRASTRUCTURES (PKIS): WHAT ARE THEY?

Jean Carlo Binder

To mitigate the security risks of conducting business in an open environment while at the same time maintaining the cost advantages of doing so, enterprises are turning their attention to an emerging segment of the security market known as public key infrastructure (PKI). The purpose of PKI is to provide an environment that addresses today's business, legal, network, and security demands for trust and confidentiality in data transmission and storage. PKI accomplishes these goals for an enterprise through policy and technology components. These components determine and identify the roles, responsibilities, constraints, range of use, and services available. This introductory chapter identifies the key concepts and issues surrounding the technologies and policies required to implement and support an enterprise PKI.

PKI is a system for supporting digital signatures and document encryption for an organization. It is fast becoming essential for an effective, secure E-commerce and to fulfill general security and authentication requirements over non-secure networks (such as the Net). The banking services are the most popular usage of this technology, a technology that is quickly spreading over all the applications that need security to be fully operational.

This chapter also aims to be a good starting point for those interested in the PKI concepts, without analyzing specific implementations that are discussed throughout this book. References at the end of each chapter are provided to allow more in-depth investigation about each of the PKI topics, as well as to give credit to where the information was obtained from or based on. Some references to specific software implementations are given only to serve as a reference for a technical analysis, and will not be used as a "recommendation" of such products or vendors.

So, without further ado, the burning question must be asked: What really is PKI? What does it have to offer? Let us take a look!

WHAT IS PKI?

A PKI enables users of an insecure public network such as the Internet to securely and privately exchange data through the use of a public and a private cryptographic key pair that is obtained and shared through a trusted authority. The PKI provides for digital certificates that can identify individuals or organizations and directory services that can store and, when necessary, revoke them. The PKI is the underlying technology that provides security for the Secure Sockets Layer (SSL) and Hypertext Transfer Protocol Secure Sockets (HTTPS) protocols, which are used extensively to conduct secure E-business over the Internet.

The PKI assumes the use of *public key cryptography*, which is the most common method on the Internet for authentication of a message sender or encryption of a message. Traditional cryptography involves the creation and sharing of a secret key for the encryption and decryption of messages. This secret key system has the significant flaw that if the key is discovered or intercepted by someone else, messages can easily be decrypted. For this reason, public key cryptography and the public key infrastructure is the preferred approach on the Internet. A public key infrastructure consists of:[1]

- A certificate authority that issues and verifies digital certificates
- A registration authority that acts as the verifier for the certificate authority before a digital certificate is issued to a requestor
- One or more directories where the certificates (with their public keys) are held
- A certificate management system

WHAT DOES PKI OFFER?

The five requirements for E-security are non-repudiation, privacy, integrity, accountability, and trust. A successful PKI implementation plays a major part in satisfying all five of these requirements.

Non-Repudiation

For a business transaction to be valid, neither party can later deny the existence or execution of that transaction. PKI uses digital signatures to bind the identity of a party to the transaction so that knowledge of the transaction cannot later be denied.

Privacy

PKI offers privacy through public and private key encryption. This system enables unrelated parties to conduct business securely across an unprotected network.

Integrity

PKI offers integrity through digital signatures, which can be used to prove that data has not been tampered with in transit. This is important in its own right, but also for non-repudiation.

Accountability

PKI offers accountability by verifying the identity of users through digital signatures. Because digital signatures are more secure than username/password combinations, users are more likely to be held accountable for their actions.

Trust

The whole concept of a PKI is based on trust. You trust the issuing certificate authority (CA). If you have no faith in the issuing CA, then you cannot trust any of the certificates that they have issued, or the organizations to which they were issued. This is not the fault of the organizations, but of the CA itself.

So, with the preceding in mind, the objective of this introductory chapter is to first briefly describe the general and basic concepts of the PKI to individuals interested in security and secure commerce (sometimes called S-commerce), but with a low level of knowledge about Internet security. Next, this part of the chapter introduces some basic security concepts, which are needed to understand the PKI topics discussed later in this chapter and in later chapters throughout the book.

BASIC SECURITY CONCEPTS

To be able to access data and applications from within a company, a user must first be authenticated, and then needs to be authorized to perform the operation. *Authentication procedures* perform the former task, and *access control decision* functions perform the latter task as shown in Exhibit 1.[1]

Access Control Policy

The authentication procedures are responsible for the verification of the identity of the user (if that person really is who she or he says she or he is) because the access control functions depend on this. Three different types of information or factors can be used:[1]

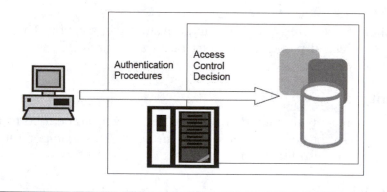

Exhibit 1   Authentication and Access Control

1. Something the user knows
2. Something the user possesses
3. Something the user is

Something the User Knows

This is the traditional way to validate any user based on a password or a "shared secret." It is usually the weakest authentication solution for the following reasons. First, it can be stolen from the computer by cracker programs (as in a dictionary attack), where an attacker tries to gain access by using a program that cycles through all the words in a dictionary, and their combination with numbers and special characters as possible passwords. Second, the user identifications and passwords can be intercepted on the network via sniffer programs.

Something the User Possesses

Here, the user could possess a physical token, like a proximity card, a smartcard (like a Visa card), a private key, or a passport. This factor is normally combined with something the user knows for authentication purposes.

Something the User Is

Here we are dealing with biometrics, which can be used for both local and network authentication. This is the strongest form of authentication because it is very difficult to steal the authentication token (a fingerprint, ten fingerprints, DNA, retina) from the user. But, there is one main disadvantage. They are not secret; therefore, if a user's biometric signature (or its digital representation) is stolen, it can never be replaced. Second, they are not an exact match (like passwords, smartcard identifications, or

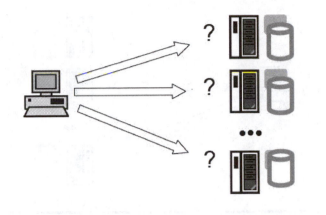

Exhibit 2   Multiple Systems and Multiple Access?

tokens), but a fuzzy match, meaning that a certain number of false positives and false negatives may arise. Even stronger procedures use a combination of two or three factors, as previously described.

Distributed Systems and Password Authentication

When a company has several applications hosted by different systems and servers, there are several ways of identity authentication. Exhibit 2 illustrates this type of authentication.[1]

Multiple Passwords: One for Each System/Application

This is the standard. However, it is more cumbersome for the users and increases the problems of forgotten passwords (see Exhibit 3).[1]

Same Password: Replicated in Each System

This is not usual, although possible. It is considered extremely vulnerable because knowledge of a single password (obtained by an attack to the weakest system) gains access to all the systems. The benefit is that users with multiple IDs over the systems only have to remember one password (see Exhibit 4).[1]

Single Sign-On Software

These systems are able to store different usernames and passwords for each system the user is allowed to use. The single log-on software shows a list of authorized applications (menu style) and is able to retrieve the username/password pair needed to log on to the application. The weak

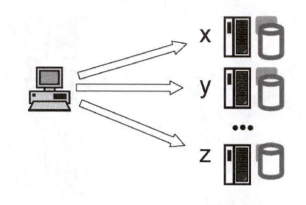

Exhibit 3   Multiple Systems and Multiple Passwords

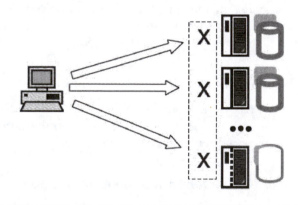

Exhibit 4   Password Replication

points are the password database (protected by cryptography) and the network communication between the single log-on server and the other applications (must be a secure network). The strongest implementations of this method are called Secured Single Sign-On (SSO) (see Exhibit 5).[1]

Directory Server

Each user usually has only one password, which is stored in a central system (System A), as shown in Exhibit 6. The user logs on to the trusted central system, which validates its identity (Step 3). When the user logs on to a second system (System B), this one authenticates itself to the central system, informing the user and password and asking for a response. If user Joe is not listed on the access list in the central system for System B, he will be denied access to System B and its applications, as shown in Exhibit 6.[1]

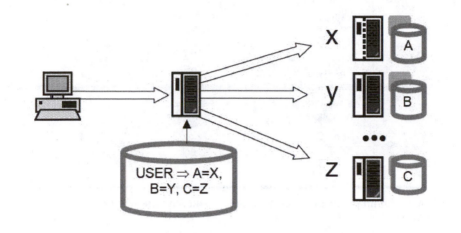

Exhibit 5 Single Log-On Software

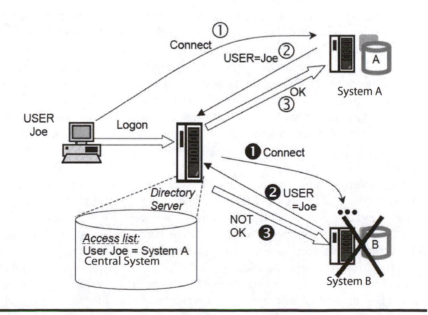

Exhibit 6 Directory Server

Symmetric and Asymmetric Encryption

The objective of encryption is to transform a message (which may contain plaintext, images, sound, or other binary objects) to a ciphertext, ensuring confidentiality. It is mainly used to protect passwords and extremely sensitive information stored in databases or transmitted in unsafe networks.

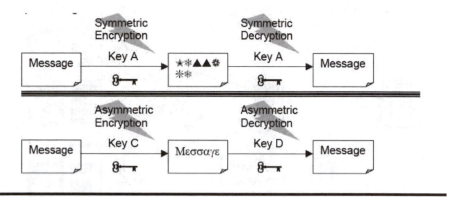

Exhibit 7   Comparison between Symmetric and Asymmetric Encryption/ Decryption

A decryption key allows the algorithm to reverse the encryption and is needed to read the message. Two different types of encryption exist — symmetric and asymmetric — as shown in Exhibit 7.[1]

In symmetric encryption schemes (the classical form of cryptography), the same key (called the secret key) is used to both encrypt and decrypt the text. The problem with these systems is that of transporting the secret key from the sender to the receiver, without security exposures. Some systems (notably MIT's Kerberos system) use only symmetric secret-keys to communicate securely over public networks, but they are difficult to implement in large organizations and need some extra security procedures such as a central "trusted and secure" server. The Data Encryption Standard (DES) algorithm is a good example of the symmetric encryption implementation.

Asymmetric cryptosystems (also called *public key* cryptosystems) use one key (the public key) to encrypt a message and a different key (the private key) to decrypt it. Given an encryption key, it is virtually impossible to determine the decryption key (and vice versa). The main disadvantage is its slower computing speed when compared to the symmetric encryption (due to its computing complexity). Two different asymmetric algorithms include the Rivest–Shamir–Adleman (RSA) algorithm, which is permutable (one key can either encrypt or decrypt), and the Elliptic Curve Digital Signature Algorithm (ECDSA — a variant of the well-known Digital Signature Algorithm [DSA]), which may implement existing algorithms using elliptic curves. The keys are smaller (without compromising security) with consequently faster processing times. This difference in speed and computing power requirements lead the implementation of secret-key systems to encrypt the message, and the public key systems to encrypt the secret key (usually shorter than the message, and often limited to 1024 bits = 128 bytes), as shown in Exhibit 8:[1]

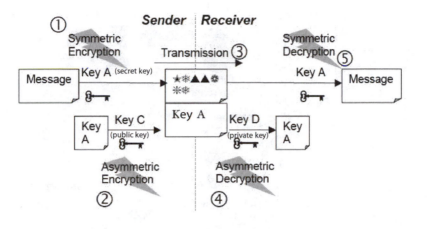

Exhibit 8 Secret-Key Systems Structure

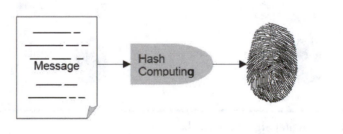

Exhibit 9 Hashing

Exhibit 8 shows the sender encrypting the message (step 1). The randomly chosen secret key used for this step is also encrypted using the receiver's public key (step 2). The encrypted message and secret key are sent to the receiver (step 3), which uses his or her private key to decrypt the secret key (step 4), and then uses this one to decrypt the message (step 5).

Hashing

Hashing is the method used to obtain a "digital fingerprint" (hash) for a given message, which can be used to validate the message integrity but not to reproduce it (see Exhibit 9).[1] The hash code has a fixed length (normally 128 or 160 bits) and is designed to be unique (different messages produce different hashes).

Hashing algorithms are also called one-way hash functions, message digest algorithms, cryptographic checksum, digital fingerprint, message integrity check (MIC), and manipulation detection code (MDC). Some

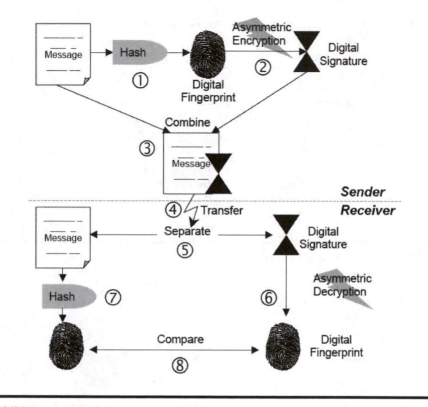

Exhibit 10   Digital Signature Mechanism

examples include MD2, MD4, and MD5 (which use 128 bits and were created by Ron Rivest) and Secure Hash Algorithm (SHA1), which uses 160 bits and was invented by the U.S. National Institute of Science and Technology)

Digital Signature

To obtain a secure digital signature, several steps (which mix the concepts explained above) must be executed: Exhibit 10 illustrates these steps.[1]

At first, the message is hashed (step 1), creating a digital fingerprint that is encrypted using the receiver's public key (step 2) and creating a digital signature. The clear message is combined with the digital signature (step 3), and the result (an authenticated message) is sent (step 4). After the reception, the message is separated from the digital signature (step 5), which is decrypted using the receiver's private key (step 6). The message is hashed into a "temporary" digital fingerprint (step 7), which is used to validate the received fingerprint (step 8). If the message has not been modified during the transfer process, it is authenticated.

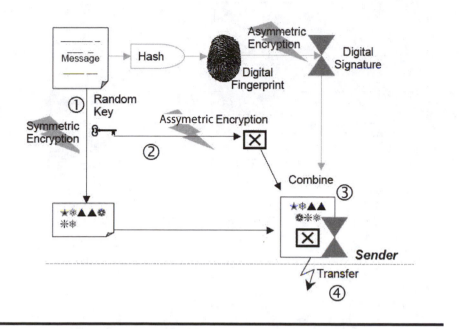

Exhibit 11   Digital Signature with Message Encryption

Digital Signature Associated with Message Encryption

The digital signature (as previously explained) validates if the message has not been corrupted during the transmission (integrity). To ensure the confidentiality of the message, some additional steps must be executed, as shown in Exhibit 11.[1]

The message is encrypted using a random key (step 1). This random key is then encrypted using the receiver's public key (step 2). This encrypted random key will be combined with the digital signature and the encrypted message (step 3). This package is sent via an unsecured network (step 4).

As shown in Exhibit 12,[1] after the reception, the encrypted message and random key are separated from the digital signature (step 5). The random key is decrypted using the receiver's private key (step 6). The message is decrypted using the random key (step 7) and after that is hashed into a "temporary" digital fingerprint, which is used to validate the received fingerprint (step 8). If the message has not been modified during the transfer process, it is authenticated.

So, with the preceding in mind, three different formats of messages can be used in public-key cryptosystems:[1]

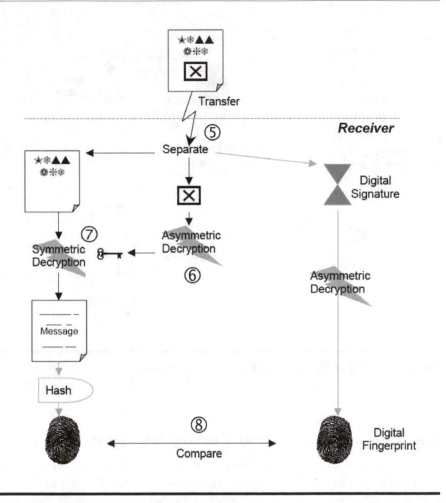

Exhibit 12   Digital Signature with Message Encryption

1. *Encrypted message.* A symmetric key encrypts the message (as previously explained) and the public key encrypts the symmetric key.
2. *Signed message.* The message is hashed into a digital fingerprint, which is encrypted into a digital signature (as previously explained) using a private key.
3. *Signed and encrypted message.* A combination of the preceding concepts, in which the message is signed using the private key of the sender and then encrypted using the public key (as previously explained).

Having been introduced to some basic security concepts, you are now ready to look at how public and private key cryptography really works.

HOW PUBLIC AND
PRIVATE KEY CRYPTOGRAPHY WORKS

In public key cryptography, a public key and a private key are created simultaneously by a certificate authority (CA). The private key is given only to the requesting party and the public key is made publicly available in a directory that all parties can access. The private key is never shared with anyone or sent across the Internet. By first encrypting data using an organization's or individual's public key, it is possible to safely send the data across an insecure network such as the Internet, because only the holder of the associated private key will be able to decrypt it.

The public keys must be stored in a directory to ensure their worldwide availability. As they are accessible via unsecured networks (Internet), an infrastructure must be set up to allow them to be undoubtedly trusted. This is the main objective of the Public Key Infrastructure (PKI). This part of the chapter discusses the way this trusted relationship is implemented.

Furthermore, in addition to decrypting messages, private keys can also be used to digitally sign data as a way of both authenticating its origin and proving that the data has not been tampered with. To create a digital signature, the sender passes the data through a "hashing" algorithm, which returns a value known as a one-way hash. The one-way hash is unique to the data but cannot be used to reproduce it. A sender encrypts the one-way hash using his private key to create a digital signature. The digital signature is sent, in addition to the data.

The digital signature can be decrypted to obtain the one-way hash using the sender's public key (available from a global directory of public keys). By passing the data through the same hashing algorithm and comparing the result with the one-way hash extracted from the digital signature, the recipient can prove that the data was sent by the owner of the public key and has not been tampered with.

This dual use of keys leads to a conflict in terms of key lifetime. For example, if a private key that is used for digital signatures is stolen, it could be used to forge the owner's identity, and should immediately be destroyed. In contrast, if a key pair is used for encryption, the private key should be archived for as long as possible; because, if the private key were ever lost, it would be impossible to retrieve messages encrypted with its public counterpart. It is therefore sensible to keep multiple copies of this private key.

For this reason, it is considered good practice to use two private keys: one for the decrypting of data and the other for the purpose of digital signatures. Now let us look at PKI entities — which are instrumental in the operation of encrypting and decrypting data.

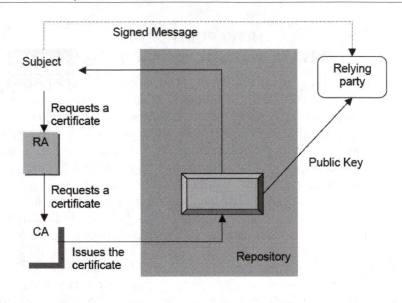

Exhibit 13   PKI Basic Entities and Operations

PKI Entities

The following are basic PKI entities:

- Certification authority (CA)
- Registration authority (RA)
- Subscriber
- Relying party
- Repository

Exhibit 13 illustrates how these entities work together.[1]

Certification Authority (CA)

The certification authority (CA) is the entity that issues the certificates (see certificates later in the chapter) to the subscriber. It may be online (the certificates are obtained via the network infrastructures [e.g., VeriSign]) or offline (the certificates are kept locked in a room and sent by floppy disks using secured transport services [e.g., European Sesame Project]).

Registration Authority (RA)

The registration authority (RA) is an optional local agent that authenticates the subscriber and issues requests for certification to the CA on behalf of the subscriber. The RA may be authenticated face-to-face by the CA staff, issued with a certificate, and then trusted to perform face-to-face authentication of the subscribers. A digitally signed message from the RA to the CA will be as good as if the CA had performed face-to-face authentication of the subscriber. One CA can operate several RAs.

Subscriber

The subscriber is also called a certificate user (or simply a subject). A subscriber is the entity who has been issued a certificate and whose name appears in its subject field.

Relying Party

The relying party is the user receiving the digitally signed information from the subscriber. The user also needs to use the PKI to verify the signature.

Repository

The repository holds the Certification Revocation Lists (CRLs) and certificates (see Revocation later in the chapter). It is usually an X.500/Lightweight Directory Access Protocol (X.500/LDAP) directory, but it could also be a Web site.

Certification

Certification is the fundamental function of all PKIs. The certificates provide a secure way of publishing public keys, so that their validity can be trusted.

Subject Certification

The initial procedures used to certify the user's public keys are the most important, because a successful "masquerade" attempt during this phase may be difficult to subsequently detect. This may be done automatically by "internal" PKIs (run by a company for its employees), but in other cases it may require "face-to-face" authentication by either the CA or the RA, and even some "real" (or physical) document validation, like passports or identity cards.

Certificates

A certificate contains (at least) the basic information needed to provide a third-party entity with the subject's public key (see Exhibit 14):[1]

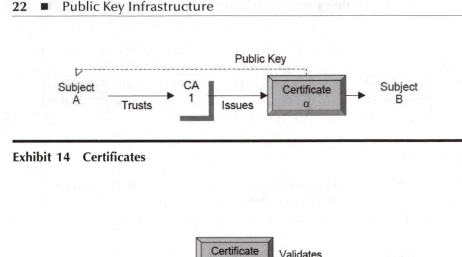

Exhibit 14   Certificates

Exhibit 15   Cross Certificates (Pair of Trusted CAs)

1. CA identification information (CA1) as shown in Exhibit 14
2. Subject identification information (Subject A) as shown in Exhibit 14
3. Subject public key as shown in Exhibit 15
4. Validity (time) as shown in Exhibit 15

The certificates can be used to identify an *entity* (the identity certificates) or *non-entities*, such as permissions or credentials — the credential certificates. A *true certificate* is trusted to identify the subject and its public key or credentials and can then be used by other subjects.

Cross Certification

Not all the entities will trust the same CA to hold their certificates. *Cross certification* is used to create the certificate between two CAs (CA1 and CA2) as shown in Exhibit 15.[1] If both CAs trust each other, a cross certificate pair is established. In other cases, only one certificate would be created, and not a pair.

Certification Path

In a universe composed of several different CAs (and in which not all of them are connected to each other via a cross certification), an arbitrary

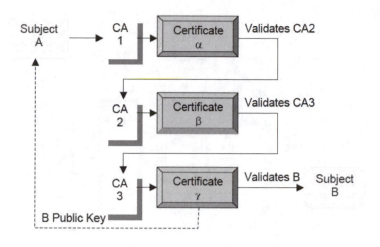

Exhibit 16   Certification Path Validation Process: Example with Three Different CAs

number of CAs must validate each other, until a certificate is obtained. This process is called *certification path validation* as shown in Exhibit 16.[1]

Exhibit 16 shows that the subject A needs the public key from the subject B. As the subject A does not "trust" the CA3 (at least not directly), it needs to use the CA1, who "trusts" the CA2, who trusts CA3. This one knows the public key from the subject B that is then sent to the subject A.

CA Relationships of a PKI

The CA relationships of a PKI govern its scalability. For a PKI to operate globally, its functions must scale up to a large number of users while keeping the size of the certification paths acceptable. Depending on the general relationships among their subjects, the CAs of a PKI can be arranged within a general hierarchy, a top-down hierarchy, or a web of trust.

General Hierarchy

Each CA certifies its parent and children, and some extra cross certificates can additionally link the CAs, as shown in Exhibit 17.[1] In this example, let us suppose that the subject B needs to certify a message from the subject D. It will need to go through the certification path composed by CA5-CA2-CA1-CA3-CA6. But, if several subjects from CA5 must certify messages coming from subjects from CA6, a cross certificate may be established and then the path is reduced to CA5-CA6.

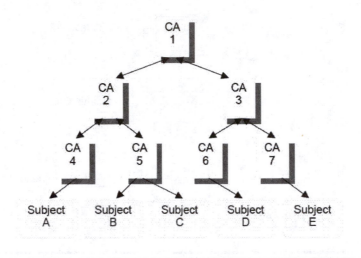

Exhibit 17   Example of a Three-Level General Hierarchy with Cross Certificates

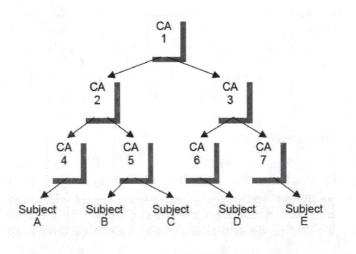

Exhibit 18   Example of a Three-Level Top-Down Hierarchy

Top-Down Hierarchy

There is a top-level CA, and each CA certifies only its children. All users must use the top-level CA as their root CA. This requires all users to obtain a copy of the top-level CA's public key prior to using the PKI, as shown in Exhibit 18.[1]

In this example, let us suppose that the subject B needs to certify a message from the subject D. It will need to go through the certification path composed by CA1-CA3-CA6, which is shorter than the previous example (see Exhibit 17). As all users must fully trust the top-level CA for all purposes, this type of hierarchy may be impractical for a worldwide PKI.

Web of Trust

Some PKIs have no structure at all, depending exclusively on the cross-path certificates between the CAs. This structure can be called a "web of trust" (because each CA must base its trust on the certificates of other CAs), and is used by the PGP program (explained later on in the chapter). The users exchange keys and sign each others' keys to establish a trust relationship.

Validation

Validation is the process that ensures that the certificate information is still valid, as it can change over time. Either the user can ask the CA directly about the validity (every time it is used) or the CA can include a validity period in the certificate. This second alternative is also known as *offline* validation.

Revocation

Closely related to the validation method, revocation is the process of informing the users when the information in a certificate is not valid (either because the information has been corrupted or stolen, or simply because some basic user information has changed). This is especially interesting in the absence of online validation approaches, and the most common revocation methods consist of publishing Certification Revocation Lists (CRLs). A CRL is a "black" list of revoked certificates that is signed and periodically issued by a CA.

In the initial PKI implementations, there were several problems related to the "time-granularity" problem (wrong information may be given during the time between the certificate's being revoked and its appearing in the CRL) and the size of the CRL. The risk of exposure by the first issue has been reduced using "Delta-CRL," which is simply a list of changes that have occurred since the last full CRL was published. The second issue is addressed by partitioning the CRL into different lists (e.g., one containing the CRL for the end-user subjects, another with the certified CAs).

Exhibit 19   Examples of Key Pair Models

Mode	Example	Non-Repudiatable	Encryption/ Decryption	Access Control
One key	VeriSign (class 1) and PGP	One pair		
Two keys	Entrust	One pair	One pair	
Three+ keys	SmartTrust	One pair	One pair	One or many pairs

Authentication

As previously explained in this chapter, in order for the subject to gain access to its private key, it must possess something (like a smart card or an encrypted key file). It also must know something (PIN or password) or be something (a particular fingerprint).

Keys and Key Pair Models

To increase the security level, different key pairs might exist for different functions, which may be divided into the following categories (see Exhibit 19):[1]

- Authentication only (LOG ON functions): used in cases where a user is not aware of the actual contents of the message that is digitally signed at log-on time.
- Encryption/decryption functions.
- Non-repudiatable message signing (e-mail): once the message is signed, the subject cannot refuse to be its author.

Key Management

These are the main steps performed in a PKI structure to handle the key pairs:

- Key generation
- Storage of private keys
- Revocation of public keys
- Publication of certificates and CRL
- Key update
- Backup and recovery
- Escrow and recovery

Key Generation

There are (at least) two different ways of generating the keys (centralized and basic authenticated), but the common steps to be performed are:[1]

- Subject identification (discussed previously in the chapter).
- CA sends a secret information (normally off-line) to the subject.
- The key pair generation is performed (by the CA or by the subject).
- A connection is established between the subject and the CA (using the secret information to ensure privacy), and either the public key is sent to the CA or the private key is sent to the subject.
- The disadvantage of sending private keys is the loss of the non-repudiation function.
- Sometimes the CA sends the certificate to the user, asking for an acknowledge message.

Storage of Private Keys

To increase the security, the private keys can be stored in smart cards (something that the subject possesses). The CA root private keys must be strongly protected (if they are compromised, the entire PKI is lost) and, for ultimate security, should ideally be stored in special hardware devices, which are tamper proof, climate proof, and that may destroy the key in case of attack.

Revocation of Public Keys

The revocation process must be easy but also secure; if anyone can revoke anyone else's certificate "too" easily, this will lead to denial-of-service (DoS) attacks; and, if the revocation is "too" secure, this may lead "masquerade" attacks to be held before the revocation can be completed. Some suggested methods are a telephone call from the user, validated by a secret token, or a signed message.

Publication of Certificates and CRLs

Because the issuing CA signs the certificates and CRLs, they are tamper proof and can be authenticated. Because they do not need to be transferred securely, they may then be:[1]

- Published in a LDAP/X.500 directory (explained later in the chapter)
- Published on a Web site
- Transferred directly to relying parties (using e-mail or FTP)

Key Update

As the certificates only have a limited lifetime (typically a year), there is a need for an easy process to update the subject's key pair(s) and issue new certificates periodically. This is far from being an issue and may be fully automated, as the user is already trusted (by a certificate), so he or she can send a signed message asking for a new certificate.

However, the update for a root CA key is operationally more difficult because, during the transition (also known as rollover), some users will trust the new key and others still use the old key. This implies that some certificates will be signed by the old CA root key, and others with the new CA root key. The solution is to create and publish three temporary certificates:[1]

1. *Old CA root Certificate:* signed by the new CA root and with a validity period from date of creation of the old certificate to date of expiration of the old certificate.
2. *New CA root Certificate:* signed by the old CA root and with a validity period from date of creation of the old certificate to date of expiration of the old certificate (or until rollover is finished).
3. *New CA root Certificate:* signed by the new CA root, this is the "permanent" one and will be valid until the following update operation is needed.

Backup/Recovery

The backup and recovery functions allow recovery of encrypted data if a subject loses its private decryption key. The backup is performed by a trusted internal third party (CA) that keeps a secure copy of the subject's private key. The subject who needs a recovery simply retrieves its private key from this third party (either offline using a floppy disk or CD-ROM, or online).

The backup is sometimes regarded as a bad thing because it might allow a dubious third party to act as the subject, but corporate environments are accepting it as a good policy to avoid loss of information (e.g., by using keys for people who already left the company). The organization owns the information, even if the non-repudiation function is not fully guaranteed.

Escrow/Recovery

Technically, these functions act similarly to the backup/restore functions, but as this may imply several privacy issues, they are often regarded as a *bad thing*. The trusted third party in this case is a company related to government or law enforcement agencies, which allow the key recovery to be done by an external organization (such as the police) to retrieve the subject's private key without its (the subject) knowledge or authorization.

Certificate Life Cycle

Exhibit 20 provides a short summary of the main activities covered in this part of the chapter:[1]

RELATED TECHNOLOGIES

Now take a look at some of the latest related PKI technologies:

- Cryptographic Message Syntax (CMS)
- Secure Sockets Layer (SSL)
- Secure e-mail/S/MIME
- Virtual private network (VPN)
- Pretty Good Privacy (PGP)

CMS: Cryptographic Message Syntax (CMS)

The Cryptographic Message Syntax (CMS) is used to digitally sign, digest, authenticate, or encrypt arbitrary messages. Its main goal is to define the data structures and processes for digitally signing and encrypting other data structures (also called encapsulation syntax); and it can support a variety of architectures for certificate-based key management, such as the one defined by the PKIX Working Group.

Secure Sockets Layer (SSL)

The Secure Sockets Layer (SSL) protocol runs above Transmission Control Protocol/Internet Protocol (TCP/IP) and below higher-level protocols such as HTTP or Internet Message Access Protocol (IMAP). It allows a server to authenticate itself to a client, allows the client to authenticate itself to the server, and allows both machines to establish an encrypted connection.

Originally developed by Netscape, SSL has been universally accepted on the World Wide Web for authenticated and encrypted communication between clients and servers. The SSL protocol includes two sub-protocols: the SSL Record protocol and the SSL Handshake protocol. The SSL Record protocol defines the format used to transmit data. The SSL Handshake protocol involves using the SSL Record protocol to exchange a series of messages between an SSL-enabled server and an SSL-enabled client when they first establish an SSL connection. This exchange of messages is designed to facilitate the following actions:[1]

Exhibit 20 Summary of Basic PKI Entities and Activities

Activity	CA	RA	Subject	Directory
Verification of applicant (registration and initialization)	Validates (face-to-face or via RA)	Validates (ideally face-to-face)	Provides information to RA or CA	—
Certificate generation	Generates or receives from user	May store a local copy	Receives from CA or generates and sends it	Stores new certificate
Certificate publication	Publishes certificate (Intranet, Web, floppy)	May store a local copy	—	Makes certificate available
Certificate revocation	Publishes CRL	May inform CA in case of problems and perhaps ask for a new certificate	Informs CA or RA in case of problems and perhaps asks for a new certificate	Makes CRL available
Certificate expiration	Updates certificate's expiration status	May update the local copy	Perhaps asks for a new certificate	Reflects certificate's expiration status into the database (or simply discards certificate)
Certificate archiving	Keeps (offline) a copy of the certificate to be used to recall or certify old messages	May store a local copy	Asks for the certificate if needed	Cleans up the online certificate

- Authenticate the server to the client
- Allow the client and server to select the cryptographic algorithms, or ciphers, that they both support
- Optionally authenticate the client to the server
- Use public-key encryption techniques to generate shared secrets
- Establish an encrypted SSL connection

Secure E-mail/S/MIME

Security services can be added to each communication link along a path, or can be wrapped around the data being sent so that it is independent of the communication mechanism. This latter approach is often called "end-to-end" security and it has become a very important topic for users.

Short for Secure Multipurpose Internet Mail Extension (a new version of the MIME protocol that supports encryption of messages), S/MIME is based on RSA's public-key encryption technology (it was originally developed by RSA Data Security, Inc.). Secure messaging, in compliance with the S/MIME standard, is drawing a lot of interest, especially in industries where regulations regarding privacy and security are causing changes. Using PKI, messaging systems can digitally sign messages, encrypt messages, or both, providing the authentication, integrity, and confidentiality that companies need in an asynchronous world. To enable these functions, however, the companies must first enable basic PKI functions, such as issuing and managing key pairs and digital certificates. That has many organizations considering how they will support PKI, either internally or through outsourced services.

Virtual Private Network (VPN)

A virtual private network (VPN) is a private data network that makes use of the public telecommunication infrastructure — instead of owned or leased lines — maintaining privacy through the use of a tunneling protocol and security procedures. The idea of a VPN is to give a company the same capabilities at much lower cost by using the shared public infrastructure rather than a private one.

VPNs are an important part of an E-business strategy. Some companies are using VPNs to network remote employees, driving down response times and improving access to business information. Other companies are using VPNs to tie their customers, partners, and suppliers into their network as part of an overall E-business strategy. VPNs require a PKI to authenticate connection points and, as a result, organizations using VPNs are starting to evaluate their overall PKI architectures because a VPN eliminates hard-to-manage modem banks.

Pretty Good Privacy (PGP)

Pretty Good Privacy (PGP) is a product family that enables people to securely exchange messages, and to secure files, disk volumes, and network connections with both privacy and strong authentication. PGP is a freely available encryption program that protects the privacy of files and electronic mail, using powerful public key cryptography and working on virtually every platform. It has become a *de facto* standard for e-mail security.

Finally, in an organization using a PKI with X.509 certificates, it is the job of the CA to issue certificates to users. And, in an organization using PGP certificates without a PKI, it is the job of the CA to check the authenticity of all PGP certificates and then sign the good ones. PGP defines its own PKI built on a "web of trust" (as previously explained in the chapter).

SUMMARY

Public Key Infrastructure (PKI) is a system for supporting digital signatures and documenting encryption for an organization. It is fast becoming essential for an effective secure commerce and to fulfill general security and authentication requirements over non-secure networks (like the Net). The banking services are the most popular usage of this technology, which is quickly spreading over all the applications that need security to be fully operational.

Finally, PKI is a complicated but sound solution to a difficult problem, namely enabling two parties to exchange data securely over an insecure medium without the benefit of prior communication. It has been adopted by the popular Web browsers and is widely used for business-to-customer (B2C) transactions. In general, however, PKI still faces challenges in terms of application support, interoperability between vendors, differing government legislation, and practical key management. Large-scale PKI implementations therefore demand careful planning and management if goals are to be realized within the desired time scales. Where possible, companies developing these large-scale implementations for the first time should pilot the solution on an isolated, non-critical area of the business and always be realistic about what they hope to achieve.

References

1. Jean Carlo Binder, "Introduction to PKI — Public Key Infrastructure," version 1.1, © 2002 Jean Binder [The Knowledge Binder SPRL] URL: http://www.k-binder.be/Papers/, 2003.

2

GROWING A TREE OF TRUST

Mark Merkow

The Internet community needs to explain to consumers that Internet security is only as good as the individual Web site's commitment to making transactions and information secure for their customers. Until then, the whole community suffers from this bad perception that the Internet as a whole is not secure.

— Andrew DeMeo
President of Electronic Commerce Marketing Systems,
a NY-based consultancy

We have previously looked at dozens of ways that adversaries might launch attacks on systems, data, and even personnel. We have now shifted the focus to solutions that mitigate many of the risks and threats. We have described how security is implemented as a series of layers, building upon the layers below moving from the physical to the logical. Atop the highest layer, a public key infrastructure (PKI) completes the security picture with a comprehensive solution that permeates all processing — person to person, person to resource, and resource to resource.

With the appropriate layers of security throughout the network, a PKI can put to rest the concerns of how to protect assets, freeing you to concentrate on adding value to your employees, your customers, and your business partners. It also helps you announce to the world that your site's security — and your customers' interests — are taken to heart.

In this chapter we take a close look at what constitutes effective PKIs, why their protection is crucial to success, and some thoughts for your consideration prior to implementing your own PKI.

WHAT ARE PUBLIC KEY INFRASTRUCTURES?

Using applied cryptography, PKIs govern the distribution and management of cryptographic keys and digital certificates that allow you to take advantage of several fundamental features:

- *Confidentiality of information* assures users that their communications are safe and readable only by the intended recipients. Message encryption using digital certificates assures this confidentiality.
- *Integrity of data* guarantees that message contents are not altered during the transmission between the originator and the recipient. PKIs provide for digital signatures to ensure the integrity of all transmitted information.
- *User authentication* enables systems and applications to verify that users are who they claim they are and have the authority to access the resource. PKIs use digital signatures and user certificates to assure the authentication of all end entities and system resources.
- *Non-repudiation* prevents users of the PKI to deny that they have participated in a transaction or sent a message to another user or resource. With a legitimate digital signature in hand and the legitimate digital certificate that accompanies it, the chances that a message is forged or originated elsewhere approach zero.
- *System interoperability* — due to strict standards compliance — enables a PKI's operation across a variety of hardware and software systems without concern for incompatibilities.

Effective PKIs are based on the public key cryptographic standards (PKCS), a family of standards that includes:

- *RSA encryption* provides for the construction of digital signatures and digital envelopes.
- *Diffie-Hellman key agreements* define how two people, with no prior arrangements, can agree on a shared secret key that is known only between them and used for future encrypted communications.
- *Password-based encryption* hides private keys when transferring them between computer systems, sometimes required under public-private key cryptography.
- *Extended certificate syntax* permits the addition of extensions to standard X.509 digital certificates; these extensions add information such as certificate usage policies, other identifying information, etc.
- *Cryptographic message syntax* describes how to apply cryptography to related data, including digital signatures and digital envelopes.
- *Private key information syntax* describes how to include a private key along with algorithm information and a set of attributes to offer a simple way of establishing trust in information provided.

■ *Certification request syntax* describes the rules and sets of attributes needed for a certificate request from a certificate authority.

Recall that a digital certificate binds a previously authenticated private key holder (a person) to the public key that accompanies it. This attestation, performed by a trusted party, creates a message containing the person's identification information, his or her public key, certificate usage rules, and other information. This message is then signed using the CA's private key and returned to the private key holder. PKI hierarchies of trust use this concept to manage the public keys for all users, both internal and external. With a PKI in place, a "tree of trust" is formed to represent how certificate authorities (CAs) control certain aspects of other CAs in the branches below them. Constructing this tree is one of the first activities in developing a PKI and these are embodied in the Certificate Practices Statement (CPS) discussed later.

WORK PERFORMED BY CERTIFICATE AUTHORITIES

Key and certificate management are not tasks to be taken lightly — nor are they for the faint-of-heart. Extremely tight security is an imperative to maintain the trust that PKIs require. At their essence, CAs provide three basic services to the entities (other CAs or end entities) directly below them in the tree:

1. Certificate issuance
2. Certificate renewal
3. Certificate revocation

Root Certificate Authority

The highest level, or root, of the hierarchy of trust is the *root certificate authority*. It is normally maintained offline and only accessed when needed for signing purposes. Root CA responsibilities also include the generation and distribution of the Certificate Revocation List (CRL) in cases of any private key compromise in the branches directly below the root. Root certificates are self-signed. Their presence is required for validating a PKI certificate chain. Enterprise root certificates will normally be embedded in the Web browsers used to access PKI-protected resources.

What Is a Certificate Revocation List (CRL)?

The idea behind CRLs is to stop the uses of any digital certificates that are related to a set of private keys that were compromised (stolen). If a thief gains a copy of a private key and possesses its accompanying certificate, that thief has essentially stolen the identity of the private key holder. If the theft is not detected, the thief could use the key-pair (certificate and private key) to either (1) masquerade as the legitimate keyholder without any suspicion or (2) use the private key to sign forged certificates (if a CA key was stolen). Once a theft or compromise is detected, it is critical that the CA that signed the key-pair knows about it and places the certificate's serial number on the CRL immediately and republishes the list.

CRLs are defined by the X.509 Standard for publication and distribution of the identity of revoked, unexpired certificates. CRLs are composed of the serial numbers for all revoked certificates, with the CA that signed those certificates responsible for their near-real-time maintenance to prevent any fraud or abuses using compromised private keys.

PROTECT THOSE KEYS!

Protecting the private keys that are tied to a digital certificate's public key, especially those keys that are used to sign lower-level digital certificates, is very serious business under any PKI uses. Without this protection, the notion of any trust goes out the window and the infrastructure will inevitably fail. Stolen (copied) private keys from any end entity could be used to transact or communicate without any cause for suspicion. It is the same as a stolen identity, where a thief masquerades as the legitimate key holder without any reason to suspect wrongdoing. Similarly, if the keys for a certificate authority were compromised, the repercussions could be severe. With a stolen (copied) CA key in hand, a would-be forger could issue bogus certificates without any way to detect the forgery. Protection of all CA keys is absolutely critical to maintain the PKI's level of trust.

The more a private key is used to sign messages, the more instances a would-be attacker can obtain for cryptanalysis. If these keys are changed often and regularly, stored under NORAD-like conditions, and managed well they'll remain safe from all forms of attack.

PKI cryptographic keys are extremely sophisticated in deterring would-be cryptosystem attackers. Because of their robustness, it is not really worth the effort to try breaking the cryptography. Even with all the computers on the planet working in tandem, an attacker would still find it tough to reverse-engineer or attempt brute-force methods (trying all possible combinations of a key) to determine the key. CAs will normally guard against such attacks anyway by using extremely long keys. They will also change their keys regularly and re-issue new certificates whenever they do. Rather than try to discover the key, thieves are better off trying to steal the actual key from where it is stored, so extra precautions must be taken to ensure that this cannot happen. Because CAs clearly understand the value of the keys in their possession they go out of their way to keep them safe from all possible attacks, physical and logical.

Every end entity under a PKI is responsible for the safety of its own keys and certificates. This is a central theme and cannot be overemphasized. A PKI's ability to guarantee assurances of authentication, message integrity, privacy, and security cannot be realized once keys get into the wrong hands. Private keys are valuable. Although some are considered more valuable than others, that does not lessen the degree of care required for all keys at all times.

ATTACKING THE CERTIFICATE AUTHORITY

CA systems may be the subject of attacks through several different ways. In addition to hacker attacks from the outside, CA operations are vulnerable to collusion, sabotage, disgruntlement, or outright theft by employees from within.

External Attacks on the CA

External attacks attempt to steal private keys using computers located outside the physical CA system environment. They may arrive via the Internet, break-ins to private lines, or backdoor methods through a local area network within the CA. The break-ins might attempt to foil Web page security, try to exploit known operating system flaws, or try and gain control of the server.

Internal Attacks on the CA

At least as great a threat to private keys lies with those employees responsible for operating and maintaining the CA system. CA private keys are an attractive target to those who work with them.

CAs can help lessen their attractiveness to internal theft by limiting their access and ensuring that that no one person has full knowledge of a complete key. Beyond storing them across several hardware devices (crypto-boxes), the environment in which the hardware itself resides should be ultra-secure. Strict access control, electronic monitoring, and intruder detection on each device should deter even the most tenacious would-be thieves.

WHAT CAN BE DONE WITH STOLEN PRIVATE KEYS?

In the unlikely event of a private key compromise, the effects differ, depending on which keys were stolen, who performed the theft, and what their motivation was.

The theft of a user's private key could occur if the user's PC was stolen or was used by someone else. Although some form of an electronic wallet will store the keys and certificates, and are usually protected by a password, if a correct guess does open the E-wallet, the thief instantly assumes the identity of the authorized keyholder. If the theft is not reported, message and transaction recipients are left with no other choice than to believe that they were performed in earnest. At certificate-issuance time, users must be made aware of these consequences when they agree to the Use Policies before accepting their certificates.

Theft of a CA private key is a whole other matter. With the proper systems, a CA key thief could establish himself as a CA, ready to issue certificates. These forged certificates would be undetectable as forgeries and could be used without question.

CERTIFICATE PRACTICE STATEMENTS (CPSs)

Beyond the limits of physical and logical protection of keys used to sign certificates, CA policies and procedures are clearly spelled out in Certificate Practice Statements (CPSs). CPSs consist of detailed descriptions of certificate policies and how they are implemented by a particular CA.

The American Bar Association defines them this way:

> A CPS is a statement of the practices that a certification authority employs in issuing certificates.

When CAs negotiate cross-certification services, they will examine and compare each other's CPS. The liability that certificate issuers and end entities assume plays a role in the degrees of trust.

X.509 certificates contain certificate policies that allow certificate holders to decide how much trust to place in their certificates. According to X.509, Version 3, a CPS is:

> A named set of rules that indicates the applicability of a certificate to a particular community or class of application with common security requirements.

DETERMINE YOUR PKI READINESS

You might be ready to embark down the PKI path if several of the following conditions are true:

■ You have migrated your application interfaces to Web browser technology, including the access to mainframe and midrange system applications. This is a requirement to permit the use of directory services, such as LDAP, to enable a single sign-on capability that not only identifies the requester, but also determines their rights and provides for access control.

■ You have migrated to browser-based e-mail systems that support S/MIME and digital signing of messages.

■ You have migrated to application software that can deal with signed documents and messages to eliminate the routing of paperwork for authority determination purposes.

■ You are prepared for logical access controls via smart cards or token devices that store private keys and digital certificates.

Build or Buy?

As you see from the PKI dissection, developing one is far from trivial. More than a few companies have tried to build one on their own, only to discover that trust is tenuous without the ultimate protection of CA private keys. Many have turned to outside firms that specialize in offering CA services to corporations around the world.

3

IN PKI WE TRUST?

Mike Fratto

When public key infrastructures (PKIs) hit the streets a few years ago, a media frenzy ensued — remember 1999, the year of the public key infrastructure? Now it is the morning after, and we have gotten a dose of reality when it comes to the cost and complexity of rolling out a PKI. But one thing remains constant: positive authentication is vital for doing business, regardless of whether you are express-mailing paper contracts and purchase orders or sending those documents electronically. A PKI offers a way to transmit data securely over insecure networks, extending user credentials across an enterprise or to extranet partners.

Sounds good, but a PKI implementation should not be undertaken lightly. The preparation involved is daunting, no matter which vendor or technology you choose. Success or failure will hinge on whether or not you have done your homework — make sure you know what services you want from your PKI, what applications you must support, what policies and procedures will be defined for the care and feeding of the PKI, and how the PKI will be integrated into your security and operational plans. Only after these and other policy issues have been resolved are you ready.

A fundamental question is whether to outsource all or some of your PKI. This is a difficult business decision; and once you start down one path, it is difficult to change course. Why outsource? After all, if you do your homework, deploying a PKI is not difficult. If you can install an application, you can install a CA (certificate authority). The trick, however, is ensuring the security and integrity of the CA while providing adequate uptime. We say let outsourcers build and support secured facilities, complete with redundant network connections and disaster-recovery plans. Then you can spend your time where it counts: creating and instituting certificate policies and applications that rely on your PKI.

LOOKING OUTWARD

To determine how well an outsourced PKI might perform, we created a simple scenario. Our hypothetical organization supports an initial user base of 1000 to 5000 clients on Microsoft Windows NT/2000 and Sun Microsystems Solaris. We specified S/MIME (Secure MIME) using Microsoft Exchange and Outlook, and support for a remote-access VPN using a Check Point Software Technologies' VPN-1 installation. We chose these applications because they are ready to integrate with a PKI. The participating vendors have active partner programs ensuring integration with VPN, e-mail, ERP (enterprise resource planning), and a host of other applications. In addition, each vendor offers APIs so developers can customize applications as needed. You give up a lot of control when you outsource critical services, so we asked vendors to provide auditing information, descriptions of their networks, information on how they will guarantee uptime, and a description of development APIs.

Answering our call were Baltimore Technologies, with its Managed PKI Service; Entrust Technologies, with Entrust@YourService; and VeriSign, with its OnSite 4.6 offering. We based our fictitious organization in our Syracuse University Real-World Labs®.

A BIG DECISION

Outsourcing a PKI is not like hiring an ISP to host a Web site posting the cafeteria menu. Your PKI — and the individual CA digital certificates and corresponding key-pairs — is your organization's digital identity. Moreover, your PKI is vouching that the certificates it signs are given to the appropriate end users or devices. Digital certificates are not just for identification and authorization; attributes in the certificates can be used by PKI-aware applications to determine access control and authorization. For example, a bank could use your digital certificate to determine what kind of customer you are and provide differentiated services, or an online order-entry system could use information contained in the certificate to determine your spending limit. As long as the signing CA is trusted, certificates issued by that CA will be trusted as well. Because so much trust, and thus risk, is tied to a CA, you must protect it and the certificates it issues just as you would HR records, existing contracts, and other data.

Likewise, the certificates stored on user computers need to be guarded. Using smart cards or requiring that users password-protect digital-certificate stores will provide reasonable protection. Digital certificates issued to Microsoft clients, such as Internet Explorer and Outlook, can carry an attribute requiring the use of a password-protected store.

Managed PKI services remove much of the burden of securing and maintaining a PKI by hosting the server hardware and software in secure, monitored, and well-maintained facilities. Procedures are in place for every process the service provider performs, from adding new administrators to generating audit logs, and these processes are audited.

While vendors will claim good practices, you should get copies of their most recent security audits or ask that your auditors be allowed to perform their own audits. We were unable to get SAS-70 audits from VeriSign or Baltimore. (A Statement on Auditing Standards No. 70, or SAS-70, allows an auditing organization to evaluate and state an opinion on a service provider's internal controls. It also provides an audit report that a customer can use during due diligence when evaluating a provider.) VeriSign and Baltimore, sensitive to risk, said the security audits contain confidential information that is disclosed only on a need-to-know basis. Both companies assured us that they are SAS-70-certified; Baltimore submitted a summary of a recent audit, which we took on trust, and VeriSign pointed us to its WebTrust audit report.

Entrust@YourService, which is hosted at a FirstData Corp. C2-certified facility, says it is planning to initiate an SAS-70 audit but was unable to give us any details. While we believe the vendors in this review operate in good faith, we would not want to base a customer financial statement audit on such assurances.

SERVICE FEATURES

A number of service features — including supporting simple or complex PKI architectures, extensive preplanning, formalized change requests, service redundancy, and customized PKI designs — are common to all three vendors' offerings. Like nearly all outsourced services, your application goals should drive the end result.

We chose a simple PKI architecture. We had a single subordinate CA, which was signed by one of the root CAs for each respective service. Operationally, we could conduct the review with this simple model. However, for a real deployment, you will need a multi-tiered architecture. Your organization's digital identity is tied to your root CA; so if the root CA is compromised, all the certificates it has created must be revoked and replaced. To limit the risk and damage of a compromise, at minimum a two-tier, and ideally a three-tier, PKI should be deployed.

In a two-tier PKI, your root CA issues certificates to its own administrators and any subordinate CAs below it. The subordinate CAs issue user certificates, while the root CA can be kept offline in a locked and monitored room, which should assure security. If a subordinate CA is compromised, only the certificates it has signed need to be replaced. And a multi-tier PKI can more closely model your organizational requirements — each major department can run its own CA.

The hosted PKI process begins with a planning phase, where you meet with the service provider to discuss your specific needs, including application support, and develop change-management policies, both for the CA service and for locally hosted processes such as user registration. Enter these meetings with clear objectives and technical knowledge. The more prepared you are, the more productive your planning will be, making it less likely that you will need costly rearchitecting down the road. The vendors' professional services include consulting, ranging from architecture to application development. The key is to make sure the service is developed with your initial goals and future plans in mind.

The planning stage is also when you make decisions about when and how revocation data is published. The vendors whose products we review here support certificate revocation lists, certificate-revocation distribution points, and OCSP (Online Certificate Status Protocol). Entrust's and Baltimore's service offerings let revocation data be published once a certificate is revoked. VeriSign issues revocation data every 24 hours or every hour, depending on the level of service, or immediately when using OCSP. OCSP is only as valuable as certificate revocation is timely.

After planning is complete, your interaction with the service provider will be limited largely to maintaining certificate life cycles. VeriSign offers the widest array of management features, even letting you change certificate elements and service parameters when needed. More extensive changes may or may not be billable, depending on how the service is negotiated. Both Entrust and Baltimore perform on your behalf all service modifications, such as adjusting certificate attributes or customizing the certificate enrollment pages. For the most part, service modifications will take place within a few days; noncritical changes that require CA downtime will take place during scheduled downtime.

All three service providers ensure connectivity and uptime using multiple links to the Internet and redundant hardware. Entrust@YourService and VeriSign OnSite host multiple customers on a single hardware platform, so the entire platform, including secure key storage, is redundant. Baltimore charges extra for redundant hardware. In addition, all three service providers can create any kind of PKI you require — from a simple, single CA to a full-blown, three-tiered architecture with multilevel CAs. One major benefit of a hosted PKI is that you spend your time on the important stuff, like architecture and policy, while the service provider does the grunt work of installing and maintaining the PKI. Your point of contact with the PKI involves managing certificates.

You can subordinate your CA to one of the public CAs, leveraging the power of a larger PKI. However, you will have to subordinate your policies under the vendor's PKI policies because your certificates are ultimately under the authority of the topmost CA. All three vendors also host private

PKIs, where you have a self-signed root CA and the trust stops there. The service provider manages and maintains the infrastructure in its secure facility, but your organization not only is responsible for developing policies regarding certificate life-cycle management, but must also distribute your root CA certificate to the users and applications to make use of it.

TAKE YOUR PICK

Each provider has strengths and weaknesses. VeriSign's base package offers the most complete management front end and provides plug-ins for common applications in its Go Secure line but lacks some of the advanced features offered by its rivals. Entrust, with its desktop applications, has the best client and certificate life-cycle support but that adds to both the purchase price and support costs. Baltimore offers a great deal of flexibility with its various modules, but the base offering is not as complete as the other two.

VeriSign took our Editor's Choice award, but each vendor's strengths make its service more compelling in specific applications. You need to do the homework and decide on the best fit for your organization.

VeriSign OnSite 4.6

VeriSign's name is synonymous with Web server certificates — chances are that your favorite online store uses a server certificate issued by the company. VeriSign is far from being a one-trick pony, however. Its OnSite hosted PKI offering takes top honors, just slightly ahead of Baltimore and Entrust, because of the service's comprehensiveness. VeriSign's management for LRAs (local registration authorities) is unmatched. Audit logs, complete certificate life-cycle management, and the ability to alter the configuration of OnSite are other pluses.

During the planning phase of the installation, we talked with OnSite engineers and developed a plan for the service offering. Our scenario was simple, but expect to spend a lot of planning time with VeriSign before rolling out OnSite. Keeping in mind that you should separate duties among administrators — so that no one person can hide actions from others — decide who will be your local security officer, the person who is authorized to set policy and direct the PKI deployment; your LRAs, responsible for issuing certificates and managing the server (often not the security officer); and what application support is needed.

Administration is through RA Control Center, a Web-based management system hosted at VeriSign's secure facility. LRAs are vetted by VeriSign Security Officers prior to being issued a VeriSign Class 3 administrator certificate. Once the LRA has a certificate, he or she can issue, revoke, suspend, audit, and configure certificates.

OnSite also beats Entrust@YourService and Managed PKI Service (see Exhibit 1) because of its Local Hosting option, whereby you can customize and alter OnSite to suit your needs rather than having to submit change requests to VeriSign. For example, we started out hosting everything at VeriSign's location. That was good in that no applications had to be hosted locally, but it also left us with few customization options for the enrollment page and for automatic enrollment. After we became familiar with OnSite, we decided to install Local Hosting, which let us host user registration pages on a local Web server.

The installation process first stepped us through installing the required Web site, pages, scripts, and executables, and then had us modify the Web server configuration to support Local Hosting (we used Windows 2000 with IIS 5). We then reconfigured OnSite service via the policy wizard in the RA Control Center for Local Hosting and downloaded the configuration file to the local Web site. Once we had the configuration file from OnSite, we ran a script, supplied by VeriSign, to apply the configuration file to our Local Hosting site. We customized the enrollment pages for our organization, added the ability to authenticate users against existing user databases, and integrated with Exchange 2000. Installing Exchange integration is similar to installing Local Hosting except for the extra step of configuring the OnSite policy file for Exchange. The process was smooth.

LRAs can issue certificates three ways: manually, automatically, or via PassCode. With manual issuance — the simplest method but one ill-suited to bulk enrollments — users connect to an enrollment page and fill out the information, including name, address, and organization. The browser generates a public/private key-pair and a certificate request and sends them to the RA, who then reviews each certificate request. Once the enrollment was approved, our users received e-mails with URLs from which to download certificates. Simple, but cumbersome.

If you have a lot of users to certify, OnSite's two other methods allow for automated registration. We tested PassCode registration and found it simple and easy to implement. We created a CSV (comma-separated value) file with the user's last name, e-mail address, and pass code. We then reconfigured OnSite for PassCode authentication and uploaded the file to VeriSign. After the file was checked for syntax, users were added. It is your responsibility to distribute the pass codes to users securely; OnSite does not e-mail pass codes (Exhibit 2). When users apply for certificates, they must enter their pass codes. If the pass code is successful, VeriSign issues a certificate immediately. We liked being able to view and manipulate the pass-code list so we could delete users and see which pass codes had been used.

Exhibit 1 PKI Service Pricing

	Baltimore Technologies Managed PKI Service	Entrust Technologies Entrust@YourService	VeriSign OnSite 4.6
Installation	Included	$120,000 (flat fee)	$2000 per day for PSO (number of days depends on user volume purchased); $10,000 for 1000 certs; $30,000 for 10,000 certs
1000 certificates	$65,000 per year	$38,250 per year	$70,000 per year
5000 certificates	$129,000 per year	$157,000 per year	$170,000 per year
10,000 certificates	$168,000 per year	$247,500 per year	$220,000 per year
25,000 certificates	N/A[a]	$450,000 per year	$280,000 per year
Consulting per person	Professional services range from $1050 to $3500 per day, depending on person's role	$2000 to $2200 per day	$250 per hour
Price for modules to support third-party applications	Included	Entrust ID: $18 to $45 per user based on volume; application plug-ins: $15 to $33 per user based on volume	Free: Go Secure for Exchange, Go Secure for Lotus Notes, Go Secure for Check Point, Go Secure for Nortel, Go Secure for Web Applications, Go Secure for SAP
Training included in service price	No	Yes: an administrator CBT (computer-based training) CD is included; additional Internet security training is available for a fee	No

[a] Alternative pricing available.

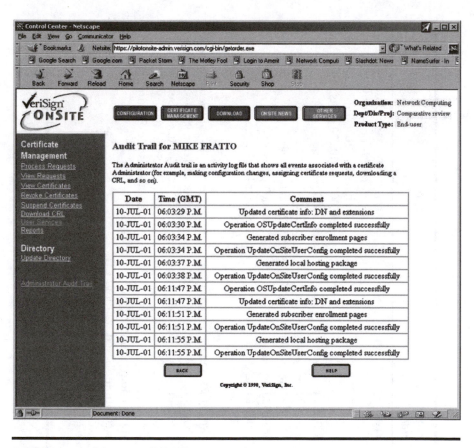

Exhibit 2   VeriSign's Audit Trail (Screen View)

We were also pleased with the auditing functions available in OnSite, with on-demand Administrator Audit Trail logs and activity reports. The logs provided a full audit trail, indicating which administrator performed each function. We also generated reports detailing certificate activity.

> OnSite 4.6. Available: Now. VeriSign, (650) 961-7500; fax (650) 961-7300. http://www.verisign.com/products/onsite/index.html

Entrust Technologies Entrust@YourService

Entrust@YourService (Exhibit 3) is a managed variety of Entrust/Authority. The services and plug-ins Entrust offers for Authority, including the Web Connector and VPN Connector applications, are not yet included in Entrust@YourService, although the company says these will be made available in future releases. Entrust's big claim to fame is the advanced certificate life-cycle management it provides. Automated certificate and

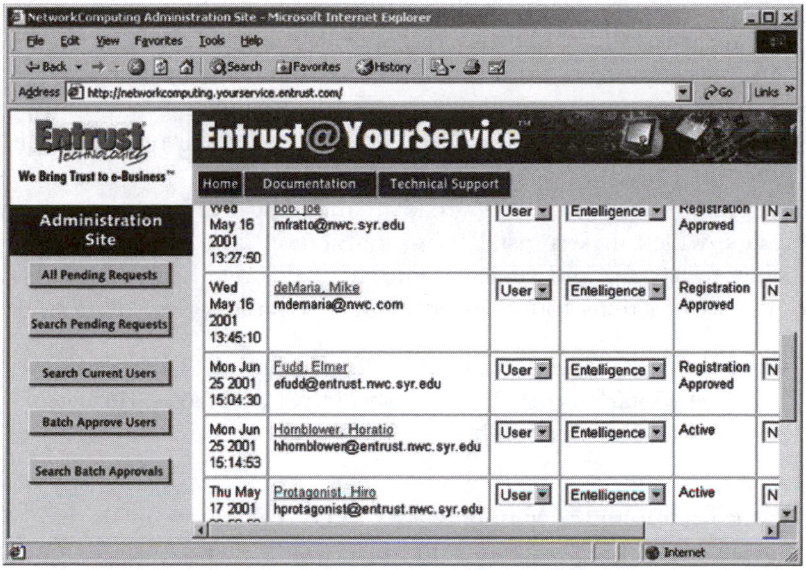

Exhibit 3   Entrust@YourService (Screen View)

key updates, automated key escrow, automatic revocation checking, and other services required to roll out a PKI earned Entrust top scores in our features and certificate life-cycle categories. This functionality, however, comes at a price: You must purchase, install, and manage Entrust client software on every computer. Support for unmanaged certificates or certificates used without Entrust client support should be available soon, if they are not already.

Entrust installs each CA on a shared Solaris server (as many as five CAs per server), each with its own Chrysalis-ITS high-security module to hold the private keys. The CAs are configured according to the security policy developed by you with one of Entrust's engineers. All the LRAs need be concerned with is certificate management. Changes to the CA configuration must be requested in writing and sent to the security officer assigned to your account. Timeframes for changes depend on the type of changes to be made. For example, simple policy changes can take less than 24 hours, while more complex policy changes can take longer, either because an Entrust security office needs to approve the change or because the change may need to wait for the scheduled downtime.

Entrust@YourService is managed via a Web front end and requires Entrust Direct to authenticate and secure the session with the RA (registration authority) in Entrust's secure facility. Once the first LRA is configured, users can register through a customized page. In our test, we had users fill out just a few fields — such as first and last name, e-mail address, and a password — to retrieve the certificate. Once the request is made, the LRA approves it and the user receives via e-mail a URL where he or she can pick up the certificate. At this point, a key-pair and digital certificate and an Entrust Profile file are generated and stored on the hard drive. We were able to send and receive secure e-mail using the plug-in for Outlook.

Applications that are Entrust-ready can request and be issued digital certificates, which makes installation, integration, and certificate life-cycle management a snap and removes much of the overhead involved with ongoing PKI functions found in VeriSign's or Baltimore's solutions.

> Entrust@YourService. Available: Now. Entrust Technologies, (972) 943-7300; fax (972) 943-7305. http://archive.entrust.com/yourservice/introduction.htm

Baltimore Technologies Managed PKI Service

Baltimore's strengths are in its add-on features and certificate life-cycle support. Like Entrust's offering, Managed PKI Service (Exhibit 4) is a centrally managed instance of Baltimore's commercial CA software, with the CA installed on dedicated hardware in Baltimore's secure facility. Baltimore's service — including which Baltimore PKI applications will be hosted on the customer premises and which will be hosted by Baltimore, defining certificate revocation rules, and deciding how often audit logs are created and sent to a designated administrator — is customized during the service planning phases.

Baltimore's WebRAO (Registration Authority Operator) interface (Exhibit 5) is limited to a few basic functions regarding certificate issuance, approval, and lookup. Managed PKI Service enables multiple certificate policies to be active at any time, meaning we could issue a customized certificate based on the application using it. For example, we might issue a certificate with attributes indicating spending limits or have a certificate profile defined specifically to control access into a Web application. This is one way to tailor certificates to specific users without having to fill in meaningless fields. Certificate policies are built by Baltimore technicians based on customer definitions and pushed out to WebRAO. We had several policies defined for our installation so we could generate certificates for Outlook or Web servers and create new RAOs.

Baltimore's was also the only service in which we could register users face to face by having WebRAO generate public/private key-pairs and the related digital certificates and present them to the user. This capability is useful in authenticating a user in person before issuing a digital certificate. Face-to-face registration is also used for processing PKCS (Public Key Cryptography Standard) #10 certificate requests.

Exhibit 4 PKI Service Features

	Baltimore Technologies Managed PKI Service	Entrust Technologies Entrust@YourService	VeriSign OnSite 4.6
Enrollment:			
Manual/auto enrollment	Y/Y	Y/Y	Y/Y
Bulk load of users	Y	Y	Y
PKCS #10	Y	Y	Y
Other	Y	N	Y (XKMS-based enrollment — Q3)
Certificate Issuance:			
Online/offline	Y/Y	Y/Y	Y/Y
PKCS #7	Y	Y	Y
Other	Y (DER, PEM, PKCS #12)	N	N
Generation and distribution of key-pairs	Y	Y	Y
Certificate Services:			
Roaming	Y	Y	Y
Suspension	Y	Y	Y
Archiving	Y	Y	Y
Escrow/recovery	Y	Y	Y
Renewal	Y	Y	Y
Other	Y (smart card issuance)	N	N
Tiered administration availability	Y	Y	Y

Exhibit 4   PKI Service Features (continued)

	Baltimore Technologies Managed PKI Service	Entrust Technologies Entrust@YourService	VeriSign OnSite 4.6
Audit Logs Availability:			
Online/on demand/periodic	N/Y/Y	Y/Y/Y	Y/Y/N
Client software requirement/availability	N/Y	N/Y	N/Y
Types of available CAs:			
Self-signed root	Y	Y	Y
Sub-CA	Y	Y	Y
Ability to Build Complex PKIs:			
Hierarchal	Y	Y	Y
Peer to peer	Y	Y	Y (not standard)
Ability to cross-certify self-signed root CAs with external CAs	Y	Y	Y
Ability to issue certificates to external directories	Y	Y	Y

Revocation Methods Supported:		
CRL	Y	Y
CDP or CRDP	Y	Y
OCSP	Y	Y (through partner)
Other	N	Y (Identrus OCSP, XKMS-based certificate validation)
Issue Frequency of Revocation Data:		
On demand/on revocation/periodic	Y/Y/Y	Y/Y/Y
Ability to migrate root keys and certificates to customer-owned CAs	Y	Not standard
Programming API availability for developers	Y	Y

Note: Y = Yes   N = No

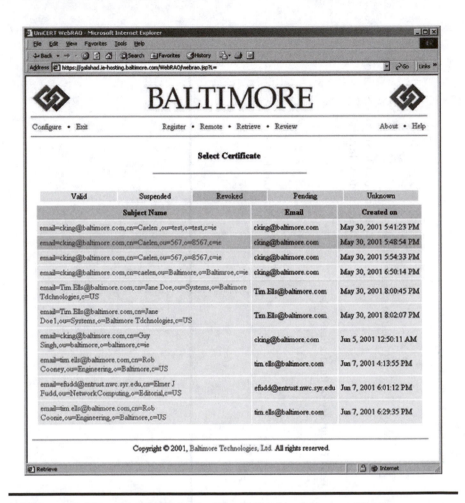

Exhibit 5   Baltimore's WebRAO Certificate Retrieval (Screen View)

Registering a user is a simple process. We selected the certificate policy we wanted to generate, entered the data, and submitted the request. WebRAO generated a public/private key, issued the certificate request, and submitted it to the CA. In a few moments, the certificate was ready for downloading. Once a certificate is downloaded, WebRAO saves it in the PKCS #12 file; that file, along with a password to unlock it, can be given directly to the user. All your registration can be done face to face, provided passwords are distributed separately from the PKCS #12 file.

What helps Baltimore also hurts it, however. While Managed PKI Service is flexible, you pay for that flexibility. It is especially important here to go over all the deployment options available during the planning stages. For example, if you want to do bulk enrollment, easily accomplished with Entrust and VeriSign, Baltimore has to deploy — at a cost — its ARM (Advanced

Registration Module), which can be programmed to pull authorization information from external user databases, regardless of where the module is located. It might make more sense to put ARM on the local network to ensure uptime and accessibility. Conversely, hosting ARM at Baltimore's secure facility means one less server to maintain.

> Managed PKI Service. Available: Now. Baltimore Technologies, http://www.baltimore.com

PKI SERVICES

While not quite at the "if you have to ask, you can't afford it" level, outsourcing a PKI is a considerable investment in both money (the cost can approach six figures for a midsize shop, depending on the services you choose) and time (you will need to do your homework and have your technology ducks in a row going into negotiations). But in return you get the invaluable benefit of having your IT staff able to devote itself to your business rather than a PKI infrastructure.

At our Syracuse University Real-World Labs® we set up a fictional organization with 1000 to 5000 users on Windows NT/2000 clients, the need for S/MIME on Microsoft Exchange and Outlook, and a remote-access Check Point VPN in the works. The desired architecture was simple. We took a look at Baltimore Technologies, with its Managed PKI Service; Entrust, with Entrust@YourService; and VeriSign, with its OnSite offering. The race was neck and neck; and while we found VeriSign the best fit for our organization and gave it our Editor's Choice award, only three-tenths of a point separated the three contenders on our score sheet. Your needs, and thus your pick, may differ.

4

PKI STANDARDS

Many government agencies and private-sector companies are exploring the use of Public Key Infrastructure (PKI) technology to provide the security foundation for their Web services, electronic commerce applications, and other information technology needs. As they explore the technology through pilots and small-scale production use, users often want solutions built to standards, but standards supporting PKI technology are still emerging. At the same time, vendors are developing PKI products and Web services for today's electronic commerce applications. It can be costly to update PKI solutions when standards change; yet new standards are developed to provide new functionality. New features in PKI standards can also create greater complexity, yet many commercial offerings still implement only basic functionality.

The purpose of this chapter is to explore issues related to this evolution process by providing perspectives from the standards community and from the vendor community, as well as a discussion of why PKI standards are changing. This chapter briefly describes why some products and Web services do implement standards and why some vendors implement their own solutions. Furthermore, the chapter briefly compares the security and cost implications of building standards-based PKI solutions and proprietary approaches. As a related issue, the chapter briefly provides a perspective on the interoperability implications between products and Web services as PKI standards continue to emerge. Finally, the chapter briefly discusses the future of PKI standards and projects what, if any, non-traditional PKI standards approaches may be viable in future PKI products and Web services.

With the preceding in mind, most of the work surrounding standards that support PKI technology are in the Public Key Infrastructure for X.509 Certificates (IETF) or PKIX areas. Let us now take a look at a brief overview of the PKIX approach.

0-8493-0822-4/04/$0.00+$1.50
© 2004 by CRC Press LLC

GENERAL PKIX STANDARDIZATION REQUIREMENTS

To describe public-key infrastructures, PKIX uses the terms "PKI" and "Privilege Management Infrastructure" (PMI). Between the two, one can find similarities. The main difference is that while the PMI handles the attribute certificates, the PKI handles the public key certificates. A good metaphor to distinguish between the two is to associate the latter with the visa and the former with the passport of a person. The one provides permission and the other provides identity.

Standardization Areas of PKIX

The general requirements of a PKIX often involve working on the following five areas:

1. Profiles of X.509 v3 public key certificates and X.509 v2 certificate revocation lists (CRLs)
2. Management protocols
3. Operational protocols
4. Certificate policies and Certificate Practice Statements (CPSs)
5. Timestamping and data certification/validation services

Profiles of X.509 v3 Public Key Certificates and X.509 v2 Certificate Revocation Lists (CRLs)

PKIX describes the extensions and basic certificate fields to be supported for the Certificate Revocation Lists and certificates. Then, PKIX describes the extended and basic certificate path validation. Finally, it covers the supported cryptographic algorithms.

Management Protocols

First, PKIX discusses the restrictions and assumptions of the protocols. Then, PKIX defines the functions that conforming implementations must carry out and provides the data structures used for the PKI management messages. Finally, it describes a simple protocol for transporting PKI messages.

Operational Protocols

Currently operational protocols describe how Lightweight Directory Access Protocol version 2 (LDAPv2), File Transfer Protocol (FTP), and Hypertext Transfer Protocol (HTTP) can be used as operational protocols.

Exhibit 1   RFCs for PKIX Documents

Subject	RFC
Certificate policy and certification practices framework	RFC 2527
Operational protocols	RFC 2559, RFC 2585, RFC2 560
PKIX certificate management protocols	RFC 2510
Profiles of X.509 v3 public key certificates and X.509 v2 certificate revocation lists (CRLs)	RFC 2459
Timestamping and data certification services	No RFCs yet, only Internet Drafts available

Certificate Policies and Certificate Practice Statements

The purpose of this document is to establish a clear relationship between Certification Practice Statements (CPSs) and certificate policies. Furthermore, the purpose is also to present a framework to assist the writers of certificate policies or CPSs with their tasks. In particular, the framework identifies the elements that may need to be considered in formulating a certificate policy or a CPS. The purpose is not to define particular certificate policies or CPSs, per se.

Timestamping and Data Certification/Validation Services

Because the documents are still classified as Internet Drafts, there are no Requests for Comments (RFCs) on these services yet. To indicate that data existed at a particular point in time, the timestamping services define a trusted third party that creates timestamp tokens. The data validation and certification services provide claim of possession of data, certification of possession of data, and validation of digitally signed certificates and documents. The relevant RFC documents are depicted in Exhibit 1.

The specification of the X.509 certificates is very extensible and general. The PKIX Working Group (the PKIX WG is discussed in detail later in the chapter) defined a *profile* to ensure interoperability between different Internet-centric implementations. This is a description of the format, semantics of certificates, and certificate revocation lists for the Internet PKI.

The operational protocols are the protocols that are required to deliver certificates and CRLs (or status information) to certificate-using client systems. For the certificates and the CRLs, there is an emphasis to have a variety of distribution mechanisms, using, for example, LDAP, HTTP, and FTP. For example, what constitutes an operational protocol is the retrieval of the CRL by a merchant to check whether a certificate is valid.

The protocols that are required to support online interactions between PKI user and management entities are known as management protocols. The possible set of functions that can be supported by management protocols includes:

- *Certification:* the issuance of the certificate.
- *Cross certification:* when two certification authorities (CAs) exchange information to generate a cross certificate.
- *Initialization:* for example, generation of a key-pair.
- *Key-pair recovery:* the ability to recover lost keys.
- *Key-pair update:* when the certificate expires and a new key-pair and certificate must be generated.
- *Registration of entity:* takes place prior to issuing the certificate.
- *Revocation request:* when an authorized person advises the CA to include a specific certificate into the revocation list.

So, with regard to the usage of the certificate, the certificate policies and the certificate practice statements are recommendations of documents that will describe the obligations and other rules.

Functionality of Public Key Infrastructure

The functionality or operations of a PKI are as follows:

- Registration
- Initialization
- Certification
- Key-pair recovery
- Key generation
- Key update
- Key expiry
- Key compromise
- Cross certification
- Revocation
- Certificate and revocation notice distribution and publication

As previously explained in Chapters 1 and 2, a PKI is a set of hardware, software, people, policies, and procedures needed to create, manage, store, distribute, and revoke public key certificates (PKCs) based on public key cryptography. Thus, a PKI consists of five types of components, as shown in Exhibit 2.

The architectural model assumed by the PKIX Working Group depicts an end entity, using management transactions to send its certificate request

Exhibit 2   PKI Components

Type of Component	Description
Certificate holders	To sign and encrypt digital documents
Certification authorities (CAs)	To issue and revoke PKCs
Clients	To validate digital signatures and their certification path from a known public key of a trusted CA
Organizational registration authorities (ORAs)	To vouch for the binding between public keys and certificate holder identities and other attributes
Repositories	To store and make available certificates and certificate revocation lists (CRLs)

to the Registration Authority (RA) for approval. If it is actually approved, it is forwarded to the Certification Authority (CA) for signing. The Certification Authority verifies the certificate request and if it passes the verification, it is signed and the Certificate is produced. To public the Certificate, the CA sends it to Certificate Repository for collection from the end entity.

Thus, the end entity can communicate directly with the CA. It is possible to implement the functionality within the CA, according to the PKIX recommendations.

Additionally, both the CA and RA deliver Certificates to the repository. Depending on the implementation, one of the two is chosen.

A similar course with the generation of the Certificates is taken for the issue of the revocation of the certificates. The end entity asks the RA to have its certificate revoked, the RA decides and possibly forwards it to the CA, and the CA updates the revocation list and publishes it on the CRL repository. Then, using an operational protocol, the end entities can check the validity of a specific certificate.

Privilege Management Infrastructure (PMI)

PMI is the set of hardware, software, people, policies, and procedures needed to create, manage, store, distribute, and revoke *attribute certificates* (ACs). Thus, a PMI consists of five types of components, as shown in Exhibit 3.

There are two types of attribute certificate distribution: *push* and *pull*. It is suitable for a client to *push* an AC to a server in some environments. This means that no new connections between the client and server are required. It also means that no search burden is imposed on servers, which improves performance.

Exhibit 3   PMI Components

Type of Component	Description
Attribute authorities (AAs)	To issue and revoke ACs (also called attribute certificate issuer)
Attribute certificate users	To parse or process an AC
Attribute certificate verifier	To check the validity of an AC and then make use of the result
Clients	To request an action for which authorization checks are to be made
Repositories	To store and make available certificates and certificate revocation lists (CRLs)

It is also more suitable for a client simply to authenticate to the server, and for the server to request or *pull* the client's AC from an AC issuer or a repository in other cases. A major benefit of the *pull* model is that it can be implemented without changes to the client or to the client/server protocol. It is also more suitable for some inter-domain cases where the client's rights should be assigned within the server's domain, rather than within the client's domain.

Now let us briefly look at the PKIX Working Group and discuss the future of PKI standards and projects. The PKIX Working Group was established in the fall of 1995 with the intent of developing Internet standards needed to support an X.509-based PKI.

WORKING GROUP DESCRIPTION

The scope of the PKIX Working Group (WG) has expanded beyond its initial goal. PKIX not only develops new standards apropos to the use of X.509-based PKIs in the Internet, but also profiles ITU PKI standards.

In support of the original and revised scope of the WG, PKIX has produced several informational and standards track documents. For use in the Internet, the first of these standards, RFC 2459, profiled X.509 version 3 certificates and version 2 CRLs. Profiles for the use of Attribute Certificates (RFC XXXX [pending]), LDAP v2 for certificate and CRL storage (RFC 2587), the Internet X.509 Public Key Infrastructure Qualified Certificates Profile (RFC 3039), and the Internet X.509 Public Key Infrastructure Certificate Policy and Certification Practices Framework (RFC 2527 — Informational) are in line with the initial scope.

The Certificate Management Protocol (CMP) (RFC 2510), Online Certificate Status Protocol (OCSP) (RFC 2560), Certificate Management Request Format (CRMF) (RFC 2511), Time-Stamp Protocol (RFC 3161), Certificate

Management Messages over CMS (RFC 2797), Internet X.509 Public Key Infrastructure Time Stamp Protocols (RFC 3161), and the use of FTP and HTTP for transport of PKI operations (RFC 2585) are representative of the expanded scope of PKIX. These are new protocols that have been developed in the WG, not profiles of ITU PKI standards. A roadmap, providing a guide to the growing set of PKIX documents, also has been developed as an informational RFC (see Exhibit 4).

PKIX Ongoing Work Items

An ongoing PKIX task is the progression of existing, standards track RFCs from proposed to draft (see Exhibit 5). Also, it is necessary to track the evolution of the other protocols and produce updated RFCs, to the extent that PKIX work relates to protocols from other areas (LDAP). For example, the LDAP v2 documents from PKIX are evolving to address LDAP v3. Furthermore, the WG will continue to track the evolution of these standards, and incorporate changes and additions as appropriate, because the profiling of X.509 standards for use in the Internet remains a major focus.

PKIX New Work Items

The following work items may become standards track, informational or experimental RFCs. Or, it is quite possible that they may not even be published as RFCs:

- Development of a logotype extension for certificates
- Development of a proxy certificate extension and associated processing rules
- Development of an informational document on PKI disaster recovery
- Production of a requirements RFC for delegated path discovery and path validation protocols (DPD/DPV) and subsequent production of RFCs for protocols that satisfy the requirements

Finally, as extensions are proposed, other deliverables may be agreed upon. Before inclusion on the charter or IETF meeting agendas, new deliverables must be approved by the Security Area Directors (see Exhibit 6).

SUMMARY

This chapter described the important concepts with regard to the PKI standards. A public key infrastructure does not only need an infrastructure to handle identities, but also needs an infrastructure to handle privileges. The distinction between the two became more evident in this chapter.

Exhibit 4   Request for Comments

Description	URL
Internet X.509 Public Key Infrastructure Certificate and CRL Profile (RFC 2459) (278,438 bytes)	http://www.ietf.org/rfc/rfc2459.txt
Internet X.509 Public Key Infrastructure Certificate Management Protocols (RFC 2510) (158,178 bytes)	http://www.ietf.org/rfc/rfc2510.txt
Internet X.509 Certificate Request Message Format (RFC 2511) (48,278 bytes)	http://www.ietf.org/rfc/rfc2511.txt
Internet X.509 Public Key Infrastructure Certificate Policy and Certification Practices Framework (RFC 2527) (91,860 bytes)	http://www.ietf.org/rfc/rfc2527.txt
Internet X.509 Public Key Infrastructure Representation of Key Exchange Algorithm (KEA) Keys in Certificates (RFC 2528) (18,273 bytes)	http://www.ietf.org/rfc/rfc2528.txt
Internet X.509 Public Key Infrastructure Operational Protocols — LDAPv2 (RFC 2559) (22894 bytes) obsoleted by RFC 3494	http://www.ietf.org/rfc/rfc2559.txt and http://www.ietf.org/rfc/rfc3494.txt
Internet X.509 Public Key Infrastructure Operational Protocols: FTP and HTTP (RFC 2585) (14,813 bytes)	http://www.ietf.org/rfc/rfc2585.txt
Internet X.509 Public Key Infrastructure LDAPv2 Schema (RFC 2587) (15,102 bytes)	http://www.ietf.org/rfc/rfc2587.txt
X.509 Internet Public Key Infrastructure Online Certificate Status Protocol — OCSP (RFC 2560) (43,243 bytes)	http://www.ietf.org/rfc/rfc2560.txt
Certificate Management Messages over CMS (RFC 2797) (103,357 bytes)	http://www.ietf.org/rfc/rfc2797.txt
Diffie-Hellman Proof-of-Possession Algorithms (RFC 2875) (45,231 bytes)	http://www.ietf.org/rfc/rfc2875.txt
Internet X.509 Public Key Infrastructure Qualified Certificates Profile {RFC 3039) (67,619 bytes)	http://www.ietf.org/rfc/rfc3039.txt
Internet X.509 Public Key Infrastructure Data Validation and Certification Server Protocols (RFC 3029) (107,347 bytes)	http://www.ietf.org/rfc/rfc3029.txt
Internet X.509 Public Key Infrastructure Time Stamp Protocols (TSP) (RFC 3161) (54,585 bytes)	http://www.ietf.org/rfc/rfc3161.txt

Exhibit 4   Request for Comments (continued)

Description	URL
Algorithms and Identifiers for the Internet X.509 Public Key Infrastructure Certificate and CRI Profile (RFC 3279) (53,833 bytes)	http://www.ietf.org/rfc/rfc3279.txt
Internet X.509 Public Key Infrastructure Certificate and CRL Profile (RFC 3280) (295,556 bytes)	http://www.ietf.org/rfc/rfc3280.txt
An Internet Attribute Certificate Profile for Authorization (RFC 3281) (90,580 bytes)	http://www.ietf.org/rfc/rfc3281.txt
Delegated Path Validation and Delegated Path Discovery Protocol Requirements (RFC 3379) (32,455 bytes)	http://www.ietf.org/rfc/rfc3379.txt

At the heart of recent efforts to improve Internet security is a group of security protocols such as Secure Multipurpose Internet Mail Extensions (S/MIME), Transport Layer Security (TLS), and Internet Protocol Security (IPSec). All of these protocols rely on public key cryptography to provide services such as confidentiality, data integrity, data origin authentication, and non-repudiation. The purpose of a PKI is to provide trusted and efficient key and public key certificate management, thus enabling the use of authentication, non-repudiation, and confidentiality.

Note: Essential Web services to ensure the security on the Internet are confidentiality, data integrity, data origin authentication, and non-repudiation. These can be achieved with protocols such as S/MIME, TLS, and IPSec. The protocols need a PKI to function effectively.

Users of public key-based systems must be confident that, any time they rely on a public key, the associated private key is owned by the subject with whom they are communicating. This applies whether an encryption or digital signature mechanism is used. This confidence is obtained through the use of *public key certificates* (PKCs), which are data structures that bind public key values to subjects. The binding is achieved by having a trusted *certification authority* (CA) verify the subject's identity and digitally sign each PKC.

A PKC has a limited valid lifetime, which is indicated in its signed contents. Because a PKC's signature and timeliness can be independently checked by a certificate-using client, PKCs can be distributed via untrusted

Exhibit 5   Internet Drafts

Description	URL
Internet X.509 Public Key Infrastructure:RoafhAv,-tp- (154,861 bytes)	http://www.ietf.org/internet-drafts/ draft-ietf-pkix-roadmap-09.txt
Simple Certificate Validation Protocol (SCVP) (99,732 bytes)	http://www.ietf.org/internet-drafts/ draft-ietf-pkix-scvp-12.txt
Internet X.509 Public Key Infrastructure Certificate Management Protocols (203,274 bytes)	http://www.ietf.org/internet-drafts/ draft-ietf-pkix-rfc2510bis-08.txt
Internet X.509 Public Key Infrastructure Permanent Identifier (30,964 bytes)	http://www.ietf.org/internet-drafts/ draft-ietf-pkix-pi-07.txt
Internet X.509 Public Key Infrastructure Repository Locator Service (7262 bytes)	http://www.ietf.org/internet-drafts/ draft-ietf-pkix-pkixrep-01.txt
Internet X.509 Public Key Infrastructure Certificate Request Message Format (CRMF) (50,610 bytes)	http://www.ietf.org/internet-drafts/ draft-ietf-pkix-rfc2511bis-06.txt
Internet X.509 Public Key Infrastructure Proxy Certificate Profile (99,230 bytes)	http://www.ietf.org/internet-drafts/ draft-ietf-pkix-proxy-08.txt
Internet X.509 Public Key Infrastructure Certificate Policy and Certification Practices Framework (206,938 bytes)	http://www.ietf.org/internet-drafts/ draft-ietf-pkix-ipki-new-rfc2527-02.txt
Internet X.509 Public Key Infrastructure: Logotypes in X.509 Certificates (47,335 bytes)	http://www.ietf.org/internet-drafts/ draft-ietf-pkix-logotypes-11.txt
Internet X.509 Public Key Infrastructure Operational Protocols: Certificate Store Access via HTTP (40,450 bytes)	http://www.ietf.org/internet-drafts/ draft-ietf-pkix-certstore-http-05.txt
X.509 Extensions for IP Addresses and AS Identifiers (52,360 bytes)	http://www.ietf.org/internet-drafts/ draft-ietf-pkix-x509-ipaddr-as-extn-01.txt
Policy Requirements for Time-Stamping Authorities (88,965 bytes)	http://www.ietf.org/internet-drafts/ draft-ietf-pkix-pr-tsa-05.txt
Internet X.509 Public Key Infrastructure Warranty Certificate Extension (17,798 bytes)	http://www.ietf.org/internet-drafts/ draft-ietf-pkix-warranty-extn-03.txt

Exhibit 5 Internet Drafts (continued)

Description	URL
LDAPv3 DN strings for use with PKIs (9024 bytes)	http://www.ietf.org/internet-drafts/draft-ietf-pkix-dnstrings-02.txt
Attribute Certificate Policies extension (12,016 bytes)	http://www.ietf.org/internet-drafts/draft-ietf-pkix-acpolicies-extn-03.txt
Certificate Extensions and Attributes Supporting Authentication in PPP and Wireless LAN (14,586 bytes)	http://www.ietf.org/internet-drafts/draft-ietf-pkix-wlan-extns-04.txt
Certificate Validation Protocol (70,631 bytes)	http://www.ietf.org/internet-drafts/draft-ietf-pkix-cvp-02.txt
Internet X.509 Public Key Infrastructure Subject Identification Method (SIM) (27,017 bytes)	http://www.ietf.org/internet-drafts/draft-ietf-pkix-sim-00.txt
X.509 Internet Public Key Infrastructure Online Certificate Status Protocol, version 2 (67,658 bytes)	http://www.ietf.org/internet-drafts/draft-ietf-pkix-ocspv2-ext-01.txt
Additional Algorithms and Identifiers for RSA Cryptography for use in the Internet X.509 Public Key Infrastructure Certificate and Certificate Revocation List (CRL) Profile (48,591 bytes)	http://www.ietf.org/internet-drafts/draft-ietf-pkix-rsa-pkalgs-00.txt
NIST Recommended EC Domain Parameters for PKIX (8673 bytes)	http://www.ietf.org/internet-drafts/draft-ietf-pkix-ecc-nist-recommended-curves-00.txt
DPV and DPD over OCSP (20,270 bytes)	http://www.ietf.org/internet-drafts/draft-ietf-pkix-ocsp-dpvdpd-00.txt
Internet X.509 Public Key Infrastructure LDAP Schema for X.509 CRLs (27,550 bytes)	http://www.ietf.org/internet-drafts/draft-ietf-pkix-ldap-crl-schema-01.txt
Internet X.509 Public Key Infrastructure LDAP Schema for X.509 Attribute Certificates (32,113 bytes)	http://www.ietf.org/internet-drafts/draft-ietf-pkix-ldap-ac-schema-00.txt
Trusted Archive Protocol (TAP) (69,676 bytes)	http://www.ietf.org/internet-drafts/draft-ietf-pkix-tap-00.txt
Internet X.509 Public Key Infrastructure: Qualified Certificates Profile (68565 bytes)	http://www.ietf.org/internet-drafts/draft-ietf-pkix-sonof3039-01.txt

Exhibit 5   Internet Drafts (continued)

Description	URL
Internet X.509 Public Key Infrastructure: Certification Path Building (159,204 bytes)	http://www.ietf.org/internet-drafts/ draft-ietf-pkix-certpathbuild-00.txt
Subject Certificate Access Extension (7915 bytes)	http://www.ietf.org/internet-drafts/ draft-ietf-pkix-sca-00.txt

communications and server systems, and can be cached in unsecured storage in certificate-using systems.

PKCs are used in the process of validating signed data. Specifics vary according to which algorithm is used. There is no specific order in which the checks below must be made. Implementers are free to implement them in the most efficient way for their systems, but the general process works as follows:

- The recipient of signed data verifies that the claimed identity of the user is in accordance with the identity contained in the PKC.
- The recipient validates that no PKC in the path is revoked (by retrieving a suitably current Certificate Revocation List [CRL] or querying an online certificate status responder), and that all PKCs are within their validity periods at the time the data was signed.
- The recipient verifies that the data is not claimed to have any values for which the PKC indicates that the signer is not authorized.
- The recipient verifies that the data has not been altered since signing, by using the public key in the PKC.

If all of the preceding checks pass, the recipient can accept that the purported signer signed the data. The process for keys used for encryption is similar.

Note: It is, of course, possible that someone very different from the signer signed the data — if, for example, the purported signer's private key was compromised. Security depends on all parts of the certificate-using system, including but not limited to physical security of the place the computer resides; personnel security (the trustworthiness of the people who actually develop, install, run, and maintain the system); the security provided by the operating system on which the private key is used; and the security provided the CA. A failure in any one of these areas can cause the entire system security to fail. PKI is limited in scope, however, and only directly addresses issues related to the operation of the PKI subsystem. For guidance in many of the other areas, see RFC 2527.

Exhibit 6   Goals and Milestones

Completion Date	Goals and Milestones
Done	Complete approval of CMC, and qualified certificates documents
Done	Complete time-stamping document
Done	Continue attribute certificate profile work
Done	Complete data certification document
Done	Complete work on attribute certificate profile
Done	Standard RFCs for public key and attribute certificate profiles, CMP, OCSP, CMC, CRMF, TSP, Qualified Certificates, LDAP v2 schema, use of FTP/HTTP, Diffie-Hellman POP
Done	INFORMATIONAL RFCs for X.509 PKI policies and practices, use of KEA
Done	Experimental RFC for Data Validation and Certification Server Protocols done
Done	Production of revised certificate and CRL syntax and processing RFC (son-of-2459)
Done	DPD/DVP Requirements RFC
Done	Certificate Policy & CPS Informational RFC (revision)
Done	Progression of CRMF, CMP, and CMP Transport to DRAFT Standard
Done	Logotype Extension RFC
Done	Proxy Certificate RFC
Done	SCVP proposed Standard RFC
March 2004	Progression of CMC RFCs to DRAFT Standard
March 2004	Progression of Qualified Certificates Profile RFC to DRAFT Standard
March 2004	Progression of Certificate & CRL Profile RFC to DRAFT Standard
March 2004	Progression of Time-Stamp Protocols RFC to DRAFT Standard
June 2004	Progression of Logotype RFC to DRAFT Standard
June 2004	Progression of Proxy Certificate RFC to DRAFT Standard
June 2004	Progression of SCVP to Draft Standard of Attribute Certificate Profile RFC to DRAFT standard

Many systems use the PKC to perform identity-based access control decisions (the identity can be used to support identity-based access control decisions after the client proves that it has access to the private key that corresponds to the public key contained in the PKC). For many systems, this is sufficient; but increasingly, systems are beginning to find that rule-based, role-based, and rank-based access control are required. These forms of access control decisions require additional information that is normally not included in a PKC because the lifetime of the information is much shorter than the lifetime of the public/private key-pair. To support binding this information to a PKC, the attribute certificate (AC) was defined in ANSI and later incorporated into ITU-T Recommendation X.509. The AC format allows any additional information to be bound to a PKC by including, in a digitally signed data structure, a reference back to one specific PKC or to multiple PKCs — this is useful when the subject has the same identity in multiple PKCs. Additionally, the AC can be constructed in such a way that it is only useful at one or more particular targets (Web server, mail host).

Finally, users of a PMI must be confident that the identity purporting to possess an attribute has the right to possess that attribute. This confidence may be obtained through the use of PKCs or it may be configured in the AC-using system. If PKCs are used, the party making the access control decision can determine "if the AC issuer is trusted to issue ACs containing this attribute."

5

TYPES OF VENDOR AND THIRD-PARTY CA SYSTEMS

For many years Public Key Infrastructure (PKI) deployments were the provenance of governments and large, security-conscious corporations and financial institutions. These organizations have the financial and human resources necessary to successfully manage the complexities of a public key system. Lately however, several forces have converged to encourage a broader base of enterprises to take a closer look at PKI.

The first is the rise of E-commerce. PKI's first foot into the enterprise door is often via Secure Sockets Layer (SSL), the protocol that authenticates servers and encrypts traffic in Web-based transactions. A company engaged in E-commerce is, by association, exposed to the basic underpinnings of a PKI, such as digital certificates and public/private key-pairs.

The second force is the widespread deployment of Internet Protocol Security (IPSec) virtual private networks (VPNs). Any significant VPN rollout requires the enterprise to set up a Certificate Authority (CA) to deploy digital certificates to remote users. Once that CA is in place, the certificates generated for the VPN can be applied elsewhere.

According to PKI software vendor Entrust (htpp://www.entrust.com), VPNs are often the first application into the enterprise. The beauty is that it scales. That same PKI could be used for secure e-mail or paperless transactions. It might be one application that can scale to hundreds of applications.

The third force is the PKI vendors. In the past, enterprise PKI was often sold as a security black box. Rather than tailoring the solution to business applications, companies were expected to fit their applications to the solution. According to PKI service pr ovider GeoTrust (http://www.geotrust.com), the industry did not focus on building PKI for applications. People sold PKI for the sake of PKI.

0-8493-0822-4/04/$0.00+$1.50
© 2004 by CRC Press LLC

Now, all of that has changed. PKI vendors are demonstrating to customers how they can make essential business applications faster and more efficient by moving them to the Internet — without sacrificing security. Those applications usually include secure remote access, secure messaging, electronic document exchange, transaction validation, and network authentication.

PKI BASICS

As explained in previous chapters, PKI relies on a pair of keys: one key is publicly available and the other is kept private. These keys are independent but mathematically related, which gives them asymmetric properties; that is, any data encrypted with one key can be decrypted by the other. Conversely, whatever key encrypts data cannot decrypt it.

Asymmetric key pairs are only the beginning of a PKI. Digital certificates and digital signatures are essential parts of the infrastructure. Digital certificates contain a public key and identify the owner of the corresponding private key.

A certification authority (CA) issues digital certificates. A CA can be run from a server in an enterprise, but governments, financial institutions, and PKI vendors also act as CAs. Digital certificates follow the X.509 standard, which defines the contents of a certificate, including a serial number, the subject of the certificate, the subject's public key, an expiration date, and the CA's digital signature.

In addition to issuing certificates, a CA must also be able to revoke certificates; for example, if private keys are compromised or an employee leaves a company. Like a database of bad credit cards, a certificate revocation list (CRL) allows a CA to track expired or invalid certificates.

Digital signatures are included in digital certificates to provide message integrity and some level of non-repudiation. A digital signature is created by running a hashing algorithm on the document or data being signed. This algorithm creates a message digest, a condensed version of the document. If the document remains unchanged, running the same hashing algorithm will produce the same message digest. If even one bit is altered, the algorithm will produce a different digest.

The message digest is encrypted with the sender's private key. The sender includes the encrypted digest and the hashing algorithm used to create the digest. The recipient uses the sender's public key to decrypt the digest, then runs the name of the hashing algorithm on the document. If the resulting digest matches the first, the receiver knows the document has not been altered in transit. Timestamps can also be added to a digital signature to indicate when the transaction took place.

PKI VENDOR MARKETPLACE

The products reviewed in this chapter are defined more by their similarities than by their differences. For example, all products now support Web-based registration, in which end users can apply for certificates via a Web browser. Users authenticate themselves to the registration authority (RA) as defined by the enterprise's security policy. This helps lower the rollout costs of a PKI by automating what is often a manual function.

Many offerings also support some form of roaming, in which users can access digital credentials from any Web-enabled PC, rather than being tied to a specific desktop that stores the credentials on the hard drive. This roaming function enables user mobility, a feature that would otherwise be moot without a more ubiquitous smart card infrastructure (at least in the United States).

Because the products share a similar feature set, potential customers should pay attention to other factors such as price, reputation, customer support, and support for both commercial and homegrown applications. Customers should also take advantage of the robustness of the PKI market. While Entrust, VeriSign, and Baltimore Technologies are the current (and traditional) market leaders, they are no longer the default choice. Competitive pressure from the likes of RSA, GeoTrust, and others means that all of these vendors have to work harder to meet customer needs.

Baltimore Technologies

Baltimore Technologies (http://www.baltimore.com) just recently released the newest version of its flagship PKI product called UniCERT. UniCERT is a full-fledged CA that issues, manages, and revokes digital certificates and key-pairs. The certificates support a full range of applications, including VPNs, secure messaging, digital signatures, and business-to-business and business-to-consumer transactions.

New to UniCERT is Web-based registration. As previously mentioned, Web-based registration automates the registration process. Administrators decide what information users must provide to authenticate themselves to the RA and then put those fields into a Web form. Administrators can also opt for face-to-face authorization for high-value certificates.

Also new to UniCERT is a cloning feature. This feature creates exact duplicates of either the CA or RA to improve availability and performance of certificate administration without the need for clustering hardware or software. For example, a pair of clones can share expiration and reissuing duties. The cloned CA can also be used for fail-over.

UniCERT includes a module for the Extensible Markup Language (XML) Key Management Specification (XKMS) standard being drafted by the

World Wide Web Consortium. XKMS provides PKI management functions such as certificate location and certificate validation in Web services, helping to make Web services more secure. The UniCERT XKMS server provides an interface for XML-aware business applications to utilize PKI services.

The software is available on several platforms, including Windows NT/2000/XP, Solaris, and HP-UX. It also supports both Active Directory and Lightweight Directory Access Protocol (LDAP) to store certificate information.

Entrust

Entrust (http://www.entrust.com) provides a full range of software products that apply PKI to various applications. Its product line includes Entrust Authority, TruePass, and Entelligence.

Entrust Authority was formerly known as Entrust/PKI. Central to the Authority product is the Security Manager, a CA that issues, manages, and revokes X.509 certificates. It performs key backup and recovery, updates key-pairs, and supports cross certification for compatibility with certificates from competitors such as VeriSign. It also supports Active Directory and X.500 and Lightweight Directory Access Protocol (LDAP) directories for certificate repositories.

Authority provides Web-based registration to issue first-time certificates and key-pairs. To request digital credentials, users fill in a Web form with identification information. The registration form is configurable, allowing administrators to gather data that uniquely identifies the user (e.g., mother's maiden name, employee ID number, or recent paycheck amount).

The product also supports mobile users. Through the use of the Authority Roaming Server, users can access their digital credentials (certificates and keys) from any Web browser. The credentials are delivered via a Java applet over an encrypted session, and are removed from the browser once the session is terminated.

Updated features in Authority include support for Elliptic Curve Cryptography (ECC), commonly used for wireless applications. Authority also supports dual key-pairs to separate encryption and signing functions. Backup encryption keys can be stored and encrypted via the Advanced Encryption Standard (AES), the U.S. Government's replacement for the aging Triple Data Encryption Standard (DES) encryption algorithm. Finally, according to Entrust, a single CA can support up to 20 million users.

Entrust's TruePass targets Web-based applications. Building on the Authority platform, it enables companies to move business applications to the Web, making those applications more available to employees, business partners, suppliers, and customers. TruePass provides user authentication, transaction validation through digital signatures and time-stamps, transaction logging, and encrypted communications.

TruePass does not require client-side software. Users can be enrolled via a Web form; however, companies using TruePass must determine what levels of verification they require before issuing credentials, especially when enrolling people outside the organization.

Once registration is complete, digital credentials can be stored in an Authority Roaming Server, allowing users to access those credentials from any PC. These credentials can be used for encryption and digital signatures. Optionally, digital credentials can be stored on smart cards, or securely stored on a specific desktop.

Entelligence is aimed at specific enterprise applications and consists of four modules. The first is Desktop Manager, client-based software that handles key management, backup, and certificate updates; maintains key histories; and checks Certificate Revocation Lists (CRLs) to validate incoming and outgoing certificates. Rather than require separate credentials for disparate applications, Desktop Manager lets users employ one set of credentials for a variety of services, including secure e-mail, Web access, digital signatures, VPN access, and desktop file encryption.

The second module is the Entelligence E-Mail plug-in, which enables users to digitally sign and encrypt e-mail. It interoperates with Microsoft Outlook and Exchange and Lotus Domino and Notes. Encryption keys are backed up and stored so that enciphered e-mail can always be recovered. The module also interoperates with content-filtering software from Tumbleweed. Mail can be scanned for viruses and for content violating company policies, such as sexual language, before being sent.

The third module helps secure enterprise Web applications and E-commerce. Transactions can be encrypted using Triple DES or CAST 128 algorithms; and users can digitally sign HTML documents for transaction verification. The module supports HTTP as well as the Internet Explorer and Netscape Navigator browsers.

The last Entelligence module is a file plug-in. It encrypts and decrypts files and folders stored on desktops, laptops, and network drives. Users select the file to be encrypted and then choose an encryption option from a menu. The module can also be configured to automatically encrypt files saved in designated folders. Numerous encryption algorithms are supported, including Triple DES and ECC.

GeoTrust

As previously mentioned, GeoTrust (http://www.geotrust.com) is a pure-play PKI service provider. The company recently announced a partnership with Register.com in which merchants who register a domain name with

Register.com can get Secure Sockets Layer (SSL) certificates from GeoTrust. This partnership is a direct challenge to VeriSign's registration and SSL certificate business.

GeoTrust's product line includes SSL certificates for E-commerce, site identity verification, and PKI services for enterprise applications. Its enterprise-focused offering is called True Credentials. GeoTrust divides True Credentials into three targeted services: paperless transactions, secure access, and secure messaging.

Paperless transactions provide authentication and digital signatures for companies that want to move paper-based processes to electronic forms. Secure access focuses on remote employees and trading partners. It uses a Web-based interface to provide intranet and extranet users access to enterprise applications. It also works with VPN hardware and clients to provide remote users secure network access. Secure messaging enables encryption and digital signing of e-mail, and is compatible with Microsoft Exchange and Outlook, LotusDomino and Notes, and Eudora.

GeoTrust does not issue management software to its enterprise customers. Rather, a designated administrator or administrators control policies for key recovery, key revocation, and certificate renewal through a browser that points back to GeoTrust's facility. Certificates are issued to end users through a Web browser, and the digital credentials are stored on the desktop.

RSA Security

RSA's (http://www.rsasecurity.com) Keon is an enterprise-focused PKI system. It is designed for secure e-mail, secure application access, reduced sign-on, and desktop file encryption. It is also appropriate for Web-based SSL transactions and can produce certificates for IPSec VPNs.

RSA divides Keon into components that can be applied to various business processes and applications. Buyers only have to purchase the components that meet their applications' requirements.

RSA's Keon system provides credential storage. A user's key credentials can be stored in a smart card or in an encrypted container that can be transferred to the user's desktop when needed.

The certificate server (CS) is the heart of RSA's product line. The CS issues and revokes certificates, acts as the certificate repository, and registers users. The CS distributes industry-standard X.509 v3 certificates for SSL, Secure Multimedia Internet Message Extensions (S/MIME), and IPSec applications, and can also be integrated with other Keon components to provide PKI for other applications. Because the certificates are standards based, they are interoperable with certificates issued by other major PKI vendors, including VeriSign.

Users enroll for certificates via a Web browser. Certificates are stored in a Netscape LDAP server or other LDAP-compliant directories. The CS includes an embedded LDAP client to communicate with the directory.

An optional component to the CS is a hardware-based key archive system, called the Key Recovery Module (KRM). The KRM securely stores a copy of the private keys used to encrypt data. These copies ensure that encrypted data can be recovered in the event of lost or corrupted private keys.

Note: Private keys that are used for digital signatures are never duplicated because this violates a digital signature's quality of non-repudiation.

Access to duplicate keys is controlled by a private key that is divided among a number of individual smart cards. A specific number of administrators in possession of the smart cards must be present at the same time to get a complete key.

Next is the Keon Security Server (SS). The SS offers authentication, authorization, certificate validation, credential store management, and other services. The SS also promotes mobility by storing user keys and certificates that users can download via a Web browser using SSL.

Whenever a user needs his or her credentials, he or she accesses the SS from a PC running the Keon Desktop client software. After the user authenticates to the SS, the credentials are transferred in an encrypted container and can be stored temporarily on the user's desktop.

Keon Desktop is client software that runs on desktops or laptops. It gives users access to their keys and certificates for applications such as network authentication, secure e-mail, and IPSec VPN. Keon Desktop also allows for local file encryption.

Keon Desktop also supports multiple authentication methods, including smart cards, tokens, biometrics, and passwords. Administrators who want strong non-repudiation should activate the second key-pair to separate encryption and digital signing functions.

Note: In default mode, Keon creates two key-pairs for either standard or virtual smart cards, but uses only one pair for both encryption and digital signatures.

VeriSign

VeriSign (http://www.verisign.com) is the market leader in outsourced PKI services. The heart of its enterprise offering is the Managed PKI service. While VeriSign generates the keys and certificates used in the infrastructure, the enterprise retains complete control over the registration and revocation process, including how users apply for certificates (e.g., via a customized Web form) and what authentication procedures they undergo.

VeriSign supports dual key-pair generation to separate encryption and digital signing functions. A user's private keys can be deployed to a smart card or token, but most often they are stored locally on the hard drive.

A key management system allows the enterprise to back up private keys that are used for encryption. The backup keys are stored in an encrypted form at the enterprise — VeriSign does not store copies of private keys on its premises. However, the key to unlock the encrypted backups is stored by VeriSign. This eliminates a single point of failure regarding key storage.

With the Managed PKI service deployed, companies can then integrate the certificates into various applications, including E-commerce transactions, VPNs, secure document signing and transmission, and secure e-mail.

For example, VeriSign's Go Secure for Microsoft Exchange lets users encrypt and digitally sign e-mail using a standard Outlook 98/2000/XP client. An Exchange Server directory stores digital certificates so that a sender can access the recipient's public key to encrypt a message. Private keys are stored on a hardware device or locally on the PC for digital signing. Go Secure is also available for Lotus Notes.

VeriSign also offers a roaming solution for mobile end users. A browser plug-in known as a Personal Trust Agent prompts the user for a password. Once the user authenticates him- or herself, the plug-in accesses the user's certificate and private key, and performs any signing or encryption functions required by the application on the user's behalf.

The certificate is never stored on the local machine's hard drive. It is wiped from memory either at the end of the transaction or if the session times out. The roaming service supports both Internet Explorer and Netscape.

OTHER PKI VENDORS

While PKI has its big three providers — Entrust, VeriSign, and Baltimore Technologies — the market is alive with other competitors. Here are several other companies that offer PKI solutions, and a brief summary of their products.

nCipher

As the number of users and frequency of transactions in your PKI grow, the processing demands on your infrastructure can grow exponentially, threatening the overall performance of your online application and the response time experienced by your users and customers. nCipher's (http://www.ncipher.com/) Hardware Security Modules (HSMs) combat PKI performance challenges through high-speed transaction acceleration capabilities. By offloading processor-intensive tasks such as creating digital signatures from your secure servers to an nShield HSM, you can increase server processing capacity. This frees the CPU to respond to more user requests and interact with other PKI resources, such as databases, directories, and applications.

In fact, you can achieve sustained throughput of up to 400 signatures per second from a single nShield HSM or chain multiple HSMs together to handle additional signing needs. NShield UltraSign delivers the processing capacity of multiple high-powered servers.

NCipher is a developer of hardware and software Internet security products that help global E-businesses maximize information security, system scalability, and transaction processing performance in electronic commerce and public key infrastructure applications. Many organizations requiring the highest level of online security from Microsoft to Barclays Bank to the U.S. Navy use nCipher products to protect their information assets and global networks from external and internal security risks. NCipher's products are particularly well suited to organizations seeking to manage risk, boost system performance, or innovate new online services, such as financial institutions, E-retailers, and online service providers (ISPs/ASPs).

Certicom

Well-known vulnerabilities in the Wired Equivalent Privacy (WEP) standard have prompted many companies to seek additional layers of security. Certicom (http://www.certicom.com) offers both managed and in-house PKI solutions to provide stronger authentication and better-implemented encryption for wireless LANs than WEP. Certicom offers both Elliptic Curve Cryptography (ECC) and RSA algorithms. ECC, which uses shorter keys, is faster and less computationally intensive, and is often more appropriate for wireless devices.

Computer Associates

Recently, Computer Associates (CA) (http://www.ca.com) announced eTrustPKI, a software-based PKI solution for the enterprise. ETrust issues X.509 digital certificates that can be used for various applications, including VPN, single sign-on, and Web access. However, eTrust is designed to integrate most closely with products from CA, and may be less appropriate for companies that have not deployed other CA solutions.

Digital Signature Trust (Identrus)

Digital Signature Trust (DST) is a PKI service provider. Its core product is the TrustID platform, which issues digital certificates to an enterprise that wants to move business transactions online, use digital signatures, and securely store data. Recently, DST (http://www.digsigtrust.com) announced that it was being acquired by Identrus (http://www.identrus.com). Identrus is a global trust broker that manages the contract infrastructure for major banks to issue digital certificates both to each other and consumers.

Novell

The Novell Certificate Server (http://www.novell.com) is an enterprise PKI solution that integrates with the Novell Directory Service (NDS). It acts as a Certificate Authority and can issue certificates to both end users and Web servers for SSL transactions.

Windows 2000/XP

Finally, Microsoft's Windows 2000/XP OS can issue X.509 digital certificates to other PKI-enabled Microsoft (http://www.microsoft.com) applications such as Exchange and Outlook. However, Microsoft's solution offers limited management capabilities and is most suited for a homogenous Windows environment.

SUMMARY

The market for PKI solutions remains in a state of anticipation; and, as vendors await the explosion of demand that has been expected for several years now, they are jockeying for position with a variety of acquisitions and partnerships. The leading vendors of PKI solutions discussed in this chapter provide several types of PKI solutions, including outsourced solutions in which the vendor manages the infrastructure and issues the certificates; in-house solutions in which the customer issues the certificates; and merchant certificates used mainly for business-to-consumer (B2C) transactions. While the leading vendors have historically emphasized different types of solutions, they have started to converge in terms of their offerings. In addition, they have been busy rectifying perceived weaknesses, expanding geographically, and experimenting with new types of integrations. While revenues for all vendors are still low (less than $400 million), they are enjoying rapid growth. Meanwhile, several other vendors also want to play in this space, and some of them are quite competitive.

The vendors discussed in this chapter have led the market for PKI solutions during the past several years. Some of these vendors include Entrust, Baltimore Technologies, and VeriSign. These vendors initially established strengths in different areas (in-house solutions, outsourced solutions, merchant certificates), but pigeonholing any one of them as a provider of a certain kind of solution is becoming less and less appropriate. All of them are beginning to offer a full range of offerings as they position themselves for the takeoff that is anticipated in the PKI market. As you continue to await this explosion of demand, these vendors, and especially Entrust, will continue to dominate the market, bolstering their positions with a variety of acquisitions and partnerships.

Numerous other vendors are entering the PKI market, and some of them offer notable strengths in certain areas. But it will be some time before they are able to win sufficient mindshare to represent a serious challenge to the dominant players.

Finally, companies considering a PKI should, first of all, establish clearly that they need a PKI and that they are prepared to incur the costs of implementation. If a PKI is really warranted, Entrust, Baltimore Technologies, and VeriSign should definitely be among the companies on their short list. Other vendors might also deserve consideration for certain specialized strengths, such as Certicom's expertise in wireless PKI or RSA's ability to deliver PKI-enabled single sign-on for employees.

6

UNDERSTANDING DIGITAL CERTIFICATES AND SECURE SOCKETS LAYER (SSL)

Peter Robinson

DIGITAL CERTIFICATES

What are they? Digital certificates are electronic files that are used to uniquely identify people and resources over networks such as the Internet. Digital certificates also enable secure, confidential communication between two parties.

When you travel to another country, your passport provides a universal way to establish your identity and gain entry. Digital certificates provide similar identification in the electronic world. Certificates are issued by a trusted third party called a Certification Authority (CA). Much like the role of the passport office, the role of the CA is to validate the certificate holder's identity and to "sign" the certificate so that it cannot be forged or tampered with. Once a CA has signed a certificate, the holder can present their certificate to people, Web sites, and network resources to prove their identity and establish encrypted, confidential communications.

Note: For more information on trust, refer to the White Paper *The Concept of Trust in Network Security,* available at: http://www.entrust.com/resourcecenter/whitepapers.htm

A certificate typically includes a variety of information pertaining to its owner and to the CA that issued it, such as:

- The name of the holder and other identification information required to uniquely identify the holder, such as the URL of the Web server using the certificate, or an individual's e-mail address.

- The holder's public key (more on this below). The public key can be used to encrypt sensitive information for the certificate holder.
- The name of the Certification Authority that issued the certificate.
- A serial number.
- The validity period (or lifetime) of the certificate (a start and an end date).

In creating the certificate, this information is digitally signed by the issuing CA. The CA's signature on the certificate is like a tamper-detection seal on a bottle of pills — any tampering with the contents is easily detected.

Digital certificates are based on public key cryptography, which uses a pair of keys for encryption and decryption. With public key cryptography, keys work in pairs of matched "public" and "private" keys. In cryptographic systems, the term "key" refers to a numerical value used by an algorithm to alter information, making that information secure and visible only to individuals who have the corresponding key to recover the information.

Note: For more information on public key cryptography, refer to the White Paper *An Introduction to Cryptography,* available at: http://www.entrust. com/resourcecenter/whitepapers.htm

The public key can be freely distributed without compromising the private key, which must be kept secret by its owner. Because these keys only work as a pair, an operation (for example, encryption) done with the public key can only be undone (decrypted) with the corresponding private key, and vice versa.

A digital certificate securely binds your identity, as verified by a trusted third party (a CA), with your public key.

WEB SERVER CERTIFICATES

A Web server certificate is a certificate that authenticates the identity of a Web site to visiting browsers. When a browser user wants to send confidential information to a Web server, the browser will access the server's digital certificate. The certificate, which contains the Web server's public key, will be used by the browser to:

- Authenticate the identity of the Web server (the Web site)
- Encrypt information for the server using Secure Sockets Layer (SSL) technology (more on SSL below)

Since the Web server is the only one with access to its private key, only the server can decrypt the information. This is how the information remains confidential and tamper-proof while in transit across the Internet.

CA CERTIFICATES

A CA certificate is a certificate that identifies a Certification Authority. CA certificates are just like other digital certificates except that they are self-signed. CA certificates are used to determine whether to trust certificates issued by the CA.

In the case of a passport, a passport control officer will verify the validity and authenticity of your passport and determine whether to permit you entry. Similarly, the CA certificate is used to authenticate and validate the Web server certificate. When a Web server certificate is presented to a browser, the browser uses the CA certificate to determine whether to trust the Web server's certificate. If the server certificate is valid and trusted, the browser and Web server will establish an SSL connection. If the server certificate is not valid, the server certificate is rejected and the SSL session is stopped.

CA certificates come pre-installed on most popular Web browsers, including those from Microsoft® and Netscape®.

SECURE SOCKETS LAYER (SSL)

What is SSL? Secure Sockets Layer (SSL) technology is a security protocol. It is today's *de facto* standard for securing communications and transactions across the Internet. SSL has been implemented in all the major browsers and Web servers and, as such, plays a major role in today's E-commerce and E-business activities on the Web.

The SSL protocol uses digital certificates to create a secure, confidential communications "pipe" between two entities. Data transmitted over an SSL connection cannot be tampered with or forged without the two parties becoming immediately aware of the tampering. The newest version of the SSL standard has been renamed TLS (Transport Layer Security). You will often see these terms used interchangeably. Since the term SSL is more commonly understood, we will continue to use it throughout this chapter.

How Certificates Are Used in an SSL Transaction

Suppose Alice wants to connect to a secure Web site to buy something online:

- When Alice visits a Web site secured with SSL (typically indicated by a URL that begins with "https:"), her browser sends a "Client Hello" message to the Web server indicating that a secure session (SSL) is requested.
- The Web server responds by sending Alice its server certificate (which includes its public key).

- Alice's browser will verify that the server's certificate is valid and has been signed by a CA whose certificate is in the browser's database (and who Alice trusts). It will also verify that the CA certificate has not expired.
- If the certificates are all valid, Alice's browser will generate a one-time, unique "session" key and encrypt it with the server's public key. Her browser will then send the encrypted session key to the server so that they will both have a copy.
- The server will decrypt the message using its private key and recover the session key.

At this point Alice can be assured of two things:

- The Web site she is communicating with is really the one it claims to be (its identity has been verified).
- Only Alice's browser and the Web server have a copy of the session key.

The SSL "handshake" — the process of identifying the two parties that want to establish an SSL connection — is complete and a secure communications "pipe" has been established. Alice's browser and the Web server can now use the session key to send encrypted information back and forth, knowing that their communications are confidential and tamper-proof. The entire process of establishing the SSL connection typically happens transparently to the user and takes only seconds.

A key or padlock icon in the lower corner of the browser window identifies the security mode of a browser. When the browser is running in "normal" mode, the key looks broken or the padlock looks open. Once an SSL connection has been established, the key becomes whole, or the padlock becomes closed, indicating that the browser is now in "secure" mode.

SSL is supported in the vast majority of browsers, which means that almost anyone with a browser can reap the benefits of SSL encryption. SSL is also incorporated into most Web servers on the market.

WHAT'S NEXT?

The Internet, intranets, extranets, and wireless networks are redefining how companies communicate and do business. As the value of business relationships and transactions increase, so do the associated risks and security requirements. Entrust provides the world's most advanced security solutions for protecting business relationships and transactions with a full range of products based on public key infrastructure (PKI) technology.

To learn more about PKI and how it can help your business grow, please refer to the Entrust Web site at http://www.entrust.com.

Entrust is a registered trademark of Entrust, Inc. in the United States and certain other countries. Entrust is a registered trademark of Entrust Limited in Canada. All other Entrust product names and service names are trademarks or registered trademarks of Entrust, Inc or Entrust Limited. All other company and product names are trademarks or registered trademarks of their respective owners.

7

CA SYSTEM ATTACKS

Deloitte Touche Tohmatsu

Certificate Authority (CA) systems may be the subject of attacks through several different ways. Besides hacker attacks from the outside, CA operations are vulnerable to collusion, sabotage, disgruntlement, or outright theft by employees from within.

EXTERNAL ATTACKS ON THE CA

External attacks attempt to steal private keys using computers located outside the physical CA system environment. They may arrive via the Internet, break-ins to private lines, or back-door methods through a local area network within the CA. The break-ins might attempt to foil Web page security, try to exploit known operating system flaws, or try and gain control of the server.

INTERNAL ATTACKS ON THE CA

At least as great a threat to private keys lies with those employees responsible for operating and maintaining the CA system. CA private keys are an attractive target to those who work with them.

CAs can help lessen their attractiveness to internal theft by limiting their access and ensuring that that no one person has full knowledge of a complete key. Beyond storing them across several hardware devices (crypto-boxes), the environment in which the hardware itself resides should be ultra-secure. Strict access control, electronic monitoring, and intruder-detection on each device should deter even the most tenacious would-be thieves.

With the preceding in mind, let's take a detailed look at how to protect CAs from internal and external attacks. As previously explained, the heart of trust in a public key infrastructure (PKI) is the certificate authority (CA).

Fundamental to this trust is the CA's root cryptographic signing key, which is used to sign the public keys of certificate holders and, more importantly, its own public key. The compromise of a CA's root key by malicious intent, inadvertent errors, or system failures can be of catastrophic proportions. Hence, this root signing key must be diligently protected by the best technologies and practices within the cryptographic community.

PROTECTING THE CA ROOT KEY FROM ATTACK

Today many organizations are grappling with the issue of implementing digital certificate-based authentication for E-business purposes. This can be accomplished by becoming their own certificate authority (CA) or by utilizing the services of a public CA. In either case, there is explicit reliance on a public key infrastructure (PKI), internal or external, of which the CA is a critical element. Such a PKI comprises the technology, procedures, and security practices for generating and managing certificates in a trustworthy fashion.[1]

The heart of trust in a public key infrastructure is the certificate authority (CA). Fundamental to this trust is the CA's root cryptographic signing key, which is used to sign the public keys of certificate holders and, more importantly, its own public key. The compromise of a CA's root key by malicious intent, inadvertent errors, or system failures can be of catastrophic proportions. Hence, this root signing key must be diligently protected by the best technologies and practices within the cryptographic community. Exhibit 1 shows the processing context for a CA.[1]

Leading security product manufacturers believe that such protection can be provided by placing all cryptographic key management and encryption/decryption functions into a hardware device rather than residing in software on a host computer. By using a trusted hardware cryptographic module in conjunction with tamper-proof tokens, the sensitive cryptographic processing, key generation, verification, storage, and deletion functions can be offloaded from the CA server.[1]

This offloading not only protects the critical keying data, but also provides the benefit of backing up the keying material for disaster recovery. To uniformly evaluate security modules (whether hardware, software, or some combination), the U.S. National Institute of Standards and Technology (NIST), the U.S. National Security Agency (NSA), and the Canadian Communications Security Establishment (CSE) have developed a set of criteria. These criteria are documented in Federal Information Processing Standard (FIPS) 140-1 — Security for Cryptographic Modules. The criteria are broken into four levels; Levels 3 and 4 address the requirements for cryptographic modules that provide, for example, high assurance cryptographic key protection, trusted software mechanisms, and strong authentication.[1]

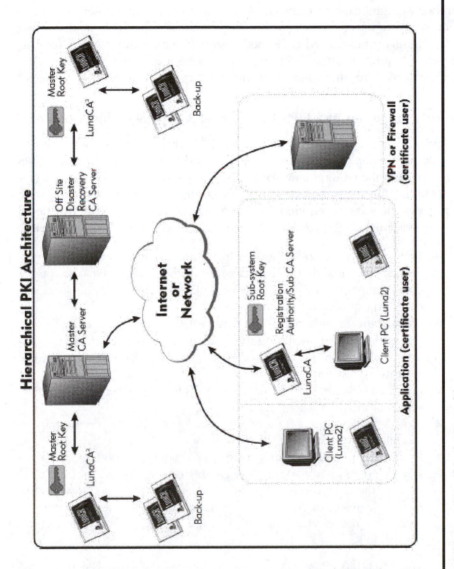

Exhibit 1 Hierarchical PKI Architecture

Devices capable of meeting the FIPS 140-1 Level 3 or higher standards are required to provide cryptographic key generation and transport in hardware. In this manner, a trusted path from CA key generation to key backup to key operational usage can be assured.

A FIPS 140-1 Level 3 validated cryptographic module (VCM) has a number of significant security and operational properties over an equivalent software-based cryptographic implementation, which is discussed next. These properties, when joined together with tamper-proof tokens, pair-wise key backup mechanisms, and independent channel authentication methods, offer the potential to provide scalable, secure PKI services.[1]

Security Properties of a FIPS 140-1 Level 3 Cryptographic Module

A device awarded the FIPS 140-1 Level 3 Validation has been proven to provide a number of important security properties. As noted earlier, FIPS 140-1 specifies the requirements for four security levels, but does not describe in detail the threats mitigated, or conversely the security benefits accrued, by meeting the security requirements for a given level. The overall functional security objectives (FSO) for a FIPS 140-1 Validation comprise the following:

- Protect a cryptographic module from unauthorized operation or use.
- Prevent the unauthorized disclosure of the non-public contents of the cryptographic module, including plaintext cryptographic keys and other critical security parameters.
- Prevent the unauthorized and undetected modification of the cryptographic module, including the unauthorized modification, substitution, insertion, and deletion of cryptographic keys and other critical security parameters.
- Employ FIPS approved security methods for the protection of unclassified information.
- Provide indications of the operational state of the cryptographic module.
- Ensure the proper operation of the cryptographic module.
- Detect errors in the operation of the cryptographic module and prevent the compromise of sensitive data and critical security parameters as a result of those errors (this is referred to as "failsafe;" — that is, if the device fails, it will fail in such a way as not to compromise its secrets).[1]

To pass FIPS 140-1 Level 3 Validation, the manufacturer of the cryptographic module must demonstrate that the module has the properties as shown in Exhibit 2.[1]

The key items recommended to assure CA root key protection include physical tamper protection, attack resistance, and trusted path access. By

Exhibit 2   Cryptographic Module Properties

Properties	Description
Crypto module	Specification of cryptographic module and cryptographic boundary; description of cryptographic module, including all hardware, software, and firmware components; statement of module security policy.
Module interfaces	Data ports for critical security parameters physically separated from other data ports.
Roles and services	Identity-based operator authentication.
Finite state machine	Specification of finite state machine model; required states and optional states; state transition diagram and specification of state transitions.
Physical security	Tamper detection and response for covers and doors.
Software security	High-level language implementation.
Operating system	Labeled data protection; trusted communication path.
Key management	Entry/exit of keys in encrypted form or direct entry/exit with split knowledge procedures.
Random number generator	Provide capability for performing statistical tests for randomness on demand.
Cryptographic algorithms	FIPS approved cryptographic algorithms for protecting unclassified information.
EMI/EMC	FCC part 15, Subpart J, Class B (home use).
Self-tests	Power-up test and conditional tests.
Authentication	Identity-based authentication: Must authenticate the identity of an operator Must verify that the identified operator is authorized to assume a specific role and perform a corresponding set of services

using hardware root-key protection from the beginning of deployment, an organization can achieve FIPS 140-1 Level 3 security at the outset. The inherent risks associated with software are mitigated because the root key will always have been stored in protected and trusted FIPS 140-1 Level 3 validated hardware.[1]

Physical Tamper Protection

The Validated Cryptographic Module has "tamper" protection, such that any attempt to open or modify the device will immediately be evident. Additionally, the Level 3 device is so constructed that if one tries to open it, the device destroys any of its cryptographic secrets so that the secrets cannot be recovered.[1]

Attack Resistance — Cryptographic Solutions in FIPS Validated Hardware

Cryptographic software is vulnerable to a number of attacks that cannot be perpetrated on a FIPS 140-1 Level 3 Cryptographic Module. Such attacks include the following:

- The copy attack
- Modification attacks
- Theft of the PC or computer containing the cryptographic software[1]

The Copy Attack

The copy attack occurs when someone surreptitiously copies the software. There is frequently no evidence of the attack. For example, an attacker could insert a diskette into a crucial PC and copy the encryption files. Having the copy permits the attackers to study all aspects of the software at their leisure.[1]

To mount an attack on copied software, the attacker would look for "buried" or hidden secrets, which contain or are crucial security information such as passwords and secret keys. One method of analysis is to examine the software code for stretches that appear to be random strings. These are frequently the secrets or transformation of the secrets. Once identified, the attacker can launch a number of attacks to disclose these secrets. Having these secrets, the attacker can eavesdrop into what is thought to be secure communication and, if the attacker desires, the attacker can masquerade as a *bona fide* user.[1]

Modification Attacks

A sophisticated attacker can introduce eavesdropping programs. These programs can be introduced by virus infection, or by having an unsuspecting user accept a "Trojan horse." A Trojan horse is a program that performs useful functions for the user, but, as an "extra-added" function, does things that the user is unaware of. The added "feature" could be eavesdropping software within the machine. The software could read the plaintext as it transverses the internal communications within the computer. Or, the devices could monitor the registers that perform the cryptographic calculations, capturing the intermediate values. Periodically, the introduced software sends to the attacker a message containing its ill-gotten information. Using the intermediate values, an attacker can reconstruct the cryptographic process and the cryptographic keys.[1]

Another modification attack is for the attacker to change the cryptographic algorithms, such that the algorithms appear to be running correctly but, in reality, are not. For example, an attacker can change a counter to a static number, so that a cryptographic key never changes. Additionally, once the attacker forces the software to use a never-changing key, the attacker can force the software to use a key that the attacker knows. Now, the attacker can, again, listen in to a supposedly secure communication, and if the attacker desires, send bogus but authentic looking messages.[1]

Theft of the PC or Computer Containing the Cryptographic Software

Once in possession of the PC, the attacker can use a multitude of techniques to analyze the cryptographic algorithms and extract the secrets. A FIPS 140-1 Level 3 Validated Cryptographic Module negates this attack by its self-protecting anti-tampering defenses that obliterate any secrets if the module detects someone attempting to open it. Additionally, the module requires identity-based authentication from its users. Only when a user presents the proper identification will the module permit the user to interact with the module.[1]

Trusted Path

For certificate authorities in particular, the concept of trusted path is a critical one. The root signing key must be generated securely; a backup key, stored securely in a trusted crypto module at an alternate site for disaster recovery purposes, and, finally, it must be securely entered into the CA's signing engine. Hence, the preservation of the trust level of the CA's key occurs both within and without the cryptographic processing environment.[1]

A FIPS 140-1 Level 3 validated cryptographic module enables a "trusted path" that cannot be compromised to reveal the secrets, such as cryptographic keys and protecting critical data. This precludes attacks such as eavesdropping on the transmissions between the various components needed to generate cryptographic keys and conduct secure encryption and decryption. In less secure systems, the transmission of information into and out of a machine is a target for a cryptographic attack. For example, in many systems, the cryptographic keys are stored encrypted under a secure key, but the keys must be decrypted and transported in plaintext ("naked" or in the usable form) into memory or registers that are used in the cryptographic process. If attackers can "capture" these transmissions, they have the plaintext keys and can read the secure transmissions and even send fake "authentic" messages.[1]

The same vulnerability can occur when one loads the cryptographic keys, passwords, or other critical secrets into a machine. This concept is illustrated in Exhibit 3, which shows the trusted path associated with the generation, storage, and distribution of the root signing key for a certificate authority.[1]

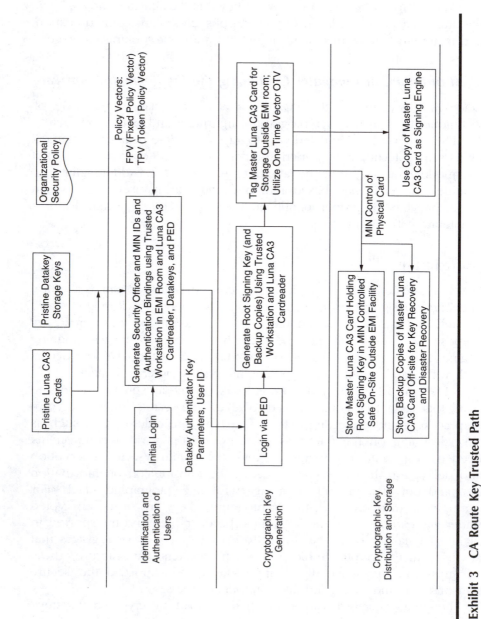

Exhibit 3 CA Route Key Trusted Path

Additionally, the module must be so constructed that no "plaintext" ("naked") secret key can ever be exposed. If secret keys are exported (for secure distribution or for backup), the secrets are either encrypted or "split" into key "parts." The key parts are constructed such that the compromise of individual key parts will not reveal the original secret. The original secret can only be reconstructed in a secure trusted environment from a prerequisite set of key parts. This process of splitting the keys into parts is frequently referred to as "split knowledge" and is combined with a second security principle called "nperson control (n > 2)." Dual control, for example, requires collusion to compromise a secret (that no single person [or machine] can compromise the secret). For example, a secret key might be split into two parts, with each part given to a different trusted courier. A courier might be forced to compromise his or her part; but because he or she does not have or control the second part, the secret is not compromised.[1]

For example, in the Chrysalis-ITS system (www.chrysalis-its.com), within the Luna CA3 Cryptographic module, the private key (secret PK) is encrypted under a "master" symmetrical key (M-key) card:[1]

$$\text{M-key}$$
$$\text{secret PK} \rightarrow {}_{\text{M-key}} \{\text{secret PK}\}$$

Then the cryptographic module "splits" the M-key into n parts, such that m of these parts are needed to reconstruct the original M-key:[1]

$$\text{M-key} \rightarrow \text{m-key1, m-key2, ..., m-key}_n$$

Now, the encrypted secret PK ($_{\text{M-key}}$ {secret PK}) can be safely transported without fear of it being compromised, even if intercepted. Furthermore, when the encrypted secret PK ($_{\text{M-key}}$ {secret PK}) arrives at its destination, it can be decrypted only when a sufficient number of the M-key's key parts are assembled.[1]

$$\text{m-key1 + m-key2 + ...+ m-keym} \rightarrow \text{M-key}$$

then,

$$\text{M-key}$$
$$_{\text{M-key}} \{\text{secret PK}\} \rightarrow \text{secret PK.}$$

The preceding sequence of events and secure processes to enforce the principle of preventing any single individual from being able to compromise the security and secrets of a system, is also called the principle of

Exhibit 4 Hardware versus Software Efficacy and Resilience to Attack

Attack Situation	Hardware	Software

Detection of modification:
Introduction of "Trojan horses"
Program modification such as:
  Changing counters to a constant value
  Substituting a known value for a secret (cryptographic value)
	Tamper evidence: FIPS 140-1 Level 3	Difficult to detect or prevent

Detection of copying of secrets (permitting masquerade attacks)	Tamper evidence: FIPS 140-1 Level 3	Difficult; must have constant physical protection and surveillance of the computer
Detection of reading intermediate calculations (registers)	Tamper evidence: FIPS 140-1 Level 3	Difficult; must have constant physical protection and surveillance of the computer
Detection of eavesdropping of intra-device communication (from registers to memory devices along internal buses)	Tamper evidence: FIPS 140-1 Level 3, "Trusted Path"	Difficult; requires constant physical protection and surveillance of the computer
Detection of eavesdropping of inter-device communication (data moving from the computer to an external)	Tamper evidence: FIPS 140-1 Level 3, "Trusted Path"	Difficult; must have constant physical protection and surveillance of the computer
Protection of secrets, even if device is stolen	FIPS 140-1 Level 3 controls (requires two-factor authentication)	None; data is always vulnerable to dictionary attacks

Prevention of sabotage	Tamper evidence: FIPS 140-1 Level 3	Difficult; must have constant physical protection and surveillance of the computer
Separation of duties	Physically different and differentiated Datakeys	Difficult
Parallel processing	Hardware cryptographic accelerators! Off-loading from processor! Accelerated processing	Requires intensive CPU processing

the "separation of duties," although the phrase "n-person control" seems to be more prevalent.[1]

This is exemplified in the Chrysalis-ITS Luna CA3 security key management system. It uses various colored Datakeys, secure cryptographic key transport devices, to bind users, duties, and cryptographic privileges. The Chrysalis-ITS system ascribes specific colored Datakey tokens to specific user ids, tasks, and security roles in order to provide strong authentication binding.[1]

SUMMARY

Based on the preceding observations, the following specific recommendations hold with regard to CA root key protection:

- The root key should be generated in a FIPS 140-1 Level 3 or higher security module.
- The root key should never exist in plaintext outside the cryptographic boundary of a FIPS 140-1 Level 3 or higher module.
- Movement or backup of the CA root key should not expose the root key.
- Access to the root key security module should require strong authentication and m/n access control splits where m > 2, n > 4 (3/5).
- Physical attack to the security module should disable the cryptographic functions and destroy the keying data.[1]

Finally, providing the preceding functionality at the required level of security for CA operations requires that these functions all be performed in hardware meeting FIPS stringent requirements. Through the use of FIPS approved hardware, it is possible to enhance the security of CA cryptographic processing and key management functions over those provided by software-only solutions across a wide spectrum of attack situations. Exhibit 4 illustrates such a comparative summary.[1]

REFERENCES

1. "CA Root Key Protection — Recommended Practices," ©2003 by Deloitte Touche Tohmatsu. All rights reserved. Deloitte & Touche (National Office), Deloitte & Touche Security Services, LLC, 1633 Broadway, New York, New York 10019-6754, United States, 2003.

8

KEY ESCROW VERSUS KEY RECOVERY

Bob Walder

INTRODUCTION

Information is at risk today as never before.

Data that is the lifeblood of The NSS Group is being sent on its journey down the *information superhighway* in the back seat of a convertible rather than in the back of an armored car. Anyone who is interested in The NSS Group's private data can simply reach into the car as we pause at the traffic lights and help himself.

Of course, we may see him doing this in the rear-view mirror; but by the time we spot the intrusion and turn around to do something about it, the lights have changed and the perpetrator is on his way — and we cannot even report the infraction because he does not have any license plates!

We are constantly being reminded that it is information that gives us our competitive edge in today's marketplace. Yet we are oftentimes prevented from protecting that information to the extent it deserves.

When information was represented almost entirely as words on paper documents, security was relatively simple. Because there was no means to glean the information without physical access to the documents, all you had to do was lock them away in a safe or filing cabinet and ensure that only trusted personnel had a key. By carefully controlling the number of copies produced and physical access to those copies, you could thus fully control the dissemination of corporate information.

Once computers started to appear on the scene, it became far easier to make vital information readily available to a greater number of people. At the same time, security became correspondingly more difficult, although in the early days, at least the centralized computing model enforced by the mainframe made it possible to apply the same sort of access controls we had used before.

With the PC came the distributed computing model. This introduced a myriad of potential security problems, none of which were irresolvable given the control we still had over our own networks. Yet with the Internet, this distribution became global. Now, any organization could find itself transmitting vital data across a public network that is anything but secure.

Given the fact that we can no longer keep our information locked away in a filing cabinet, we must implement other means of security. We cannot ignore the convenience of the Internet, nor the cost-effective way in which it allows us to link together remote networks, sharing data around the world as if we were all connected via a single corporate intranet.

However, we also cannot ignore the fact that there is a whole sub-culture that has evolved in tandem with the Internet — a sub-culture that is bent on invading our privacy, reading our mail, and stealing our corporate secrets. Privacy should be a serious concern for anyone who uses the Internet.

Every time you engage in a commercial transaction of any sort on the Web, send sensitive information via e-mail, or even simply browse a Web site, you are in danger of revealing private information about yourself or your company to individuals or groups who will modify that information, sell it to third parties, or otherwise use that data for malicious purposes.

The necessity of reliable, fast data interchange is the reason for the Internet's existence. But if you cannot preserve the confidentiality and integrity of your data, then the Internet potentially can cause you more harm than good.

To move our information from the back of the convertible to the back of the armored car, we need just one tool — *encryption*.

AN ENCRYPTION PRIMER

In the best tradition of the James Bond novel, encryption is all about secret codes, transforming plaintext into a form unreadable by anyone without a secret decryption key. It thus allows secure communication over a general-purpose, insecure channel such as the Internet.

Although the mathematics behind it can be very complex, encryption itself is pretty straightforward. Cast your minds back to when you were kids and you wanted to send secret messages to each other. The simplest form of encryption was the one where every letter of the alphabet was substituted for the one "n" positions following it.

Here we are introduced fairly painlessly to the two most important buzzwords in the cryptography world: the "key" is the number of positions we are shifting the letters, while the "algorithm" is simply the idea that the encrypted letter is the one "n" places following the plaintext letter.

There are two ways you can beef up security on this: increase the length of the key and devise ever more complex algorithms. Luckily, we do not have to get involved in creating our own algorithms, because there are some perfectly acceptable standards out there, the main ones being DES (Data Encryption Standard), Triple DES, IDEA (International Data Encryption Algorithm), and RC4 (an algorithm developed by Ron Rivest of RSA as a stream cipher with a variable key length).

Whereas the original DES algorithm used 56-bit keys, later and more powerful systems use much longer ones, forcing potential hackers to run through trillions of combinations in any attempt to find the right one by brute force. Triple DES is an enhanced version of the original DES algorithm and encrypts data three times using three different keys (providing an effective key length of 112 bits). IDEA is a 128-bit mechanism developed by the University of Zurich in 1992 and is a favorite of European financial institutions.

SECRET KEY CRYPTOGRAPHY

As you might imagine, the longer the key length, the more secure the encryption. Going back to our simple cipher, if our single-digit key is represented by a letter of the alphabet, a potential hacker only has to try 26 possible combinations in order to crack the cipher using brute force. Now, if we increased the length of the key and wrote it beneath our original message (repeating the key over and over until it was equal to the length of the message), each character in the key would represent a different shift for the letter above. Of course, if short keys are used, then repeating patterns may begin to emerge in the message — the most secure method is to use a key that is the same length as the message itself, but this is impractical in real-life situations. Combine long keys with sophisticated algorithms, however (something a little more complex than "shift each letter of the message by the value of the key character beneath"), and you are in business.

Unfortunately, "secret key" or "symmetric key" cryptography (as it is known) clearly relies on both parties involved having access to the same secret key, because the sender uses the key to encrypt the message, and the receiver uses the same key (together with the same algorithm in reverse) to decrypt the message. This naturally introduces a potential problem — how do we ensure that the key is distributed in a secure manner?

If we have regular contact with the person, we can pass the key face to face — you cannot get much more secure than that. In business terms, secret keys (such as bank PIN numbers) are often distributed by mail in special tamper-proof envelopes, or can be encapsulated in hardware devices such as smart cards, where the issuing authority never gives the customer access to the key information.

But in the case of one-off Internet transactions with hitherto unknown parties, we do not have that luxury, because as a result of the unique key-pair arrangement between the two parties, it is impossible to exchange data with someone to whom you have not already been "introduced."

Neither of you has a shared secret key, and there is no secure channel over which to exchange one. For this reason, secret key cryptography works best when a single issuing authority is maintaining a service for a user base where there is some kind of registration process that takes place prior to the exchange of information.

PUBLIC KEY CRYPTOGRAPHY

With "public key" or "asymmetric key" cryptography, however, each person gets a pair of keys, known as the *public key* and the *private key*. The public key is generated from the private key using a complex algorithm, following which the public key can be published, while the private key remains secret.

The mathematics behind public key cryptography are exceedingly complex and beyond the scope of this chapter, so you are simply going to have to trust me on this one — any message encrypted with a given public key can only be decrypted using the corresponding private key, and there is no known way to derive the private key from the public key. Honest — this really works.

Now, if Bob wishes to send a message to Alice (Bob and Alice are the cryptography industry's favorite couple), he will encrypt it using Alice's public key (which can be published in a directory or distributed via unsecured e-mail). The only person who can decrypt the resulting message is the holder of the appropriate private key — Alice. The need for sender and receiver to share secret information is eliminated because all communications involve only public keys, and no private key is ever transmitted or shared. The best-known and most widely used asymmetric key technologies are Diffie-Hellman and RSA.

Although providing the highest levels of security, public key cryptography is notoriously heavy on system resources, particularly when working on large messages. For performance reasons, therefore, RSA is usually used only to exchange keys, while a conventional secret key cryptosystem (such as DES) is used for the bulk of the message.

Suppose Alice wishes to send an encrypted message to Bob. She first encrypts the message with DES, using a randomly chosen DES "secret" key that can be different for every message sent. Then she looks up Bob's public key and uses it to encrypt the DES key. The DES-encrypted message and the RSA-encrypted DES key together form a "digital envelope" and are sent to Bob. Upon receiving the digital envelope, Bob decrypts the DES key with his private key, finally using the DES key to decrypt the message itself.

WHY IS ENCRYPTION A THREAT?

Modern cryptography is very advanced, allowing us to produce encrypted data which is — for all intents and purposes — uncrackable.

Given that it is impossible to determine a private key from either the encrypted data or the public key by any straightforward computational means, the only recourse for the would-be cracker is a "brute-force" attack. This involves trying all possible key combinations one after another until the message is readable; and given that we can use computers for such tasks, it is certainly possible to crack any message — eventually.

The critical factor here is key length. Each "bit" added to the key makes brute-force attacks twice as difficult. Using a 56-bit key, for instance, makes the task of cracking the key 2^{16} (or 65,536 for the non-mathematicians among you) times as hard as with a 40-bit key. This means that DES is over 65,000 times more secure than 40-bit RC4.

ARE EXPORT CONTROLS THE ANSWER?

Imagine, therefore, how difficult it would be to crack a 128-bit or a 1024-bit key! This is the unpalatable prospect facing the world's law enforcement organizations, keen to protect their respective countries from the threats of terrorism, drug smuggling, money laundering, child pornography, etc. With a burgeoning security industry, the U.S. Government therefore imposed export controls on such products, limiting export to products incorporating specific algorithms with fairly small key sizes (RC2 and RC4 algorithms with a 40-bit key maximum).

U.S. companies were only allowed to ship more advanced encryption products — based on 56-bit DES — out of the United States if they were destined for foreign subsidiaries (more than 50 percent U.S.-owned) or to banks. Even then, banks are only permitted to use strong encryption for actual financial transactions — they still cannot use it for normal e-mail or EDI. The American-imposed export restrictions were therefore often seen as a major barrier to the widespread adoption of electronic commerce outside the United States, given that 40-bit encryption is seen as too weak for commercial use in connection with financial transactions.

For instance, in January 1997, a student at Berkeley, California, successfully "broke" a 40-bit key in 3.5 hours, using 259 Unix scale computers. This means that it would take a single computer over 37 days to decrypt just **one** session, which is hardly likely to provide a huge incentive for criminals to start hacking away — after all, by the time the session could be cracked, the data would be out of date or redundant. However, the mere fact that a 40-bit key has been proved to be crackable within a reasonable amount of time is enough to render it useless for many applications — particularly those in the financial sector.

This makes all commercially available products exported from the United States less than attractive to a world intent on maintaining its privacy. Of course, the financial world could still use 56-bit DES — in theory, given the time to break the 40-bit key and the fact that DES is 65,535 times more difficult to crack than RC5, it would take one computer over **6,780 years** to decrypt a **single** session.

"STRONG CRYPTOGRAPHY MAKES THE WORLD A SAFER PLACE"

In June 1997, however, in response to the RSA Secret Key Challenge, a team from Colorado harnessed the power of tens of thousands of computers across the Internet to break a 56-bit DES encrypted message (which ironically read "*Strong cryptography makes the world a safer place*"). Although the team had to search just 18 quadrillion out of a possible 72 quadrillion keys, and although such a task is clearly beyond the realms of the average hacker, such feats only serve to highlight the need for stronger encryption — particularly for financial applications.

Certain other countries — the notable exceptions being the Scandinavian nations — are considering similar legislation to that in the United States. In March 1997, a Public Consultation Paper entitled Licensing of Trusted Third Parties for the Provision Of Encryption Services was put before the U.K. Government by Ian Taylor, Minister for Science and Technology. In it, Taylor states that:

> These proposals — aimed at facilitating the provision of secure electronic commerce — are being brought forward against a background of increasing concern, not about the technology, but about the security of information itself. In a world where more and more transactions are taking place on open electronic networks like the Internet, there has been a growing demand from industry and the public for strong encryption services to help protect the integrity and confidentiality of information. These proposals have been developed to address those concerns, but at the same time are aimed at striking a balance with the need to protect users and the requirement to safeguard law enforcement, which encryption can prevent.

The document goes on to voice the concern as to how:

> the spread and availability of encryption technology will affect the ability of the authorities to continue to fight serious crime and terrorism, and protect U.K. economic well-being and national security. In particular, **the Government considers it essential that the ability of security, intelligence and law enforcement agencies to conduct effective legal interception of communications under the Interception of Communications Act 1985 is preserved in any policy proposals.**

But in light of recent events, does the argument for export controls of strong encryption hold water? At this point, things get very political, so you have to make your own decision. It is difficultto believe, however, that any criminal organization would choose to make use of an encryption technology that is known to be susceptible to data or key recovery in any form. It should also be remembered that it is possible to obtain strong encryption products anywhere in the world — Pretty Good Privacy (PGP) is the obvious example.

In other words, the only people affected by such legislation are the law-abiding citizens and organizations who wish to make use of readily available, standards-based products.

HOW CAN THE THREAT BE COUNTERED?

As the U.S. administration bows to commercial pressure from domestic encryption companies unable to compete effectively in foreign markets, there are signs that things are changing.

An executive order — regarding Administration of Export Control on Encryption Products — took effect in the United States on January 1, 1997, effectively allowing all vendors to begin shipping 56-bit key encryption products worldwide providing they agree to add key recovery to their products within two years. Once fully compliant with the U.S. Government-imposed *key management infrastructure* (KMI), vendors are then at liberty to begin exporting stronger encryption, using unlimited key lengths.

"TRUSTED THIRD PARTY"

Initial proposals for key recovery are based on the use of the "trusted third party" (TTP). There are a number of implementations of this, each of which involves providing a licensed *key recovery center* (KRC) with the means to decrypt your encrypted sessions.

KEY ESCROW

This was the first proposal, which involves lodging copies of your private keys with the TTP, a secure facility that exists for the purpose of storing such keys.

Should access be required by a law enforcement agency (LEA) or other government agency, then some form of court order or official warrant is served on the TTP. The appropriate keys are then turned over to the LEA, following which the encoded sessions can be decrypted.

In the United Kingdom, TTPs would be licensed by the Department of Trade and Industry (DTI), and the job of issuing warrants requiring disclosure of keys to law enforcement agencies would rest with the Home Secretary.

Although the very idea of depositing private keys with a third party in this manner is unacceptable to many organizations, there is one other alarming factor that is often overlooked.

Because keys must be deposited with the TTP in advance of any encrypted communication (otherwise there is no point in making the deposit), the only keys that can exist to be deposited at that stage are the masters.

Once any third party has access to your master private keys, it is possible to recover the keys of *any* session that has been encrypted using keys derived from the master. You would thus be entrusting the TTP with the means to access *all* of your encrypted data — this requires a high degree of trust, indeed. It also raises the question of how the TTP facilitates the provision of decrypted data to the LEA. It is unlikely, for example, that the LEA would supply copies of the potentially incriminating sessions to the TTP, meaning that the TTP would be forced to turn over the master keys themselves. Yet once in possession of these, the LEA can decrypt *all* sessions — past, present, and future — encrypted using keys derived from those masters without obtaining individual warrants.

The other point to bear in mind is that if you are the "innocent" party in a series of encrypted communications with someone whose keys have been turned over to a LEA, then all *your* sessions with that party are open to being decrypted without *your* knowledge — no one has to ask *your* permission to decrypt those sessions.

In general terms, *key escrow* represents an unacceptable invasion of privacy, and an equally unacceptable risk in lodging *master* keys with a third party.

KEY RECOVERY

Given the strong resistance to key escrow by both end users and the cryptography industry alike (only the NSA seems to be really in favor of it!), the TTP idea was watered down somewhat to produce the *key recovery* proposal.

With key recovery, it is not necessary to lodge copies of keys with the TTP. Instead, the keys used to encrypt each session are themselves encrypted using the public key of the TTP and then embedded within the session data in a *Key Recovery field*.

Should the LEA require access to encrypted data, the captured session Key Recovery field is supplied to the TTP, which uses its own private key to decrypt it. This provides the LEA with the private keys necessary to decrypt that particular session, and *only* that session, and is thus slightly less invasive than Key Escrow.

Key Recovery also has the advantage that your keys are never actually stored at the TTP's facility. Thus, should that facility become a target for hackers, your own information is less likely to be compromised as a result. Of course, once the TTP's keys are compromised, a determined hacker could use them to decrypt previously recorded sessions; and because the same private keys could be used to cover a number of clients, the loss of even one private key could leave a number of organizations open to attack.

At the present time, products incorporating Key Recovery can make use of one of three proprietary, dynamic key management protocols: Internet Security Association/Key Management Protocol (ISA/KMP) Oakley (backed mainly by Cisco); Simple Key Exchange Internet Protocol (SKIP), backed by Sun; and Photuris Session Key Management Protocol, backed by Radguard.

THE CASE AGAINST TRUSTED THIRD PARTY

Trusted third party (TTP) has been heavily criticized by most of its likely users due to the potential for the criminal element to target TTP facilities in an attempt to gain access to thousands of sets of data in a single swoop. To the hacker, TTPs represent an extremely valuable potential single point of failure for the system as a whole, made worse by the proposal that some TTPs would use a single key for many users. It would take only a single error or disgruntled employee at one of the TTPs in order for a large number of keys to be compromised, with disastrous consequences.

There is also the feeling, of course, that it does not make commercial sense to allow *any* third party — even a "trusted" one — to hold keys that could provide access to our most sensitive corporate data.

Furthermore, in both the Key Recovery and Key Escrow cases described above, it would be possible to investigate one of the users of an information system without the knowledge or awareness of the organization or the individuals being investigated. Only the Key Recovery Agent and the courts granting access would be aware that the data had been revealed to the LEA.

A report released by a number of industry experts and scientists earlier this year cautions that "the deployment of a general key-recovery-based encryption infrastructure to meet law enforcement's stated requirements will result in substantial sacrifices in security and cost to the end user. Building a secure infrastructure of the breathtaking scale and complexity demanded by these requirements is far beyond the experience and current competency of the field."

It is worrying also that even as we see the U.S. administration preparing to adopt a more sensible and commercially aware approach to export controls of strong encryption, the U.K. Government is about to embark on its own attempt at Orwellian legislation.

The proposal by Ian Taylor MP is somewhat misleading (those paranoiacs among the general populace might say deliberately so) in its confusion of several important terms and issues. For instance, it talks rather grandly of a Key Recovery scheme that is of great benefit to mankind — promising that TTPs will be able to offer interoperability of secure services hitherto unavailable. This claim is clearly spurious, given that interoperability of encryption services actually stems from adopting standard encryption algorithms (DES, IDEA, etc.) and building products to a common architecture — in other words, such interoperability is available right now, without the hindrance of TTPs. On closer inspection, in fact, it turns out that Taylor's proposal is nothing more than Key Escrow, which offers no significant benefits to either end users or vendors.

It also rather worryingly confuses the roles of certificate authorities (CAs) and trusted third parties (TTPs), implying that these are one and the same. Whereas, admittedly, it would be possible for a single organization to offer both services, it would not be wise to confuse the valuable role of the CA with the unwelcome one of the TTP.

It is almost inevitable that the introduction of TTP schemes will be viewed as an intrusion into individual privacy, and will thus lead to a loss in confidence in the use of cryptographic techniques. Far from encouraging electronic commerce, such an approach is likely to stifle it before it gets off the ground.

TRUSTED FIRST PARTY

Trusted first party (TFP) is a much more sensible approach, and one that is receiving the backing of vendors and end users alike. The latter, while not exactly happy about any enforced method of data recovery, are at least prepared to accept TFP in the spirit of compromise, and as the only means to gain access to strong encryption previously denied to them.

The U.S. Government, for example, now requires only that an acceptable key management infrastructure (KMI) is implemented before software products containing strong encryption are exported. While a KMI may be based on key escrow if required, the U.S. administration has also accepted the idea of a KMI using a trusted first party implementation.

With trusted first party, it is still possible to retrieve keys and thus decrypt data from a particular captured session, yet this time the entire process is under the control of the end user organization. There is no need to deposit any keys with third parties, and only the end user can obtain access to session data.

The key (pardon the pun!) to the flexibility of trusted first party is the idea of unique session keys. These are generated from encrypted "challenges" exchanged between the communicating parties as a means of mutual authentication at the start of the session. These challenges are combined and encrypted using the users' secret key, and the resulting "hybrid" key is used for the duration of that session only — no two session keys are ever identical. Meanwhile, the plaintext version of the challenges is included as part of the session data — this is quite safe, because it is impossible to determine the actual session keys from these without access to the secret key also.

Should an LEA wish to gain access to an encrypted session, then an electronic "recording" of that session is presented to the customer's key recovery agent (KRA) — along with a valid warrant, of course. Because the recorded session will include the plaintext challenges, and because the KRA obviously has access to the secret keys, then the KRA has everything he needs to recreate the session keys.

Once those keys have been regenerated, they can be supplied to the LEA, who will then have the means to decrypt that particular session — and *that session only* (in stark contrast to a TTP situation). Knowing one or more keys gives no information about any of the other keys for that user or any other, and the master keys from which the session keys are derived are never revealed. All other messages that are encrypted with keys derived from the same master key thus remain fully protected.

Providing that the end user has been approved by the U.S. Bureau of Export Administration (BXA) and fully auditable key recovery procedures have been put in place, the U.S. Government will allow export of encryption products using any key length. Full support for the trusted first party within encryption software would allow such procedures to be implemented, thus providing the necessary ability to respond to a legally sanctioned request for keys while allowing the end-user organization to retain complete control over the process.

ADVANTAGES OF TRUSTED FIRST PARTY

The advantages of the TFP approach are numerous and very clear — especially when compared to TTP.

The first and most obvious advantage is that there is never a need to expose master keys to anyone outside the end-user organization. It is no longer necessary to lodge copies of keys with third parties, nor is it necessary to provide master keys on even a temporary basis to LEA's in order to recover an encrypted session.

Should a law enforcement agency ever request access to encrypted data, the end user can be sure that only the specific session presented by the LEA can be decrypted, because only the session keys are released. This approach also provides tremendous flexibility over how the LEA recovers the session data.

For example, the session can be provided to the customer's key recovery agent, who decrypts it and passes it back. This might not suit the LEA, however, who might prefer that the KRA did not have sight of the decrypted session. In this case, the session keys themselves could be released, allowing the LEA to decrypt the data at a later date. If even this level of exposure is worrying to the end user, then another option would be to have the whole process carried out by e-mail and under the control of some key recovery software.

In this case, the LEA could provide the recorded session along with a copy of its own public key. This package could be further encrypted using the end user's public key before being transmitted to the KRA. The KRA would decrypt the package and process the recorded session using the key recovery software. The software would automatically recreate the session keys, decrypt the session, and then re-encrypt it using the LEA's public key before transmitting it directly to the LEA. This is certainly the most flexible approach, because it allows access to the decrypted session by the LEA without providing the KRA with sight of the suspicious session, and without releasing even the unique session keys to a third party.

Although most of the arguments for key recovery concentrate on the need for access by LEAs, it should be remembered that it also provides one major advantage to end users — that of protection against key loss. The ability to recover any encrypted session internally, even when the required keys have been mislaid or deliberately hidden by a disgruntled employee, is an extremely valuable feature.

In the future, it will be necessary to forge an agreement between the customer and the U.S. Department of Commerce Bureau of Export Administration before trusted first party key recovery can be implemented.

Most of that agreement will deal with secure operation of the key recovery software and ensuring best practices of operation. There must be a willingness to accept the legal authority's warrant (or other document) and provide a timely response to a request for access. Once such an agreement is in place, there is nothing to prevent the supply of strong encryption software with *any* key length required.

THE ROLE OF CERTIFICATE AUTHORITIES

Rather than concentrating on licensing TTPs to operate key escrow systems, it would be preferable for the various governments of the world to help to create a hierarchy of recognized certificate authorities (CAs).

One potential barrier to the widespread take-up of electronic commerce is the inability to reliably identify potential users of such systems. Digital certificates bind a user identity to a public key and are then signed by the relevant CA — the resulting block of data provides the means to identify any user absolutely.

Currently, these CA requirements are being met by commercial initiatives such as VeriSign and Entrust. Some European countries, however (notably Scandinavia), are already working to establish a network of CAs, and other countries should follow suit if the global electronic economy is to flourish.

Present uncertainty over the legal status of electronic signatures is also a potential barrier to the development of electronic commerce. Legislation to force legal acceptance of digital signatures would provide the required legal status of "signed" electronic documents, thus allowing them to be used to form the basis for legally binding contracts and agreements.

These measures would provide a framework for the increased use of electronic commerce, and together would be far more helpful than legislation of key escrow systems.

CONCLUSION

The almost universally hostile reaction to suggestions that encryption keys should be deposited with a U.S. agency has led to a more considered approach by the U.S. administration. Key escrow — particularly where the escrow agency may be located overseas — is simply not a viable consideration for most commercial organizations.

The draconian legislation that existed prior to 1997 has done considerable harm to the encryption industry, certainly preventing the export and use of U.S.-produced strong cryptography products around the world. If the U.K. introduces key escrow as detailed in Taylor's current proposal, then U.K encryption vendors will face the same problem. Rather than promoting the export of robust encryption, these proposals will damage it.

The U.S. administration has now recognized the commercial reality of the situation, and requires only Key Recovery and not Key Escrow for export of strong encryption. This is the only method allowing recovery of the transmitted session under the full control of the organization operating the security system. It also provides much greater protection to individual privacy, and is thus much more acceptable to commercial organizations implementing electronic commerce.

9

AN APPROACH TO FORMALLY COMPARE AND QUERY CERTIFICATION PRACTICE STATEMENTS

Stephan Grill

Public key infrastructures (PKIs) are gaining importance in today's IT environment for managing certificates and keys. Much effort is devoted to understanding and standardizing protocols to manage this infrastructure. However, it is equally recognized that the quality and trustworthiness of certificates depend to a large extent on the practices and procedures a certification authority applies when issuing certificates. These procedures are documented in so-called Certification Practice Statements (CPS), which are generally text-based documents and therefore cannot be processed by machines. This chapter describes a framework, based on knowledge representation techniques, which addresses this situation. Subsumption will be used to compare and query CPS. Based on a case study of modeling a real CPS, some features of this framework will be described. An outlook of future work conclude this chapter.

INTRODUCTION

Public key infrastructures (PKIs) are emerging as an important cornerstone of today's communications systems. X.509 certificates are envisioned to provide a wealth of services ranging from electronic ID cards, digital signature, authorization schemes, etc. Processes and protocols to manage and use private keys and certificates are well understood and corresponding standards[1] are currently in the process of being defined.

0-8493-0822-4/04/$0.00+$1.50
© 2004 by CRC Press LLC

The degree to which a certificate user can trust the binding embodied in a certificate depends on several factors (e.g., practices followed by the CA in authenticating the subject, the subject's obligations in protecting the private key, the legal obligations of a CA, etc.).

X.509 provides two means to bind this kind of information to certificates:

1. Certificate Policy
2. Certification Practice Statement

A Certificate Policy (CP) essentially is a unique, registered Object Identifier (OID), which can be included in the certificate. A Certification Practice Statement (CPS) may be published or referenced by a CA and may contain a more detailed description of the practices a CA follows when issuing certificates. The objectives and the contents of a CP and a CPS are described in RFC 2527.[2]

Both formats have weaknesses, including:

■ A CP is based on numbers (OID), which only support equality comparisons. However, it is not possible to retrieve specific detailed information related to a CP/CPS and it is also not possible to apply relational operators other than equality (e.g., is one CP/CPS more trustworthy than another?).
■ A CPS is based on textual descriptions, which cannot be automatically processed by machines. End users have to read each CP/CPS and judge whether or not associated certificates are trustworthy. However, the length of a CPS will usually lead users to refrain from reading and understanding it when receiving a certificate.

A framework to improve this situation will be suggested in the following sections. The section entitled "Requirements for the Representation of a CP/CPS" discusses requirements for a structured and formal representation of information typically contained in a CP and CPS (from now on denoted by CP/CPS). The section entitled "Solution Approach" explains the general approach that was taken to address this problem. And the section entitled "Case Study" highlights some examples based on a case study that was performed by modeling real CP/CPS. A summary with learnings and an outlook for future work concludes the chapter.

REQUIREMENTS FOR THE REPRESENTATION OF A CP/CPS

To define requirements for a CP/CPS, representation cases for using these models are discussed first:

- Relying parties should be enabled to *retrieve* specific aspects of a CP/CPS of a received certificate (e.g., they want to check where the associated private key of a certificate is generated and stored).
- Relying parties might want to *specify conditions or policies* a CP/CPS of a certificate must match in order to be accepted (e.g., they want to specify that certificates are only accepted if the associated private key is generated and stored on a smart card).
- These comparisons might be based on equality comparisons, but also on other *comparison operators* that might be applicable for the quality of certificates (e.g., practices described in a CP/CPS might indicate that associated certificates are more trustworthy than certificates issued according to another CP/CPS; as an example, a certificate for an associated private key that is generated and stored on a smart card might be more trustworthy than a certificate whose associated private key is generated in software and stored on a hard disk).
- Certification Authorities (CAs) might be interested to better investigate CP/CPS of another CA when engaging in cross certification.

From these possible use cases a set of requirements can be derived:

- A representation of a CP/CPS exists primarily in the realm of the Internet. Hence, it must support the flexible nature of the Internet. It must be possible to construct a CP/CPS from existing definitions. It must be possible to derive a new CP/CPS from an already-existing CP/CPS. Building blocks of a CP/CPS can be shared and might be stored in a distributed manner.
- Current text-based CP/CPS describe complex objects and complex practices. A formal model must support this complexity. The representation has to support *<attribute, value>* pairs, which might be organized in a hierarchical structure, and where *value* by itself might be a complex object. A wide range of data types must be supported.
- The representation must allow one to define a metric or classification scheme to support not just equality comparisons, but also additional relational operators.
- The representation must be declarative (as opposed to a procedural representation) in order to support operations on this representation.
- Based on the possible uses of a CP/CPS representation described above, operations like projection, equality comparison, and relational comparison ought to be possible.

SOLUTION-APPROACH

A two-phased approach was chosen to address this problem. In the first phase, a possible semantic representation is investigated; and in the second phase, the syntactical representation of the defined semantics is defined.

Semantic Representation Using Description Logics

Based on the identified requirements regarding the possible complexity of the models that must be represented, it appeared natural to use known techniques from the Knowledge Representation community. After reviewing different representation paradigms (procedural, logic-based, frame-based/object-oriented), the decision was taken to use a Description-Logics-based model. Description Logics combine the strengths of a logic model, which is formally well understood, and the object-oriented model, which provides good means of structuring the modeling domain.

Formal Knowledge Representation was first pursued using Semantic Networks and Frames. However, both of these techniques do not provide sufficient formal semantics. KL-ONE[3] tried to add a formal semantics to frames and semantic networks and initiated research in what was subsequently called Description Logics (DL) — or terminological systems. Consequently, several systems were devised and studied: KRYPTON,[4] NIKL, BACK, LOOM, CLASSIC, KRIS, etc. Hence, capabilities and restrictions of DL-based systems are, in the meantime, well understood.

Description Logics Overview

A thorough discussion of DL goes beyond the scope of this chapter and can be found in others;[5] but to subsequently describe the case study, a very brief overview of the architecture and capabilities is given.

The core of a DL-based system is a *concept language*. The major constructs of this language are *concepts*, *roles*, and *individuals. Concepts* are used to represent classes as sets of individuals. *Roles* describe properties (attributes) of concepts in the form of binary relations between classes. *Individuals* are instances of classes. From now on *concepts* and *classes*, *individuals* and *instances* are used synonymously.

As an example, the following DL statement defines the concept Father-OfGirls as the set of individuals that are parents (belongs to the class Parents), are male (belongs to the class Male), and all of whose children are female (the individuals have the property CHILD, and all values of this property are individuals that belong to the class Female).

```
FatherOfGirls  ≡ Parent  ∩Male  ∩ ∀CHILD.Female
```

It can be seen that the structure of a DL statement is based on first-order logic and a formal semantic of DL statements can be given. The most commonly used connectives in DL are shown in Exhibit 1.

DL Reasoning Services

In addition to being able to explicitly define concepts, DL provides interesting reasoning services; that is, new information can automatically be derived from explicit specifications:

Exhibit 1   Commonly Used Connectives in DL

Concept definition	$\equiv$
Conjunction	$\cap$
Disjunction	$\cup$
Negation	$\neg$
Universal quantification	$\forall$
Existential quantification	$\exists$
Number restriction	$(<= n), (>= n)$
Enumeration of individuals	$\{ a1, a2, ..., an \}$

- *Concept assurance.* Given a concept C and given a set of individuals I, check if there are any individuals that belong to C (based on their described properties).
- *Equivalence checking.* Given two concepts C and D, check whether their descriptions are equivalent.
- *Subsumption.* Given two concepts C and D, check if D subsumes C; that is, if all individuals that belong to C also belong to D (intuitively it could be said that D is a super-class of C). Subsumption supports the definition of a partial ordering scheme, where the underlying ordering relationship is Generalization-Specialization.
- *Instance checking.* Given a concept C and an individual I, check if I is an instance of C.

There are additional reasoning services available, but they will not be used in the following paragraphs. Because of the formal foundation of DL, these reasoning services can also be formally investigated to verify their correctness and completeness.[6]

These reasoning services provide the required means to implement the operations previously mentioned as requirements:

- *Equivalence checking* can be used to determine if two descriptions of a CP/CPS are equal.
- *Subsumption and instance checking* can be used to determine the relationship of two CP/CPS descriptions.

The strength of the subsumption reasoning service is that, in contrast to commonly used object-oriented class-definition, the super-class/sub-class relationship does not need to be specified manually, but can be derived automatically from the given class definitions and instance descriptions.

A case study that has been performed will show how this can be used on a real CP/CPS.

Syntactic Representation

Currently, an investigation is ongoing to identify means to represent a model in a DL-based language suited to the environment where certificates are used. Currently, the focus lies on studying the Resource Description Framework[7] of the W3C.

CASE STUDY

To verify the applicability of this approach, some CP/CPS have been modeled using an implemented DL system. The CP/CPS chosen include:

- Certificate Policies for the Government of Canada (GoC) public key infrastructure[8]
- SEIS Certificate Policy[9]

The GoC PKI Policies actually define eight different policies — four designed for digital signature certificates and four designed for confidentiality certificates. These four policies cover different assurance levels: rudimentary, basic, medium, and high. In the following examples these policies will be identified with the prefixes `GocSign[1234]` and `GocConf[1234]`, respectively.

The reason for choosing these policies was that both are based on the framework suggested in RFC 2527 — and therefore provide some possibility to make them comparable.

The DL system chosen was NeoClassic.[10] NeoClassic is one of the more widely used DL systems.

First, the syntax of NeoClassic is briefly shown. Then the methodology for performing the case study is described; and finally, some examples are shown and explained.

NeoClassic

NeoClassic implements the connectives shown in Exhibit 2.

Syntactically, the above DL statement

```
FatherOfGirls ≡ Parent ∩ Male ∩ ∀CHILD.Female
```

is represented as:

```
( createConcept FatherOfGirls
  ( and Parent
    Male
    ( all CHILD Female ) ) )
```

Exhibit 2 NeoClassic Connectives

Concept definition	≡
Conjunction	∩
Universal quantification	∀
Existential quantification	∃
Number restriction	(<= n), (>= n)
Enumeration of individuals	{ a1, a2, ..., an }

Methodology

One of the objectives to formally represent CP/CPS is to make them better comparable. Therefore, it is necessary to use a common structure: the same topics must be described, the same attributes must be used, the same sets of values must be used, etc.

Consequently, a reference description must be defined first. This description is based on RFC 2527. It defines concepts and individuals, which can be refined and combined by subsequent CP/CPS descriptions using specialization and the definition of new concepts, respectively. These concepts and individuals define a core terminology, which should be accepted as a common framework. In practice, it will possibly be the case that several of such reference frameworks will be developed and a combination of these frameworks will be possible. This approach is quite similar to the definition of classification schemes in Library Science.[11]

During the definition of such frameworks, it is also possible to define some primitive taxonomies, which will then support the creation of more complex taxonomies. This will be exemplified further below.

Based on the established reference ontology (RFC 2527), specific CP/CPS (GoC, SEIS) have been modeled.

Examples

The following examples show this approach more specifically.

Asymmetric Key Sizes

The first example is rather simple — as it is using the predefined properties of the built-in concept `Integer`.

The core terminology based on RFC 2527 requires describing the minimal length of the used keys:

```
( createConcept Rfc2527AsymmetricKeySizes
  ( all keyLength Integer ) )
```

Concept Rfc2527AsymmetricKeySizes has one role (attribute) named key-Length, which is of type/concept Integer (a primitive NeoClassic concept).

The Government of Canada PKI CP/CPS defines the following restrictions on the above concept:

```
( createConcept GocSign1AsymmetricKeySizes
  ( and Rfc2527AsymmetricKeySizes
    ( all keyLength ( minimum 512 ) ) ) )
```

Concept `GocSign1AsymmetricKeySizes` is a sub-class of `Rfc2527AsymmetricKeySizes` with the additional restrictions that all values of the attribute `keyLength` must be greater-equal 512.

```
( createConcept GocSign2AsymmetricKeySizes
  ( and Rfc2527AsymmetricKeySizes
    ( all keyLength ( minimum 1024 ) ) ) )

( createConcept GocSign3AsymmetricKeySizes
  ( and Rfc2527AsymmetricKeySizes
    ( all keyLength ( minimum 1024 ) ) ) )

( createConcept GocSign4AsymmetricKeySizes
  ( and Rfc2527AsymmetricKeySizes
    ( all keyLength ( minimum 2048 ) ) ) )
```

The SEIS policy is denoted as:

```
( createConcept SeisAsymmetricKeySizes
  ( and Rfc2527AsymmetricKeySizes
    ( all keyLength ( minimum 1024 ) ) ) )
```

Using the built-in properties of NeoClassic's type Integer, an ordering scheme is predefined: Rfc2527AsymmetricKeySizes defines a class of instances with the attribute keyLength, which may take all integers as value; GocSign1Asymmetric-KeySizes restricts the values to greater-equal 512; GocSign[23]Asymmetric-KeySizes restricts the values to greater-equal 1024; GocSign4AsymmetricKey-Sizes restricts the values to greater-equal 2048. Because of the properties of Integer the application of the subsumption reasoning service results in the following ordering:

```
Rfc2527AsymmetricKeySizes subsumes
  GocSign1AsymmetricKey-Sizes
which in turn subsumes GocSign[23]AsymmetricKeySizes
which in turn subsumes GocSign4AsymmetricKeySizes
```

NeoClassic also automatically finds that:

```
GocSign[23]AsymmetricKeySizes is equivalent to
   SeisAsymmetric-KeySizes
```

If the only requirement would be to compare numeric values, the general subsumption mechanism would not be necessary — PICS[12] does something similar. However, not all properties described in a CP/CPS can be represented by numeric values, which can be seen in the next examples.

Activation Actions

Often, constructs comparable to object enumeration are required. Enumerations (oneOf) do not define any order relationship.

RFC 2527 recommends specifying how a private key can be activated, that is, accessed by the user:

```
( createConcept Rfc2527MethodOfActivatingPrivateKey
  ( and
    ( all activationAgent Rfc2527Agents )
    ( all activationActions Rfc2527ActivationActions)
    ( all activationPeriod Rfc2527ActivationPeriod )))
```

The above concept definition creates a concept with three properties describing who may activate (agent), how the activation is done (action), and how long the activation may be valid (period) with respective types.

An agent can be the end entity, RA, CA, or the directory:

```
( createConcept Rfc2527Agents
  ( oneOf ENDENTITY RA CA DIRECTORY ) )
```

Activation actions are defined below:

```
( createConcept Rfc2527ActivationActions
  ( oneOf POWER-ON LOGIN INSERT-TOKEN PIN AUTOMATIC ) )

( createConcept GocSign2MethodOfActivatingPrivateKey
  ( and Rfc2527MethodOfActivatingPrivateKey
    ( all activationActions ( oneOf PIN ) )

( createConcept SeisMethodOfActivatingPrivateKey
  ( and Rfc2527MethodOfActivatingPrivateKey
    ( all activationActions ( oneOf PIN ) )
```

NeoClassic would determine that
GocSign2MethodOfActivatingPrivateKey and
SeisMethodOfActivatingPrivateKey are equivalent.

Key-Pair Generation

To support comparison operations, it is necessary to define an order relationship among newly defined concepts. For example, a key-pair generated in HW might be more trustworthy than a key-pair generated in SW.

```
( createConcept Rfc2527Hw       Rfc2527ModuleTypes )
( createConcept Rfc2527HwOrSw  Rfc2527Hw )
( createConcept Rfc2527Sw       Rfc2527HwOrSw )
```

The above statements define that:

- Rfc2527Hw, Rfc2527HwOrSw, Rfc2527Sw are sub-classes of Rfc2527ModuleTypes.
- Rfc2527Hw subsumes Rfc2527HwOrSw.
- Rfc2527HwOrSw subsumes Rfc2527Sw.

This subsumption relationship can be associated with an interpretation of *trustworthiness*: module types whose concept descriptions subsume others are more trustworthy than the module types associated with the subsumed concepts.

Using this taxonomy, Rfc2527KeyGeneration can be defined with two attributes: caKeyGen and eeKeyGen. Both require values that belong to the concept/class Rfc2527ModuleTypes.

```
( createConcept Rfc2527KeyGeneration
  ( and ( all caKeyGen Rfc2527ModuleTypes )
    ( all eeKeyGen Rfc2527ModuleTypes ) ) )
```

The Government of Canada Policy can be specified as:

```
( createConcept GocSign2KeyGeneration
  ( and Rfc2527KeyGeneration
    ( all caKeyGen Rfc2527HwOrSw )
    ( all eeKeyGen Rfc2527HwOrSw ) ) )

( createConcept GocSign3KeyGeneration
  ( and Rfc2527KeyGeneration
    ( all caKeyGen Rfc2527Hw )
    ( all eeKeyGen Rfc2527HwOrSw ) ) )
```

```
( createConcept GocSign4KeyGeneration
  ( and Rfc2527KeyGeneration
    ( all caKeyGen Rfc2527Hw )
    ( all eeKeyGen Rfc2527Hw ) ) )
```

NeoClassic will determine that GocSign4KeyGeneration subsumes GocSign3-KeyGeneration, which subsumes GocSign2KeyGeneration. This can then, in turn, be interpreted in such a way that certificates associated with CP GocSign4 are more secure than certificates associated with CP GocSign2.

The SEIS policy can be described as:

```
( createConcept GocSign2KeyGeneration
  ( and Rfc2527KeyGeneration
    ( all caKeyGen Rfc2527HwOrSw )
    ( all eeKeyGen Rfc2527HwOrSw ) ) )
```

NeoClassic will recognize GocSign2KeyGeneration as being equivalent to Goc-Sign2KeyGeneration.

SUMMARY

In this chapter it was shown how techniques from the area of formal knowledge representation could be used to better represent the information contained in Certificate Policies and Certification Practice Statements. It has been discussed how subsumption can be used to compare the quality and trustworthiness of certificates.

Performing the case study of modeling different CP/CPS, the following observations have been made:

- The definition of a core terminology in the form of an ontology is necessary. RFC 2527 actually provides some kind of framework that can be followed to specify such a reference terminology.
- It also became clear that CP/CPS that follow RFC 2527 are difficult to compare because this framework leaves too much room for interpretation and expressing different aspects.
- This shows that users who want to compare the quality of certificates actually do face a major problem, as existing CP/CPS are difficult to compare.

Planned work comprises the specification how a DL-based language like NeoClassic can best be syntactically represented in an environment where certificates are being used. While performing this work, it also became apparent that different domains are using different models to represent authorizations, capabilities, rights, etc. These different representations, in turn, require domain-specific processing models. It seems promising to study how a DL-based system can be used as a unifying scheme for a generic policy specification.

REFERENCES

1. Housley, R., Ford, W., Polk, W., and Solo, D. Internet X.509 Public Key Infrastructure: Certificate and CRL Profile, IETF RFC 2459, 1999.
2. Chokhani, S. and Ford, W. Internet X.509 Public Key Infrastructure: Certificate Policy and Certification Practices Framework, IETF RFC 2527, 1999.
3. Brachman, R.J. and Schmolze, J.G. An Overview of the KL-ONE Knowledge Representation System, Cognitive Science, 9(2), 171–216, 1985.
4. Brachman, R.J., Pigman-Gilbert, V., and Levesque, H.J. An Essential Hybrid Reasoning System: Knowledge and Symbol Level Accounts in KRYPTON, in *Proc. of the 9th Int. Joint Conf. on Artificial Intelligence (IJCAI-85)*, 1985, 532–539.
5. Donini, F.M., Lenzerini, M., Nardi, D., and Schaerf, A. Reasoning in Description Logics, CLSI Publications, Principles of Knowledge Representation and Reasoning, 1994, 193–238.
6. Borgida, A. and Patel-Schneider, P.F. A Semantics and Complete Algorithm for Subsumption in the CLASSIC Description Logic, *Journal of Artificial Intelligence Research*, 1, 277–308, 1994.
7. Lassila, O. and Swick, R. Resource Description Framework (RDF): Model and Syntax Specification, W3C Recommendation, 1999.
8. Treasury Board of Canada, Secretariat. Digital Signature and Confidentiality Certificate Policies for the Government of Canada Public Key Infrastructure, Version 3.02, 1999.
9. Secured Electronic Information in Society. SEIS Certificate Policy SeisS10-1: 1.0, High Assurance General ID-Certificate with Private Key Protected in an Electronic ID-Card, Version 1.0, 1998.
10. Brachman, R.J., McGuinness, D.L., Patel-Schneider, P.F., Resnick, L.A., and Borgida, A. Living with CLASSIC: When and How to Use a KL-ONE-Like Language, John F. Sowa, Ed., *Principles of Semantic Networks — Explorations in the Representation of Knowledge*, Morgan Kaufmann Publishers, 1991, 401–456.
11. Nabil, A. and Yelena, Y. Strategic Directions in Electronic Commerce and Digital Libraries: Towards a Digital Agora, *ACM Computing Surveys*, 28(4), 818–835, 1996.
12. Krauskopf, T., Miller, J., Resnick, P., and Treese, W. PICS Label Distribution Label Syntax and Communication Protocols, W3C Recommendation, 1996.

10

MANAGED PUBLIC KEY INFRASTRUCTURE: SECURING YOUR BUSINESS APPLICATIONS

VeriSign, Inc.

To operate business-critical applications over the Internet, enterprises need high-level, certificate-based security provided by a public key infrastructure (PKI). PKI protects applications that demand the highest level of security, enabling online banking and trading, Web services-based business process automation, digital form signing, enterprise instant messaging, and electronic commerce. In addition, it protects firewalls, virtual private networks (VPNs), directories, and enterprise applications. The PKI should offer comprehensive functionality, integrate easily with internal and external applications, scale to millions of users, operate flawlessly 24/7, and ensure military-grade physical security. In addition, it should allow enterprises to easily create communities of trust with partners, customers, and suppliers.

In selecting a PKI to provide these critical capabilities, enterprises must choose between deploying PKI software in-house or outsourcing PKI services to a reliable provider. In-house deployments often have inherent drawbacks — proprietary software, limited physical security, and poor redundancy — that impede successful PKI implementation. Outsourced PKIs offer a number of advantages, including lower cost of ownership, rapid deployment, and reduced risk.

The VeriSign Managed PKI service is an outsourced offering that enables enterprises of any size to rapidly and confidently deploy PKI services. It alleviates the burden of planning, building, and maintaining a public key infrastructure, while allowing enterprises to maintain internal control over digital certificate issuance, suspension, and revocation. Using the Managed PKI, enterprises can securely move valuable data online to lower costs, streamline processes, and strengthen relationships with partners, customers, and suppliers.

PROTECTING INFORMATION ASSETS

As financial institutions, manufacturers, government agencies, healthcare organizations, and other enterprises leverage the Internet to link business processes, streamline communications, and conduct commerce, the protection of information assets has become a vital, yet increasingly complex component of online data exchange. Enterprises not only must safeguard sensitive information and maintain the trust of online trading partners, but also must comply with government and industry regulations related to online data. Meanwhile, virus distribution methods have evolved, the hacker arsenal has grown, and technology advances such as wireless communications have created parallel environments that must also be protected. In protecting information assets, enterprise security is now expected to provide gatekeeping functions such as data protection and network isolation, as well as facilitative functions such as exposing enterprise data to outside applications, connecting users for extended collaboration, and enabling online transactions and communications.

INTRODUCING ENTERPRISE PKI

The foundation for providing application and network security in these multifaceted environments is public key infrastructure (PKI). PKI protects applications that demand the highest level of security, enabling online banking and trading, Web services-based business process automation, digital form signing, enterprise instant messaging, and electronic commerce. In addition, it protects firewalls, virtual private networks (VPNs), directories, and enterprise applications.

Technically, PKI refers to the technology, infrastructure, and practices that support the implementation and operation of a certificate-based public key cryptographic system. The system uses a pair of mathematically related keys — called a private key and a public key — to encrypt and decrypt confidential information and to generate and verify digital signatures. (Digital signatures are used to sign transactions or to authenticate users or machines prior to granting access to resources.) The main function of PKI is to distribute public keys accurately and reliably to users and applications that need them. The process employs digital certificates, which are issued to users or applications by an enterprise certificate authority (CA). Issuance of a certificate requires verification of the user's identity, usually by a registration authority (RA).

An enterprise PKI uses digital certificates to protect information assets via the following mechanisms:

- ***Authentication:*** validates the identity of machines and users.
- *Encryption:* encodes data to ensure that information cannot be viewed by unauthorized users or machines.
- *Digital signing:* provides the electronic equivalent of a hand-written signature; also enables enterprises to verify the integrity of data and determine whether it has been tampered with in transit.
- *Access control:* determines which information a user or application can access and which operations it can perform once it gains access to another application; also called authorization.
- *Non-repudiation:* ensures that communications, data exchanges, and transactions are legally valid and irrevocable.

Critical Factors in Running an Enterprise PKI

In selecting an enterprise PKI solution, enterprises must consider the following factors, which span PKI technology, infrastructure, and business practices:

- *PKI functionality.* For strong security, easy administration, and hands-on control of certificate management, an enterprise PKI must be based on a modular design that includes reliable, high-performance support for certificate issuance and life-cycle management, protocols and processing capabilities for diverse certificate types, comprehensive administration functions, records retention, directory integration, and key management.
- *Ease of integration.* To minimize costs, leverage existing investments, and ensure compatibility in diverse environments, enterprises should choose a PKI that integrates easily with all the new and legacy applications it is intended to support. The PKI should not lock end users into proprietary PKI desktop software. In addition, it should be able to accommodate the varying desktop policies of not only internal IT departments, but also partners, suppliers, and customers.
- *Availability and scalability.* The PKI must be available to its user community around the clock. In addition, it must be able to scale to millions of users, if necessary, to keep up with enterprise growth.
- *Security and risk management.* To preserve trust and minimize financial and legal liability, enterprises running an Internet-based PKI must safeguard the PKI infrastructure, private keys, and other valuable assets from not only network-based attacks, but also threats to the physical facility housing the assets.

■ *Expertise.* To ensure that the PKI is properly deployed, maintained, and protected, enterprises should have security professionals who are extensively trained in PKI.

■ *Scope of operation.* To maximize ROI (return on investment), promote collaboration, and ensure business agility, enterprises investing in PKI should ascertain that the offering can be easily enabled to operate across intranets, extranets, instant messaging communities, Web services networks, Internet marketplaces, VPNs, and other communities of interest.

These factors, which are strongly influenced by the PKI deployment model chosen, determine the success or failure of an enterprise PKI and impact an enterprise's immediate and long-range plans for the exchange of high-value data.

Two Models for PKI Deployment

When deploying a PKI, enterprises must choose between purchasing stand-alone PKI software for in-house deployment and outsourcing an integrated PKI platform. In addition to their differing capabilities to meet the challenges discussed in the preceding section, the two approaches vary in their total cost of ownership (TCO), time to implementation, likelihood of success, use of in-house talent, degree of risk, and brand value.

In-House Deployment of Stand-Alone PKI Software

In an in-house deployment, an enterprise purchases stand-alone PKI software and creates a stand-alone PKI service. In this scenario, the enterprise assumes 100 percent responsibility for provisioning, deploying, and maintaining the PKI itself, as well as all the surrounding technology, including systems, telecommunications, and databases. The enterprise is also responsible for providing a secure facility. A secure facility must have physical site security, Internet-safe network configurations, redundant systems, disaster recovery, viable PKI legal practices, financially sound liability protection, and highly trained personnel. If any of these components are weak, the enterprise may be compromised.

Regardless of the in-house PKI's capability to address critical success factors, adoption of PKI-enabled services by partners, customers, and suppliers may be hindered by lack of confidence in the unproven PKI or unfamiliarity with the enterprise itself. In addition, non-repudiation — the capability to provide third-party auditing and corroboration of transactions — may not exist in an in-house implementation, further diminishing the

PKI's value. Finally, the process of planning, purchasing, implementing, deploying, and testing an in-house PKI can take many months, delaying the deployment of strategic business initiatives as well as the return on existing investments.

Outsourced Deployment to an Integrated PKI Platform

In an outsourced deployment to an integrated PKI platform, an enterprise delegates PKI construction, deployment, and maintenance to a trusted third party whose services include certificate processing, root key protection, and security and risk management.

Because it is their core business, integrated PKI platform providers can devote a greater percentage of their resources to state-of-the-art PKI technology, security, and training than is feasible for most enterprises. In addition, security practices, procedures, and infrastructure have been tested over time. This accelerates deployment and helps ensure that the PKI operates at the highest levels of availability and security. Because billing for outsourced services is based on flat rates, the number of digital certificates issued, or a combination of the two, the enterprise can predict costs more accurately and simply add PKI capability as business expands.

An important differentiator among outsourced PKI platforms is the enterprise's capability to control and execute its security policies with respect to user authentication and certificate life-cycle management.

The VeriSign Value Proposition

As an industry leader in Internet security and public key infrastructure, VeriSign builds state-of-the-art integrated PKI service platforms for enterprises of all sizes. Real-world experience serves as the foundation for the design and support-readiness of the VeriSign Managed PKI service. By leveraging VeriSign's expertise and infrastructure, enterprises alleviate the burden of building, deploying, and maintaining an in-house infrastructure while retaining complete control over certificate life-cycle management, including issuance, renewal, and revocation. Enterprises can rapidly secure Web services, instant messaging, online forms exchange, legacy, and other applications, yielding faster return on investment and enabling agile response to evolving business strategies.

The VeriSign Managed PKI meets all the critical requirements of a successful PKI deployment, while providing the following advantages:

- *Lower TCO:* VeriSign invests millions of dollars in building, maintaining, updating, securing, and externally auditing its PKI platforms, as well as in staffing its operating centers. By leveraging the VeriSign Managed PKI, enterprises save significantly on secure facilities, infrastructure, and staffing. In fact, TCO of an in-house PKI system is greater than outsourcing to VeriSign, even if the insourcer's software costs are zero.[1]

■ *Rapid deployment:* Because the platform, policies, and procedures are already in place, the Managed PKI can be implemented in less than one-third the time of a typical in-house, software-based PKI.

■ *Proven success:* The Managed PKI is based on a proven back-end infrastructure, helping to ensure the implementation's success.

■ *Minimum impact on staff:* Day-to-day operation and maintenance of the PKI are handled by VeriSign's security professionals, allowing in-house IT resources to focus on core business.

■ *Strong security:* VeriSign's commitment to military-grade facilities and industry-leading certificate practices ensures the highest level of security.

■ *Brand value:* By using a recognized, trusted brand, enterprises more easily gain the confidence of suppliers, partners, and customers.

Exhibit 1 summarizes the fundamental differences between stand-alone PKI software and the VeriSign Managed PKI services platform.

ELEMENTS OF ENTERPRISE PKI

The VeriSign approach to enterprise PKI distinguishes itself from the build-it-yourself approach by giving enterprises control over policy and day-to-day decision making but delegating back-end processor tasks to VeriSign. To explain the VeriSign difference, the following sections discuss the complete PKI solution in terms of the critical success factors already identified: functionality, ease of integration, availability and scalability, security and risk management, expertise, and scope of operation.

Managed PKI Functionality

At the core of PKI lie software and hardware that implement CA and RA functions, enrollment processes, certificate renewal and status-verification services, directory and application interfaces, private key management, and so on. This technology must support strong security, high availability, and multiple application interfaces. Most importantly, it must have a modular design, permitting PKI functions to be distributed between enterprise premises and a supporting secure data center.

The VeriSign Trust Network (VTN) architecture, on which VeriSign Managed PKI services are based, is robust and comprehensive. It supports the PKI service center needs of enterprises, commercial CAs, and Web

Exhibit 1   Stand-alone PKI Software versus the Verisign Managed PKI Services Platform

Success Factor	Integrated PKI Platform	Stand-alone PKI Software
PKI functionality	Fully-featured PKI, proven in world's largest 24/7 PKI service centers. Leveraged experience from hundreds of enterprises.	Enterprise designs, builds, and deploys supporting infrastructure, and assumes 100 percent implementation risk. Software vendor has no PKI operating experience.
Ease of integration	Seamless integration with standard best-of-breed applications, including standard Web browsers, mail clients, and enterprise applications.	Requires proprietary client software for all users and applications.
Availability and scalability	Contractually guaranteed PKI backbone services and disaster recovery. On demand scalability. Leverages high-capacity, fault-tolerant infrastructure.	Enterprise provides 100 percent of services infrastructure and disaster recovery. Assumes 100 percent operational risk. Redundancy difficult. Scalability limited.
Security and risk management	Contractually guaranteed PKI backbone security. Mature, industry-leading certificate practices. Externally audited.	Enterprise provides 100 percent of security infrastructure; must design own operational policies and practices; assumes 100 percent of risk.
Personnel	Rigorous screening process. Highly trained security professionals; core focus is security and PKI; up-to-the-minute knowledge base and skill sets.	Personnel must receive regular training to keep up with evolving technology, standards, and risks. Inexperience may slow deployment, cause downtime, and create gaps in security.
Scope of operation	International network of CAs. Enterprise can select private or public trust networks (largest in world).	Private cross certification only. Enterprise builds 100 percent custom solution each time. Partners assume 100 percent of the risk.

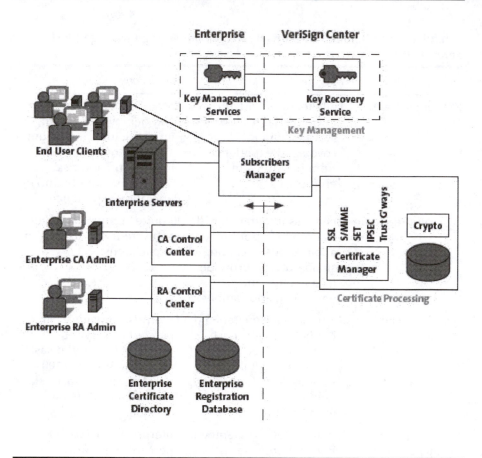

Exhibit 2   VeriSign's WorldTrust Architecture

sites worldwide, satisfying the most stringent security, commercial, legal, and best practices requirements.

The Trust Network architecture (Exhibit 2) is comprised of the following module families:

- *End-user Enrollment Pages:* provide localizable and brandable enrollment pages for end-user registration and other end-user services such as certificate renewal.
- *Managed PKI Control Center:* provides in-house certificate management functions, such as certificate issuance approval, revocation approval, and general administration functions; can be fully automated.
- *CA Control Center:* enables enterprises to establish local CA policy, such as certificate content rules and administration authorizations.

- *Certificate Processing:* includes certificate issuance, certificate life-cycle compliance and protocol support, premium validation services such as Online Certificate Status Protocol (OCSP), cryptographic key management, records storage, and other core functions.
- *Certificate Manager:* allows enterprises to choose the types of certificates to be issued, for example, SSL, S/MIME, IPSec, or VeriSign Trust Gateway certificates.
- *Key Management Services:* provide maximum-security generation, backup, and recovery of user key-pairs; includes dual-key (separate key-pairs within a single application) support.
- *Enterprise Integration:* provides interfaces to enterprise databases to support automated certificate issuance and other administration functions, automated posting of certificates to enterprise directories or databases, and access to certificate revocation information by enterprise Web servers.
- *Application Integration Toolkits:* enable commercial application vendors and enterprises to enable PKI-ready applications.

Ease of Integration

One of the biggest challenges in a PKI deployment is PKI-enabling applications, both within and outside the enterprise. The architecture that the PKI vendor uses — proprietary or standards-based — influences the ease and cost of integration.

- *Proprietary.* Proprietary PKI software is installed on every desktop. Applications that use the PKI require a proprietary software interface from the PKI vendor, making it costly, complex, and usually unfeasible to extend applications to other areas of the intranet or to partners, customers, and suppliers. In addition, upgrades to any application may be incompatible with the existing PKI.
- *Standards based.* Native applications interface to the PKI using industry-standard interface protocols or tailored standards-based interfaces provided through PKI-application vendor partnerships. No proprietary PKI software is needed on the desktop.

VeriSign uses a standards-based approach to PKI and works with over 100 independent software vendors to provide built-in support for the Managed PKI; applications are PKI-enabled as shipped from these vendors. To further ensure seamless operability with virtually any application, the Managed PKI also includes easy-to-use application programming interfaces (APIs) for PKI-enabling customer-written applications.

Availability and Scalability

A PKI supporting mission-critical applications must be available around the clock and must be able to smoothly grow to support large numbers of users and applications.

Availability

To ensure continuous availability, VeriSign Managed PKI has a fully redundant infrastructure with guaranteed 24/7 service levels for all critical components. Back-up disaster recovery sites operate 24/7 in geographically separate locations. By contrast, stand-alone PKI products frequently are not designed for redundancy, predisposing them to unplanned downtime. In addition, disaster recovery capabilities may be limited, unless arrangements are made for a separate secure location.

Scalability

VeriSign digital certificate issuance has been proven under real-world conditions to scale smoothly from hundreds to millions of users. Stand-alone PKI software is known to encounter scaling limits at the tens of thousands due to lack of a transaction-optimized architecture and scaling and resiliency limits with database and directory systems.

Security and Risk Management

Protecting root and private keys and providing continuous service are two critical aims of enterprises deploying a PKI. To ensure strong security and 24/7 availability, an enterprise must have airtight physical security and sound certificate practices. However, physical security is one of the largest expenses in a PKI deployment, and well-designed certificate practices require a mature, carefully delineated approach to security and risk management. VeriSign's significant investments in security technology and its industry-leading certificate practices statement enable a level of security that exceeds the capabilities of most enterprises operating stand-alone PKIs. Leveraging the VeriSign Managed PKI, enterprises can alleviate not only the costs, but also the risks of establishing and operating a high-security, high-availability facility.

Physical Security

Because software-based cryptography implementations are prone to tampering or misuse, a fundamental requirement of a CA supporting business-critical applications is that it employ hardware cryptographic modules for certificate signing. In addition, root keys (which provide the basis for linking together multiple CAs) require special precautions. Their private key must be stored in a secure, offline hardware unit; multiple key shareholders must be employed to enable the key for signing; and all processes must be tightly controlled and audited. In addition to the specific mechanisms used to protect keys, the facility housing critical PKI functions must be impenetrable. In addition, it must have redundant power, redundant heating, air conditioning, and ventilation (HVAC), and specialized fire systems to prevent heat and water damage.

VeriSign locates critical PKI functions in a secure data center operated by VeriSign or an affiliate on a 24/7 basis. To ensure the highest levels of security and availability, all PKIs implemented through VeriSign Managed PKI services employ hardware-based cryptography, highly screened and trained personnel, a military-grade secure facility, and a rigidly audited system of procedural controls. Round-the-clock service levels are supported.

Customer Practices Support

To guarantee non-repudiation and win the trust of partners, customers, and suppliers, enterprises must have well-defined, audited processes for cryptographic PKI management, day-to-day operations, and record-keeping. This is particularly important when enterprises use PKI-based digital signatures to electronically sign electronic transactions, documents, and other information. In this case, sound practices and independently audited processes are essential to ensure that transactions are legally binding.

VeriSign is a world leader in the development of PKI practices, with audited business processes that meet the most stringent industry standards. VeriSign's Certification Practices Statement (CPS), which delineates the practices underlying the VTN public CA services, is recognized as the most comprehensive document of its type and is used internationally as a foundation for enterprise PKI practices.

VeriSign's practices include witnessed and audited processes for CA key establishment and management, and rigid multi-party controls over all key materials. VeriSign undergoes an annual, independent security audit against established WebTrust for CA and SAS 70 security guidelines, and has been approved to issue certificates consistent with the policies and procedures defined by the Department of Defense. VeriSign's processes are certified by KPMG in accordance with AICPA SAS-70.

Expertise

Proper planning, implementation, and maintenance of a PKI requires highly trained personnel with hands-on experience. To assemble a security team for an in-house PKI deployment, enterprises must divert development and IT staff from their core strengths, train existing personnel for the job, or screen and hire new resources. Once the PKI is deployed, ongoing staff training is necessary in order to keep current on rapidly changing security trends and technology. Overall inexperience, unfamiliarity with specific technology, and untested security policies may expose an in-house deployment to delays, unexpected downtime, and flawed security.

By outsourcing PKI deployment to VeriSign security professionals with in-depth experience, enterprises minimize personnel costs, reduce risks, and speed deployment. As the leading provider of Internet trust services,VeriSign has extensive experience developing, implementing, and maintaining a PKI. The VeriSign Managed PKI team focuses solely on security and PKI, and its skill set is updated constantly to incorporate state-of-the-art technology and security practices.

Scope of Operation

PKI can potentially span communities of any size, from enterprise extranets that include select partners, to industry-specific Web services networks that span multiple enterprises, to global communities that include all comers, for example, for instant messaging. VeriSign facilitates the development of communities beyond the intranet through broad community enablement and cross-certification.

Broad Community Enablement

While some enterprises require closed, private PKIs, others want their certificates to be recognized and trusted by out-of-the-box commercial Web browsers or other desktop applications. This greatly facilitates the establishment of extended PKI communities, by obviating the need for special software installation or configuration in the desktop systems of organizations that are not under the administrative control of the PKI-operating enterprise. VeriSign Managed PKI gives enterprises the option of establishing an isolated private PKI, a community or industry-wide PKI, or a PKI linked into the VTN. The VTN is a global, cross-certified PKI operated by VeriSign and its worldwide affiliates. Root keys of the VeriSign Trust Network are pre-installed in all major commercial desktop products, including Microsoft and Netscape clients, allowing the certificates issued in the PKI to be immediately recognized by the users of these products. With an in-house PKI, community building can be unwieldy, involving manual exchange and installation of cross certificates or root keys.

Cross Certification

Cross certification is the process whereby one CA issues a certificate for another CA, allowing certificate chains to link PKI communities that may span multiple enterprises.

Cross certification involves more than just issuing a certificate. It is a special business arrangement, involving agreements on issues such as security practices and liability apportionment. VeriSign has built numerous multi-enterprise cross-certified CA structures, linking groups of financial institutions, commercial CAs, and other enterprises worldwide. In addition, its Managed PKI is certified by the Federal Bridge Certificate Authority (FBCA), allowing government agencies to securely exchange information. VeriSign can help enterprises establish or integrate cross-certification practices and agreements that address the security requirements of all participants. With a stand-alone PKI software product, enterprises must develop and execute cross-certification processes on their own.

FEATURES SUMMARY

VeriSign is the only vendor in the PKI space offering a complete enterprise PKI solution — based on the PKI service platform concept. Exhibit 3 summarizes some major features of the VeriSign offering.

CONCLUSION

As the role of Internet security has evolved to include gatekeeping functions as well as network facilitation, protecting information assets has become more costly and complex. The foundation for providing application and network security in this dynamic environment is PKI. Because a successful PKI requires state-of-the-art technology, sophisticated certificate practices, and highly trained personnel, in-house deployment of PKI services involves significant investments of time and money. In addition, enterprises deploying stand-alone, in-house PKIs often cannot provide the same levels of security as service providers dedicated solely to PKI and security.

The VeriSign Managed PKI service is an outsourced offering that alleviates the burdens and risks of building, deploying, and maintaining an in-house PKI while allowing enterprises to maintain internal control over vital aspects of security such as certificate issuance, suspension, and revocation. By leveraging VeriSign's industry-leading technology, expertise, and certificate practices statement, enterprises not only reduce costs, speed time to deployment, and strengthen security, but also win the confidence of partners, customers, and suppliers who recognize and trust the VeriSign name.

Exhibit 3   Major Features of the Verisign Offering

PKI Component	VeriSign Managed PKI
PKI Functionality	
Cryptographic hardware for certificate signing	All CAs use hardware cryptography, FIPS 140-1 level 3 endorsed (averts risks of tampering and disclosure of private CA key inherent in software cryptography)
Root key protection	Root keys always network in isolation and in secure facility; activation by regimented, audited secret sharing (averts risks of penetration and disclosure of private root key by intruders/administrators if private root key held in on-line, operational environment)
User key management	User encryption keys backed up at enterprise; full key histories; strong protection using distributed key recovery technology
Dual-key support	Supports single or dual key-pairs for any application (dependent on application requirements and capabilities)
Revocation	Certificate revocation lists issued regularly; revocation enabled for Web servers and standard browsers; supports OCSP
Ease of Integration	
Standards-based versus proprietary PKI	Standards-based PKI; no proprietary software on desktops; 100+ ISV partners; 120+ applications enabled
Directory/database technology	Enterprise choice of LDAP, X.500, SQL, or legacy DBMS; no directory schema restrictions
Availability and Scaleability	
Redundancy	Guaranteed 24/7 service levels, redundant servers, database, ISPs, telecommunications
Disaster recovery	Guaranteed 24/7 disaster recovery backup at remote secure site
Security and Risk Management	
Facility security	Fortified construction, five-tier security; dual biometric access control, 24-hour monitoring, motion detect, network security audit
Personnel security	Investigative screening, specialist training, retraining

Exhibit 3   Major Features of the Verisign Offering (continued)

PKI Component	VeriSign Managed PKI
Independent audit	Independent SAS-70 audit by KPMG
Customer practices support	Enterprise CA may join VTN with proven established practices, or may establish own practices; VeriSign offers practices consulting or CPS
Non-repudiation	Evaluated/audited cryptographic materials management and secured records retention provide independently verifiable evidence for dispute resolution
Expertise	
Dedicated staff	Highly screened and trained security professionals focus solely on security and PKI
State-of-the-art skill set	Refresher courses and ongoing updates to maintain proficiency
Scope of Operation	
Global community enablement	Enterprise has option of joining PKI structure with roots pre-installed in all commercial Web/mail clients
Cross certification	Can cross-certify enterprise Managed PKI CA into established VTN or private network; can cross-certify private Netscape or Microsoft certificate server; cross-certification includes all phases, including support for practices establishment

VeriSign, and other trademarks, service marks and logos are registered or unregistered trademarks of VeriSign and its subsidiaries in the United States and in foreign countries. WP 025 0403

NOTES

1. Total Cost of Ownership for PKI, VeriSign, and BlueBridge, February 2002.

11

PKI READINESS

More than a few enterprises have tried to build a PKI readiness solution on their own, only to discover that trust is tenuous without the ultimate protection of a real PKI solution. Many have turned to outside firms that specialize in offering PKI readiness solution services to enterprises around the world. With the preceding in mind, let us now look at whether you should build or buy your PKI readiness solution. In other words, PKI readiness solution options abound for digital certificates, but so do security concerns and design headaches.

PKI READINESS SOLUTION

Imagine a technology that authenticates virtually any transaction, enables E-commerce applications, and is available to any user, anywhere. Now imagine a technology that can lead to fraud, is expensive to implement, and requires serious retooling of enterprise hardware and software to be effective. Which one would you pick?

Actually, both descriptions apply equally well to the same technology: public key infrastructure (PKI). As previously explained, PKI can help anywhere strong authentication is needed — in business-to-business transactions, in bank exchanges, and in communications involving human resources data. These types of transactions are usually encrypted using digital keys, and PKI comprises the policies and equipment to manage those keys.

In recent history, PKI has taken its place alongside firewalls and VPNs as a security must-have for a growing number of enterprise networks. But PKI design remains something of a black art, forcing network professionals to wade through a thicket of acronyms and algorithms. It is little wonder many enterprises opt to outsource the entire process. Others, mistrustful of delegating too much security, muddle through rolling out their own.

0-8493-0822-4/04/$0.00+$1.50
© 2004 by CRC Press LLC

For network managers opting to build their own PKI readiness solutions, the biggest risk is compromised certificates resulting from network, physical, or personnel security that is not up to a specification. Outsourcers are usually strong in these areas, but any enterprise going with a commercial certificate authority provider still needs to be vigilant that the provider keeps the enterprise's data private.

Deciding whether to build or buy is probably the most important step in any PKI implementation. Neither route is easy, and both pose serious security risks if poorly implemented.

Designing Issues

For build-and-buy decisions, network executives will need to understand the various PKI components, the elements of PKI design, and the ways in which PKI interacts with existing applications and network infrastructure. By mixing and matching the basic building blocks, network designers can put together a PKI for a department, an enterprise, many enterprises, or many individuals. The design phase is where PKI gets tricky.

In the most basic case, all users request certificates from one certificate authority. This design is simple, but also unrealistic in most enterprise settings because it may not scale to encompass multiple offices or large numbers of users.

A more common type of PKI design involves a hierarchy of certificate authorities with a "root" certificate authority at the top of a tree. A hierarchical design is relatively simple but on the downside, it does not provide for direct any-to-any connectivity among certificate authorities.

Using this model, any PKI-enabled application must first verify the authenticity of a certificate before using it. This involves the certificate application walking the tree of certificate authorities and thereby establishing a so-called certification path. In a hierarchical design like this, all certification paths must begin at the root certificate authority as a design restriction — in this case, the root certificate authority is the one vouching for all the certificate authorities below it. The deeper the hierarchy, the more complex the certification paths become.

An alternate design employs a mesh topology, with all or most certificate authorities directly connected to each other. Here, certification paths may begin at any point. Accordingly, the certification paths are more varied than in the hierarchical model, but they may actually be simpler for the certificate user. The benefits of a shorter certification path are that authentication may happen more quickly and management traffic is reduced.

Unfortunately, most certificates do not offer clues as to whether they belong in a hierarchy or mesh, or at which point along the certification path they should begin to make a query to the originating certificate authority. For security, it probably will not be apparent to end users exactly who is doing the certifying. For performance, longer look-up paths take more time to traverse. Some implementations build a "certificate cache" in PKI-enabled applications (a store of all previously used certificate paths) to speed future attempts at certificate path construction.

It is important to note that these are design and not product issues. Any commercial certificate authority product will work in either design.

The PKI market includes software and equipment vendors and out-sourced service bureaus. Software and equipment vendors offer tools such as certificate authorities, smart cards, and encryption algorithms (see sidebar "Tokens"). Major vendors in this area include Baltimore Technologies, Entrust, RSA Security, and VeriSign. Service bureaus such as Electronic Data Systems, IBM, the Big 5 consulting firms, and numerous ISPs offer the same tools as equipment vendors, along with value-adds such as integration.

Tokens

If your organization is like most, your users log into your enterprise system with user names and passwords. And they probably log into multiple accounts, with each account requiring its own user name–password pair. Some applications employ authentication, asking for another user name–password set, and now your users are up to their necks in passwords. How do most users remember them all? They write their passwords on little Post-It® notes and paste the notes under their keyboards or on their monitors, of course. Unfortunately, and obviously, that poses a significant security risk.

Single sign-on systems can alleviate some password management problems for end users, but single sign-on is expensive and complicated to deploy, and does not address the fundamental problem — the ease with which passwords are lifted via shoulder-surfing by keystroke loggers or by a variety of other techniques. In contrast, security tokens can replace user name–password pairs or can be used in two-factor authentication schemes where authentication is dependent on the user having both an authentication token and a PIN/password.

Authentication tokens function on two levels. First, only the authorized user should possess the token and the password that unlocks it. Second, tokens protect secret data (the shared secret or the public/private key-pair) by performing cryptographic functions, such as key generation, key negotiation, and authentication, within the token circuitry. Neither the end user nor the OS can access the shared secret or public/private key-pair.

Two-factor authentication provides twice the assurance of a single password scheme that your users are who they say they are. The qualitative measurement goes like this: single-factor authentication (password only) is easy to steal and, in turn, use. It provides minimal assurance that the person using that user name–password is not an impostor. A user would not know if his or her password had been stolen — after all, nothing physical is taken.

With two-factor authentication, your users must possess both the tokens and the PIN/passwords to log on. A user would know if his/her token were stolen or missing. Therefore, adding tokens as a second layer to your security schemes may decrease the likelihood of an attack.

The integrity of a two-factor authentication scheme is wholly dependent on users handling their tokens and PINs responsibly, however. This involves not losing the authentication token, changing the PIN periodically, and notifying the appropriate people immediately if the token is missing. If a determined attacker gets a user's PIN and authentication token, that user is easily impersonated — think of someone walking around with your PIN number and your ATM bank card. This exposure lasts from the time the token and PIN are stolen to the time the legitimate user notifies the appropriate authorities and the authentication token is invalidated.

Authentication tokens come in many forms, including magnetic-strip cards, USB devices, micro-chip cards with readers, and contact-less cards that use radio to transmit data. But the function of the token is more important than its form: the token is worthless if it does not do what is required.

Choose devices based on your application and policy needs. Some authentication tokens generate random passwords that are keyed into the authenticating application. Others generate and store public keys while holding the certificates based on the keys. Still others perform all cryptographic functions on the token. Additionally, the API will determine how easily you can integrate token authentication into existing applications. For example, Microsoft's Crypto API (CAPI) for Windows and RSA Laboratories' Public-Key Cryptography Standards (PKCS) #11 both define APIs for accessing tokens and let vendors integrate security products into the OS — token developers need not write separate drivers for each application. Likewise, application developers should support any CAPI-, PKCS #11-, or PKCS #12-compliant token.

API and standards specifications can be interpreted, and misinterpreted, so vendor certification will add another level of assurance that authentication tokens and applications work together. Nearly all vendors have partnership certification programs; RSA Secured and the Microsoft Certified Partner program are two. Careful review of the certificate program and the products certified can clue you into limitations and potential problems when integrating products. Additionally, there are certification programs designed to provide assurance that token products perform securely.

Traveling users are limited to what is supported on today's laptops. Many laptops (including the IBM T21 I use) have USB, serial, parallel, and mouse ports at the back of the case. But devices that are plugged into those ports can become misaligned, or worse. And they can be damaged if deflected upward in the socket. For laptop users, the PC card and USB form are the best choices. Both are widely supported, offer plug-and-play connectivity, and can be hot-swapped.

Microchip, magnetic-strip, and contactless cards all require external readers. You can avoid this option with traveling users because often there is no place to lay the reader while in use. But if your road warriors must use external readers, laptop-to-reader interface options include PC Card, serial port, and mouse-port adapters.

Desktop users have more reader-interface options. These interfaces are often on the back of the PC and require the use of extension cables to bring the USB ports or external card readers to a location where users can access them. Obviously, you do not want your users going butts up over a PC to plug in an authentication token.

The logistics of distribution and user training are difficult, no matter the product; and everyone expects a certain amount of pain with the initial rollout, but the costs will really accumulate with ongoing maintenance.

An authentication token must be initialized when the user first gets it. In many cases, tokens can be bulk-loaded or initialized by the user remotely, regardless of whether the token uses a shared secret or digital certificates. If the authentication token uses shared secrets, make sure methods are in place for remotely initializing the token. This will be especially helpful if and when a user forgets his/her password or the token data somehow becomes corrupted.

If the authentication token uses digital certificates, the user will have to request a new certificate. If your organization supports key recovery, the digital certificate and key-pair may be recoverable. In regard to digital certificates, certificate management (issuance, revocation, and renewal) is handled separately from authentication-token management. However, processes for managing digital certificates must be coordinated among administrators who manage tokens and those who manage the CA registration process.

Any authentication system must support common functions, such as the ability to monitor user logins, implement time-of-day policies, and lock/unlock user accounts. Automatic lockout due to authentication errors should be available as well. Develop policies beyond the scope of the token-management system to ensure that authentication lockouts are generated by a legitimate user making a mistake versus an attacker trying to authenticate with a stolen token.

From the Buy Side

Service bureaus will integrate PKI into just about anything — be it an enterprise application, a router, a set of VPN gateways, or a wireless infrastructure. Service bureaus also manage the certificate authority and handle the issues surrounding certificate management, such as obtaining a certificate (called "enrollment" in PKI-speak) and keeping certificate revocation lists current. Outsourcing also moves the responsibility for securing the certificate authority away from the enterprise.

Many enterprises find it more convenient to hand over these tasks than to manage their own certificate authorities. It is still hard to do enrollment and revocation, partially because the protocols are hard and partly because they are not implemented in a neat, tidy way.

Another plus for service bureaus is they set up and manage public certificate authorities, an important consideration for E-commerce applications. Public certificate authorities give customers a ready means of mutual authentication without the need to expose an enterprise's internal network.

One last consideration in favor of service bureaus is that PKI standards are still a moving target. Going with a service bureau could relieve an enterprise of having to keep current with the alphabet soup of PKI protocols and the politics that surround them.

Consider the two competing proposals for "certificate life-cycle" issues — enrollment, revocation, and expiration. Entrust and Baltimore Technologies back a specification called certificate management protocol, while VeriSign, Cisco, and Microsoft support a competing specification called certificate management protocol using cryptographic message syntax. The two protocols differ in the extensions and cryptography standards they support (see sidebar, "Crypto Standards"). Enterprises without an abiding interest in these topics may find it more worthwhile to pay someone else to sort it out.

Crypto Standards

One of the better-known certifications in this country is Federal Information Processing Standards (FIPS) 140-1 (http://csrc.nist.gov/

publications/fips/fips1401.htm). The levels of FIPS 140-1 range from 1 to 4.

- FIPS 140-1 Level 1 means the device uses FIPS-approved algorithms. This level does not stipulate requirements for hardware security, tamper detection, or resistance.
- FIPS 140-1 Level 2 requires tamper-resistant seals on hardware tokens.
- FIPS 140-1 Level 3 specifies, among other things, that tampering be detectable and that intrusion attempts will cause the token to zero-out its contents. Also, users must authenticate to the token and be assigned permissions for accessing the token.
- FIPS 140-1 Level 4 adds protection against environmental attacks, such as super-cooling a token to thwart defensive mechanisms.

An up-and-coming certification is the Common Criteria for Information Technology Security Evaluation (CC 2.1). Common Criteria (http://www.commoncriteria.org) is an attempt to merge multinational security standardization into an international standard. ISO specification 15408:1999 is a clone of CC 2.1.

The biggest downside for buying a managed PKI readiness solution service is the farming out of trust. Some enterprises will not outsource any security function because they are not comfortable delegating security to outsiders.

Builder's Choice

That does not mean outsourcing is automatically the best choice. Arguments for rolling out your own PKI readiness solution include project scope and a desire to control all aspects of key management.

A project involving one certificate authority, a small set of users, and a simple security policy may not justify bringing in a service bureau. For more complex situations, the buy/build decision may be a question of deciding whose time is more valuable — the internal staff or the outsourcer.

Finally, building one's own PKI readiness solution has its advantages; the learning curve is definitely steeper. Network executives will need to learn PKI protocols and design issues that can make even the most complex lower-layer network design look like child's play.

SUMMARY

Regardless of which way you go with the buy/build decision, there are serious issues of trust management that need to be addressed in any PKI design. These issues include the security of the certificates and certificate authorities; the authority of the certificate authority; the uniqueness of certificates; and the degree to which integration of other systems into PKI may compromise the system.

Certificates are assumed to be secure because they are issued by an authority and signed with a user's private key. But the vast majority of users store certificates on conventional computers or smart cards, both of which are prone to attack. As in any system design, security is only as strong as the weakest component. If the storage medium is vulnerable to viruses, other malicious code, or even physical attacks, the certificate is vulnerable too.

In some states, the holder of a key certified by an approved certificate authority is responsible for whatever that key does. The problem with this is that it does not matter who was at the keyboard or what virus may have done the signing.

PKI vendors generally consider non-repudiation (the inability of a certificate holder to deny a transaction took place) to be a benefit. However, non-repudiation is not a valid practice in all cases. For example, users can repudiate unauthorized charges with regard to credit cards. There is not yet a similar mechanism in most PKI designs.

Of course, securing the certificate authority is also a major issue in the case of buying or building. A compromise of the certificate authority's private key would be a disaster in security terms because it means the attacker could issue bogus certificates.

But attackers can compromise the certificate authority's authority even without compromising the certificate authority. In an alarmingly high-profile case in 2001, attackers posing as Microsoft employees successfully extracted bogus certificates from a certificate authority run by VeriSign. Microsoft was forced to issue a security bulletin stating that the vulnerability could affect "all customers using Microsoft products." VeriSign determined the breach occurred because humans did insufficient checking on the validity of the attacker's request.

Although the bogus certificates apparently were never used, they could have been used for anything — and that raises the issue of certificate legitimacy. For example, your assistant could pose as you and say to your bank: "Withdraw all my money;" or to your doctor, "send all my medical records to XYZ address."

Microsoft asks users to decide whether they trust Microsoft content when they download bug fixes. Few users actually inspect the digital signature to verify its content, making it just as easy to accept forged certificates as legitimate certificates.

For example, the Secure Sockets Layer encryption is used to secure Web transactions. There are Web pages whose certificate is for the Web hosting enterprise, not for the enterprise whose logo is on the pages. In such situations, it is not clear with whom the end user is having a "secure" conversation. Most end users cannot or will not be bothered to find out.

Yet another generic problem with certificates is that they may not be unique. For example, if you have a certificate for someone named John Robinson (even if a user knows only one person named John Robinson), the certificate authority may know dozens. The X.509 format allows the use of many other attributes in addition to the "Common Name" for identifying a certificate holder, but this practice assumes the certificate user also knows how to use those other means when looking for the correct John Robinson.

A final issue is that of integrating PKI with existing applications, especially authentication schemes. Consider single sign-on (SSO) authentication mechanisms. It is possible to integrate a certificate-issuing smart card into an SSO system so that a user only has to authenticate once a day to reach all the computing resources in the enterprise. While it sounds convenient, it also defeats the PKI's intent of validating every transaction at the time of the transaction. For an office clerk, it may not be a big deal if someone "borrows" the computer, while he or she is at lunch. However, in the boiler room of a brokerage-trading floor, the stakes could be different.

Properly implemented, PKI can deliver a powerful means of making any transaction so secure that it is virtually immune from attack. It can also pose some of the thorniest security challenges network designers have ever faced. Getting it done right is difficult and requires taking the time to understand and implement the various pieces of the PKI infrastructure in a truly secure way.

II

ANALYZING AND DESIGNING PUBLIC KEY INFRASTRUCTURES

With regard to PKI architectural design considerations, the system administrator for the network server must install and configure the necessary security software in various secure locations, and make this software accessible to the security officers. System resources and network bandwidth must be available for the certificate issuance, verification, storage, and revocation processes. Thus, the PKI architecture's four functional design components are:

1. A certification authority (CA)
2. Optionally, one or more registration authorities (RAs)
3. Public directories
4. Client-side software

The CA system is established on a secure server that houses software for issuing and signing certificates and publishing certificate information in the directory server. If needed in larger environments, a hierarchy of CAs can be established. The CA is managed by a principle security officer who is responsible for the overall security and maintenance of the PKI.

One or more RAs can be established to process user requests for certificates and other certificate management functions. Security administration officers can be chosen and assigned routine certificate management functions, such as manual issuance and revocation of user certificates.

Directories must be configured for storing certificates, and for synchronizing this information as needed to distribute certificates throughout an enterprise. The system administrator responsible for the directories must be made aware of the requirements of the directory for storage and maintenance of the certificates. The directories may need to be upgraded to use the Lightweight Directory Access Protocol (LDAP) standards, or reconfigured to enable security. Thus, a comprehensive PKI architecture design solution includes client-side software that operates consistently and transparently with existing applications to take advantage of encryption and digital certificates.

With the preceding in mind, this section begins with Chapter 12, which concentrates on a small but interesting area of software security based on public key cryptographic technology. Next, Chapter 13 is not about PKI technology; rather, it is about time and money. Then, Chapter 14 discusses why a number of enterprises develop the many significant standards related to PKI. Finally, Chapter 15 discusses PKI architectural design considerations. The first part of the chapter describes the requirements of a public key infrastructure. Next, the chapter presents the high-level structure of the PKI architecture by grouping the architecture's design components into broad functional categories. The third part of the chapter enumerates the design components in each of the architecture's functional categories; describes the functionality of each design component and lists existing specifications that could serve as candidate standards for each design component's interfaces and protocols; identifies where negotiation facilities are required to deal with the probable existence of a multiplicity of security mechanisms; enumerates important public-key-related protocols, and discusses the need for environment-specific profiles. Finally, the chapter discusses the use of hardware security devices in the architecture.

Tip: To be considered a "candidate" for purposes of the public key infrastructure architecture, an interface or protocol must be described by a publicly available specification, and support a significant fraction of the functionality of the PKI design component for which it is proposed as a candidate.

12

PKI DESIGN ISSUES

Douglas P. Barton, Anthony S. Moran, and Luke O'Connor

Computer security is a vitally important consideration in modern systems. Until recently, typically only the military and banking areas have had detailed security systems. However, with advances in technology and new paradigms, security is becoming a more widely considered concern, particularly with the massively growing interest in E-commerce.

System security is a broad term that covers all areas of security within information technology, from physical security, such as locks on doors, through software to perform cryptographic functions. This chapter concentrates on a small but interesting area of software security based on public key cryptographic technology.

CRYPTOGRAPHY AND PUBLIC KEY TECHNOLOGY

Cryptography is the enciphering of data using some well-known function to ensure the privacy of that data. Typically, cryptographic functions require "keys" that are used to "encrypt" and "decrypt" the data and are known only by trusted entities. There are two commonly known flavors of key-based cryptography, known as symmetric key and asymmetric key. As the names suggest, symmetric key cryptography uses the same key to encrypt and decrypt data, while asymmetric key cryptography uses two keys that are mutual inverses (one decrypts the other's encryption). Asymmetric cryptography is known as "public key" cryptography because one half of the key-pair can be published without compromising the overall security of the system.

Public key technology is seen by many to be both more cryptographically secure than symmetric key techniques and more easily scalable. Several reasons exist in support of these beliefs:

- Public keys can be more easily published without compromising the security of the private key or the overall system.
- Keys maintain at least an implicit identity by association of particular key-pairs with specific entities.
- Unlike the majority of symmetric key cryptography systems, key lengths are not fixed and may be increased for added cryptographic strength (security).[1]

Public key technology does, however, suffer from similar problems to those experienced by symmetric key systems such as Kerberos, Sesame, and standard UNIX login security. The most obvious problem is that of key management, where keys must be generated and passed around throughout the system. The problem is somewhat different between symmetric systems and public key systems. Key negotiation is required in symmetric systems so that the secrecy of keys is maintained, while in public key systems, broadcast of public keys and establishing trust in the public key are the main requirements. Symmetric key systems use trusted third parties, sometimes called Key Distribution Centers (as in Kerberos), to manage this process and an analogous technique can be used in public key systems.

Public keys may be maintained in a database with associated subject identity and other information; each record is known as a certificate. Certificates, however, do not by themselves enhance the trust in the system as a trusted third party is still required to create the certificates and prove trust. The trusted third party is known as the Certification Authority (CA) and it enables trust using a public key technique known as digital signatures (see Exhibit 1).[1]

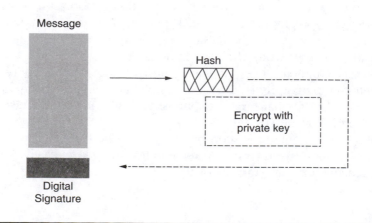

Exhibit 1   Digital Signatures

Digital signatures constitute a technique that uses an entity's private key to encrypt a message digest (checksum or message hash) calculated on a message. This enables other entities to verify the signature by decrypting the signature using the signing entity's public key and comparing it with a message digest calculated on the message locally. Digital signatures prove integrity of the message and authenticity if the public key can be trusted to be authentic.

Because the CA's public key must be well-known by all clients, and because it is a cryptographically strong ("hard to guess") key, the CA can provide trust within the system by signing all the certificates it issues. As long as the signing CA's public key for any certificate is known and trusted, the certificate can be trusted and used as proof of a binding between a client and a particular public key.

The key management problem is now apparent. How are certificates passed around a public key system, and how is the CA's public key, which is used to verify certificates, broadcast/published securely? These problems can be resolved by the provision of a public key infrastructure (PKI) that supports certification and broadcast of certificates using a simple architecture. It is a desirable feature of this PKI architecture that it be easily scalable to enable support for very large network environments such as the Internet.

PKI DESIGN ISSUES

There are a wide variety of issues presented when designing and implementing PKI, ranging from common issues encountered in all areas such as language choice and design methodology through specifics such as interdomain hierarchy structures and revocation techniques. This part of the chapter considers the difficult questions that are treated with little or no depth by existing documentation, and yet which present the greatest impact on design and implementation of PKIs. First, this part of the chapter outlines the existing standards documents and bodies working in the public key arena and then presents a discussion of the difficult issues.

Standards and Crypto

Public key authentication technology cannot be discussed without mention of the X.509 standard Open Systems Interconnection (OSI). The OSI "Directory" standard specifies, in extensive detail, the use of Abstract Syntax Notation (ASN), data structures, protocol exchanges, and other important information for the implementation of the X.509 directory services. The X.509 standard has gone through several cycles of revision and major changes affecting the proposed certificate structure.

There are a number of working groups on the Internet that are primarily concerned with public key technology and infrastructure. The most notable of these is the PKIX Working Group. Recently, the Open Software Foundation (OSF) published an architecture specification for PKI that details a basic PKI framework and considerations.

Due to the likelihood of public key uptake in electronic commerce systems of the future, there is significant interest in the legal issues involved. Various countries have developed or are developing frameworks, including legal specifications, for the use and regulation of public key technology. Australia, for instance, recently published a document called The Australian PK Authentication Framework (TAPKAF) and a corresponding request for comments. This document discusses the legal ramifications of various uses of public keys, such as non-repudiation and digital signatures.

On the technology side of the public key arena, there are a number of major players. The cryptographic techniques are patented and copyrighted by a U.S. company called RSA. RSA-based public key cryptography is the most common, but there are other similar public key techniques based on similar concepts such as El Gamal. Pretty Good Privacy (PGP) by Phil Zimmerman, based on RSA techniques, is one of the most widely used of these public key technologies. PGP is now widely accepted on the Internet, largely because it is freely available and runs on many platforms including PCs. A variety of message digest technologies are available; again, the most common techniques, such as Message Digest 5 (MD5), are produced by RSA.

PKI Structure

The basic structure of any PKI requires at least two functional blocks. First, certificates must be created and destroyed (revoked) somewhere within the system; and second, certificates must be stored and made available to clients. The Certification Authority (CA) provides all the required services of the former, and the Certificate Server (CS) the latter.

Because trust in a PKI system resides within the certificates themselves, the CA must be a trusted entity, but no such requirement need be placed on the CS. The CA must reside within the trusted computing base of the installation and be maintained by a trusted administrator. Two interfaces to the CA are provided to clients: one to create certificates and one to revoke certificates. The CA has no other interfaces to external clients. Certificates and Certificate Revocation Lists (CRLs) are registered with the CS by the CA.

The CS receives Certificates and CRLs from the CA and stores these items in the corresponding database. The CS provides several other interfaces to clients within the local domain as well as an interdomain interface. Clients may contact the CS, requesting certificates by subject name or serial number. They may also request CRLs from the CRS interface. Interdomain clients may access the same facilities through the local CS. The CS may reside anywhere within the installation and need not be trusted, as it merely stores certificates in which the trust is inherent.

The provision of services from separate server entities facilitates the partitioning of the larger network into localized domains. Smaller domains enable local security management and reduce the administration overhead to achievable levels. Each domain would maintain its own internal PKI structure of CA and CS/CRS servers and certified clients. Interdomain trust, however, becomes somewhat more difficult to resolve. For two clients to establish trust, each must be able to retrieve and verify the other's certificate. This process follows the outline:

- Obtain the public key for the CA that certified the other client.
- If clients are from different domains, then the CAs of each domain must be certified within the local domain, or some path of CA/domain certification must exist between the client domains, a process known as cross certification;
- Each client must then obtain the certificate of the other client, and can check its validity using the public key of the issuing CA obtained in the previous step.
- Once valid certificates have been shared, the public keys within the certificate may be used for secure exchange of information such as session keys and other encrypted data.[1]

PKI Functional Blocks

The fundamental PKI structure can be extended with the addition of two extra functional blocks: the Certificate Revocation Server CRS and the client block application programming interface (API) (see Exhibit 2).[1] Each of these blocks interacts with one or more of the other blocks (and itself in the case of the client block) to achieve successful PKI operation.

The CA is the trusted third party within the system by which all trust is propagated. It is a highly trusted and secured piece of software and must reside within the trusted computing base of the installation to maintain the trust in the local PKI domain and overall PKI hierarchy (see a discussion of hierarchies later in the chapter). The CA certifies clients within the domain, proving in a trustable manner that the holder of the private key matching the certificate is indeed who they claim to be. This can be achieved in a variety of ways.

First of all, the primary process of certification is offline, requiring an entity to physically consult the security administrator and apply for a

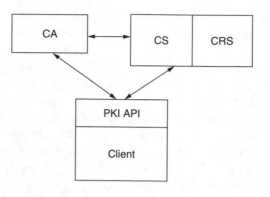

Exhibit 2   PKI Basic Functional Units

certificate. The process is somewhat akin to applying for a passport, driver's license, or credit card. Clients desiring certification must provide proof to the security administrator that uniquely and incontrovertibly proves the client's identity.

Second, an alternative process, and one that is more open to attack and compromise, is online certification. A client interface is provided by which the client forms a certificate request containing all the required information. The interface passes the request to the security administrator for actioning. The client interface must ensure the authenticity of the client, which is often very difficult and the main reason why offline certification is generally held to be more secure.

The CS and CRS are servers that interface the clients with the back-end certificate and revocation list databases (which could be as simple as files). These servers are quite simple and need not be trusted, as all trust resides within the certificates or CRLs by the CA signature. Clients make requests of these servers and verify the return data using the CA public key, which must be a well-known and widely published data and which may be retrieved with high assurance of authenticity. Because of the similar nature of the CS and CRS, these servers may execute as a single entity, running separate threads for the two different roles.

Clients are provided with an API that may be used within applications to interface with a variety of PKI services and public key functions. Certificate and CRL manipulation, as well as public and symmetric key cryptographic functions, are provided within the API.

Interdomain

As previously discussed, the PKI provides the facility to partition the world into localized security domains. Domains are typically localized within organization boundaries, encompassing the trust region of that organization

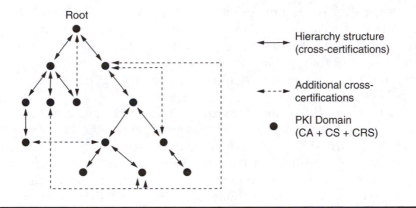

Exhibit 3 PKI Domain Hierarchy and Cross Certification

only. Domains may contain from one to many hosts and many clients, although the purpose of domains is to localize a manageable number of clients and machines within the scope of a security administrator.

The simplest PKI system is comprised of only a single domain within which all entities exist. This simplifies certificate validation issues, such as locating the CA public key, but cannot be used in the real world as the sheer size of the domain would be unmanageable; and very few, if any, entities are willing to share trust in a single CA. Each organization has its own unique set of trust requirements that can easily be localized within its own domain, but not in a single super-domain.

Splitting the world into domains alleviates some problems but creates others. How does one domain establish trust with other domains? How does a large collection of domains interwork? How are certificates passed around between domains, and how are they verified? These problems can be resolved by addressing the routing problem inherent in all these questions. A domain needs to be able to establish trust, via cross certification, with other domains. Each domain may opt to use its own ad hoc routing method, or a global hierarchy can be established within which every domain resides, cross certified with at least one other domain (see Exhibit 3).[1]

Certificate Retrieval

Certificate retrieval is an important issue in PKI systems as verification of certificates requires public key decryption that can be a potentially high-cost operation. It is therefore desirable to optimize the certificate retrieval process to reduce waiting times and overheads.

Retrieval of a certificate from within the local domain is a straightforward operation. The client contacts the CS, outlining the details, either subject name or serial number, of the desired certificate. The CS checks the request; if valid, it searches the certificate database and returns the certificate, if found. The client must then verify the certificate for authenticity using the CA's public key to verify the digital signature on the certificate. This is the expensive operation, decrypting the signature using the public key.

A subsequent check on a certificate with a valid signature is to check whether it has been revoked. The client must contact the CRS, requesting a copy of the latest CRL. Once it receives a copy of the CRL, the client must verify the signature on the CRL using the CA's public key. If the CRL is valid, then the client searches for the certificate serial number in the CRL. If the serial number is found, then the certificate has been revoked and may only be usable for decrypting data encrypted (or verifying data signed) by the certificate owner before the certificate was revoked.

Certificate Chains and Trust

The case of interdomain certificate (and CRL) retrieval is more complicated and depends heavily on the domain interconnection strategy adopted within the PKI. To retrieve a certificate from a remote domain requires that the CAs of the local and remote domains are cross certified (see "Cross Certification" later in the chapter) or there is a path of cross-certified domains linking the local and remote domain's CAs.

Retrieving a certificate from a remote domain yields a chain of certificates corresponding to the path of cross certification of CAs/domains through the hierarchy and the desired certificate. Validating the certificate chain requires that each certificate's digital signature is verified with the issuing CA's public key. This process begins with the first certificate in the chain, which is generated by the local CA, yielding the public key of the issuing CA of the next certificate in the chain. The process continues, validating certificates in the chain using previous certificates in the chain until the final certificate can be verified. If the certificate chain is ten certificates long, then ten digital signatures need to be verified, and possibly ten CRLs retrieved and verified, totaling up to twenty digital signature verifications and quite a delay.

It is obvious from this example that certificate chains need to be kept as short as possible to ensure timely retrieval. This hinges upon a domain hierarchy that optimizes the hop distance between domains.

Cross Certification

Cross certification performs two essential operations within the PKI domain hierarchy (see Exhibit 3). First, it propagates trust between domains, enabling interdomain communications secured using PKI services. Second, it enables short-cuts through the domain hierarchy, speeding up certificate retrieval between any two domains by reducing the hop distance between the two domains through the hierarchy to a single hop. Cross certification has the side effect of shortening the hop distance between two domains that are not cross-certified if intermediate domains in the path are cross-certified in such a way as to provide a more direct path through the hierarchy.

Trust is the primary factor, and it must be maintained to ensure the integrity of each domain. Cross certification occurs in much the same manner as client certification, except that there must be a higher assurance of authenticity of each party. Typically, security administrators of each domain must meet, agree on policies and other details, and then exchange CA public keys for certificate creation.

Revocation

Once created, a certificate remains valid for the duration between its inception/creation and expiry times. However, there are reasonably foreseeable situations in which the certificate may be compromised either through owner carelessness, system compromise, or mandatory retirement of the certificate. In these circumstances, a facility is required to enable cancellation of certificates. This process is known as revocation.

Online

Revocation is a process, like certification, that requires a minimum amount of authentication and authorization. Only the owner of the certificate or the administrator of the CA should have the authorization to revoke a certificate. Digital signatures can be used to determine whether a revocation request should succeed.

As with certification, revocation may occur online or offline; however, unlike certification, either method can be trusted. Clients requesting revocation of their own certificate must digitally sign the request that contains the certificate. Because revocation requires generation of a CRL signed by the CA, the CA is the revocation agent to which all revocation requests are sent. The CA can verify the revocation request and also the certificate within the request. If both are valid, then the certificate details are added to the most recent CRL and the CRL is signed by the CA and issued to the CRS.

In the process of administering the local domain, the administrator may find reason to revoke a certificate. This may be due to suspicion of compromise by disclosure or attack, certificate expiration, or possibly that the client owning the certificate has left the company. In such situations, the administrator must have the authority to revoke certificates.

Revocation Lists and Deltas

Revocation information must be publicly available exactly as for certificates. This information is typically represented as a list, signed by the CA, with each entry detailing a revoked certificate. Information contained in each list entry includes certificate serial number, revoker identity, time and date of revocation, and reason for revocation. This list is known as a Certificate Revocation List (CRL), is issued by the CA, and is made available to clients via the CRS.

The CRL is maintained by the CA and as each revocation occurs, an entry is added to the list. As the CA's domain ages, the CRL grows, listing all revoked certificates. It is obvious that, as time goes by, the CRL may become quite large — especially in a domain with a large client base and high turnover of certificates. As a mechanism, CRLs are the most obvious solution to the problem of storing and relaying revocation information; however, the obesity of CRLs needs to be addressed.

Delta CRLs have been proposed as a solution to the CRL problem. In this idea, CRLs are issued over short timeframes, with each CRL adding to the revocation database comprised of all previous CRLs. Hence, each CRL issued is effectively a delta or update of previous revocation information. Delta CRLs have achieved some popularity in the PKI world; however, there are substantial arguments against their use.

First of all, when retrieving revocation information for a particular certificate, it is impossible to guess whether it has already been revoked and when that revocation might have occurred. Delta CRLs are issued as updates over the last (short) period of time and hence are indexed on time of issue. To make use of delta CRLs, a search mechanism would be required so that clients could be provided with the appropriate revocation information. This increases the workload of the CRS and goes against the design philosophy of moving work to the client side wherever possible.

Second, delta CRLs are also open to man-in-the-middle attacks. It is not clear what data should be returned to the client when there is no revocation information regarding the certificate being verified. What is returned must not be open to replay and must prove that the certificate is valid and not currently revoked. In the case of CRLs, this is simple because the whole CRL is provided and revocation status is determined by existence of a matching revocation entry. However, delta CRLs are partial lists, and non-existence on the list is not proof that the certificate is not revoked.

Revocation Notices

An extension proposed here is Certificate Revocation Notices (CRNs). In this proposal, revocation information is added to certificates when they are revoked. The certificate is re-signed and updated within the certificate database. It becomes a simple matter then for clients to verify a certificate by checking for revocation information in the certificate extensions.

CRNs are, however, not a problem for all the troubles of revocation. Under this proposal, certificates could not be cached by clients or within domain CSs because, while cached, they may be revoked. This means increased load on certificate retrieval, but reduced load on CRL retrieval; and implementation would depend on the trade-off between these two loads. Of course, fetching and verifying a certificate would require only the single network operation and a local check for the revocation notice within the certificate.

Policy

Policy is a generic problem within the area of information security. It is the specification of local requirements and processes for specified levels of trusted operation. Policy applies to the PKI because a variety of algorithms, key lengths, certificate structures, and extension fields are available for use.

PCAs

The PKAF specifies the use of Policy CAs (PCAs) which provide policy defaults for CAs lower down in the PKAF hierarchy. The PCAs are servers that respond to policy queries, providing trusted default policy information to subordinate CAs and clients.

Domain Policy

PKI domains divide the wider network into localized security domains under the control of local authorities and within which the same local policy holds. Typically, an organization would maintain its own domain or may locate each department within its own domain in a subordinate hierarchy, and the organization will enforce its own particular policies within its domain(s).

As domains fit into a larger hierarchy, so too does policy. Default policy would flow through the "root" of the hierarchy down into subordinate domains — from parent domain to child domain. Policy specified locally within a domain would override any policy default inherited from higher in the domain hierarchy; and where no local policy exists, inherited policy would be used.

Policy Negotiation

Finally, policy, being typically specific to domains, is not likely to be identical between entities from different domains wishing to communicate. An integral role of policy is to specify local details in a manner that enables negotiation of the default characteristics that entities must use to communicate across the arranged channel. If the negotiation process cannot be resolved, in instances where policies are mutually exclusive, then the options of an unsecured connection or termination of the session should be provided.

SUMMARY

The proposed structure of CA, CS, and CRS, where the CA is the trusted third party, maintains a very localized trusted computing base and minimizes the risk of compromise. Offline certification and secured communications channels also add to the security of the servers within the domain unit. Interdomain security is maintained through limited access via the CS and cross certification between the CAs of trusting domains.

Finally, policy remains an unresolved problem. Two main problems exist: how policy is managed within the PKI (including policy propagation and inheritance) and how policy is specified. The former has a variety of proposed solutions such as local domain-based policy or policy CAs that specify default policy within the PKI hierarchy. The latter is a question of what language is satisfactory for specifying policy. Subsequently, this begs the question of what aspects of the PKI can and should be specified by policy and what policy choices different types of organizations might wish to specify.

REFERENCES

1. Barton, Douglas P., Moran, Anthony S. and O'Connor, Luke, Queensland University of Technology, DSTC Pty Ltd., "Design Issues in a Public Key Infrastructure (PKI)," Gale Information Technology, 33 King Street, Caboolture Qld, Australia 4510, 2003.

13

PKI RETURN ON INVESTMENT

Derek Brink

Many organizations struggle to quantify their return on investment (ROI) for technology purchases. In fact, the technology industry is rife with analyst organizations and consulting groups that spend tremendous amounts of money researching the topic for organizations worldwide. In this guest-written chapter by RSA Security Director of Product Marketing, Derek Brink, we bring you a primer on how to begin assessing and planning for ROI when you are thinking of implementing a public key infrastructure. For a more detailed discussion of this topic, please reference the RSA Press/McGraw-Hill book titled *PKI: Implementing and Managing E-Security*, by Nash, Duane, Joseph, and Brink.

This chapter is not about technology; it is about time and money. That is, organizations often ask for help with not only the technology case, but also the business case for their investments in public key infrastructure (PKI). In other words, what is the return on investment (ROI) for PKI?

This is not always an easy question to answer. PKI is an E-security infrastructure, and the ROI for infrastructure of any kind can be extremely difficult to quantify. Some do not try, and have implemented PKI based on a leap of faith. At some point, however, we can observe that the ROI for infrastructure often becomes unnecessary to quantify because the capabilities it enables are both mission critical and well understood. For example, when was the last time any large business required a return on investment analysis to determine whether or not it should invest in infrastructures such as telephones, facsimile machines, or e-mail?

This chapter is developed from the present perspective that ROI for PKI is somewhere between too difficult and not necessary, somewhere between a leap of faith and a matter of course.

TOTAL COST OF OWNERSHIP: THE "I" IN ROI

How much does public key infrastructure really cost? When the financial returns are difficult to quantify, the investment side of the ROI equation — that is, the total cost of ownership (TCO) for a particular implementation of PKI — is usually the initial subject of focus and scrutiny.

The most important point for developing a meaningful TCO for PKI is to consider all relevant costs in the following high-level categories: ***Products/Technologies, Plant (Facilities), People,*** and ***Process***. Cost estimates should be captured for a reasonable period of time, typically three to five years. This time period is helpful for time-based budgeting and expectation setting, and it provides the foundation for more detailed investment analysis such as net present value, etc.

In considering this cost framework, however, there are three obvious but important caveats to keep in mind:

1. *Use incremental analysis.* TCO calculations should include only those investments that are incremental to those that have already been made.
2. *Use the line-item veto.* PKI is a sophisticated technology with many available options, and obviously not all options are required for every business process. If the TCO framework lists a particular cost element that does not apply to the particular business environment under analysis, simply cross it out.
3. *Keep things in perspective.* TCO is a perfectly appropriate metric for PKI ROI calculations, but cost is certainly not the sole criteria for selecting a PKI vendor. Other important vendor selection criteria include product functionality, technical architecture, strategic vision, financial strength, reputation, and service and support. In fact, according to one industry analyst, the cost should represent only 8 percent of the total consideration in the selection of a strategic PKI supplier.

You should also remember that people with hands-on experience in PKI implementations are now generally available. If not you, then someone in your organization; if not someone in your organization, then someone from a trusted E-security supplier or a respected professional services organization can provide what you need. Get them involved!

With the denominator of the ROI equation on firm ground, we can now turn our attention to the part that tends to generate the most enthusiasm in the corner offices: the ***financial returns*** made possible from PKI-enabled business processes.

FINANCIAL RETURNS: THE "R" IN ROI

What financial returns does public key infrastructure really provide? As PKI becomes more widely deployed, and as more hands-on experience makes the TCO for PKI more accurately understood, our focus turns inevitably to the more exciting but previously elusive "R" side of the PKI ROI equation.

The most important points for developing meaningful financial returns for PKI-enabled applications are to focus on the business process, establish appropriate metrics, and look for all relevant returns in the following high-level categories: **Revenues, Costs, Compliance,** and **Risks**. In considering this framework, the following simple, step-by-step approach should be kept in mind:

1. *Focus on the business process.* It is worth repeating that PKI is an E-security infrastructure, and infrastructure in the absence of a specific business process returns nothing. For example, if we invest in telephones, facsimile machines, and e-mail systems but never place a call, transmit a document, or send a message, what have we gained? Moreover, returns from E-security infrastructure are generally difficult, if not impossible, to separate from the returns from the business processes themselves. The primary focus — once it has been determined that authentication, data privacy, data integrity, digital signature, or other E-security capabilities provided by PKI are important business requirements — should therefore be on the financial returns from the successful implementation of a particular (security-enabled) business process. This approach also accommodates the reality that financial returns are typically application specific, company specific, industry specific, and so on.

2. *Establish appropriate metrics.* With a proper focus on a security-enabled business process, the next step is to establish the appropriate metrics for determining potential financial returns. The metrics chosen will logically be a function of not only the particular business process under analysis. For example, questions asked might include whether this is an internal process, customer-facing process, or partner-facing process. In addition, specific business objectives should be outlined; that is, are you aiming to increase revenues, lower costs, or improve efficiency?

3. *Establish a baseline for the current state.* Having established an appropriate set of metrics, the next step is to use them to establish a baseline for the business process under analysis, based on the way things are today. This is the "business as usual" scenario.

4. *Compare to the desired future state.* The same metrics can then be used to compute the financial impact of implementing a new or improved business process that meets the specific business objectives we have in mind. This is the "business as a result of" scenario, or desired future state, that will result from the successful implementation of a new or improved PKI-enabled business process.

If this straightforward approach sounds familiar, it should come as no surprise; it is a time-honored method for establishing value, a process we have all gone through (consciously or otherwise) countless times before. We can observe that PKI is not uniquely complex or difficult to analyze in this regard. On the contrary, this approach for computing financial returns for PKI-enabled applications is the same one used for virtually any other significant investment. By properly framing the ROI discussion in the context of the key E-security enablers for a particular E-business process, we can very quickly begin to quantify financial returns using a straightforward, widely accepted approach.

With the numerator of the ROI equation well established, all that remains is to put it all together — to compare the investment represented by our TCO analysis with the sum of the financial returns made possible by PKI-enabled applications.

PKI AND RETURN ON INVESTMENT: SUMMARY

What is the return on investment for PKI? The only credible response is "it depends," but the frameworks discussed in this chapter can help us generate a more definitive answer. On the one hand, we have a framework for capturing the various elements of cost currently involved with implementing a PKI. It presumes a particular application architecture, and aims to include all relevant costs for products, plant (facilities), people, and process. On the other hand, we have a widely accepted methodology for quantifying the potential financial returns from particular PKI costs, better compliance, and mitigated risks. On balance, your personalized comparison of the two halves of the ROI equation will determine your own ROI for PKI. In general, however, we believe that the benefits from PKI-enabled applications significantly outweigh the costs of PKI implementation. Yes, Virginia, there is a strong ROI for PKI.

As said at the beginning, this is not about technology; it is about time and money. To put things in perspective, consider the parallels between current thinking about E-security infrastructure and the thoughts about various quality initiatives in manufacturing (just-in-time manufacturing, total quality management programs, etc.) in the 1980s. A common business issue for pragmatic, nontechnical executives at that time was the "cost of quality," as in "Quality programs sound great, but how much will they really cost, and will there really be a return on my investment?". Then a provocatively titled little book, *Quality Is Free*, helped business people to better understand and quantify the financial effects of poor quality: scrap, rework, longer cycle times, product returns, poor word-of-mouth, higher customer support costs, etc. So the phrase "Quality is Free" was really a concise summation of the concept that the cost of implementing quality programs was significantly less than the financial returns made possible by producing high-quality products in the first place.

And so it is with E-security: the total cost of ownership for implementing an E-security infrastructure such as PKI is significantly less than the financial returns made possible by PKI-enabled applications. In other words, "E-Security is Free." *Plus ça change, plus c'est la même chose.*

AUTHOR NOTE

RSA, Keon, SecurID, ClearTrust, and BSAFE are either registered trademarks or trademarks of RSA Security Inc. in the United States or other countries. All other products and services mentioned are trademarks of their respective companies.

14

PKI STANDARDS DESIGN ISSUES

During the design phase, a standards-based approach is essential to ensure the interoperability and complete security of your PKI. In many cases, a PKI represents a large, diverse system spread out across an enterprise. It is important that standards be followed during the design phase, so that your internal PKI systems can work together and continue to offer full security. If you decide to partner with another firm and use cross certification to extend your PKI, this is only possible through the use of standards.

A number of enterprises develop the many standards related to PKI. The enterprises and their most significant standards are given next.

ITU-T STANDARDS

The International Telecommunications Union (ITU) is an international organization that coordinates global telecommunications networks and services. Its Telecommunications Standardization Section (ITU-T) issues and maintains telecommunications standards. The standard format for digital certificates is defined as ITU-T standard X.509.

PKCS

RSA Laboratories coordinates the development and maintenance of Public Key Cryptography Standards (PKCSs), a series of public key cryptography specifications produced in cooperation with systems developers worldwide. PKCSs have become part of many formal and *de facto* standards. They define many of the standards upon which a PKI is based.

0-8493-0822-4/04/$0.00+$1.50
© 2004 by CRC Press LLC

Of particular interest are PKCSs #10, #7, and #12. PKCS #10 is the Certification Request Syntax Standard: a standard syntax for requesting certification of a public key, a distinguished name, and optionally a set of attributes, using automated electronic means. The request is processed by a CA to create and issue a digital certificate in the X.5009 standard format. The attributes may provide additional information about a given entity for inclusion in a certificate.

PKCS #7 is the Cryptographic Message Syntax Standard, providing a general syntax for data that may have cryptography applied to it, such as digital signatures (see sidebar, "The Digital Signature Act"). The syntax allows recursion, which means that data may be signed more than once. It also allows arbitrary attributes, such as signing time, to be authenticated along with the content of a message.

PKCS #12 defines the Personal Information Exchange Syntax Standard, which specifies a portable format for storing or transporting a user's private keys and certificates. Systems that support this standard will allow a user to import, export, and use a single set of personal identity information. Personal information can thus be transferred securely between systems.

Together, these PKCSs define a standard and secure means of requesting and obtaining digital certificates, employing public key cryptography to encrypt data, and distributing digital certificates and CRLs.

The Digital Signature Act

Companies work hard to establish trust in business relationships. Negotiations that end with a handshake come only after many hours of face-to-face meetings and telephone conversations. These meetings detail the boundaries of an agreement and clarify a system of personal trust between the parties. The trust, established through personal contacts, however, does not easily transcend to E-business, where documents are exchanged over intranets, extranets, and the Internet. The Electronic Signatures in Global and National Commerce Act (E-Signature Act or Digital Signature Act) aims to bridge the gap, but companies still should proceed with caution.

The E-Signature Act went into effect in October 2000. Its goal is to put contracts in electronic form with electronic signatures on equal footing with their paper-based counterparts. The act states that an electronic contract, signature, or record is legally equivalent to a hard-copy contract, signature, or record. But the act does not detail the technical requirements of an electronic or digital signature and does not recommend implementation models. This lets vendors offer a range of options for signing electronic documents. Many of these options, however, do not take into account the risks inherent in electronic signatures, including fraud and the liability for insecure signatures. Companies need to know when it makes good business sense to use electronic signatures and proper implementations that reduce their risks.

Electronic Contracts and Agreements

Many electronic transactions are agreed on when terms are offered and accepted or when the parties' actions demonstrate recognition of a contract. Contracts can be formed through an exchange of e-mail or by accepting an online order, such as when you shop online with a user name and password linked to directory and credit information. In the future, the Uniform Computer Information Transaction Act (UCITA) may apply a law that recognizes the formation of electronic contracts in any manner that shows agreement. It also allows independent, electronic agents to act or respond to electronic messages to form the basis of a contract.

In many cases, however, the law requires a contract to be in writing and signed by the person bound by the contract. For example, commercial law requires that contracts for the sale of goods priced at $500 or more and contracts for services lasting more than one year, are not enforceable unless they are in writing, signed "by the party against whom enforcement is sought." With the E-Signature Act, the traditional definition of "in writing" includes electronic documents and their associated signatures.

The E-Signature Act will not impact infrequent, high-value transactions, such as contracts for mergers and acquisitions. The risk of loss is too high. It could, however, have a noticeable impact on high-volume transactions with low values, such as contracts in sales and order fulfillment. The risk of loss is reduced and spread across multiple transactions. The act could also help in the transmission of insurance forms, negotiable instruments, and secured transactions; and pave the way for other E-commerce services related to trust and security, such as electronic performance bonding and transaction insurance.

During the past century, the U.S. legal system relaxed many rules governing commercial transactions. A signature has come to mean any symbol that is used to authenticate writing. Names on letterhead, mailgrams, telegrams, and fax transmissions have passed muster as signatures.

However, signatures do not have a bearing on the substance of a contract, agreement, or transaction. They are representations or forms that authenticate a contract by identifying the signer as well as providing a ceremony that brings the signer's attention to the legal significance of his or her act. For example, mortgages and wills often require witnesses when the parties sign. These ceremonies reduce the chance that someone will later repudiate his or her intention to be bound to a contract.

To make repudiation of a contract difficult, enterprises can set up their own ceremonies for electronic signatures. Such a ceremony goes beyond electronic and digital signatures per se and includes a PKI (public key infrastructure) system.

A PKI system can include a framework of policies and procedures to initially authenticate a person and, based on that authentication, issue a digital ID (see RFC 2527 at http://www.ietf.org/rfc/rfc2527.txt). Digital signatures in a PKI system can authenticate a document and provide sufficient evidence of a signer's intent to hold him or her bound to an agreement. They can also maintain the integrity of the writing and guard against alterations and amendments to the original agreement.

Electronic Signatures

Electronic signatures use a variety of methods and are created using different technologies. Although all electronic signatures are represented in digital or binary form, at base an electronic signature indicates who signed a document and, ideally, when that document was signed. An electronic signature can be the name in the body of an e-mail message, a digitized image of a handwritten signature attached to an electronic document, or a unique biometric authentication such as a fingerprint or a retinal scan.

Note: Biometric devices that use fingerprints show promise, but iris- and facial-recognition systems are drastically affected by lighting conditions and have not been thoroughly tested in the real world.

Short of using cryptography, most electronic signatures can be obtained easily on public networks and fraudulently reproduced, leaving an enterprise holding the bag as a buyer or seller. Assume that someone obtains the electronic signature with which you identify yourself. Suppose also that person uses your signature and other information obtained from a message to impersonate you and obtain valuable equipment from a vendor under the pretext of a review.

Six months later, you receive a call from the vendor asking for the publication date of the review. Excuse me? In this scenario, the vendor would have to look elsewhere for a remedy. The risk of fraud, however, is greatly reduced if applied cryptography was used to create my digital signature.

A signature should make reproduction or forgery of a signature without authorization difficult. And a signature should identify the document signed and make it problematic to alter the text of the document without detection, such as with signatures created using public key cryptography.

Digital Signatures

Creating digital signatures with public key (asymmetric) cryptography uses two different but mathematically related keys: A private key encrypts a message and a public key decrypts it. The private key is known only to the signer and is used to create the digital signature. The public key is distributed widely or kept in an online repository and is used to verify the signature. If the system is designed properly, deriving the private key from the public key to forge a signature is very difficult. In fact, the risk of loss due to a fraudulent or invalid signature is inversely proportional to the number of bits used in the signing algorithm.

A hash function (algorithm) is used to create and verify digital signatures. The algorithm operates on a message to create a digital representation or a fixed-length hash value unique to a particular message. Then you sign the hash value with a private key using, for example, the Digital Signature Algorithm (DSA) or RSA algorithm. The resulting signed hash becomes the digital signature.

The signature can be verified by referring to the size of the original message using the public key that corresponds to the private key. Any change in the message would produce a different hash result using the same algorithm. Although this ensures that a signature will match a certain message, an enterprise may still lack the confidence that the signature identifies the party to be bound to the message. For example, someone might be sitting at your computer with direct access to your private key. Using a PKI system with tokens can add the requisite assurance.

Digital signatures in a PKI system are created using a digital ID, a combination of public and private keys, and an associated digital certificate. A certificate is a document associated with the keys that contain an identity and with its public key signed or certified by a recognized certificate authority (CA), such as VeriSign.

Certificates are public documents that should always conform to the X.509 standard. They can be stored on a hard drive, in a browser or directory, or on a token. A token, such as a smart key or smart card, can create a digital signature with a private key without revealing the private key. Digital signatures can be created on a computer without a token. However, this exposes the private key to potential theft by direct access to the computer or from a virus like the Love Bug, which was designed to compromise user credentials.

Using a digital signature generated from a token in a PKI system would make repudiation of a contract very challenging. By entering a passphrase known only to the token and the signer, a signer engages a ceremony to authorize a token to make a digital signature. Hence, a potential fraud would require physical access to the token and knowledge of the passphrase.

You can build a PKI system. It is, however, a complex security initiative that can be costly and time-consuming to implement for users and customers. Alternatively, you could buy a commercial product or service from companies such as Baltimore Technologies, Entrust, or VeriSign.

Configuring a PKI system for digital signatures sets up an electronic ceremony to authenticate documents, identify the signature parties, and reduce the risk of repudiation and loss from invalid or fraudulent signatures. A PKI system can instill trust that a signature was created from a unique token and authorized by a certain signer known to a CA.

For low-volume, high-value transactions, you may still want to meet to create a binding agreement between parties. But for high-volume, low-value transactions, E-signatures in a PKI system can enable E-commerce transactions and pave the way for other services to add trust and security in agreements.

What Effect (If Any) Does the E-SIGN Legislation Have on PKI?

The Electronic Signatures in Global and National Commerce Act (e-Sign Act) went into effect as law on October 1, 2000. The law is expected to enable the rapid adoption of digital signatures by providing a legal foundation within the United States for the technology's implementation.

Digital signatures using PKI (public key infrastructure) software represent the most effective and feasible solution for authenticating (or identifying) users and binding them to online transactions. Customers in a wide variety of vertical markets are actively using digital signatures today to securely streamline their E-business processes. E-Sign Act customers are a testament to the ongoing adoption of digital signatures across a broad spectrum of vertical industries, including financial services, insurance, healthcare, pharmaceuticals, telecommunications, and the public sector. Some industries, such as healthcare through the Health Insurance Portability and Accountability Act (HIPAA), have already recommended security standards to develop and maintain the security of all electronic information exchanged.

The e-Sign Act of 2000 gives people a foundation to modernize their businesses and validates the increasing importance of trusted E-business solutions, including electronic forms, document management, e-mail, and various Web applications. The underlying technology of digital signatures provides the foundation to enable the following types of business benefits:

- Consumers can purchase products and services online more conveniently and with confidence.
- Governments and businesses can streamline operations and reduce costs.
- E-businesses can strengthen and streamline online relationships with suppliers, customers, and partners.
- E-businesses can be deployed more quickly, bringing information to market faster and enhancing competitiveness and innovation.

Digital signatures that provide proof of identity and integrity of the transaction are superior to all other forms of electronic signatures, which can include merely signing an electronic tablet at the point of sale or capturing and appending a graphical signature to a file. Whereas digital signatures cannot be forged or copied, other forms of electronic signatures can be easily copied and do not ensure validity of the information contained within the transaction.

Digital signatures can be used to solve one of the most important challenges of the Internet — identifying the parties before, during, and after the completion of a transaction. They are cryptographically generated based on PKI technology, providing proof that a specific person authorized a specific transaction and that the data contained within that transaction has not been altered since it was sent. The ability to generate a digital signature can be complemented by additional means of authentication such as smart cards or biometric devices, including fingerprint scanners, retinal scanners, or voice recognition technology.

IETF STANDARDS

The Internet Engineering Task Force (IETF) establishes many of the standards related to the Internet. The IETF is a large, open, international community of network designers, operators, vendors, and researchers who are concerned with the evolution of the Internet. The actual technical work of the IETF is done in its working groups, which are organized by topic into several areas. Working groups issue new standards as Requests For Comment (RFCs).

The PKIX working group of the IETF develops the Internet standards needed to support a PKI based on X.509 certificates and CRLs, and are based on the ITU-T and PKCSs. The first of these standards, RCF 2459, profiles the X.509 v3 certificate and X.509 v2 CRL for use on the Internet. Other standards include the Certificate Management Protocol (CMP), based on PKCS #7 for online interactions of PKI components. It provides for such interaction as between a client and a CA, or between two CAs when establishing cross certification. The Cryptographic Message Syntax (CMS) standard, based on PKCS #12, provides for basic cryptographic services, including encryption and signing.

Work of the PKIX group is ongoing, as it aims to establish additional protocols that are either integral to PKI management or closely related to PKI use. The group has developed a profile for X.509 attribute certificates, which has been published as a new RFC, and necessitates extensions to existing certificate management standards to accommodate differences between attribute certificates and public key certificates.

With the preceding in mind, a common mistake in implementing PKI trust services is to make them proprietary. This part of the chapter now addresses not only why this is undesirable, but also offers hints on how to design a PKI in a fully standards-compliant manner.

COMPLIANT PKI STANDARDS DESIGN ISSUES

The idea behind this part of the chapter is to make heads or tails of how to handle cross certification. Cross certification is an easy idea in concept — you trust me and I trust you, so let's sign each other's certificates and then different third parties whom you each trust can derive utility from the fact of your trust for the other party. From a corporate point of view, the problem comes when you try and define the word "trust" (it is ephemeral) — you can not measure it? So, how can you determine if what you mean by "trust" is the same as what your cross-certification partner means by "trust"? The solution lies in encouraging all parties that set up public key infrastructures to follow the same set of standards and, more importantly, to follow them in the same way. The remainder of this part of the chapter deals with what standards should apply to all public key infrastructures, how they should be interpreted, and how these interpretations should be followed.

PKI Assumptions

Everyone comes to PKI with certain assumptions. So that you know and understand where this part of the chapter is coming from, it is going lay out where the prejudices are with regard to PKI. Some people view PKI as the "holy grail of computer security" that will enable E-commerce, give instant security, stop "crackers" cold, cure cancer, and eliminate world hunger. Others view it as a very expensive way of replacing a user's login name and password. Thus, PKI has a useful place alongside intrusion detection, effective change management, and user security awareness training. It is not a panacea that will render an enterprise instantly secure, but that it is a necessary step along the security road.

For example, suppose you are trying to design a PKI for a trusted third party for large multinational corporations involved in a multitude of projects at a variety of locations around the world. Here you would have had to deal with many issues, including wading through the many cryptography restriction and digital signature laws that currently serve as the minefield through which all PKI implementers must tread. Add to that privacy laws and requirements, the need for liability assignment, and the requirement for near 100 percent availability, and one quickly comes to the conclusion that this entire field of endeavor is perhaps best avoided.

PKI is 90 percent procedure and 10 percent technology, and in practice, by far, this is the toughest part of any PKI design issue — obtaining the necessary approvals, writing all of the procedures, and assuring the necessary levels of training. The technology, while undoubtedly the coolest part of a PKI project, is almost secondary to its operation. That said, however, the security school to which you should subscribe is that everything can be made secure and auditable given enough political will and money (the first being far more important than the second) — and, if you cannot make it secure, eliminate it. This means quite a bit of time thinking through every possible attack on the systems involved in delivering your PKI service and working on ways to make them immune, if they are not, or at least highly resistant. It also means ensuring that all possible attack vectors are closed — both physical and logical. The result of this is an increase in the required technology, the number of procedures to protect the technology, and a commensurate increase in systems awareness to guarantee that the technology and procedures were utilized correctly.

Now let us move on to how standardization can help with the nice, clean running of the PKI and ease the transition from being an island of trust, to becoming a part of a larger trust community.

Building Compliant Certificate Policies and Certification Practice Statement

In March 1999, the Internet Engineering Task Force (IETF) officially published the "Internet X.509 Public Key Infrastructure Certificate Policy and Certification Practices Framework," better known as RFC 2527. Its purpose, as previously stated, was to "assist the writers of certificate policies or certification practice statements for certification authorities and public key infrastructures."

This was (and still is) an excellent document (RFC 2527), which, as the rest of this part of the chapter shows, allows PKI policy makers to ensure that all possible angles and situations are covered. Unfortunately, the majority of the prominent PKI vendors to date have not adopted this document as their standard (the most notable being VeriSign, which is strange considering that one of the authors of RFC 2527 is one of VeriSign's prominent researchers).

Nevertheless, RFC 2527 becomes very important when you are thinking about cross certifying with another PKI. At that point, you either need to come up with some common criteria upon which to establish your mutual trust, or you have to start doing some rather exotic things like Bridge Certification Authorities managed by jointly held corporations. In other words, if all parties involved in cross-certification discussions had the same format, it would make the task of determining specific trust equivalencies very easy. The other thing that this facilitates is the creation of specific "cross-certification certificates" — which would be, in essence, a jointly developed Certificate Policy, which then would be integrated into each other's PKI without affecting any of the other existing certificate types. And, because some of the best minds in the field of PKI architecture and management created a template that could be used in such a way, and created it as the recognized standard, why not adopt it as such?

BS7799 Security Compliance

The preceding dealt with the procedural aspects of the PKI and addressed the concept of trust equivalencies. This part of the chapter deals with the issue of overall security compliance, which should be the other factor in determining the amount of trust that is capable between enterprises. If one is selling trust, then one should have a demonstrably secure foundation upon which to build that trust. And, in the computer business, *trust* and *security* go hand in hand. In the absence of an official ISO computing security standard, the BS7799 is widely regarded as the best gauge of judging an enterprise's security posture. By adopting the stance that in order for any enterprise to cross certify with you, they must have the same BS7799 profile as you, a corporation can rapidly see if there is an equivalent potential level of trust, and where to focus their energy when there is not. The BS7799 mechanism is a valid tool in this context because an accredited third party must audit a corporation in order to claim BS7799 compliance. The likelihood of misrepresentation is extremely low in these circumstances.

What about the Technology?

If you will notice, the one thing that this chapter has avoided discussing, is the purely technical aspect of cross certification. This is because once a coherent set of policies is defined, the technology aspect of the work is usually fairly easy. Even in a world where the party that you are trying to trust uses a "VeriSign?" CA and you use an "Entrust?" CA, there are ways of making these "see" each other and be able to sign each other's certificates.

Note: PKCS #10 Certificate Signing Requests come readily to mind. They are supported by both camps.

It is far more difficult for the implementer to resolve the political and connectivity issues that surround PKI, rather than the technical ones. For example, trust partners must provide each other with some kind of directory access. The contract between the two parties will force them to then define and fulfill mutual auditing requirements and procedures. As previously explained, PKI is 90 percent procedure and 10 percent technology.

Tying It All Together

Once you have the standardized policies (and the means for two certificate authorities to cross certify), this leaves you with one final (albeit technical) problem. That is, once you have established that two certificate policies are, in fact, equivalent, how do you let applications know this. This is where the last critical bit of standards compliance falls. You must use the appropriate extensions for their associated purpose. This means that the object identifier for each certificate policy should be registered under the X.509 Certificate Policy Extension; and applications should use that extension to determine the trust level of that particular certificate. Once you have established this as your go-forward position, it becomes a trivial exercise to implement certificates in a cross-certified environment. All one has to do is add your partner's object identifier to this extension (which the X.509 architects so conveniently designated as an ASN.1 Stack of Certificate Policies), and the problem is solved. This is not possible using the current (and incorrect in this author's opinion) way of identifying which policy the certificate is issued under.

Finally, the current thinking on this is to put the Certificate Policy or type information in either the Certification Authority name, or worse, as part of the Distinguished Name of the user. These fields should only have the Certification Authority Name (VeriSign, Entrust, SITA, Equifax) or

Subscriber information, respectively. So, by using the fields as they were intended, you can easily establish certificate equivalencies, and still maintain who issued any given certificate.

Caution: o=Verisign Class 1 is not a valid use for the X.500 naming scheme.

SUMMARY

So where does this leave you? Until there is an acceptable standard to which all PKI providers adhere, a lot of confusion as to how to properly deal with cross certification and the trustworthiness of certificates will exist in the PKI space. Once a standard for PKI cross certification has been adopted (as the accounting trade has adopted standard ways of reporting financial information [the Generally Accepted Accounting Principles, or GAAP]), it will be much easier to accomplish what everyone wants from PKI — namely, trust you can trust. And, as providers of trusted services, you should all want to make sure that your customers can make clear, concise choices when considering their PKI investment. At the risk of sounding redundant, the only way you can accomplish this is through the common adoption of an established standard. Finally, you know that the implementation of the ideas put forward in this chapter will be difficult or costly to some enterprises; but until these standards are adopted, you will never realize the full potential and see widespread acceptance of PKI technology.

15

ARCHITECTURE FOR PUBLIC KEY INFRASTRUCTURE (APKI)

The Open Group

1: REQUIREMENTS ON A PUBLIC KEY INFRASTRUCTURE

1.1 Baseline Requirements for a Global PKI

An interoperable global PKI is required to provide privacy and digital signature services in support of international commerce, balancing the legitimate needs of commerce, governments, and privacy of citizens. The global PKI must support multiple governance policy models within a single global PKI framework, and must enable the enforcement of all existing governance policy mandates.

1.1.1 Required Services

- Establishment of domains of trust and governance
- Confidentiality (sealing)
- Integrity and authentication (signing)
- Non-repudiation
- End-to-end monitoring, reporting, and auditing of PKI services

1.1.2 Required Functionality and Characteristics

Key Life-Cycle Management

The actual life cycle of a key depends on whether it is used for confidentiality or signature purposes. Key life-cycle facilities to be supported are:

1. Key Recovery Facilities   The PKI shall specify key recovery functionality for use in environments that require such functionality. This chapter takes no position on key recovery policy issues. Implementations of the PKI may omit key recovery functionality, or may disable its use, in environments in which it is not required. PKI implementations that provide key recovery functionality should do so using the interfaces or protocols specified herein. Key recovery facilities shall provide the following functionality:

- Use of key recovery facilities implies acceptance of a mandatory policy for the protection and recovery of keys. The policy defines how the keys are to be protected and under what conditions and to whom a key will be made available. The mandatory aspect of policy arises as the operations of a key recovery facility may be regulated by legislation or procedures required under commercial contracts for liability management.
- It must be possible to ensure that only key recovery enabled systems shall be usable within a PKI implementation, where this is required.
- A key recovery facility shall be unconditionally trusted and be liable to uphold the stated policy with redress for loss arising from failures to uphold policy through contractual liability and penalties.
- A key recovery center shall be able to verify the legitimacy of a key submitted to it for storage.
- A user of a key recovery repository shall be able to verify that it is an authorized repository.
- The PKI shall provide for coordination between the management of public and private keys in PKI and in data recovery centers.

Note: Public and private key parts do not have the same life cycle and key parts may be archived.

- The PKI shall support aging, revocation, and repudiation of keys.
- The PKI shall support discretionary key fragmentation between key recovery facilities.

2. Key Generation Facility   The method of key generation shall be discretionary, subject to commercial decision and business requirement. Selection of key quality, uniqueness, secrecy, and recoverability of keys must be left to the discretion of the organization generating the keys (and any governance authorities to which it is subject).

3. Key Distribution, Revocation, Suspension, Repudiation, and Archive   The PKI must support the following functionality:

- Facilities for the distribution of keys to appropriate storage devices and directories
- Ability of a certification authority to revoke certificates for individual keys under the terms of the applicable policy
- Ability of a certification authority to suspend and reactivate certificates for individual keys under the terms of the applicable policy
- Ability of a certification authority to force delivery of revocation, suspension, and reactivation notices
- Facilities to enable a user to repudiate his public key under the terms of the applicable policy
- Facilities to enable a user to suspend and reactivate his public key under the terms of the applicable policy
- Facilities to enable the user and subscriber to retrieve revocation, suspension, and reactivation notices.
- Facilities to enable the user and subscriber to determine the status (e.g., revoked or suspended) of a specific certificate
- Facilities to enable the archive and subsequent retrieval of certificates in support of the retrieval and verification of long-term information in accordance with governance policy
- Warranted retrieval: the PKI must support implementations that enable the following warranted retrieval scenarios:
  - Law enforcement retrieval (subject to policy conditions)
  - Corporate agency retrieval (subject to policy and authorizations)
  - Individual retrieval (subject to policy and authorizations)

The following functionality is required in support of warranted retrieval:

- An electronic vehicle is needed for the delivery of a notarized electronic warrant, to support the automation of key retrieval under due process (this must be able to take advantage of existing legal agreements).
- A permanent, non-repudiable and independently verifiable record of key retrieval operations must be maintained.

Note: Warranted retrieval policy includes policy regarding disclosure or non-disclosure of key retrieval to owner of the retrieved key.

Distributed Certificate Management Structure

The PKI must provide distributed Certificate Management functionality, driven by the requirements of the transaction or business domain. The following Certificate Management functions must be provided by the PKI:

1. Policing and policy enforcement (governance model), including the following:
   - Policy creation and maintenance: the policies include those covering key generation, key recovery, key distribution, revocation, suspension, repudiation, archive, and warranted retrieval
   - Ability to register a key and the binding between the key and a name
   - Ability to query which keys are bound to a name
   - Policies (for services built on PKI access control) must not be required to be based on individual identity
   - Certification of the binding between a public key and a directory name shall be mandatory
   - Certification of the binding between additional attributes and a directory name shall be discretionary
   - Auditing and support for the monitoring of policy compliance is required
2. Concurrent support of multiple policies.
3. Exchange of certificates.
4. Support for continuance of service in the event of transfer of certificate services from one certification authority to another.
5. Certificate authority policy mapping services to establish cross certification between CAs.
6. Support for arbitration to determine acceptability of certificates in the event of multiple conflicting certification paths.
7. Support for separation of the certification authority and repository functions in accordance with the governance policy. Changes to certificate repositories must be transactional (e.g., two-phase commits).

Security of the PKI

The PKI itself must be secure. In particular, the PKI must:

1. Protect the confidentiality, integrity, and availability of the PKI services, for example, key generation, key distribution, and key storage.
2. Provide strong non-repudiation services for actions of certificate services.
3. Prevent PKI services themselves from repudiating their own actions.
4. Prevent users and subscribers from repudiating their own actions.

Time Service

A universal, networked time service must be available for timestamping.

Interoperability

PKI elements provided by different vendors must interoperate. In support of interoperability, PKI elements must:

1. Support international standards for certificates and associated data
2. Support international standards for certificate services
3. Support internationalization of all certificates and associated data
4. Support internationalization of all certificate services

1.1.3 Known Issues

For interoperability there is a dependency upon the definition of standard application program interfaces to and protocols between the component services of the public key infrastructure (PKI). Work is required to define and agree on profiles of option fields in certificates.

1.1.4 Recommendations

Adopt X.509 version 3 as a basis for certificates in the development of the PKI. Adopt and adapt existing standards and protocols wherever possible; invent new standards or protocols only as a last resort.

1.2 The Importance of Architecture

The APKI Working Group feels that a robust, flexible, standard, open Public Key Infrastructure Architecture is critical to the success of secure systems based on public key technology. This section explains why.

1.2.1 What Is Architecture?

The architecture of a software system is the set of interfaces through which its functions are accessed, and the set of protocols through which it communicates with other systems. The remainder of this section discusses the importance of standardizing the interfaces and protocols that comprise the public key infrastructure software architecture.

1.2.2 Interfaces

Exhibit 1 illustrates a system on which three security products have been installed. In the exhibit:

■ Product 1 includes a protocol and all the security functionality needed to protect data flowing over that protocol. Only the secure

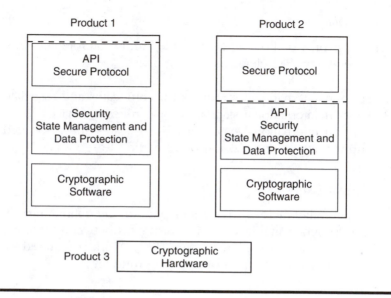

Exhibit 1   Example Security Products

protocol's interface is exposed; the underlying security functionality is not available to other applications.

■ Product 2 also includes a protocol and its requisite security functionality, but it exposes the data protection functionality through a public interface so that other applications can use it. It does not permit direct access to cryptographic functionality.

■ Product 3 is a hardware cryptographic adapter; it comes with a software driver permitting access by applications to its cryptographic functionality.

This configuration has several bad characteristics:

■ Because neither product 1 nor product 2 accesses cryptographic functionality through a standard interface, neither can use the cryptographic adapter. Furthermore, because both product 1 and product 2 embed cryptographic functionality without exposing an interface through which it can be accessed, neither can use the other's cryptographic software. The end result is that three different cryptographic subsystems (two software and one hardware) must be installed on the system, even if all three products use the same cryptographic algorithms.

■ Because product 1 and product 2 embed cryptographic functionality rather than accessing a separate cryptographic subsystem through a published interface, they will not be deployable (without

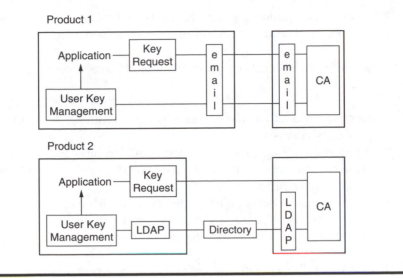

Exhibit 2   Protocols in Certificate Management

code changes) in countries whose regulatory environment restricts or forbids use of the cryptographic functions they embed.

This example illustrates some of the benefits of standard interfaces; these include:

- Replaceability of services (e.g., cryptography) without change to exploiting applications
- Elimination of duplicate service implementations in configurations in which multiple applications require the same kind of service
- Reduced programmer training costs (programmers need learn only one standard interface for a service rather than learning the proprietary interfaces of multiple products providing the same service)
- Reduced application porting complexity (code exploiting services through standard interfaces need not be changed, or requires only minimal changes, when porting from one platform supporting the standard interface to another such platform)

1.2.3 Protocols

Exhibit 2 illustrates two certificate-management products. In the exhibit:

- Product 1 communicates key requests to the certification authority (CA) via electronic mail, and receives keys and certificates from the CA via e-mail.

■ Product 2 communicates key requests to the CA using a proprietary protocol and retrieves keys from a directory service using the LDAP.

A configuration including both products would have several bad characteristics:

■ Neither product's CA could accept key requests from the other product's clients.
■ Applications using product 1 clients and wishing to advertise their certificates in the directory service would require installation of a separate directory-access product.
■ Applications using product 1 clients and wishing to retrieve partners' certificates from the directory service would require installation of a separate directory-access product.

This example illustrates the benefit of standard protocols:

■ Applications supporting standard protocols can interoperate, even if produced by different providers.

1.2.4 Profiles

Many of the services in the Public Key Infrastructure Architecture can be implemented using a variety of different mechanisms and protocols (e.g., data privacy protection can be implemented using a variety of different cryptographic algorithms). This variety of mechanisms and protocols has arisen in part because different environments impose different security requirements.

Multiplicity of mechanisms means that different providers' implementations of the PKI Architecture will not necessarily interoperate — although they support the standard interfaces and a selection of the standard protocols.

A profile defines the set of mechanisms and protocols that should be used in a particular environment. The mechanisms and protocols comprising a profile are usually chosen on the basis of their strength against the attacks that are common in the environment supported by the profile. Profiling has the following advantages:

■ Systems conforming to an environment's profile will interoperate.
■ Systems conforming to an environment's profile will be well-protected against that environment's risks.
■ Profiling helps to assure that mechanisms in use work together appropriately and securely.

1.2.5 Negotiation

Some profiles will allow multiple mechanisms and protocols in order to support different qualities of protection, or to accommodate a fragmented security product market. In these environments, it is desirable to provide a negotiation meta-protocol that allows communicating partners to determine:

- Which mechanisms and protocols they both (or all) share
- Which mechanism and protocol, among the shared set, best supports the desired quality of protection

Note: It is important to note that negotiation does not always require an on-line dialog between the negotiating entities.

2: OVERVIEW OF THE PKI ARCHITECTURE

The PKI Architecture components are grouped into the following broad functional categories:

- *System security enabling services* provide the functionality that allows a user's or other principal's identity to be established and associated with his actions in the system.
- *Crypto primitives and services* provide the cryptographic functions on which public key security is based (including secret key primitives such as DES).
- *Long-term key services* permit users and other principals to manage their own long-term keys and certificates and to retrieve and check the validity of other principals' certificates
- *Protocol security services* provide security functionality (data origin authentication, data integrity protection, data privacy protection, non-repudiation) suitable for use by implementers of security-aware applications such as secure protocols.
- *Secure protocols* provide secure inter-application communications for security-unaware and "mildly" security-aware applications.
- *Security policy services* provide the policy-related information that must be carried in secure protocols to enable access control, and provide access-control checking facilities to security-aware applications that must enforce policy.
- *Supporting services* provide functionality, which is required for secure operation but is not directly involved in security policy enforcement.

Exhibit 3 illustrates the PKI architecture.

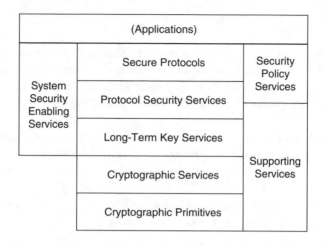

Exhibit 3   PKI Architecture Overview

Section 3 describes each of these categories in more detail (listing the components in each category), and identifies interfaces and protocols that may be candidate bases for standardization of each component.

Note: While the architecture described in this document could be implemented on insecure operating system platforms, implementors of the architecture must ensure that keys, security context data, and policy data are appropriately protected in such environments.

3: PUBLIC KEY INFRASTRUCTURE COMPONENTS

Exhibit 3 outlined the functional categories comprising the PKI Architecture and showed their relationship in the diagram.

Each of this section's subsections describes one of the architecture's categories in detail, enumerating its components and describing component functions, interfaces, and protocols.

3.1 Crypto Primitive Components

Exhibit 4 illustrates the Crypto Primitive components.

Note: The architecture's cryptographic primitives may be provided by hardware (e.g., smart cards or cryptographic modules) or by software.

3.1.1 Function

These components provide access to low-level cryptographic primitives such as key generation, hash function application to a data buffer, encryption

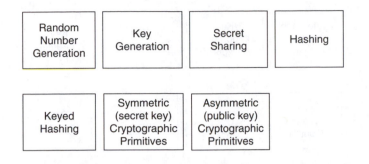

Exhibit 4 Cryptographic Primitive Components

of a data buffer using secret-key or public-key algorithms, decryption of a data buffer using secret-key or public-key algorithms, etc.

3.1.2 Protocols

Cryptographic primitives are typically called locally; it is not anticipated that any cryptographic primitive protocols will be defined.

3.1.3 Interfaces

Candidate interfaces for access to cryptographic primitives include:

- The RSA BSafe library interface
- RSA PKCS-11
- The X/Open GCS-API
- The Microsoft CryptoAPI 1.0

Other interfaces that may support some or all of the cryptographic primitive function include:

- Fortezza
- IBM CCA

Standardization of these interfaces would be of interest to developers of cryptographic service modules and to providers of cryptographic primitive modules. Standardization of an interface for access to cryptographic primitives would facilitate "pluggable" implementations of cryptographic services. The consensus of the APKI Working Group, however, is that cryptographic functionality will ordinarily be used through the cryptographic service interfaces rather than through the cryptographic primitive interfaces. Therefore, standardization of cryptographic primitive interfaces is not viewed as essential.

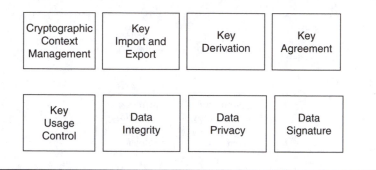

Exhibit 5 Cryptographic Service Components

3.1.4 Profiles

Most cryptographic modules provide support for multiple primitives. Many primitives are subject to legal restrictions on deployment (including both intellectual property encumbrances and national and international regulatory constraints on export, import, and deployment).

Cryptographic primitive profiles will have to be developed for PKI environments of interest (including, for example, the Internet, OMG CORBA, OSF DCE, financial, etc.).

3.1.5 Negotiation

Cryptographic primitives are ordinarily used only by the implementors of cryptographic services. Negotiation should be used to establish which cryptographic service(s) are to be used, rather than to establish what primitives should be used. Ordinarily, this negotiation will be done at a higher level than that of the cryptographic primitives and services themselves. No protocol for negotiating cryptographic primitives should be required.

3.2 Cryptographic Service Components

Exhibit 5 illustrates the Cryptographic Service components:

3.2.1 Function

These components provide access to cryptographic services such as data integrity and privacy protection ("data" here might be a file, a message, an I/O stream, etc.), key import and export, digital signature, keyed hash, etc.

Cryptographic Context Management provides the facilities through which applications initialize the cryptographic subsystem, activate keys for encryption and decryption, and clean up the state of the cryptographic subsystem after use.

Key usage controls permit control over a variety of aspects of key use, including how many times a key may be used; for what purposes it may be used (e.g., for signature only, for privacy only, for both signature and privacy, etc.), and so on.

Key derivation services permit generation of cryptographic-quality keys from non-key values such as passwords.

Crypto services are built on crypto primitives. A crypto service may support multiple implementations, each of which uses a different crypto primitive.

Descriptions of a few DES-based services will illustrate the difference between primitives and services; note that these are only examples:

- DEA is a crypto primitive that uses a 56-bit key and an initialization vector to transform a 64-bit plaintext into a 64-bit ciphertext.
- Data privacy is a crypto service. DES-CBC is an implementation of the cryptographic data privacy service that uses a 56-bit key, an initialization vector, and the DEA primitive to transform a plaintext of arbitrary length into a ciphertext of the same length subject to some rules defined by a "mode of operation." The rules describe how to "pad" plaintexts to a multiple of 64 bits, and whether and how to induce dependencies among 64-bit blocks of the ciperhtext by feeding ciphertext material from previous rounds of the encryption process into the current round.
- Data integrity is a crypto service. DES-CBC-MAC is an implementation of the data integrity service that uses the DEA primitive to generate a message authentication code given a 56-bit key, an initialization vector, and a plaintext of arbitrary length.

3.2.2 Protocols

Cryptographic services are typically called locally; it is not anticipated that any cryptographic service protocols will be standardized.

3.2.3 Interfaces

Candidate interfaces for cryptographic services include:

- Intel CSSM (CDSA)
- X/Open GCS-API
- Microsoft CryptoAPI 1.0
- SESAME CSF API

Other interfaces that may support some or all of the cryptographic primitive function include:

- Cryptoki
- RSA BSAFE

Standardization of these interfaces would be of interest to developers of long-term key service and protocol security service modules and to providers of cryptographic service modules. The APKI Working Group feels that it is important to standardize a single interface for cryptographic services, and recommends that the following interface be chosen as the basis for the standard:

- Intel CSSM

3.2.4 Profiles

Most cryptographic modules provide support for multiple services. Many Crypto Services are subject to legal restrictions on deployment (including both intellectual property encumbrances and national and international regulatory constraints on export, import, and deployment).

Cryptographic service profiles will have to be developed for PKI environments of interest (including, for example, the Internet, OMG CORBA, OSF DCE, Financial, etc.). These profiles will have to be developed with international deployment issues in mind. Each profile should be expressed in terms of the parameters used to select cryptographic services (and implementations of cryptographic services — often called "mechanisms") through the cryptographic service interface (see the next section for more information on service and mechanism selection).

Profiles will need to specify, in addition to mechanism information, the data formats that each service can accept and return.

3.2.5 Negotiation

Negotiation of cryptographic services to be used by secure protocols and other security-aware applications is generally done at a level higher than that of the cryptographic services themselves. The cryptographic service interface therefore must allow selection among available cryptographic services, and among available implementations of a single service, but it need not support negotiation.

3.3 Long-Term Key Services Components

Exhibit 6 illustrates the Long-Term Key Services components; each component is described in more detail below.

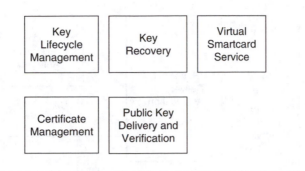

Exhibit 6 Long-Term Key Services Components

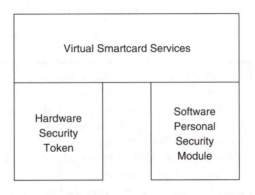

Exhibit 7 Virtual Smartcard Service Structure

3.3.1 Function

- *Key life-cycle management.* The functions this component provides include key revocation, key repudiation, key expiration, and related services.
- *Key recovery.* This component supports preparation of keys for recovery, and permits later recovery under policy control.
- *Virtual smartcard service.* This component permits users and other principals to store long-term personal security information (including private keys, certificates, and other information) in protected storage, to activate personal keys for use via an authentication procedure, and to use those keys for encryption, decryption, and signature activities. Exhibit 7 illustrates the structure of this component.
- *Certificate management.* This component allows users, administrators, and other principals to request certification of public keys and

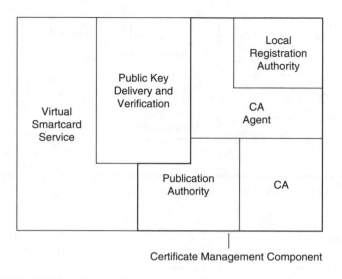

Certificate Management Component

Exhibit 8   Public-Key Delivery and Verification Structures

revocation of previously certified keys. It may optionally generate key-pairs and provide key-pair recovery services. There are four certificate management sub-components:

- The Local Registration Authority provides interfaces for requesting generation of key-pairs and corresponding certificates, requesting certification of existing public keys, and requesting revocation of existing certificates.
- The Certification Authority Agent (CA Agent) provides interfaces for certifying existing public keys, generating and returning key-pairs and corresponding certificates, and revoking existing certificates. The CA Agent implements these interfaces by using the services of a Certification Authority (CA).
- The Certification Authority (CA) certifies public keys (returning the generated certificate) and generates certificate revocation lists. In some configurations it will be "offline."
- The Publication Authority provides interfaces through which CAs and CA Agents can place certificates and CRLs into public repositories or transmit them directly to requestors.
- *Public key delivery and verification.* This component allows a program to retrieve any principal's certificate, verify its validity, and extract the principal's certified public key from the certificate. Exhibit 8 illustrates the structure and interrelationships of the certificate management and public key delivery and verification components and sub-components.

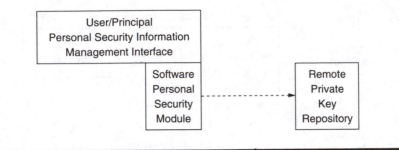

Exhibit 9   Virtual Smartcard Service Protocol

3.3.2 Protocols

Virtual Smartcard Service

When the Virtual Smartcard Service component is used for retrieval of user private keys, two models exist. One model (exemplified by PGP and Lotus Notes) manages private keys primarily on the client principal's machine (either in a software personal security module, or in a security token or other device external to the principal's workstation). In this model, no protocols are required for User/Principle Personal Security Info Management, because all operations are client-local.

The second model (exemplified by Novell NetWare) manages private keys at a central server and distributes them to client principals using a secure protocol. In this model, the client/server protocol for retrieval of private keys needs to be supported by the software personal security module subcomponent of the Virtual Smartcard Service component, as illustrated in Exhibit 9 (the dotted arrow in the exhibit represents the protocol).

The APKI Working Group does not view standardization of this protocol to be essential.

Certificate Management

Protocols must be defined to permit creation, revocation, and update of certificates. Exhibit 10 illustrates Certificate Management protocols that might be standardized; each arrow in the diagram represents a protocol.

Note: Implementations may choose to assign the responsibility for generation of private keys (through use of the key generation facilities of the PKI architecture) to the CA, the LRA, or the user workstation or smart card; additional protocols will be required to transmit the private key to the user workstation or smart card if it is not generated there in the first place.

Certificate Management

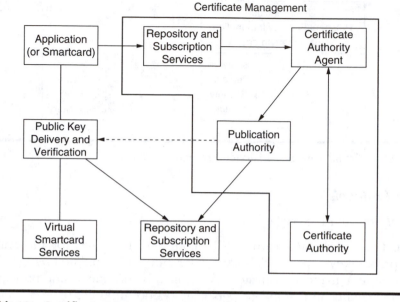

Exhibit 10   Certificate Management Protocols

The APKI Working Group feels that the following protocols should be standardized at a minimum:

- User workstation or smart card to certificate management component
- Local registration authority to CA agent

A candidate protocol specification including these protocols as well as a protocol for the Publication Authority to Public-Key Delivery protocol exists as IETF draft RFC ietf-pkix-ipki-part3-01.txt. The APKI Working Group endorses this proposal as the basis for standardization of the relevant APKI protocols.

Public Key Delivery and Verification

Protocols must be defined to transport certificates and CRLs from the repositories in which they reside to the requester's machine. In the diagram, these protocols are represented by the arrows from the Publication Authority to the Public Key Delivery and Verification component. The APKI Working Group feels that these protocols should be standardized. At least LDAP, e-mail, and HTTP versions of these protocols should be defined.

A candidate protocol specification has been published as IETF draft RFC ietf-pkix-ipki2opp-00.txt. The APKI Working Group endorses this proposal as the basis for standardization of the relevant APKI protocols.

3.3.3 Interfaces

Virtual Smartcard Service

Candidate interfaces for this component include:

- PSM (HP submission to OSF)
- SESAME CSF API

Other interfaces that may support some or all of the Virtual Smartcard Service functionality include:

- RSA PKCS-11
- PC Smartcard Consortium PC-SC specifications
- OpenCard framework
- Microsoft Wallet

The APKI Working Group feels that the Virtual Smartcard Service interface should be standardized.

Additionally, the APKI Working Group feels that the interface through which software communicates with hardware security tokens should be standardized. A candidate interface for this functionality is:

- RSA PKCS-11

Public Key Delivery and Verification

Candidate interfaces for this component include:

- SESAME PKM-API
- NSA CM-API
- Nortel CMS-API
- Intel CSSM (CDSA)

Other interfaces that may support some or all of the Public Key Delivery and Verification function include:

- Microsoft CryptoAPI version 2.0

The APKI Working Group feels that the Public Key Delivery and Verification interface should be standardized. The APKI Working Group endorses the Intel CSSM interface, with extended Certificate and Key Life-Cycle functionality currently being defined by The Open Group, as the base document for this interface standard.

Certificate Management

Candidate interfaces for this component include:

■ Nortel CMS-API
■ SESAME PKM API
■ OSF RFC 80 API
■ Intel CDSA

Other interfaces that may support some or all of the Certificate Management function include:

■ Microsoft CryptoAPI version 2.0

The APKI Working Group feels that the following interfaces should be standardized at a minimum:

■ CA agent
■ Local registration authority

The APKI Working Group endorses the Intel CSSM interface, with extended Certificate and Key Life-Cycle functionality currently being defined by The Open Group, as the base document for this interface standard.

Specification of the Publication Authority interface would also be useful to providers of repositories and communications protocols who wish to make their products available as certificate and CRL transmission media; a standard Publication Authority interface would allow them to provide Publication Authority services without requiring changes to CA Agent code.

3.3.4 Profiles

It is anticipated that multiple CAs will exist in typical PKI environments; individual servers may require the use of certificates with specific properties (signing CA, supported extensions, name format, etc.) Profiles for certificate format, contents, extensions, and policy will be needed for PKI environments of interest, including the Internet, financial industry, credit card industry (for use with SET), Government, and healthcare industry environments.

A draft profile (for the Internet PKI environment) for certificate format, contents, and extensions exists as IETF draft RFC ietf-pkix-ipki-part1-01.txt. A draft policy profile for the Internet PKI environment has been published as IETF draft RFC ietf-pkix-ipki-part4-00.txt.

3.3.5 Negotiation

It is not anticipated that any of the Long-Term Key Services components will require negotiation protocols. The Certificate Management interfaces will need to provide a mechanism through which callers can identify which CA should issue certificates and CRLs requested through its interface, in case more than one CA is available.

The Virtual Smartcard Service interface will need to support selection of user/principal certificates for environments in which users have more than one certificate.

3.4 Protocol Security Services Components

Protocol Security Services are divided into two fundamental classes:

- Session-oriented: security services that require exploiting entities to maintain security state information associated with protocol exchanges.
- Store-and-forward: security services that encapsulate all required security state information inside the protected message tokens they generate; these services do not require exploiting entities to maintain security state information. Non-repudiation services are necessarily store-and-forward services because they must allow for "protection" of the non-repudiability of a transaction after it has been completed and its state information destroyed. Non-repudiation services are depicted separately from other store-and-forward protocol security services because, unlike store-and-forward data privacy and integrity services, the use of non-repudiation services usually requires explicit user action.

Exhibit 11 illustrates the Protocol Security Services components.

3.4.1 Function

These components provide security services appropriate for use by designers of protocol stacks. Specifically, these components:

Exhibit 11   Protocol Security Services

- Provide security mechanism and quality-of-protection negotiation protocols for use by communication partners needing to agree on a common security regime
- Manage security state information (if any) needed by protocol partners wishing to set up and maintain secure associations
- Encapsulate data origin authentication, data protection, and credential and privilege transport transparently within a single service (Crypto Services, by contrast, typically provide only data protection)
- Apply security mechanisms based on administered policy information

3.4.2 Protocols

- *Session-oriented protocol security services.* A wide variety of protocol security services can be used to provide security for session-oriented protocols; examples described in existing or proposed Internet standards include the SPKM (which is public key based), Kerberos (which is secret key based), and SESAME (which has public key, secret key, and hybrid variants). Some of these services define their own protocols for runtime access to online security servers of a variety of types. All of them define formats for protected message tokens to be transported by their callers.
- *Store-and-Forward Protocol Security Services.* Only a few protocol security services suitable for protection of store-and-forward protocol messages have been defined. The IDUP and SESAME services are proposed for Internet standardization. Both of these services define formats for protected message tokens to be transported by their callers.
- *Notary and non-repudiation services.* These services must define formats for non-repudiation evidence tokens to be transmitted along with notarized data, and protocols implementing non-repudiable delivery and non-repudiable receipt.

The APKI Working Group feels that multiple protocol security services will continue to be required to meet the needs of diverse environments.

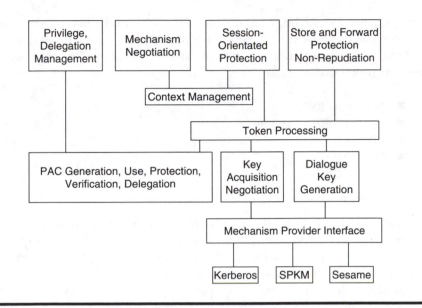

Exhibit 12   Protocol Security Service Structure

No single standard for session-oriented, store-and-forward, or non-repudiation protocol security services is proposed, therefore. The Protocol Security Services component interfaces will need to provide negotiation (for environments in which more than one service is available), and Protocol Security Service profiles will have to be established for PKI environments of interest.

3.4.3 Interfaces

The APKI Working Group feels that all of the Protocol Security Services interfaces should be standardized. The structure of the Protocol Security Services is illustrated in Exhibit 12.

- *Session-Oriented Protocol Security Services.* The preferred interface for these services is GSS-API (IETF RFC 1508).
- *Store-and-Forward Protocol Security Services* — The preferred interface for these services is IDUP-GSS- API (IETF CAT draft ietf-cat-idup-gss-07.txt).
- *Non-Repudiation Services* — The preferred interface for these services is IDUP-GSS- API (IETF CAT draft ietf-cat-idup-gss-07.txt).

In addition to these interfaces, the APKI Working Group feels that interfaces for Protection Mechanism Negotiation and Privilege and Delegation

Management should be standardized. The preferred interfaces for these services are draft-ietf-cat-gss-nego and draft-ietf-cat-xgss, respectively.

Other interfaces that may support some or all of the Protocol Security Services functionality include:

- Microsoft SSPI
- OMG CORBA Security
- TIPEM
- SHTTP

3.4.4 Profiles

GSS-API and IDUP-GSS-API are capable of supporting multiple security mechanisms; each API also allows selection of a wide range of qualities of data protection (e.g., strength of supported privacy protection, delegation mode, etc.) for each supported security mechanism.

Profiles will have to be developed to describe the set of preferred mechanisms and data protection quality parameters for PKI environments of interest. The APKI Working Group is not aware of a draft profile in this area.

3.4.5 Negotiation

Because they will be deployed in environments that require and provide multiple data protection mechanisms, the Protocol Security Services interfaces will need to support negotiation (of both protection mechanisms to be used and quality of protection to be applied).

A negotiation mechanism for GSS-API has been proposed and is described in IETF Draft draft-ietf-cat-gss-snego-04.txt.

3.5 Secure Protocol Components

There are many kinds of secure protocols. Three important categories of secure protocols are:

- *Connection-oriented peer-to-peer.* These protocols allow exactly two partners, each of which must be online, to communicate securely.
- *Connectionless peer-to-peer.* These protocols allow exactly two partners, one or both of which may be offline for some portion of the time interval during which messages are transmitted, to communicate securely.
- *Connectionless multicast.* These protocols allow one entity to communicate simultaneously and securely with several partners. Any

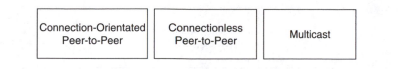

Exhibit 13   Secure Protocol Components

or all entities may be offline for some portion of the time interval during which messages are transmitted.

Exhibit 13 illustrates the Secure Protocol components.

3.5.1 Function

Secure protocols provide protected data transfer between communicating partners without requiring any calls to security services. Applications using secure protocols may have to specify a desired quality of protection before initiating a secure protocol exchange.

3.5.2 Protocols

Examples of secure protocols include:

- Connection-oriented peer-to-peer: Secure RPC, SSL, SHTTP, OMG SECIOP
- Connectionless peer-to-peer: IPSec, secure e-mail
- Connectionless multicast: secure e-mail

3.5.3 Interfaces

Each secure protocol typically has its own interface.

3.5.4 Profiles

It is not yet clear whether profiles will be established for which Web transaction security protocols (e.g., SHTTP, HTTP-over-GSSAPI, etc.) should be used in which contexts.

3.5.5 Negotiation

The APKI Working Group feels that negotiation of secure protocols is outside the scope of the public key (or even security) infrastructure effort.

Exhibit 14   System Security Enabling Components

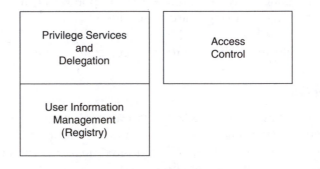

Exhibit 15   Security Policy Service Components

3.6 System Security Enabling Components

Exhibit 14 illustrates the System Security Enabling components.

3.6.1 Function

System functions (e.g., Operating System functions) are needed to support user log-on, user credential acquisition, and association of security state information with user processes and threads. For example, once a user has acquired credentials by authenticating himself to a smartcard, that user's processes should be able to use the smartcard interface to sign data using a private key stored on the smartcard. This will only be possible (and secure) if the system has maintained security state information associating the user's processes with the handle returned when the user authenticated himself to the smartcard.

It is not anticipated that the Internet public key infrastructure will define any interfaces, protocols, profiles, or negotiation mechanisms in the area of System Security Enabling services.

3.7 Security Policy Services Components

Exhibit 15 illustrates the Security Policy Service components.

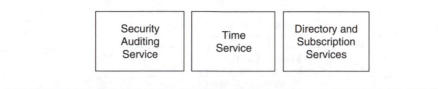

Exhibit 16 Supporting Services Components

3.7.1 Function

Security Policy services manage information about users' (and other principals') privileges and resource access control policies, and make access control decisions based on that information.

3.7.2 Protocols

Formats for privilege attribute tokens to be transported within secure protocols will need to be standardized. The most prominent existing privilege attribute format definitions today are those defined by ANSI X9, OSF DCE, SESAME, and the OMG CORBASEC standard. Privileges could be carried in X.509v3 certificate extensions, or in separate privilege attribute tokens.

3.7.3 Interfaces

It is not anticipated that the Internet public key infrastructure will define interfaces to privilege attribute services or access control services.

3.7.4 Profiles

Interoperation of systems in differing security management domains will require standardization of privilege attribute types and of the semantics of values of those types. No proposed standard profile for privilege attributes exists today.

3.8 Supporting Services Components

Exhibit 16 lists the Supporting Services components.

3.8.1 Function

These components provide functions required by the security services or required for secure operation of a networked system; however, they do not enforce security policies.

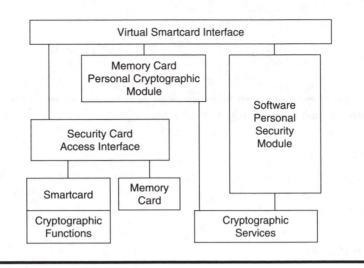

Exhibit 17   Hardware Security Devices

4: HARDWARE SECURITY DEVICES IN THE ARCHITECTURE

The architecture is intended to support at least two kinds of hardware security devices: security tokens and cryptographic modules.

Security Tokens

This class of devices includes smartcards, memory cards, time-synchronized tokens, and challenge-response tokens. These devices may provide crypto primitives and services, virtual smartcard services, and authentication functions.

Smartcards are assumed by the architecture to provide virtual smartcard services. They will also frequently provide at least the "key activation" and "signing" components of crypto services; they may also provide other crypto services.

Memory cards provide only storage; Virtual Smartcard services involving state maintenance (e.g., key activation) or cryptography will have to be provided by the memory card's software drivers. Exhibit 17 illustrates how smartcards and memory cards can be used to support the Virtual Smartcard services.

Time-synchronized and challenge-response tokens provide only authentication functionality, and will typically be integrated into the architecture through modifications to the System Security Enabling services (particularly the "log-on" and "obtain credentials" components of those services).

Cryptographic Modules

This class of devices includes chipsets, bus-connected cryptographic adaptors, and remote cryptographic servers providing crypto primitives and services, but not providing user authentication functions.

Cryptographic modules are assumed by the architecture to provide the full range of Crypto Services (and they may provide direct access to some crypto primitives for the convenience of designers of new Crypto Services).

III

IMPLEMENTING PKI

This section begins with Chapter 16, a discussion of how to implement secure Web services requirements using PKI. Next, Chapter 17 covers managed security services. Then, Chapter 18 provides readers with information that may help enterprises prepare for their pilot project or testing phase of implementing PKI. Chapter 19 discusses PKI implementation costs. Finally, Chapter 20 drills a little deeper by looking into performance expectations for a certificate authority (CA) and what a CA will expect of you with regard to a PKI.

16

IMPLEMENTING SECURE WEB SERVICES REQUIREMENTS USING PKI

Public key infrastructure (PKI) is basically dead within the client/server model but has a big role to play in Web services, and as an integral (embedded) part of applications instead of as an add-on. In fact, if you have read Chapters 1 and 2 of this book, you will see that this is being written with the preceding trends in mind.

In other words, Web services adoption is gaining speed and some Web services security specifications are growing into a new phase of maturity. While not yet standards, some specifications are leading the pack and present opportunities for connecting Web services to a trust infrastructure.

A trust infrastructure built on Web services and PKI can serve several business purposes as an integral part of applications. First of all, Web services are now being widely deployed. Enterprises are now looking for some trust mechanism to authenticate their Web services transactions as providers or consumers of a service. Although a directory scheme such as Universal Description, Discovery, and Integration (UDDI) can connect Web services providers and users, the UDDI specification has yet to finalize an authentication mechanism. So, if you use UDDI and find a new Web service to suit your enterprise needs, you will still need to make a phone call or a visit to the Web service provider to verify that the vendor offering the Web service is who they say they are. Although this extra level of personal authentication makes sense for long-term business relationships, it undermines the practicality of Web services and UDDI for smaller transactions and one-time or infrequent business relationships. To be valuable to enterprises, Web services must reflect the often subtle, complex, and,

0-8493-0822-4/04/$0.00+$1.50
© 2004 by CRC Press LLC

above all, contractual relationships of trust among enterprises. That is where a trust infrastructure, built on digital certificates and PKI, can help. And, because you would be using Web services already, a trust infrastructure built on Web services is a good fit for Web services authentication.

A Web services trust infrastructure also has broader business applications. You can streamline authentication in applications and transactions using PKI and certificates. So, providing a trust infrastructure as a Web service enables your enterprise to implement trusted transactions without investing in the development and maintenance of your own trust infrastructure. Providing this as a Web service offers the same benefits as the general promise of Web services — you can focus on your enterprise and customer expertise, and plug into a Web service without gaining that expertise yourself.

Although .NET provides a lot of native security features (.NET developers can rely on Passport for authentication (Microsoft Cryptography API [CAPI] for cryptography), and the .NET Framework XML API classes to use CAPI and Passport together — .NET does not provide the security of PKI. However, in 2001, an industry group led by Microsoft, VeriSign, and webMethods announced support for a specification, known as the XML Key Management Specification (XKMS), to deliver the PKI-based trust through the Web services framework.

XKMS combines the interoperability of XML with the security of PKI. XKMS promises to meet today's requirements for interoperability, reduced integration costs, and higher levels of trust. Using the principles of the Web services architecture, XKMS provides a way for applications to manage and exchange data about public keys. The XML Signature specification defines XML formats for describing public keys and digital certificates. XKMS uses data formats defined in XML Signature to enable applications to exchange and manage those public keys. In short, XKMS makes it easier and less expensive for applications to interface with PKIs.

MEASURE PKI'S VALUE

A PKI's value is proportional to the number of users on the network; it is very valuable if you can authenticate messages sent from anyone inside your enterprise. It becomes exponentially more valuable if you can authenticate anyone in any enterprise, such as all your partners and suppliers. Now, the Web services architecture provides an effective way to manage data in large distributed enterprises. So, would it not be nice to leverage the emerging Web services framework to make PKIs more efficient?

The PKI's ability to manage digital certificates and cryptographic keys is one of its critical features. A number of protocols have been specified for certificate management, such as Certificate Request Syntax (CRS), CMC (Certificate Management using CRS), and Online Certificate Status Protocol (OCSP). Each of these protocols presents an onerous set of requirements for those tasked with implementing them. For example, because certificates are typically shipped in Abstract Symbolic Notation (ASN.1), a binary format, certificate manipulation software is difficult to implement, extraordinarily complicated to debug, and frequently dependent on baroque, high-priced proprietary toolkits to process ASN.1 structures. Furthermore, once implemented, your homegrown PKI is unlikely to interoperate with other PKIs. Although you might be able to exchange secured messages within your enterprise, you might not be able to exchange secured electronic messages with your partners and suppliers without considerable further development. If you are considering implementing applications secured using client certificates, these are some of the challenges you will face for each client application that will depend on PKI.

Despite these apparent shortcomings, PKI provides a promising mechanism for introducing trust into the anonymous, machine-to-machine world of Web services. In the same way that Secure Sockets Layer (SSL) server certificates provide proven security to users performing transactions over the Internet, digital certificates will enable Web services to authenticate one another and to provide secure, high-value automated transactions, without requiring extensive PKI infrastructure built into a client application. The current proposal for Web services security (WS-Security) provides for digital signatures within Simple Object Access Protocol (SOAP) headers, and concretely points toward Web services transactions that are secured using digital certificates.

Nevertheless, while your .NET applications can verify the authenticity of a message locally, without some method of checking that certificate in real-time against a certificate authority (CA), you cannot be completely sure that the certificate used to create the signature is valid. The sender might have had certain privileges revoked, or the enterprise might have gone out of business (as three banks do internationally every day). Your .NET application could implement another protocol, such as the Online Certificate Status Protocol (OCSP), to do real-time validation, but OCSP requires technologies (like ASN.1 and Distinguished Encoding Rules [DER]) with which your developers are probably not completely familiar. Would it not be easier to use native tools to build Web services that use standard XML messaging to check the validity of certificates for you?

KNOW WHAT XKMS PROVIDES

The XKMS is divided into two parts: XML Key Registration Service Specification (X-KRSS) and XML Key Information Service Specification (X-KISS).

X-KRSS defines a protocol for certificate life-cycle management (registration, revocation, renewal), while X-KISS governs the retrieval of information about public keys (location and validation).

XKMS can streamline the process of certificate enrollment. If you have an enterprise messaging application that enables users to send digitally signed purchase orders, the first time a user starts the application, she or he must enroll for a digital certificate by going to the Web site of the certificate provider. With XKMS, however, the user does not have to leave the application to obtain a certificate. Rather, the XKMS-enabled application generates a key-pair, then registers the public key with a CA. The XKMS-enabled CA can be anyone from an internal PKI solution to an outsourced PKI provider such as VeriSign. If required, the CA can, in turn, generate X.509 certificate data. XKMS also specifies server-generated key-pairs. Public key revocation and renewal, also supported by XKMS, further simplify the integration of PKI functionality with enterprise administrative and account management systems. You can see how this is critical for Web services, which must be able to dynamically enroll for certificates without human intervention.

XKMS also specifies a Locate feature to provide a key directory service. Although this feature does not provide information about the validity or the status of the key, you can use it to obtain a public key for a message recipient, to encrypt a message for later delivery.

Perhaps the greatest value to Web services lies in the XKMS Validate function. Standard certificate validation methods rely on Certificate Revocation Lists (CRLs), which are typically updated only every 12 or 24 hours, creating a lag that might be unacceptable for high-value Web service transactions. XKMS enables applications to validate certificates in real-time. Rather than maintain its own certificate checking logic, a client can ask an XKMS server, "Is this certificate valid?" If, for some reason, an application needs to do more in-depth processing, the validated X.509 certificate is usually returned along with the response message. However, XKMS services are largely intended to function as a sort of litmus test. By returning an unambiguous, easily understood yes or no response to the validation query, XKMS makes it easy for developers creating diverse applications that integrate certificate-based authentication into Web services with minimal effort.

XML Signature defines a syntax for representing X.509 certificates. Depending on implementation choices made by the XKMS service provider, X.509 data may or may not be accepted or returned by the XKMS service. In general, however, enough applications use X.509 certificate that you can safely expect to get that data wherever you might need it. But one goal of XKMS is to focus applications that use PKI on the use of public keys as opposed to certificates. In an XKMS world, certificate data is managed transparently — all your application requires is the public key or the knowledge that a given public key is valid.

THE XKMS VISION: FROM SECURITY TO TRUST

The combination of .NET with XKMS benefits developers by enabling them to rapidly and efficiently incorporate formerly impractical but essential services into diverse applications. The .NET promises to lower costs of interfacing applications, while trust Web services, such as XKMS, ensure that transactions across those interfaces are secure.

Web services require a flexible, extensible trust mechanism that provides both the assurance of data integrity and identity authentication provided by asymmetric cryptography, along with the interoperability and flexibility provided by the Web services framework. Given that Microsoft is actively part of the W3's efforts, you can reasonably expect that the .NET Framework will eventually contain native support for XKMS. If so, your developers should be able to quickly take advantage of XKMS using standard mechanisms such as Web Services Description Language (WSDL).

In the future, you will probably find XKMS processing pushed down into the transport layer, away from the application layer. For example, current work within the Simple Object Access Protocol (SOAP) working group is addressing support for signatures within SOAP envelopes. Should that work come to fruition, a logical next step would be to XKMS-enable the SOAP layer, hiding XKMS from the user.

That does not mean you should have too much trouble incorporating XKMS into .NET apps. The XML Trust Center has a section devoted to developing trusted .NET applications, including how to build an XKMS service using certificate numbers.

XKMS is just the beginning. Once you have an accessible mechanism for authentication through the Web services framework, you can create rich, trusted data profiles on top of those authenticated identities. This is where security assertions enter the picture, governed by the Security Assertion Markup Language (SAML) specification. Combined with XKMS, SAML will enable your .NET-based Web services to query authoritative sources for profiles about digitally authenticated individuals and enterprises. Microsoft's role in the creation of XKMS means that IT managers and developers everywhere should take note of this maturing specification for trust in the Web services framework.

PKI WEB SERVICES

With the preceding in mind, the purpose of a PKI is to provide an environment that addresses today's business, legal, network, and security demands for trust and confidentiality in data transmission and storage. The PKI accomplishes these goals for an enterprise through embedded policy and technology components. These components determine and identify the roles, responsibilities, constraints, range of use, and Web services available.

Furthermore, PKI is a system for supporting digital signatures and document encryption for an enterprise. It is fast becoming essential for an effective secure E-commerce and to fulfill general security and authentication requirements over non-secure networks (like the Internet). The banking services are the most popular usage of this technology, which is quickly spreading over all the applications that need security to be fully operational.

As previously explained, the PKI provides for digital certificates that can identify individuals or enterprises and directory services that can store and, when necessary, revoke them. The PKI is the underlying embedded technology that provides security for the Secure Sockets Layer (SSL) and Hypertext Transfer Protocol Secure Sockets (HTTPS) protocols, which are used extensively to conduct secure E-business over the Internet.

Using PKI, messaging systems can digitally sign messages, encrypt messages, or both, thus providing the authentication, integrity, and confidentiality that enterprises need in an asynchronous world. To enable these functions, however, the enterprises must first enable basic PKI functions, such as issuing and managing key-pairs and digital certificates. That has many enterprises considering how they will support PKI, either internally or through outsourced services.

Finally, managed PKI embedded secure Web services remove much of the burden of securing and maintaining a PKI by hosting the server hardware and software in secure, monitored, and well-maintained facilities. Procedures are in place for every process the service provider performs, from adding new administrators to generating audit logs, and these processes are then audited.

17

VERISIGN'S FOUNDATION IN MANAGED SECURITY SERVICES

Allan Cary and Paul Johnson

As enterprises become increasingly dependent on the Internet, there is a growing trend among firms to open their network infrastructures to key stakeholders, including customers, employees, partners, and suppliers. By opening the enterprise environment to improve information flow and transaction capabilities, the inherent risks and vulnerabilities significantly increase as well. As a result, it is critical for enterprises to provide a secure environment that guarantees stakeholders the confidential exchange of information while ensuring data, message, and transaction integrity.

Similarly, as enterprises grant open access to their network resources, cyber-threats grow exponentially. Whether the threats originate from inside or outside the organization, enterprises are increasingly forced to deal with a variety of potentially devastating attacks and vulnerabilities such as viruses, malicious code, Web defacement, insider abuse, and theft of intellectual property. Recent statistics released by the CERT Coordination Center at Carnegie Mellon University show that the number of vulnerabilities reported in 2001 increased 124 percent compared to 2000. In addition, the number of security incidents reported increased to 52,658 in 2001, a 142 percent increase compared to 2000 (see Exhibit 1).

These dynamics are causing many organizations to engage third-party service providers to implement end-to-end services for security risk mitigation.

To that end, this white paper examines the following topics:

- Key trends in customer adoption of managed security services
- Factors to consider when transferring security functions to a third-party service provider

Number of
Incidents Reported

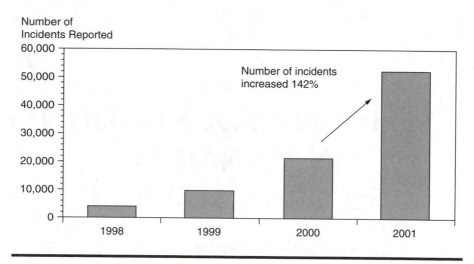

Exhibit 1   Information Security Incident Statistics (*Source:* IDC, 2002.)

- VeriSign's Managed Security Services (MSS) offerings
- Key differentiators of VeriSign's Managed Security Services

FACTORS DRIVING SECURITY SERVICES

Companies continue to invest heavily in security hardware and software solutions to minimize business risk. IDC estimates that firms spent $3.5 billion on security hardware and $6.1 billion on security software solutions in 2001. Yet, many of these solutions are implemented to address an immediate challenge (e.g., a firewall deployment to allow access for legitimate or trusted traffic while keeping illegitimate or distrusted traffic out). As various security solutions are deployed, the resulting enterprise network topology becomes a complex, multi-vendor, multi-product environment that is difficult to consistently manage and maintain with proper diligence and care.

For most enterprises, it is a daunting challenge to keep pace with both new and existing vulnerabilities, frequent technology platform software and hardware changes, and security policy changes that impact every function of E-business operations on a day-to-day basis. Significant capital investments in management technologies, facilities, and skilled personnel are required to properly and proactively secure a company's network infrastructure.

As a result, many enterprises are turning to third-party providers of managed security services. By leveraging these providers, enterprises are relying on their industry expertise and skilled resources to address the following real-world business needs and requirements:

Exhibit 2 IDC Estimate of Staffing Requirements for 24/7 Security Management and Monitoring: In-House versus MSSP

Security Staffing Assumptions	In-House	MSSP
Number of employees per shift	1	Inclusive
Number of shifts per day	3	
Average employee annual salary[a]	102,500	
Employee annual security training fees	5,000	
Monthly staffing cost[b]	26,875	Inclusive
Average monthly MSS cost		$3,000–$15,000

[a] Based on salary range average provided by Lenzner Group.
[b] Cost excludes facilities and equipment.

Source: IDC, 2002.

Return on Investment (ROI)

Enterprises want to maximize their ROI with regard to their security resources while simultaneously reducing the total cost of ownership for their security infrastructure systems. For many, this translates into rethinking their overall network and security strategies as well as their effectiveness in enabling enterprisewide business objectives.

Many enterprises struggle with the concept of measuring security ROI because of the soft metrics or "intangibles" associated with security. The biggest challenge with justifying security investments lies in the attempt to assign a dollar value to the level of security needed to adequately mitigate risk. However, with managed security services, the business case for a managed security services provider (MSSP) compared to an in-house solution is quite compelling.

IDC examines the potential cost savings associated with utilizing an external security services provider compared to managing a security solution in-house by considering the staffing requirements alone (see Exhibit 2).

The in-house monthly staffing cost of $26,875 is a relatively conservative estimate, taking into account one staff member per shift with three shifts per day providing 24/7 coverage, five days per week. More importantly, these estimates do not consider weekend shifts, additional benefits for employees, or the significant capital expenses for facilities and equipment needed to perform the security management and monitoring duties. When compared to the average monthly cost of an MSSP (typically $3,000 to $15,000 per month) delivering 24/7/365 protection, IDC believes that many enterprise customers can generate significant cost savings ranging from 40 to 70 percent in staffing alone.

Security Management and Enhancement

The challenge remains for companies to efficiently manage distributed secure internetworks. A multitude of security products are integrated over heterogeneous platforms, which require frequent upgrades, periodic testing, and reconfigurations as newly identified vulnerabilities arise. IDC estimates that security professionals may spend two or more hours each day collecting vulnerability information relevant to the network and its applications, resulting in as many as five new patches to be applied daily. Because effective vulnerability and security device management directly contributes to network performance, enhanced security services can lead to improved availability and reliability of business operations.

Consistent Security Approach

The time and expense associated with monitoring all external connections, internal activities, and vulnerabilities can overwhelm IT departments and corporate executives alike. As a result, security issues are often overlooked and never resolved. This leads enterprises to experience inconsistent security practices in an environment where consistency is a "must-have" requirement for successful business operations and, ultimately, survival in a post-9/11 economy.

Shortage of Security Professionals

Security technologies and best practices are rapidly changing to keep pace with the escalation of threats and vulnerabilities confronting the enterprise. Consequently, many in-house IT security professionals lack the core competencies or skill sets required to perform all the necessary security functions within an organization. Even more problematic, companies are challenged by the financial burden of hiring, training, and retaining skilled security professionals. According to RHI Consulting's 2002 Salary Guide, network security administrators earn between $61,250 and $84,750, depending on experience, skill sets, and region. The Lenzner Group estimates that an experienced security professional with risk assessment and intrusion detection skills can command a salary from $85,000 to $120,000. The high salaries still enjoyed by security professionals depict the true nature of the market — demand exceeds the supply.

Focus on Core Competencies

IT managers are constantly seeking ways to free operational resources for higher value-added core business activities or projects. These activities leverage the IT staff's core competencies to ensure successful execution

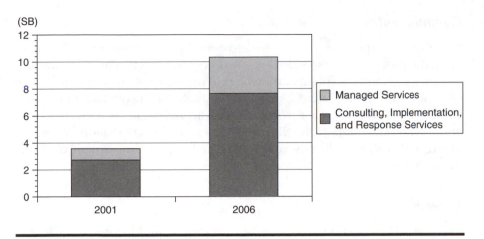

Exhibit 3   U.S. Security Services Spending (*Source:* IDC, 2002.)

of business strategies. By shifting complicated and required security activities such as security management and monitoring to an MSSP, this enables in-house IT staff to pursue a career path with more opportunities and greater responsibilities. This allows already scarce resources to provide direct, focused support for the strategic business goals of the organization.

Given the multitude and complexity of issues confronting in-house IT security operations, the business drivers for turning to third-party providers in areas that require specialized security expertise are quite clear. For example, activities including strategic security planning, penetration testing, and cyber-forensics can more easily be carried out in partnership with an information security consulting firm. IDC believes these issues are the driving forces behind the projected $7.6 billion in U.S. spending expected for security consulting, implementation, and response services by 2006 (see Exhibit 3).

Furthermore, IDC expects that demand for managed security services will result in U.S. spending of $2.6 billion in 2006, up from $860 million in 2001. By leveraging a team of dedicated security professionals managing and monitoring networks from a hardened operations center that utilizes state-of-the-art technologies, enterprises can benefit from operational efficiencies to generate significant cost savings. The ideal situation for enterprises is to receive all of their security services from one provider — a single point of contact — with whom they can build a trusted relationship.

CUSTOMER DUE DILIGENCE CHECKLIST

As an enterprise evaluates managed security service providers, there are a number of factors to consider. IDC believes the following characteristics are important to consider during the process of evaluating a credible MSSP.

Commitment

Once the enterprise has committed to security as a business-critical concern, the process begins to identify a trusted partner who can help navigate the sea of security solutions and recommend the most appropriate course of action. An MSSP should be equally dedicated to providing innovative, value-added services via a robust infrastructure, industry best practices, and highly skilled personnel. These factors reflect commitment by the MSSP, which should directly contribute to a high level of overall customer satisfaction.

Expertise

Enterprise networks typically consist of complex, multi-vendor topologies. Enterprises look to an MSSP for security expertise because they do not possess the skills or resources to adequately manage these systems in-house. Providers should possess subject matter experts with industry expertise who understand both the technology and business issues confronting the customer.

Financial Stability

One of the major concerns for customers evaluating service providers should be their overall financial stability and viability. There have been several well-publicized incidents where a provider has closed operations unexpectedly, leaving customers unprotected. The factors surrounding these business failures range from bad management and questionable accounting practices to poor strategic business planning. It is important to choose an MSSP that will be financially able to fulfill its contractual commitments.

Breadth of Services

Security is a multifaceted issue that cannot be addressed with technology alone. Enterprises must take a holistic approach by incorporating people, processes, and technology to establish a comprehensive risk mitigation program, with a heavy emphasis on people and process in the context of proactive management. A successful program must continuously assess, detect, protect, and respond against potential network vulnerabilities. In addition, with respect to detection and protection capabilities, an MSSP should exhibit the necessary and relevant industry, business strategy, technical, and educational competencies to provide end-to-end services that fully address all of a customer's evolving security needs.

Scalability

As businesses mature, their IT requirements change and grow accordingly. Companies may require additional security services to strategically plan for this growth, such as developing a technology migration path to support operational expansion. Enterprises should select a vendor with services that can easily scale to meet the new business requirements.

Service Level Agreements (SLAs)

SLAs are the benchmark by which most customers evaluate their service provider and internally justify the value received from the managed services to executive management. The vendor selection process should include two key criteria:

1. A service provider that offers consultative advice about choosing the appropriate service package
2. A service provider that commits to backing its SLAs with meaningful penalties when metrics are not met

VERISIGN'S SECURITY OFFERINGS

VeriSign is a $1 billion publicly traded company (NASDQ: VRSN) head-quartered in Mountain View, California. Since 1995, the company has invested more than $400 million in infrastructure buildout and improvements, establishing VeriSign as a global provider of digital trust and managed Internet and security services. VeriSign's digital trust services, including authentication and payment services, are provided via its global infrastructure that manages more than six billion communications and transactions per day. VeriSign's managed Internet services, including registrar, global registry, and managed domain name services provide issuance, management, and transfer capabilities of top-level dot.com, dot.net, and dot.org Web domains.

The company also has relationships with 48 affiliates worldwide that provide trust services under licensed, co-branded agreements employing VeriSign technology and business practices.

Security Consulting Services

The increasing complexity of today's global business environment, heterogeneous IT infrastructures, and cyber-threats has increased demand for comprehensive security consulting services. VeriSign's Security Consulting services incorporate a broad range of solutions — including strategic consulting, design and architecture, implementation, and customized education and training — that help organizations effectively assess, protect against, detect, and respond to security threats from inside or outside the enterprise.

By utilizing the experience and knowledge of more than 300 globally deployed security and networking consultants, these offerings enable VeriSign to mitigate customers' security risks resulting from open, Internet-connected networks.

VeriSign Managed Security Services

To successfully address customers' evolving security requirements, VeriSign continues to bolster its portfolio of security consulting services with a more robust solution set. VeriSign's Managed Security Services (MSS) have been developed as a natural extension of the company's foundation in providing managed registry, domain name (DNS), and public key infrastructure (PKI) services. In addition, VeriSign's MSS portfolio rounds out an end-to-end customer solution that augments previously established network and security infrastructures built by VeriSign for its customers. Exhibit 4 defines the services available within VeriSign's Managed Security Services offering.

In addition, VeriSign operates its Managed Security Services infrastructure 24/7/365 from a redundant system of network operations centers (NOCs) dispersed throughout the world. More than 120 technical professionals, averaging 10 years of industry experience, manage and monitor customers' network activity from these NOCs. VeriSign's technical professionals combined hold more than 364 industry (e.g., CISSP) and vendor (e.g., Check Point and Cisco) certifications.

VERISIGN'S MANAGED SECURITY SERVICES: KEY DIFFERENTIATORS

Strengths

In the highly fragmented MSSP market, each competitor provides its own set of services and capabilities, making it difficult for enterprises to scrutinize the marketing and sales rhetoric to determine the relative strengths and services that differentiate each competitor. IDC has identified the following five strengths that distinguish VeriSign in the MSSP market:

End-to-End Capabilities

With network and security assessments, architecture design capabilities, as well as management and monitoring services, VeriSign's portfolio of

Exhibit 4 VeriSign's Managed Security Services Portfolio

Service	Description
Firewall	Single or high-availability configurations; firewall policy and rule base creation; firewall logs customized and maintained to capture service-level actions and events; alert monitoring; statistics on firewall performance and security configuration
Intrusion detection	Monitored detection of distributed denial-of-service attacks, including IP spoofing and port scanning, among others; automated alerts and trouble ticket generation for critical alerts; customer notification of critical alerts
Virtual private network (VPN)	Single or high-availability site-to-site and client-to-site configurations; maintenance of IPSec-compliant tunnels; performance statistics, certificate/authentication integration; client support
Authentication	Strong, two-factor and certificate (X.509) based; key and certificate database creation and maintenance
DNS/IP	Fully redundant DNS implementation; maintenance and update of DNS zone files and IP address allocation; auditing and reporting statistics
PKI/digital certificates	PKI infrastructure creation and maintenance; managed certification process includes registration, naming, appropriate applicant issuance, revocation, suspension, repository maintenance, and audit-trail generation

Source: IDC, 2002.

security consulting and managed security services offers customers various points of entry to engage the company as a trusted advisor on any aspect of life-cycle security design, implementation, and management.

Event Correlation

The VeriSign Correlation Engine is seamlessly integrated into VeriSign's Secure Customer Management platform architecture and serves as a key enabling technology that provides event filtering and anomaly detection. The correlation engine is incorporated into each of VeriSign's managed security service offerings at no additional cost.

Proactive Management

VeriSign continues to build upon its growing repository of behavioral event models. Leveraging a customized version of Veritas' NerveCenter, tightly integrated with monitoring tools including MicroMuse Netcool and HP OpenView, these models are developed to complement the correlation engine and provide a more holistic view of threat and anomaly activity. To date, the repository contains over 80 discrete behavioral triggers that allow for automated, proactive management of customer environments. This feature allows VeriSign to detect problems before they become outages.

In addition, the distributed nature of the underlying architecture further enables VeriSign's MSS to easily scale as the customer's enterprise grows and requires increased management loads. Further illustrating the services' scalability, 1800 trouble tickets were proactively generated in 2001, which represented 96 percent of the overall total tickets generated and enabled VeriSign to meet and exceed SLA requirements (95 percent) for proactive management. During the first quarter of 2002, the number of trouble tickets managed increased by 455 percent, yet the service improved its SLA hit rate to 98 percent.

VeriSign's secure, proactive management platform architecture is outlined in Exhibit 5. The company committed $20 million to integrate the various management technologies at Step 1, which provides the foundation of the scalable, automated nature of VeriSign's MSS offerings.

Web-Based Customer Portal

VeriSign's Customer Care Web Portal provides customers with access to customizable reports to address the various needs of business constituents at all levels of the organization. The reports include detailed information such as the status of pending services delivery and service performance against SLA metrics. Customers also have the ability to request changes, ask questions, or escalate an event,as well as view current and historical management activity via the Web portal.

Service Level Agreements (SLAs)

Each managed service is backed by guaranteed SLAs with financial penalties for any missed SLA metric. Using the Customer Care Web Portal, VeriSign proactively reports against the SLAs on a monthly basis, with credits for failing to meet service levels generated automatically and proactively.

The targeted MSS metrics that are a component of every VeriSign SLA include:

- 95 percent proactive monitoring to identify a possible trouble condition
- 90 percent case assignment to a security engineer within 15 minutes of receipt of trouble

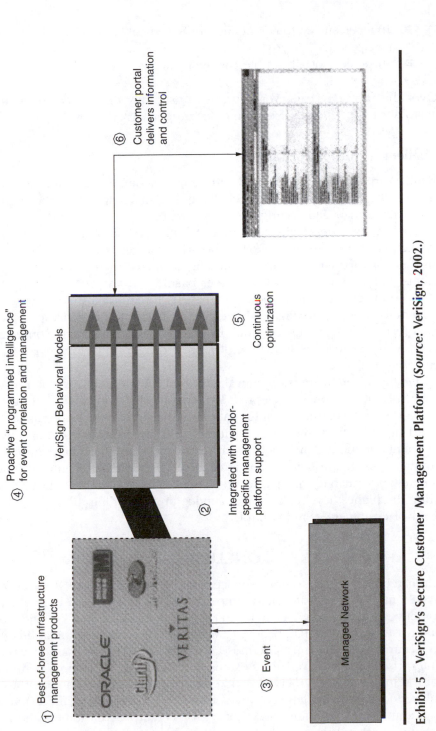

Exhibit 5   VeriSign's Secure Customer Management Platform (*Source:* VeriSign, 2002.)

- 100 percent customer notification of status within 30 minutes of receipt
- 90 percent of all trouble case tickets closed within six hours

Over the past 2½ years, VeriSign has consistently exceeded targets and customer expectations for each metric category listed above.

Challenges Moving Forward

While VeriSign boasts a rapidly growing customer base and revenue stream, the company still faces challenges as it competes in the highly competitive managed security services market.

First, it competes against a number of other established players in the marketplace. As a result, VeriSign should leverage its brand recognition and global capabilities, while continuing to focus on successful engagements within its Global 2000 customer base.

Second, the current economic climate is forcing many potential customers to consider the financial backing of its managed service provider. As a result, VeriSign must continue its pattern of demonstrating consistent year-over-year revenue growth and improved cash flows to alleviate any customer concerns.

Finally, given the mission-critical nature of security services, enterprises are reluctant to allow service providers uncontrolled, open access to their networks and confidential information. VeriSign has an opportunity to build upon its track record of having created a trusted transaction environment for more than 4,400 enterprise customers. The company must continue to demonstrate that it is capable of providing highly reliable, secure, and scalable managed security services while simultaneously delivering the highest level of customer service and providing the appropriate level of customer-desired control.

CONCLUSION

Ultimately, managed security services is a trust business. IDC believes MSSPs must demonstrate their competencies in security and their ability to deliver a high quality of service in order to win a customer's confidence and trust. In addition, IDC believes a robust, end-to-end solution approach to security risk management most effectively addresses the needs of enterprise customers. VeriSign's extension of its Security Services portfolio into Managed Security Services strategically positions the company as a full-service security solutions provider capable of addressing the expanding, immediate, and future needs of both its enterprise customers and the security marketplace overall.

18

IMPLEMENTATION AND
DEPLOYMENT

June Leung, Amir Jafri, and Andrew Farmer

Deploying a successful public key infrastructure (PKI) requires a great deal of analysis, planning, and preparation. The purpose of this chapter is to provide readers with information that may help enterprises prepare for their pilot project or testing phase of implementing PKI.

This chapter is by no means a comprehensive guide to a PKI deployment. Rather, it is intended to serve as a guide on how to adequately prepare for some of the challenges that may be encountered.

Topics such as business analysis, risk assessment, policy creation, deployment strategy, and audit considerations are discussed. This chapter assumes that the reader is already familiar with PKI theory and understands how public and private keys work. In addition, the role of a certificate authority (CA) in providing a viable trust model should be understood.

ESTABLISHING THE BUSINESS CASE: SECURITY AND BUSINESS REQUIREMENTS

PKI is a robust technology that provides a complete security solution to an enterprise. It delivers strong authentication, data confidentiality, and data integrity. It enables non-repudiation and facilitates centralized privilege management. When establishing the business case, it is important to ask:[1]

- What functionalities do the current technologies lack?
- For what applications do you intend to use PKI?
- Are all five properties (strong authentication, data confidentiality and data integrity, non-repudiation, and centralized privilege management) equally important for the applications?

- How well do you know your users? Are controls already in place to establish identity for strong authentication purposes?
- How well do your users adapt to new technology?
- Will changing existing mechanisms become a barrier to the success of your applications?
- What are the current risks associated with identity fraud in your applications? Carefully evaluate the risks associated with not using a technology like PKI to secure your enterprise.
- How onerous is the current development process for securing applications?
- Will digital signatures play an important role in the E-business strategy of your organization?
- PKI may require the storage of sensitive information about people. Will your organization be able to adhere to any applicable privacy laws?

It is important to note that technologies other than PKI can often be adequate for most security needs. The power of PKI comes from the fact that all five essential security requirements can be fulfilled with a single technology rather than with multiple solutions. In addition, a common security infrastructure is easier to administer and cheaper to maintain. The primary challenge is to determine if change is needed and how to implement that change in a cost-effective manner.

Devise a medium and long-term plan for the infrastructure. It should be clear how new and existing applications would be engineered to take advantage of the new security mechanisms and how E-business strategy of your organization will be enabled. Be careful of the "chicken-and-the-egg" syndrome. You do not want to create a solution looking for a problem. If you are unsure as to the availability of PKI applications once the infrastructure is in place, consider creating a focus group of your peers or customers to manage expectations and to get a level of commitment to the initiative. Obtaining early support of your internal IT and business units, as well as third parties, will improve your chances of success.

The selection of a suitable vendor for your PKI is extremely important. The decisions you make at the initial stages will have a significant impact on your PKI strategy. Consider the following issues when talking to vendors:[1]

- How robust are the products? Will they support the types of applications that you wish to secure? These could include Web applications, secure network connectivity, file and desktop encryption, digitally signed forms, privilege management, and registration. Look for a vendor that has strong partnerships with other software companies. This will give you flexibility and choice when implementation time comes around.

■ What is the current market share of the vendor? It obviously helps if other companies are using the vendor's products successfully. Get as many references as you can, but focus on organizations that mirror your planned implementation as close as possible.

■ The relationship with your vendor of choice will hopefully be a long-term one. Your vendor should have a proper support structure that will meet your expectations. If you will have users all over the world and your vendor does not have 24/7 coverage, then negotiate that at the beginning.

■ If your vendor prefers to use a value-add-reseller (VAR), then you must ensure that the VAR thoroughly understands your requirements.

DETERMINING TECHNICAL REQUIREMENTS

Once the pilot infrastructure has been established and a business decision has been made to implement PKI in a production environment, it is important to understand that an infrastructure that is set up for a proof of concept will almost never serve your needs in a full-blown production environment, especially if that environment is expected to pass any stringent audit requirements. Let us consider the following components that you may need in a minimal implementation:[1]

■ Certificate authority software
■ Directory
■ Registration software
■ Test applications

While Exhibit 1 shows a very simple PKI, a real-world implementation can be extremely complex when you start peeling away the layers.[1] See Exhibit 2.[1] When you consider the infrastructure in Exhibit 2, the list of components to be supported could include items such as:[1]

■ Certificate authority software
■ Master directory
■ Shadow directories
■ Registration software
■ Certificate recovery applications
■ VPN gateway
■ Firewalls
■ Application programming interface for PKI-enabling applications

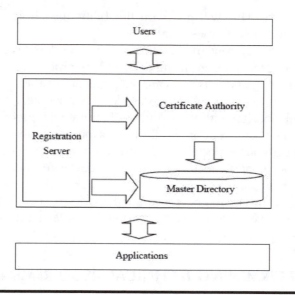

Exhibit 1   Basic PKI Components

- HSM modules for secure CA key storage
- Secure computer room

As part of your technical analysis, consider the following:[1]

- Do you have the technical skills within your organization to support a complex PKI? If not, consider outsourcing its implementation and maintenance.
- If you have internal standards for hardware, ensure that all components of your PKI will be compatible.
- Do you have an adequate business recovery plan to ensure that PKI services are unaffected in the event of system failures?

The decision of whether or not to outsource your PKI operations should be one that is made at the start. Do not conduct a pilot in-house if a third party will be providing PKI hosting and maintenance. Talk to the third-party provider about creating an appropriate test environment that will meet your needs; a pilot should attempt to mirror your production implementation as closely as possible.

DEVELOPING EFFECTIVE POLICIES, PRACTICES, AND PROCEDURES

Robust policies, practices, and procedures are integral to a successful PKI deployment. A certificate authority's purpose is to issue digital certificates

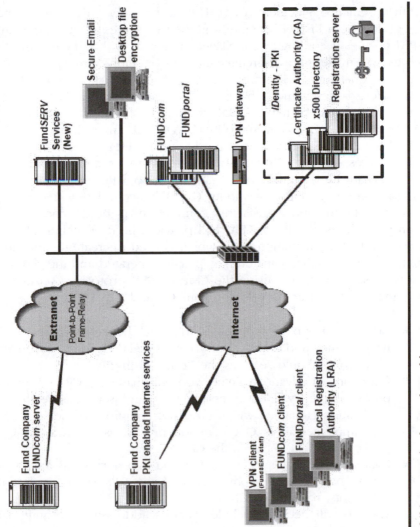

Exhibit 2   PKI in the Real World

under a trust model that allows two entities to communicate securely with each other. Appropriate controls must be established to create the required level of trust.

PKI policies refer to the business rules that will be used for the PKI implementation. These can be listed in a number of different documents, the most important of which are the Certificate Policy (CP) and the Certificate Practice Statement (CPS). The CP provides an overall business view of how your PKI will operate, and the CPS serves as an interpretation of PKI policies according to established standards within the organization such as system design and architecture and operating principles.

If you consider policies to be the "what," then practices would be the "how." Here is a statement that could be made within a CP: A request for a certificate shall be made directly to the CA by a Registration Authority (RA) or a Local Registration Authority (LRA). Such an application shall be verified with the signature key of the RA or the LRA.

The corresponding CPS could elaborate on this statement as follows: Prior to certificate issuance, a user must apply to a Registration Authority (RA) or Local Registration Authority (LRA) by completing a Certificate Registration Form. Upon satisfactory completion of the defined authentication procedures, the RA or LRA shall provide the user with a reference number and an authorization code, which is used to create the individual profile. A secure digital signature key-pair is generated and the certificate request is sent to the CA using the CMP or SEP protocol. Consider the following when you are developing your CP and CPS:[1]

- Create a group of individuals that will be responsible for the maintenance and approval of your PKI-related policy documents. This group should serve as the Policy Authority.
- Determine in advance whether you will make the CP and the CPS public. If they will be accessible by your users, ensure that the information contained within does not compromise the security of your implementation. One common practice is to make the CP a public document but keep the CPS internal.
- Establish procedures to ensure that the two documents are aligned when changes arise. Components of the CPS should reflect the statements made in the CP.
- The CP will need to include sections addressing the authorized use of the certificates and the liability for the CA in the event of abuse. Get a proper legal opinion on these sections to ensure that you are protected against damages.

Key elements of the CP and CPS would include elements such as:[1]

- CA liability, obligations, policy enforcement, publication of CA information, compliance, and data protection
- Authentication, authorization, and issuance policies for certificates
- Operational requirements
- Physical, procedural, and personnel security controls
- Technical security controls
- Policy administration

Other documents can also be created to support the CP and CPS as required. These could include:[1]

- *Sensitive password policy:* describes the controls to ensure that passwords required for sensitive PKI operations are protected.
- *Disaster recovery procedures:* formal description of procedures to recover PKI operations.
- *Emergency physical access:* policy regarding the admission of emergency support personnel into secure PKI areas.
- *Audit logging policy:* describes how PKI related logs will be reviewed.
- *Registration software policy:* policies regarding the use of certification registration software.
- *Security clearance policy:* describes the procedures required for the hiring of PKI staff.
- *System backup policy:* defines how backup media for PKI systems will be handled.
- *Visitor policy:* describes the procedures to be followed when visitors require access to secure areas.
- *PKI policy authority charter:* a formal mandate for your PKI-related policy makers.
- *Incident reporting policy:* any action that goes against defined policies may need to be formally reported to management. This policy would outline the procedures involved.

Internal Operating Procedures

When creating internal operating procedures, ensure that you balance the requirements and procedures. It is important to develop proper policies and procedures to facilitate daily operations; however, it is equally important to ensure that they are realistic to implement and adhere to.

Also, when designing access specifying the number of individuals that requires carrying out a certain act or entering a certain area (M of N rules), ensure that it is practical and meets the requirement at the same time. Keep in mind that in the event that you have to access the CA at three in the morning, all of the people involved are readily available. When creating the matrix for PKI assets, go through every operation and scenario carefully to avoid situations where one or two custodians can compromise your CA.

Furthermore, when selecting Master Users, carefully consider their job functions and responsibilities. For example, travel schedules and the inability to be physically present may negatively impact the operation of the CA.

CREATING A SUCCESSFUL DEPLOYMENT STRATEGY

Deployment strategies will vary from PKI to PKI. They are largely dependent on the level of security that needs to be attained for applications and the demographics of the community of application users. It is important for the users to understand the reasons behind selecting the PKI technology, the procedures in obtaining certificates, and the advantages in using PKI.

It is important to have an organized plan outlining the necessary steps and requirements to obtain a certificate. Training material should be simple and easy to follow. Advise users in advance if software is required to install on their desktops.

Consider the following when developing your deployment strategy: First of all, ensure that you have established an adequate education and marketing plan well in advance of rollout. People do not like sudden changes in technology. Making modifications to the security infrastructure will affect the way users conduct their daily business. Keep your message simple. Avoid unnecessary technical details about how PKI works. Focus instead on the benefits of a robust security infrastructure that protects your users and reduces time, cost, and risk. For example, talking about the benefits of single sign-on to various applications may be understood better than details about data encryption. Talk about the security requirements necessary to enable a successful E-business strategy and how PKI can meet those requirements. Increase security awareness in general. Help your users understand the need for PKI and how it will protect them.

Second of all, be prepared to encounter resistance to your PKI policies. If your infrastructure reaches out to other organizations, their security policies may be different than yours.

Third, one size may not fit all. You may encounter organizations within your user base that already have their own internal PKI implementations. They may not be eager to give up their own investment. Cross certification should be considered. In other words, create flexible policies that can be modified as required. Consider your CP and CPS to be evolving documents. The challenge will be to address the needs of your users without compromising the security standards that you set out to attain.

Fourth, do not create a trust model that cannot be realistically implemented. For example, if you require face-to-face authentication for certificate issuance, ensure that this is feasible from both a business and financial perspective.

Fifth, if your PKI includes other organizations, be prepared for scrutiny from their legal teams. If your PKI requires legal documents to be signed, your users will think twice about clauses regarding terms and conditions of use, and most importantly, liability in the event of certificate abuse.

Finally, make it easy for your users to sign up. Do not tie them up in unnecessary paperwork. Electronic agreements are a viable alternative and do not take up precious shelf space.

RESOURCE PLANNING

A key component of your infrastructure will be technical support services. Requirements will be different, depending on the type of implementation. If your PKI simply serves internal users, then existing support structures can be leveraged. However, if you have to support users in other organizations, you may require a more formal plan.

If you plan to outsource the implementation and the maintenance of the PKI, consider outsourcing the help desk as well. However, bear in mind that while the third party will most likely have the required PKI skills, it may not possess the business knowledge for application support. Another option would be to split support, addressing technical and business issues separately.

Also, if you decide to keep support in-house, you will need to consider the type of support structure you would like to create, as well as the level of support that users require. In addition, you have to evaluate the importance for the support staff to pose business versus technical knowledge. Depending on the complexity of your business area, it might be easier to train an individual who does not have in-depth technical knowledge. You might also want to develop an in-house guide to explain to the employees what this new project is all about and why the support staff locates in a locked down area. You should take the following items into consideration:[1]

- *Training requirements.* If you plan to certify your personnel, budget accordingly for the appropriate courses and examinations.
- *Skill levels.* Will your help-desk staff be expected to solve most problems by themselves, or will they escalate technical issues to the IT department or vendor support?
- *Hiring practices.* It may be difficult to hire new people who have adequate PKI-related experience. Experienced individuals may be

over-qualified for a help-desk role. You can always combat this with an aggressive training plan.

■ *Security checks.* Because PKI operations are usually considered sensitive, you may need to periodically perform background checks on your PKI staff members. Ensure that your human resources department is aligned with such policies.

AUDITING CONSIDERATIONS

Before beginning the process of deploying a production PKI, it is essential to take into consideration future auditing requirements. It is simpler and often considerably less expensive to build the system from the ground up in accordance with best practices and audit requirements rather than retrofit everything later. Consider which audits you are likely to require in the future, such as Web Trust or ISO 5900, and review the respective criteria for successfully completing these audits. Having a good understanding of audit requirements improves the ability to deliver a scalable, compliant solution. The following issues should be taken into account during the planning stages:[1]

■ Plan to conduct an audited Root Key Generation Ceremony for the initial production CA, as this is far more disruptive to do after the fact.

■ Plan to use a FIPS 140-1 Level 3 certified hardware key storage device. Migrating keys from software to hardware later will require another audited ceremony.

■ Develop CP and CPS documents that are clear and concise, while also covering all required operations aspects. Quality should take precedence over quantity, as concise documents are easier to implement, easier to enforce, and easier for auditors to review.

■ Develop supporting policy and procedure documents as the system is being built and the support systems are being implemented. This should result in a situation where, on the day the CA goes live, realistic policies and accurate procedures are already in place and staff is already familiar with them.

■ Revisit any existing corporate security-related policies and procedures and ensure that they are updated to reflect the addition of the CA infrastructure.

■ Consider having PKI administrators use FIPS 140-1 Level 2 certified hardware tokens for storage of their identities.

■ Consider redesigning physical security to be compliant with audit requirements. This generally involves building additional secured areas with electronic access control mechanisms and the installation of a wide range of additional devices, such as biometric readers and cameras.

■ Give a lot of careful thought to your M of N rules. The goal is to make it impossible for any one person to complete an end-to-end penetration of the PKI environment and systems.

■ Consider implementing a disaster recovery or business continuity strategy. This includes not only a replicated PKI environment at another site, but also the installation of additional monitoring devices at the main site, such as heat detectors and water leak detectors. If linked to a monitored security system, such devices are cheap insurance against a disruption of service.

SUMMARY

Deploying a PKI project is no different than any other business/IT project. However, the perception that PKI is a complicated technology can sometimes make deployment challenging. It is important to establish a business case that includes business needs, the scope of the initiative, and the related business, security, and technical requirements. Be sure to carry out a risk assessment of not implementing PKI as well.

A set of sound policies and procedures must be created and maintained in order to deploy a successful PKI. It is also critical to review current policies of the company and decide if additional policies and practices must be established and implemented.

Increase your users' security awareness by continued marketing and education. The success of deployment lies in gathering feedback, listening to the user community, and providing for their business needs.

REFERENCES

1. Leung, June, Jafri, Amir, and Farmer, Andrew, "PKI Deployment — Business Issues," Copyright © FundSERV Inc., 2003. All Rights Reserved. FundSERV Inc., The Exchange Tower, 130 King Street West, Suite 1730, Toronto, Ontario, Canada, M5X 1E5, 2003.

19

IMPLEMENTATION COSTS

While public key infrastructure (PKI) technology is now widely understood, it is still a very complicated IT project that costs well in excess of $800,000 to implement. Nevertheless, PKI technology has been heralded as one of the best ways to authenticate data and keep it confidential. Its major components (a registration authority that verifies a user's identity and a certificate authority that issues digital certificates and a storage repository) are now widely understood. However, understanding the components does not make PKI easy to implement. In fact, because of the technology's complexities, few enterprises have moved past pilot testing to full-scale, enterprisewide deployment.

WHAT IS INVOLVED

For one thing, setting up a PKI takes a great deal of integration. That is because the PKI requires such a complex grouping of security tools that can be difficult, time-consuming, and expensive to deploy. Enterprises must roll out digital certificates to users (including employees, partners, and even customers) and then validate those certificates.

Another hurdle is portability. Most digital certificates are used on machines. To gain portable access to PKI applications, users need smart cards, which require smart card readers. This is why PKI has been most successfully implemented on servers and firewalls and for applications such as remote access, because it can provide machine-to-machine verification.

Also, PKI tools rely on PKI applications. This means user enterprises must purchase toolkits or pay consultants to undergo a long process to "custom-integrate" the PKI to their specific applications.

0-8493-0822-4/04/$0.00+$1.50
© 2004 by CRC Press LLC

Because PKI technology is not transparent and is often difficult to work with, it is considered user "unfriendly." Users are required to answer complex or esoteric questions, sometimes requiring inane or nonsensical answers that can be frustrating when they are trying to gain access to corporate applications.

Yet another concern is that PKI requires enterprises to redevelop their directory systems. They must reengineer all the systems that maintain information on customers, suppliers, and employees. Creating that overarching enterprise directory and deciding who will manage it (human resources, security, marketing, or sales) is a huge management and political headache.

In essence, enterprises must build an online version of all their existing business relationships in the pre-Internet world. For example, banks must replace the manual process a user would normally go through to gain access to account information. Up until now, bank customers needed to physically visit a branch or use a smart card and a password on an ATM to access their account. Now, online systems handle all the steps in verifying a person's identity. Ultimately, if users do not like working with PKI and enterprises cannot develop an easily managed and maintained directory, the enterprise will not be able to move beyond the pilot-testing phase.

Finally, PKI is expensive. Even small pilot tests often cost in excess of $800,000 and can reach $5 million or higher. That does not include the cost of consulting services needed to implement PKI, which typically run as much as 50 percent of the cost of the software used.

BUILDING A CA

Despite these drawbacks, some enterprises are moving ahead with PKI implementation. For example, Barclays Capital Investment Bank of London is among those adopting the technology to develop online investment banking applications that will authenticate site users who conduct investment transactions, use a B2B application or manage their 401(k) portfolios.

In the past three years, the bank, which runs most of its applications on Windows NT servers, has developed a certificate authority (CA). Building a CA is a complex process. Consider all the steps Barclays had to take for its CA: identifying the enterprise need for developing it, selecting the best technology and supporting infrastructure, writing governing policies, installing and testing the CA and supporting infrastructure for functionality, training administrative personnel and end users, and generating public/private CA signing keys and associated CA public key certificates.

For example, Barclays is using VeriSign Inc.'s OnSite PKI tools. Recently, the bank brought in a consultant to evaluate the technical security policies of the bank's own CA, which is being used to create secure online investment-banking applications. The bank decided to build the infrastructure first so it could develop Web applications for its investors.

The bank has also completed a certification practices statement (CPS), which outlines the roles of everyone working on the project and the policies that should be followed for contingencies. For example, the CPS outlines the steps required to revoke a user's certificate should his or her private signing key be compromised.

After Barclays completes the CA review, the bank will perform remediation work, fixing any flaws in the CA. The bank must then create a database, or directory, of digital certificates, using the Lightweight Directory Access Protocol (LDAP). LDAP delineates applications that employ digital certificates and offers an easy way to help identify and search the digital certificates. Once the LDAP directory is created, consumer acceptance testing will be conducted; other pilot tests will be run before implementing Barclays' online investment-banking applications.

As previously explained, the cost of PKI is high and implementation is a big challenge. When you are talking about an enterprisewide solution involving multiple applications, LDAP servers, and certificate authorities, then the cost could be several million dollars.

This includes the personnel costs, hardware, software, training, and consulting fees. The needed PKI components are often new, still have bugs to be worked out, and often do not work with other products.

MORE PRODUCT OFFERINGS

Other enterprises are waiting to see what happens with large-scale deployments before investing in PKI. It is impossible to find any large-scale deployments that are not part of a PKI marketing scheme aimed at boosting interest in a particular PKI security supplier.

Still, security experts indicate that PKI will ultimately take hold as enterprises building B2B E-business platforms invest in stronger online security. B2B E-business is fueling PKI's adoption as a tool for building authentication, authorization, encryption, and administration into online applications.

According to industry analysts, the total market for PKI products and certificate authority services will accelerate at a compound annual growth rate of 64 percent, to $6 billion in 2007 from $514 million in 2002. Most enterprises are now using PKI in at least some smaller applications. And, most of the CIOs at enterprises with more than 1,000 employees indicate they would try to incorporate PKI in the next 12 to 24 months.

PKI Is Winning over Enterprises

Although public key digital certificate systems remain expensive and difficult to deploy, the technology is winning over enterprises. For example, Ford Motor has selected two PKI vendors — VeriSign and RSA Security — to allocate digital certificates to its 350,000 employees for signing and encrypting internal files.

Ford Motor concluded that it needed to mandate a corporate policy to encrypt everything, so that it could secure all data. Ford wanted dual partners to help ensure interoperability.

Although virtually all vendors offer standardized X.509 digital certificates, getting these products to work reliably across Netscape and Microsoft browsers, VPNs, and certificate authority and validation servers, remains dicey — this despite assurances from vendors that support for the Internet Engineering Task Force's PKIX standards solves interoperability problems.

Even as it embarks on a PKI strategy that will involve working with separate Ford divisions (and later trading partners) to promote end-to-end encryption for Web-based and proprietary enterprise applications, Ford is wondering what the total cost of the effort will be. They need to recover the costs from enterprise units, so they need to look at a cost-recovery model.

Pricing PKI

Figuring out PKI costs involves a complex equation, according to Gartner Research. An enterprise embarking on PKI must figure in much more than just each vendor's stated software prices, based on per-seat charges and amortizing them over five years or so. PKI vendors (there are about a two dozen offering full certificate authority software and toolkits) sometimes charge based on the number of applications you want to PKI-enable.

You may typically have two certificates per person, and you want encryption key recovery because people leave an enterprise and because 20 percent of users over five years forget their passwords for using their certificates. Enterprises should also have two certificate authorities (systems that issue digital certificates) in case one has problems.

Other costs include hardware, the time of enterprise lawyers involved in approving a licensing contract, and vendor software maintenance fees. In addition, enterprises may need to pay for training users and technical staff, which could include help-desk personnel and people to validate users' identities before giving them certificates.

Smart cards and readers will also be required if digital certificates are to be stored using such technology.

All in all, Gartner estimates that deploying PKI as software managed in-house typically costs $180 to $210 per user for 5,000 to 25,000 seats. However, that drops sharply for higher volumes, to an estimated $70 per user for 100,000 seats and $60 per user for 200,000 seats.

To outsource PKI as a service from VeriSign or another such enterprise costs roughly the same up to between 30,000 and 80,000 seats. Beyond that number of seats, it is less expensive to run the PKI system in-house.

If this is strategic, you may want to in-source it. However, if you trust VeriSign's people more than your own, you may want to out-source it.

Michigan Buys In

The State of Michigan's Department of the Treasury just recently finished up a 598-seat PKI deployment of RSA's Keon client and server software, which stores keys and certificates and can be used with many applications. The transition was traumatic. The Treasury department made the leap from a non-networked environment based on paper, fax, and phone, to a LAN-connected office with field auditors equipped with PCs and digital certificates for signing and encrypting all documents. The RSA Keon software constitutes "a complex product," and a sensitive one, especially with unsophisticated users.

The users, mainly auditors, are struggling to learn the new PKI methods of signing and encrypting documents. However, the Michigan government decided that digital certificates and PKI systems were worth the effort because they represented the best security technologies to safeguard sensitive financial data for transmission.

As previously stated throughout this chapter, PKI is not cheap. Michigan's Treasury Department had to add nine people to support PKI and estimates its PKI-related costs have run between $600,000 and $700,000. Michigan is now looking at having its citizens use Web-based certificates in E-commerce transactions with the government in the future.

Note: The Internal Revenue Service, which does not seem too concerned about the security implications of sending paper documents through the U.S. Mail, evinced a deep curiosity about the Treasury Department's PKI project. Michigan's Treasury Department is pushing the envelope in terms of the state government doing anything like this, with the possible exception of California.

Meanwhile, PKI testing continues and new products are emerging that ease at least some of the deployment headaches. For example, Samsung Electronics America Inc., a consumer electronics manufacturer in Ridgefield Park, New Jersey, has tested a PKI product from UniSecurity Inc. It combines PKI and biometrics.

The SecuForce Security Suite incorporates a "PKI enabler" that lets applications run secure transactions and offers user authentication through a specially designed biometric security device. UniSecurity officials indicate that customers can choose from any PKI engine as well as any biometric device, including fingerprint, iris/retina, voice, and hand.

With help from UniSecurity, the IT staff installed the product in less than a week and tested it for about ten days, using both biometric fingerprint and PKI security functions. The IT staff logged on and used both an internal e-mail system and the enterprise's SAP applications. Before the test, each user had to log on separately for access to the e-mail and SAP applications, which required a user ID and a password.

The IT staff signed on once using PKI and fingerprinting for more secure access to both e-mail and the SAP E-business applications. The test system from UniSecurity was more secure because anyone who could discover his or her user ID could access and possibly wreak havoc on Samsung's systems. The fingerprinting scanner ensured that the person accessing corporate applications was indeed the person assigned to that specific user ID or digital certificate.

Most PKI security tools still use passwords for access to digital certificates. That is a flaw biometric data eliminates by authenticating each user.

Samsung Electronics America Inc.'s IT staff considers the easier log-on and improved security to be PKI's virtues. They are now waiting for UniSecurity to integrate its software with e-mail applications from Microsoft Outlook and SAP so they can test it with a larger group of users. However, UniSecurity has offered no timeframe for Samsung's possible full-scale deployment of their product.

Conclusive Inc., another enterprise in the PKI tools market, indicates some of its customers are testing its new Open PKI software. The product promises to help enterprises testing any type of PKI software to use remote procedure calls to attach and convert code to perform PKI functions.

Finally, the software does not work with proprietary applications. But, for customers using applications developed in Java, XML, HTML, or ODBC, Conclusive's software will do the integration work to apply PKI functions to a Web application.

SUMMARY

Despite its slow acceptance, users, vendors, and analysts expect PKI implementations to increase in the next few years. Analysts indicate that more enterprises are open to outsourcing PKI than in the past, primarily because implementation is complex and it is difficult to find and keep in-house IT talent.

PKI's future depends on off-the-shelf applications coming with built-in certificates. Software tools and services that speed or ease migration will accelerate the growth and deployment of PKI security products.

Finally, acceptance is likely because there is no other obvious alternative. There is no other technology out there that will give you the ability to work with someone you do not personally know to complete secure transactions online.

20

PKI PERFORMANCE

What kind of performance should you expect from a PKI? What will a PKI expect of you? Learn the answers to these questions (and more) in this chapter.

In other words, this chapter drills a little deeper by looking into performance expectations for a certificate authority (CA) and what a CA will expect of you with regard to a PKI. The later part of the chapter looks at some commercial CA outsourcing solutions to help you focus your search for a custom PKI. Let us begin with what you should expect from a CA.

WHAT TO LOOK FOR IN A CA

Obvious expectations include an ability to operate key management under North American Aerospace Defense Command (NORAD)-like conditions, especially where root keys and certificate generation processing occurs. For most enterprises that do not normally operate the military-grade systems that are required for such work, attempting to build one is a task too daunting for most. Do yourself a favor: find a CA who specializes in security!

Another fundamental feature your CA should offer is a rich set of application programming interfaces (APIs) into the CA operation that will enable you to easily integrate your legacy systems into the PKI. You will need several interfaces from multiple systems, depending on the application mix you elect for digital certificates. The APIs should permit seamless registration authority (RA) services within a fully interactive, fully batch, or combination operating environment. Anything less only begs for problems. More on this later.

Your CA should offer digital certificates and access controls that are supportive of industry standards. Be very careful of proprietary implementations of directory services, public key cryptosystems, or secure pipes

0-8493-0822-4/04/$0.00+$1.50
© 2004 by CRC Press LLC

(aka VPNs). Rather, be sure that their products comply with protocols such as LDAP, X.500, X.509, IPSec, etc. Without assurances of standards compliance, you could well lock yourself out from communicating with customers, other enterprises, and enterprise partners.

Next, your CA should offer the highest forms of protection on key material and data that the RA needs for checking the credentials of certificate requesters. Although this is primarily under your control, the CA should provide for these activities under the tightest security.

Your CA should be able to assist you with key escrow and recovery activity. You will need these services if any of the digital certificate uses involve encrypting enterprise-owned documents or messages. To understand why this is important, it is critical to understand the distinction between message signing and data encryption. Typically, digital certificates are used for one purpose or the other — not both. Each user will possess both a signing private key and an encryption private key. It is not important to recover a signing key because the accompanying certificate is only used to verify a digital signature. If the person leaves the enterprise, there is no need to further verify his electronic signature. However, he may leave behind documents that were encrypted using the public key from his digital certificate. The only way to decrypt these documents is with the private key that accompanies the encryption public key certificate. If you are unable to recover the key from his PC's hard drive, you need a way to recover it from your CA. The common solution here is to maintain a copy of the entire key-pair (private key and public key certificate) at the time of certificate generation. The CA should be responsible for this activity. One other factor is also important. It is better to issue people key-pairs that the CA system generates if they are used for data encryption, and it is better to permit people to generate their own key-pairs when they are used for message signing. This is especially important with the concept of non-repudiation.

WHAT IS NON-REPUDIATION?

Repudiation is the principle that permits someone to disavow that a particular transaction or activity occurred — a denial that he or she has participated in some activity. Non-repudiation is the principle where repudiation is not possible — where undeniable proof exists that someone must have participated in the activity. Using digital cryptography, it operates as follows.

If a person who possesses a private key has taken adequate precautions to protect access to his key, then messages signed using that key could only have come from that person. In other words, if a digital signature is properly verified through the person's public key certificate, then only the private key could have been used to sign the message. This is especially important where digital signatures are accepted for financial transactions. Using credit cards as an example, if non-repudiation is enforced within the PKI, then the card issuer can treat any electronic transactions as though the physical piece of plastic was used to transact (credit card present versus credit card not present).

Another aspect of non-repudiation involves the process of requiring the proper mix of credentials to prove one's existence or right to request a digital certificate. If the process is such that another user could easily spoof the data requested from one user, non-repudiation will not take place. For example, in using your HR systems to verify employee data prior to issuing a certificate for secure e-mail, suppose you ask for the following information:

- Employee name
- Date of hire
- Social Security Number
- Home address

If that information is readily obtained in the offline world, another employee could simply request a certificate that permits them to masquerade as the real employee. Rather, you will want to request information that, with high likelihood, could only be known by the real employee. The following mix of attributes might be a better bet:

- Employee name
- Date of last merit increase
- Gross amount of last paycheck
- Emergency contact phone number

In the event of a full match of all these elements, you are far better assured that you are giving the certificate to the right person. In this case, you have proven (beyond a reasonable doubt) that the key holder is indeed the employee and no other non-repudiation can take root.

MORE CA REQUIREMENTS

CA systems should, as much as possible, implement the feature of Certificate Revocation Lists (CRLs) for unexpired, revoked certificates that keep them out of day-to-day operations. This function requires tight coupling with RA functions and is needed at the time certificates are shared or requested from the directory service. Many implementations do not support CRLs, but finding one that does will place you ahead of the game and adds security to the overall system. CRL update mechanisms should include an ability to alert the CA to a compromised or suspected compromise of a private key. The process should enable easy revocation and certificate replacement without undue effort. In the absence of this ability, the PKI may become next to worthless with the first private key compromise. Remember: the PKI is based on trusting the security of private keys!

Finally, you will want to make sure your CA provides sufficient training for all levels of personnel working within the PKI. This will include people who operate the RA functions, system developers, and end users. You will also want help from the CA in developing internal certificate practices statements, operating procedures, key escrow and recovery procedures, and any other documentation to support the PKI project's development life cycle.

WHAT WILL A CA EXPECT OF YOU?

Any PKI worth its salt must be rooted in appropriate and judicious uses of digital certificates. You will define what this means to you in how you will use digital certificates within (and outside) your enterprise. To that end, you must specify (in exacting detail) for what purposes digital certificates will be used (secure e-mail, access control, document signing, etc.); who is authorized to request digital certificates; what information they must present to prove their identity or their rights; how long certificates will be valid; and a host of other variables.

Because you are the one who operates the systems that contain the data that will be used to check credentials, you will need resources that can hook in to CA systems to communicate approvals and decline decisions. This activity alone is anything but trivial!

In principle, you want certificate request and fulfillment processing to occur within a single session. Doing so precludes the presence of automated processing that can obtain credentials from requesters, check them against legacy systems, and forward the results to the CA along with the data that you want contained in the certificate. If you choose to perform this work offline or in batch mode, certificate requests must operate under the following process:

1. Requester enters his request on the CA-supplied interface and terminates his secure session.
2. Credentials are forwarded to the RA for batch or offline verification.
3. RA verification results are returned to the CA system.
4. CA initiates post-processing.
5. Requester of approved request receives an e-mail message from the CA instructing them what to do.

6. Requester reestablishes a secure session with the CA.
7. Requester again proves his identity to satisfy the CA.
8. Requester downloads and stores his new certificate.

In the absence of online RA functionality, no other scenario is possible. This illustrates why the APIs into the CA systems are critical to PKI success. On small volumes, perhaps a manual RA function will work fine, but it will not scale up as certificate popularity increases. Furthermore, there is no short-cutting the process — doing so requires relinquishing some control over your internal corporate data. Extra careful thought is required here.

CAs will also expect from you a high degree of technical readiness for certificate uses. This often requires robust directory services such as LDAP and interfaces to systems that support digital certificates as an alternative to user IDs and passwords. If you intend to use smart cards, you will further need capable devices on all PCs that support system access. Remember (what you are truly building here is an infrastructure from the ground up): do not try to find shortcuts!

From certificates to encryption keys, PKI can boggle the mind. Now, let us get a handle on it in the next part of the chapter.

PKI INFRASTRUCTURE

The way to judge a successful infrastructure project is by its transparency. For example, when was the last time you thought about your city's sewage system? Unless you have suffered the plumbing equivalent of a buffer overflow, you probably do not think about it at all. And why should you? As long as the good water comes in and the bad water goes out, you can remain blissfully ignorant of the underlying structure.

Like a successful public works project, a good public key infrastructure (PKI) should also be invisible to its end users, whether they are enterprise employees, enterprise partners, or customers. Similarly, PKI and the digital certificates that are its stock in trade can be complex and complicated — the potential for messy mishaps is high.

However, such projects are undertaken because the infrastructure meets a compelling need. So, what drives PKI? The answer is E-business.

From authenticating employees, partners, and customers to securing high-value transactions conducted over the wires, PKI and digital certificates are emerging as a scalable, secure solution for enterprises that want to cut costs and integrate with partners via the Internet. The more business that gets conducted online, the more and more uses and value you will see for having a positive identification system like a digital certificate.

This part of the chapter discusses the major performance complexities of PKI and launching and managing digital certificates. Taking a good look at PKI's plumbing gives you a better chance of keeping it invisible to the people you are building it for.

More Than Just Encryption

Encryption is a prominent application of a public key system, but it has other significant uses in addition to making data illegible to outsiders. The huge benefits of PKI come from authentication, integrity, and non-repudiation, as well as identification and confidentiality. Encryption is important, but it is almost a by-product.

Identification establishes who a person is. It is especially important for electronic transactions where little to no human interaction takes place.

Authentication goes a step further by verifying that a person (or device) is who he or she (or it) claims to be. If someone identifying himself as Customer Bert transfers $8,000 to another account, you want mechanisms in place to ensure that it is really Bert, and not his evil twin Jack.

Next comes authorization, which delineates a person's privileges within a system. For example, Customer Bert may be restricted in the amount of money he can move in a single day.

Non-repudiation means that Customer Bert cannot later deny that a transaction took place. Digital signatures and timestamps in a public key transaction identify the parties involved and indicate when the transaction occurred.

Confidentiality (via encryption) prevents unauthorized parties from viewing the transaction. Integrity (also via digital signatures) ensures that a transaction was not tampered with. These mechanisms prevent mishaps such as evil twin Jack changing Bert's $8,000 transfer into an $80 transfer.

Keys, Certificates, and Signatures

The public key architecture accomplishes the preceding functions with a variety of tools, including public and private key-pairs, digital certificates, and digital signatures. The PKI's foundation is the public/private key-pair. Also known as asymmetric keys, the public/private pair is generated by independent but mathematically related algorithms. This relationship gives the key-pair its unique property: If you use the public key to encrypt data, only the private key can decrypt it, and vice versa. This is different from a symmetric key, which both encrypts and decrypts information.

For example, if you want to send a private e-mail to a confidant, you encrypt the e-mail with that person's public key, which is typically stored in a directory and made freely available to anyone who wants it. Only the person with the private key (presumably your confidant) can decrypt the message. Even if a third party intercepts the message, that third party could not unravel it using your confidant's public key.

By the same token, if you wanted to assure your confidant that a message came from you, you would encrypt it with your private key. Your confidant would decrypt the message using your public key. If the public key successfully decrypted the message, your confidant could be reasonably assured that it came from you.

One problem with this key-pair system is verifying the identity of the owner of the public key. This is where digital certificates enter the picture. Like a passport or driver's license, a digital certificate declares that the public key holder is who he or she claims to be.

Also like a driver's license or passport, a trusted authority, known as the certificate authority (CA), issues a digital certificate. In a simple PKI architecture, that CA may be the systems administrator who issues certificates to end users. In a more complex environment, a CA could be a large enterprise, a government agency, or a third-party consortium that acts as a trust agent for a specific industry.

Based on the X.509 standard, digital certificates contain a host of information, including the certificate's serial number, the CA that issued the certificate, its expiration date (also known as a validity period), the name of the certificate holder, and the certificate holder's public key.

Trusting a CA assumes that the authority has taken significant measures to verify the certificate holder's identity. For example, a liquor store uses your driver's license for proof of legal drinking age, because it trusts that the Department of Motor Vehicles has taken sufficient steps to verify your birth date.

Of course, anyone who has used an older sibling's license to buy beer knows that this system can be spoofed. Thus, PKI also relies on mechanisms to make sure that digital certificates are not forged, stolen, or out-of-date.

One mechanism is the digital signature, which verifies that a document has not been tampered with. If you have a document that you want to digitally sign, you (or, more precisely, your computer) run a hashing algorithm on the document. This hashing algorithm condenses the document into a very small file, known as a message digest. It is impossible to extrapolate the document's content from the message digest. This message digest is unique to the document; that is, if the document changes by even one keystroke and then gets run through the same hashing algorithm again, it would yield a different message digest.

The sender encrypts the message digest with his or her private key and includes it with the document, creating a digital signature. The recipient decrypts the message digest with the sender's public key, and then runs the same hashing algorithm on the document. If this new message digest is identical to the first, the receiver can be assured that the document was not changed after the sender signed it.

Both digital certificates and digital signatures are essential to gain a PKI's full benefits. Thus, certificates and signatures, and the encryption keys that underlie them, must be carefully managed. A digital certificate contains the sender's public key and also the trusted authority's digital signature. The recipient can check the authority's digital signature by decrypting the hash of the signature with the authority's public key.

Pieces of the Puzzle

As mentioned, the CA is the source of trust for a public key system. The CA issues, manages, and revokes certificates. Once the certificate is created, the CA signs it with its own private key, binding the certificate to the CA's web of trust. If for some reason a CA becomes untrusted (for example, if its private key was compromised), certificates issued by the CA after the compromise would also be untrustworthy.

The CA architecture is made up of several components, including the registration authority (RA) and the certificate repository. The RA, as its name implies, registers subscribers for a digital certificate; it gathers and verifies all information that goes into a digital certificate. RA data can be entered by a keyboard operator, by an end user via a browser, or by loading an HR or other database. The certificate policy determines what information goes into the certificate and how it gets there.

The repository houses current certificates and revocation lists. It is a publicly accessible database that distributes certificate and revocation information on request. The repository publishes its data in a directory, based on either the Lightweight Directory Access Protocol (LDAP) or an X.500 directory. All of these components may reside on the same machine, although some implementations place the CA and RA on separate devices.

The preceding components focus on issuing and maintaining certificates. The third function of the CA, and perhaps the most critical, is revocation. You may wonder at this, considering all the trouble you have gone through to hand out certificates in the first place, and because certificates have an expiration date already built in.

However, there are good reasons for revoking certificates. If an employee quits or gets fired, you will want to revoke the accompanying certificates to sever his or her authentication and authorization ties to your enterprise. Also, if a certificate holder's private key is stolen or lost, that certificate can no longer be trusted.

Thus, it is the CA's job to continually maintain and update a list of invalid certificates. The usual approach is a certificate revocation list (CRL), the electronic equivalent of a list of bad credit cards that merchants once kept near the cash register. Every time a certificate is revoked, it is added to the list. Entities can then consult the list to check a certificate's status. The CA should digitally sign the CRL so that its authenticity can be verified.

Sounds simple enough, right? Yes, but a CRL does have potential trouble spots. The first issue is the CRL's size. Depending on the number of certificates that a CA manages, CRLs can grow rather large. Transferring such a hefty file may strain network bandwidth or client processing power.

The second and more pressing issue is the timeliness of the updates. Say you update your CRL twice a day, at 11:00 a.m. and 5:00 p.m. What happens if an employee quits at lunchtime? As far as the PKI is concerned, that person has all of his or her rights associated with the certificate for another five hours — plenty of time for a disgruntled employee to wreak a little havoc.

For these reasons, there are methods to streamline the revocation process. One is the delta CRL. Periodically, a full CRL, called the base CRL, is published with a complete list of revoked certificates. In between the publication of the base CRL, a smaller list — the delta CRL — is published. This list consists of updates to the main list. Delta CRL lists are marked accordingly, so that an entity searching for a certificate's status does not mistake the shortened list for a complete CRL.

Another option is the Online Certificate Status Protocol (OCSP), which lets entities check the status of a certificate in real-time, without waiting for a CA to issue an updated CRL. OCSP has emerged as the primary technology for real-time certification checking.

When a client requests a status check from an OCSP server, there are three possible responses: good, revoked, and unknown. "Good" indicates that the certificate is not revoked, but this does not guarantee the certificate's validity — it just means that the certificate is not on a revocation list. Extensions are available that can provide additional information on a "good" response. A "revoked" response indicates that the certificate is revoked. An "unknown" response means that the server does not know about the certificate's status or existence.

Keys to the Kingdom

The structure of a public key architecture crumbles if private keys are not kept private. If a private key falls into the hands of someone other than the original key holder, it invalidates the private key's unique identification properties. For example, if Mike stole Josephine's private key, he could digitally sign documents or transactions that would appear to have come from Josephine. He could also decrypt data encrypted with Josephine's public key.

Fully protecting that private key is a critical component within PKI. Key protection is tied to the key storage method that you choose; that is, will you store end-user keys on a smart card or on the desktop? There are four general key storage methods. First is storing the private key on a smart card, which is generally regarded as the most secure because the cards are highly tamper-resistant. If you store keys on the desktop, two-factor authentication with a hardware token and a user PIN is the most secure method. Next is passphrase-based protection, which encrypts the private key on the desktop. Finally, and least secure, is storing the key in the browser in plaintext.

Although smart cards are the most secure solution, there are drawbacks. For one, desktop computers must be fitted with card readers to make the cards usable, which can be costly and time-consuming. In addition, the dirty little secret is finding LAN personnel with the appropriate skill sets for supporting smart cards. Also, if an end user loses or damages a smart card, a new card and new keys must be issued, which creates an administrative overhead.

Of course, desktop key storage also has drawbacks. Poor password choices make a key vulnerable to theft. Also, if someone broke into a desktop and took a private key out of memory, they would then be able to copy it and use it in many places.

So, which is the best solution? It really depends on what level of risk and security you are looking for, and what is best for the environment. A lot of European enterprises indicate that keys have to be stored in a hardware device, so they are looking at smart cards. Within the United States, more enterprises are comfortable with storing them in an encrypted format on the desktop.

Be aware that users may end up with more than one key-pair. Key functions are usually divided into encryption and digital signature. That is, a user may have one set of keys for encryption and another set for digital signatures. Why? If you have a backup copy of a private key used for digital signatures, it reduces the non-repudiation quality of that key because it is no longer unique to the end user. You should never have a copy of the private key for digital signatures.

Conversely, if a backup copy of a key that is used in encryption and decryption is not available, administrators may not be able to unlock files in an emergency. Say, for example, that a user loses his or her smart card, which stores his or her private key. Any files encrypted with the corresponding public key would be undecipherable. Thus, encryption keys are more likely to be archived.

Another issue with keys is the ability to share them among several applications. For example, if your end users have more than one e-mail program, it can become an administrative burden to support multiple key-pairs for each program. Thus, two interfaces — Public Key Cryptography Standard (PKCS) #11 and Microsoft's Cryptographic API (CAPI) — make keys and certificates portable among applications.

As you might guess, these are competing interfaces. PKCS #11 targets UNIX-based programs, while Microsoft developed CAPI for its own platform. PKCS #11 is an open standard. It has been around long enough that everybody writes to it.

As for Microsoft's CAPI, most of the top digital certificate vendors now work within it. The fact that it allows you to make use of digital certificates within a Windows environment (which is the common desktop now) is a huge enabler. It has come a very long way in terms of being open and useful.

So, which should you support? If you have an all-Windows environment, you would focus on Crypto-API. If you have a number of different types of computers, and if you work with a number of different enterprises, then it is PKCS #11. However, it is not really difficult to do both.

Physical Security

With all of PKI's focus on digital signatures, encryption keys, and cryptographic algorithms, it is easy to overlook securing the real-world software and hardware that makes up your infrastructure. That may be a costly oversight, especially if you are using PKI to validate and encrypt high-value monetary transactions.

The security you put in place must be commensurate with the value of the systems you are protecting. If you use PKI for single sign-on and e-mail encryption, you probably do not need motion detectors and Mission Impossible-grade booby traps in the server room. However, if your PKI is at the heart of online stock trades or international banking, something more than a locked door is recommended.

When securing your PKI systems, particularly your CA and key-generation devices, start with the administrators who maintain and manage them. Running background checks on your security personnel is a good first step. You may also want to configure your systems to require that two or more administrators be present when executing sensitive operations, such as recovering keys from the archive. Check logs and schedule audits regularly to ensure that the system is operating in accordance with predefined policies.

Finally, as for the location itself, security options include some form of electronic monitoring, such as a physical intrusion alarm with 24-hour response, video cameras at entry points, and terminals. Standard door locks can be augmented with card readers or biometrics to ensure authorized access. Last but not least, it is a good idea to have off-site backup in case of physical damage such as a fire or earthquake.

SUMMARY

Successful PKIs, by definition, require secure environments throughout. If you are unprepared to provide such an environment, it may not be worth your efforts to try. Make certain you have obtained the required support (all the way up the ladder) to assure PKI success. And be prepared to spend significant time and effort doing it. A good night's sleep is never cheap!

With these expectations in mind, you can now intelligently evaluate what is offered in today's PKI marketplace to determine suitability for your enterprise. Stay tuned.

IV

MANAGING PKI

Authorized users who know their digital certificate password and wish to revoke an existing digital certificate may do so by following the procedure described in this section. Authorized users who have lost or forgotten their digital certificate password will need to visit a local registration authority (RA) in person with their ID card in order to have their digital certificate revoked. Therefore, any digital certificate holder who experiences difficulties revoking a digital certificate they believe to have been compromised should contact the certificate authority manager immediately.

Policies and procedures must be followed when revoking a certificate. To create the trust required for digital signatures, CAs must carefully follow very specific operational rules. These procedures are usually documented in their Certification Practice Statement (CPS), a document that should be available for public review. Pay special attention to the CA's policies on security, key management (issuing, authenticating, revoking, and publishing digital certificates), confidentiality, fees, liability, and independent auditing practices. Ask the CA about recent outside audits, and request the auditors' reports.

Finally, with regard to management services: before selecting a CA, make sure that you understand the company's policies for issuing, revoking, reissuing, disabling, reactivating, and archiving digital certificate information. Make sure that the CA uses a management system that will maintain its integrity over time, one that will be able to handle changes in employees or business status (such as mergers and acquisitions).

With the preceding in mind, this section begins with Chapter 21, which is the first of five chapters that walk you through the steps of certificate management by looking first at requesting a certificate. Next, Chapter 22 discusses obtaining a certificate. Then, Chapter 23 covers the ten risks of PKI. Chapter 24 covers some of the more common things you might want to do with your personal digital certificate and, specifically, how to use it. Next, Chapter 25 discusses how to revoke a certificate. Finally, Chapter 26 contains the summary, conclusions, and recommendations for the book.

21

REQUESTING A CERTIFICATE

Previous chapters in this book have looked at public key infrastructures (PKI) from a high level, identifying its components and its value to secure private and personal communications. PKIs explicitly define how digital certificates will be used by the enterprise, how much trust users can place in them, and how to manage certificate existence (issuance, use, renewal, and revocation).

Rather than continue to delve into the nuances and esoteric details of how commercial certificate authorities (CAs) help to implement PKIs (as earlier chapters of this book have covered that topic to death), it is more instructive now to take a step back and look at digital certificates themselves in some detail. Although they are invisible and transparent when used in appropriate applications, there is still a fair amount of user interaction to manage them properly.

With the preceding in mind, this chapter is the first of five chapters that walk you through the steps of certificate management by looking first at requesting a certificate. Chapter 22 looks at "Obtaining a Certificate;" Chapter 23, "Ten Risks of PKI: What You Are Not Being Told about Public Key Infrastructure;" Chapter 24, "Using a Certificate;" and Chapter 25, "Certificate Revocation with VeriSign Managed PKI."

Once you have a taste for the types of activities necessary within a PKI, you will better appreciate what different certificate authorities (CAs) might offer and how to select the best one for your enterprise. There is little that is obvious about digital certificates. For the most part, they are invisible when their implementation is successful. That success relies on an impervious process to deliver certificates, because they involve users who must manage the key-pairs for which they are responsible. This chapter aims to remove much of the mystery surrounding the request for a digital certificate, as well as obtaining, storing, using, and removing digital certificates via browsers, which will be covered in the chapters previously mentioned.

0-8493-0822-4/04/$0.00+$1.50
© 2004 by CRC Press LLC

REQUESTING A DIGITAL CERTIFICATE

Within the PKI, the definition of the CA is well-defined, operating in conjunction with a registration authority (RA). The RA role or function makes the actual decisions of who can receive certificates and who cannot. The RA "owns" the records that dictate the proof of identity and the rights of certificate users. Usually, the RA function is performed in one of two basic ways.

Requests for certificates typically come in via Web forms operating at the CA site. The CA then forwards to the RA the information that is presented on the form. RAs then check their databases to see if the requesters have properly identified themselves, and if they have, their request is approved and returned to the CA who will generate and return the completed certificate to the requester. Normally, the CA will not operate the systems that identify requesters, so they must rely on the RA to do that for them. These RA systems may be completely manual, completely automated, or somewhere in between. In the case where manual intervention is required, the issuance process has lag time built in, requiring a wait between request and actual issuance. In those cases, an e-mail is sent when the certificate is complete, notifying the requester that his certificate is ready for pick-up. Requesters then log back on to the CA Web site, download their certificate, and install it. If the systems are automated, the entire process may be completed in a single session.

In the brief examples that follow, requests for authenticating information are minimal (just to demonstrate the technique), but in the real world, authenticating information is very specific for an application. For example, a request for a credit card digital certificate may require name, account number, any special numbers that appear on the card itself, and may even ask for your mother's maiden name or other information — presumably only what the actual requester possesses.

Now let us look at how an enterprise interacts with a customer's PKI. Rather than require a user to remember yet another password to access an enterprise's applications, an enterprise's components can use PKI to transparently authenticate the user to the enterprise itself. The outline of how this is accomplished varies, depending on whether a user is accessing the enterprise via a Web services-based client or a Telnet-based client.

REQUESTING DIGITAL CERTIFICATE AUTHENTICATION THROUGH PKI

Customers are beginning to deploy public key infrastructure (PKI) technologies within their enterprises to support a variety of Web-based services. Among those Web-based services are:

- Employees securely access corporate intranets from remote locations through PKI-enabled virtual private network (VPN) connections across the unsecured Internet.
- Business-to-business transactions are verified using PKI-enabled digital signatures.
- The disks on laptop computers are encrypted by PKI-enabled utilities to protect corporate information should the computer be lost or stolen.
- Users authenticate themselves when logging in or executing enterprise-critical operations by providing PKI-enabled credentials.
- PKI-enabled e-mail systems provide the opportunity to securely communicate via e-mail or other mediums with which no prior relationship exists.

After presenting a brief overview of PKI technology in general, this part of the chapter describes how Web-based services will extend the return on investments customers have made in PKI.

As previously explained, a PKI provides the supporting services to enable the efficient use of public key cryptographic technologies. In a public key cryptosystem, a user possesses a pair of related cryptographic keys, a *public key* and a *private key*. The private key is kept confidential to the user, and the public key can be shared with anyone. Encrypting data with a recipient's public key ensures that only the recipient, by virtue of possession of the corresponding private key, will be able to decrypt the data — this is the cryptography behind encrypted e-mail. On the other hand, encrypting data with one's private key means that anybody in possession of the corresponding public key can reliably use that public key to verify the origin of the data — this is the cryptography behind *digital signatures*.

The most-often used components of a PKI are related to retrieving public keys in a reliable manner. Public keys are encapsulated in public key *certificates*. In addition to the public key itself, these certificates contain demographic information about the owner of the public key (name, expiration date, etc.); housekeeping information about the certificate itself (serial number, issuer, etc.); and a digital signature applied by the certificate's issuer. The issuer's signature on the certificate is needed to provide some proof of the binding between an identity (owner) and a public key.

The specific details of how a PKI is constructed vary, depending upon the vendor of the PKI system. Any full-featured PKI will provide the means to retrieve a certificate for a particular user, to check that the certificate is valid (signed by an appropriate issuer, has not expired, has not been tampered with, etc.), and facilities to revoke (invalidate) a certificate as needed.

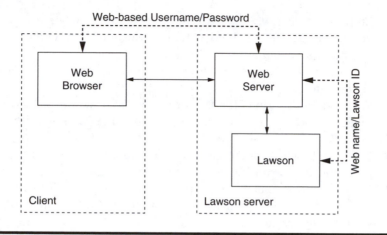

Exhibit 1 How Web-Based Clients Handle Authentication Today

PKI and Web-Based Services

If a PKI has been deployed across a customer's entire enterprise, then any participant in the PKI (anybody who has been issued a certificate) can authenticate their identity to any other entity that can avail itself of the Web-based services. Proving who you are is as (conceptually) simple as digitally signing something. This is a particularly attractive aspect of requesting a digital certificate because it can form the basis of single sign-on's capability across all of an enterprise's computer systems. Systems and applications that know how to talk to the PKI can transparently interrogate a user's desktop system and strongly authenticate the user's identity, provided that the user has been properly authenticated to the PKI.

This is how most enterprises interact with a customer's PKI. Rather than require a user to remember yet another password to access an enterprise's applications, an enterprise's components can use PKI to transparently authenticate the user to an enterprise. The outline of how this is accomplished varies depending upon whether a user is accessing an enterprise via a Web-services based client or a Telnet-based client. Details of both methods follow.

Web Services-Based Client Access

Exhibit 1 shows how Web-based client services handle authentication today. A user provides a user name and password. The Web server, represented by the heavy dashed line between the Web browser and the Web server, authenticates the user name and password.

Additionally, the Web server "translates" the user name it knows to an "Enterprise ID." The Enterprise ID is understood by the enterprise

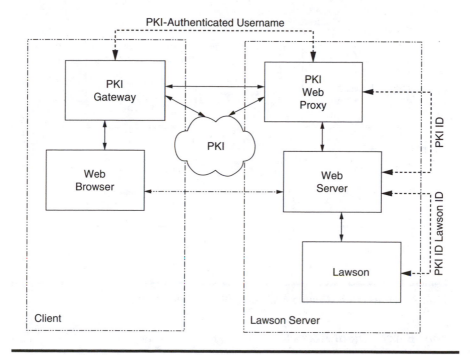

Exhibit 2 How the Introduction of PKI Components Changes How Users Are Authenticated in the Enterprise Environment

environment and business logic, as illustrated by the heavy dashed line between the Web server and enterprise.

Exhibit 2 shows how the introduction of PKI components changes how users are authenticated in the enterprise environment. A user still accesses enterprise applications via a Web browser, as in the non-PKI case. PKI authentication interposes a proxy in front of the Web server, and that proxy coordinates with a PKI component (the "PKI Gateway" in Exhibit 2). This is installed on the client system to perform the PKI authentication, represented by the heavy dashed line between the PKI Gateway and the PKI Web Proxy.

Note: These new PKI components are deployed as part of the customer's PKI rollout, and are not provided by the enterprise.

The heavy dashed line in Exhibit 2 between the PKI Gateway and PKI Web Proxy represents the PKI identity established by the PKI authentication. The PKI Web Proxy provides that identity to the (unmodified) Web Server, and that identity is translated into an Enterprise ID, analogous to the current non-PKI processing.

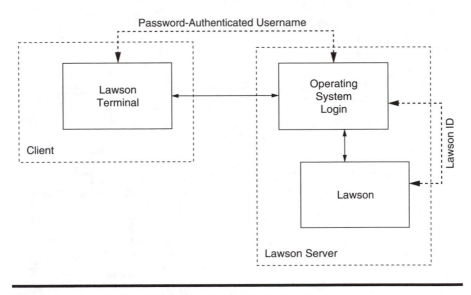

Exhibit 3 How Telnet Clients Are Currently Authenticated

Telnet-Based Client Access

When using a Telnet client, users authenticate themselves to the operating system on which enterprise is deployed. Traditionally, this authentication has been accomplished through the use of static passwords. Adding PKI to an enterprise seems to imply that it would replace the password-based authentication to the operating system with a PKI-based authentication scheme. Unfortunately, not all host operating systems are capable of performing PKI-based authentication; and even if they were, the communications path between the Telnet client and the server system would need to be extensively reworked to accommodate the PKI-based authentication.

Rather than expect (or wait for) server operating systems to perform a PKI-based authentication, a PKI-enabled enterprise Telnet client is required. Because no further development will be done to the Enterprise ID Telnet client, PKI authentication will be built into Enterprise Terminal. Enterprise Terminal is a Java applet that runs in a Web browser and serves as a Telnet client. Enterprise Terminal will then transparently handle authenticating a user via PKI means.

Exhibit 3 shows how Telnet clients are currently authenticated. A user establishes a Telnet connection with the machine that hosts the enterprise. The host machine's operating system prompts for a login name and a password. If the user provides a valid user name/password pair, the user is given a login shell. Once a user has a login shell, he can run enterprise applications and utilities under that login ID.

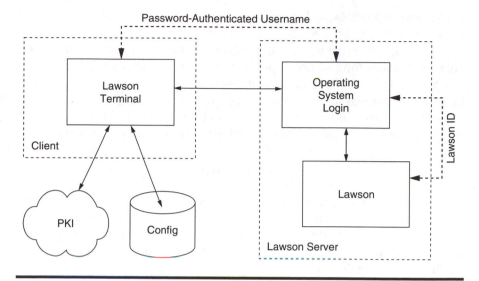

Exhibit 4   How Adding PKI Authentication Does Not Change the Picture for a Telnet Client

Exhibit 4 shows how adding PKI authentication does not change the picture for a Telnet client much. The Enterprise Terminal will handle the PKI authorization duties. Provided a user can be successfully authenticated to the PKI, the Enterprise Terminal then retrieves user information from a central configuration store. The configuration store contains the user's login name and password, encrypted under the user's public key. The Enterprise Terminal client then employs the user's cryptographic credentials to decrypt the configuration information and pass the user name and password to the operating system's prompts on the user's behalf. This approach avoids changes to the operating system login process and modifications in how users interact with the enterprise.

Configuration Store

In either of the PKI solutions described in the preceding, each user is known by at least two names: the name by which enterprise knows them ("moons") and the X.500 name (can=Dorthy Haskins, our=Women's Track and Field, o=Olympic Team 2000, c=US) found in their public key certificate. Maintaining the links between these different names will necessarily add some administrative overhead.

Finally, in the case of Web-based clients, this configuration store need only provide the ability to retrieve the enterprise user name given the X.500 name. For Telnet clients, the configuration store will hold the user's password in addition to the enterprise user name. Assuming that the configuration store is widely accessible (otherwise it would be difficult for Enterprise Terminal to use), the enterprise user name and password are stored in an encrypted format. Given a PKI, this information can be encrypted under the PKI user's public key, such that only an authenticated PKI user could properly decrypt it. Because the password sent by the Enterprise Terminal to the server's operating system is never revealed to the user, the user does not have the option to invoke a Telnet client directly, and thus bypasses the PKI-based authentication mechanisms.

SUMMARY

Once a user has successfully completed the authentication process (regardless of whether via PKI mechanisms or a password), the Enterprise proceeds as if the traditional password-based authentication had been used. PKI-authenticated and password-authenticated users can coexist in an Enterprise installation.

These PKI authentication solutions allow PKI-authenticated and traditionally authenticated users to coexist. They also provide an upgrade path by which PKI authentication can be added to an existing Enterprise installation. Enterprise customers who do not wish to use PKI authentication need not install the PKI authentication components.

Finally, regardless of the authentication mechanism used, users are administrated within the Enterprise environment as they have always been with respect to enterprise and user authentication, etc. There are no changes in Enterprise product deliverables for customers who do not wish to use PKI authentication features. PKI authentication can be provided as an add-in offering.

22

OBTAINING A CERTIFICATE

Office of Information Technologies, University of Virgina

As explained in previous chapters, a certificate is an electronic packet of information you can present that will verify your identity — similar to a passport. In fact, a certificate contains information about you, an electronic key, and a signature by a trustworthy certificate authority. To obtain one, read further.

HOW A CERTIFICATE IS USED

Once you have your certificate, you can use it in many ways, including logging into specific computers, locking and unlocking information, and accessing restricted materials. Details on the process are discussed later in the chapter.

YOU ONLY NEED ONE

For now, one certificate is enough. It is stored on your computer as a part of your Web browser; thus, it is conveniently available as you surf the Web. Your certificate is portable. Export it, make a floppy-copy, and you can take it wherever you go. You can import it to another computer's Web browser and drive away. It is best not to import your certificate to a public computer, because you must remember to remove it from the browser or your privileges could be compromised.

PERSONAL CERTIFICATES: A CLOSER LOOK

A certificate's principal function is to identify you with a key-pair. To associate a key-pair with your identity, a certificate authority (CA) issues a certificate — an electronic record that carries a public key and assurance that you hold the corresponding private key. Your digital certificate might contain your name and your public key, the expiration date of the public key, the name and digital signature of the trusted issuer of the certificate, and a unique serial number. If you present your certificate to another party, you can be challenged to make sure you have the private key that goes with the public key on your certificate. Do they trust the issuing authority? Did the alleged authority actually issue the certificate?

Format of Certificates

To verify that a certificate it issues is authentic, the certificate authority (CA) digitally signs it. As alluded to in the preceding, this CA's "stamp" on your certificate (such as, for example, the root in the University of Virginia's [UVa] certificate in Exhibit 1) can be verified by another root

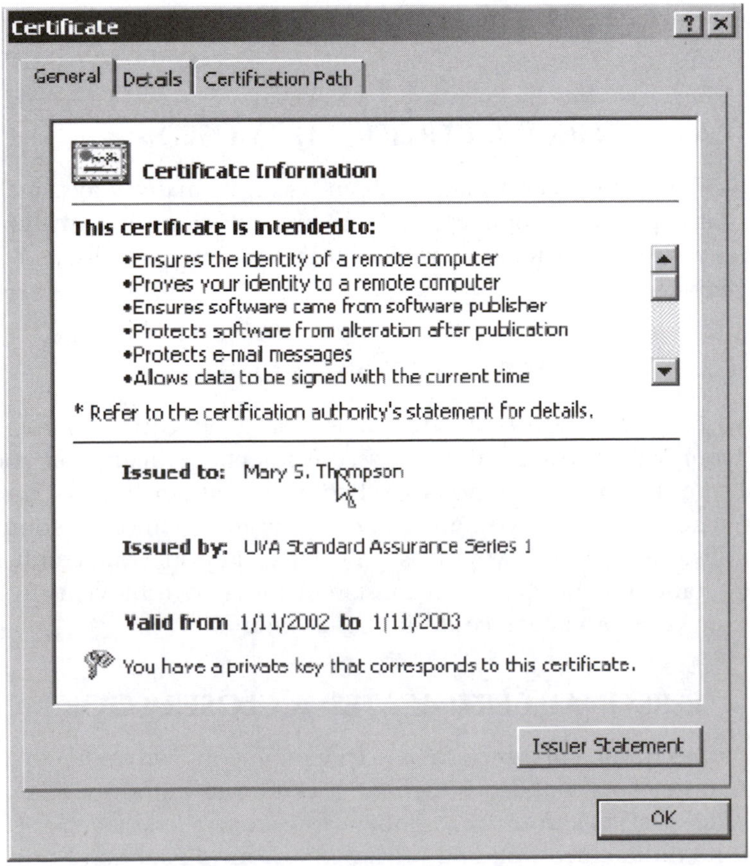

Exhibit 1   Facsimile of an Issued Certificate

certificate higher in the chain; and that other certificate can be verified similarly by yet another certificate, and so on, until the entity you are dealing with is assured that your issuing CA is genuine.[1] Exhibit 1 shows a facsimile of a certificate issued by UVa's Department of Information Technology and Communication (ITC) for user mst3k (Mary S. Thompson).

Therefore, to make your public key and its association with you available for verification purposes, the certificate can be "published" in a repository: an online database of certificates available for retrieval and use in verifying digital signatures. For example, UVa uses ldap.virginia.edu, UVa's LDAP server, because it already contains data about you that is public. In most cases, the CA includes a validation period for the certificate.

How to Acquire a Certificate

To become electronically certified by UVa, use a browser. For example, current limitations of the Cisco VPN client require that you use Internet Explorer: Obtain a "root" certificate for the UVa certificate server, and obtain a private/public key-pair and accompanying certificate for yourself.

In the Internet Explorer implementation of this process, both certificates are installed simultaneously. In Netscape (as addressed later in the chapter), two steps are necessary.

For example, if your browser is Netscape, version 6.2 and you intend to download certificates, use Internet Explorer. You can copy and paste the current URL into the "Address:" window in i.e., Then proceed with the instructions given for Internet Explorer, which are covered later in the chapter.

UVa, for example, can support the use of certificates for the browsers and platforms listed later in the chapter. The "Software" link sends you to upgrade your browser. It will take you to Software Central for Netscape, or to Microsoft for Internet Explorer. The "Obtain Certificates" option takes you to instructions for obtaining certificates with the chosen browser.

Tip: You should use Internet Explorer. Netscape Navigator is included for completeness only.

OBTAINING PERSONAL CERTIFICATES

As a first step, instructions for obtaining Personal Certificates fall into two categories: for Windows machines and for other Operating Systems (support limited to Linux and Macintosh OS X or later). For example, if you are using Netscape 6.2 under Windows, follow the instructions for certificates via Netscape later in the chapter. For now, follow the instructions for Internet Explorer coming up next.

CERTIFICATES VIA INTERNET EXPLORER

For example, certification is granted through UVa's Standard Assurance Certificate Authority. When you request a certificate, you must supply pertinent information about yourself, which is verified electronically by comparison with UVa's database. Once authorized, you will be given a public/private key-pair and a certificate as validation of your identity and affiliation with UVa. The certificate can then be used at local Web sites that require you to be affiliated with the University of Virginia as student, faculty, or staff. Examples of such sites are Software Central, which contains licensed software that must only be distributed to those affiliated with UVa, and several database and information sites accessed through the Health Sciences and Alderman Libraries. They require that you have a UVa IP address to be allowed to log in. This is a function of the Proxy Server. This is also a function of UVa-Anywhere, which uses certificates to allow its virtual private network (VPN) client to implement the IP address requirement.

About Installing Certificates

This part of the chapter includes exhibits of the GUIs for Internet Explorer. If you use a different version, the windows may differ slightly from those shown. The procedure and method of storing the certificates remain the same. If you must have multiple certificates, see sidebar on "Certificate Management."

Certificate Management

Use the same computer all the time and you will not need to manage certificates — they are always where they need to be. You should make a copy of your certificate with its private key and place it in a secure location. If you receive a message encrypted using your related public key, you must have the matching private key in order to decrypt it. To make a copy of your private key, see sidebar for instructions on "Exporting Your Personal Certificate."

Note: Certificates, Keys, and Passwords

- Your private key should be kept secret and password-protected.
- Use passwords that are difficult to guess.
- If someone obtains your private key, immediately request that the certificate be invalidated so that your communications cannot be compromised.

One Unique Certificate

In today's PKI environment, you only need one public/private key-pair and certificate. For example, the UVa Certification Authority (CA) issues Standard Assurance certificates that are accepted by their existing PKI applications and those that are planned. In the future, the UVa CA can issue High Assurance certificates, and then you will need another separate public/private key-pair that will go with the High Assurance certificate.

You should have one single certificate that you export to computers that you either have exclusive use of or for which you know and trust the other individuals who have access. If you share a computer with trusted individuals, set it up to support multiple users/accounts, so that each person has his or her own login. If you use a computer for both personal and work activities, then set up one account for personal use and another for work.

Security Recommendations

There are four security recommendations for obtaining a certificate. Remember to use Internet Explorer as the browser of choice for this set of recommendations:

- Obtain one personal digital certificate and export/import it.
- Store your certificate only on computers to which you have exclusive use, and that you share under the following conditions:
    - Computer is configured for multiple users.
    - Each person has a unique account.
    - Other users are individuals whom you trust.
- Do not import your private key/certificate to "general-use" computers.
- Do not obtain a separate certificate for each computer you use.

Create a Mobile Certificate

There are three steps to creating a "mobile" certificate. Remember to use Internet Explorer as the browser of choice for this set of instructions:

1. If you have not done so already, use Internet Explorer on a computer that is running Windows and obtain a personal certificate.

2. Export your personal certificate from Internet Explorer (see sidebar "Exporting Your Personal Certificate").
3. Import your personal certificate onto other computers you might use (see sidebar "Importing Certificates").

Multiple Computers

Do you use several computers? If so, export your certificate and private key only to those to which you have exclusive access or, if possible (Windows 2000 or XP):

- Set up an individual account for each user.
- Each user has his or her own login and password.
- Each user sees his or her own version of the desktop and has access only to his or her slice of the My Documents folder.
- Create a personal account for yourself.
- Create a separate account to use for work. Import your certificate and private key to this "work" account.

Multiple Certificates

Multiple certificates are not recommended, regardless of whether or not you use multiple computers. If you use multiple computers, there is nothing to prevent you from obtaining unique public/private key-pairs and a Standard Assurance certificate for each one, but think twice before doing this. If you have multiple certificates, you will be asked to select one as your preferred certificate, and it is this one that will be stored in the LDAP directory. When secure e-mail is implemented, it is this certificate that a person will use to send you secure e-mail and it is the corresponding private key that you will use to read it.[1]

Exporting Your Personal Certificate

Select the certificate to be exported as shown in Exhibit 2.[1] Then perform the following steps:

1. Click the Tools drop-down menu and choose Internet Options.
2. Select the Content tab at the top of the dialog box that opens.
3. Click the Certificates button, and another window should open.
4. Click the Personal tab if it is not already selected.
5. Highlight the certificate to copy and click Export.

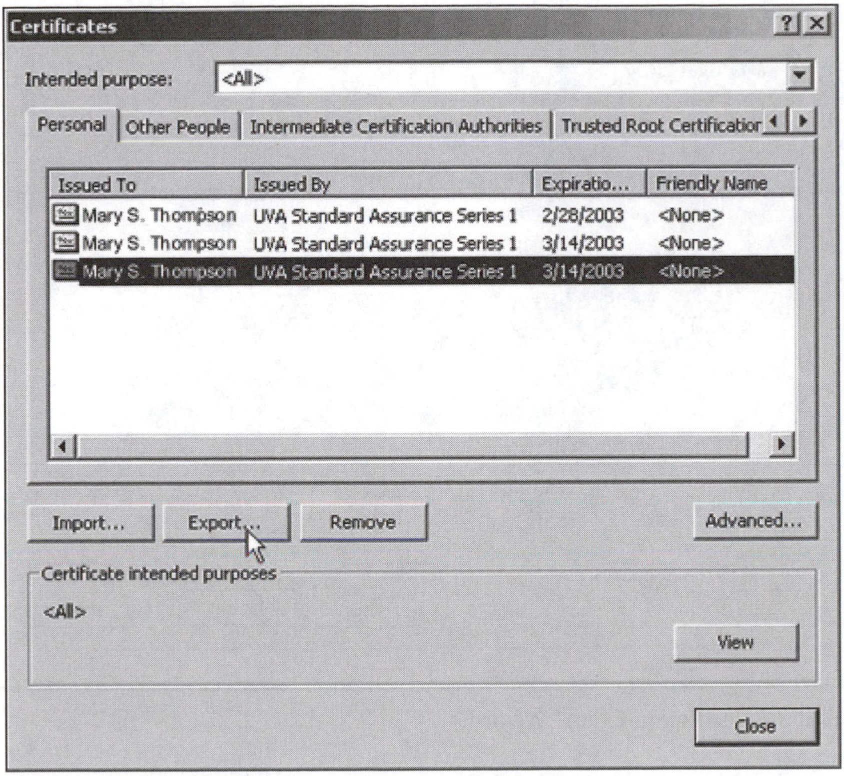

Certificates ? X

Intended purpose: <All>

| Personal | Other People | Intermediate Certification Authorities | Trusted Root Certification ◄ ► |

Issued To	Issued By	Expiratio...	Friendly Name
Mary S. Thompson	UVA Standard Assurance Series 1	2/28/2003	<None>
Mary S. Thompson	UVA Standard Assurance Series 1	3/14/2003	<None>
Mary S. Thompson	UVA Standard Assurance Series 1	3/14/2003	<None>

Import... Export... Remove Advanced...

Certificate intended purposes

<All>

View

Close

Exhibit 2 Selecting the Certificate That Is to Be Exported

Next, follow the instructions of the Certificate Export Wizard as shown in Exhibit 3.[1] Perform the following steps:

1. Click Next in the first frame.
2. Choose "Yes, export the private key" and click Next.

Choose "Personal Information" as shown in Exhibit 4.[1] Then check "Include all certificates," and complete by clicking Next.

Internet Explorer requires that a password be "attached" to the export as shown in Exhibit 5.[1] Enter a password you will remember. If you forget the password, you will not be able to retrieve the private key. After entering and confirming the password, click Next.

When prompted for a filename, specify the floppy drive (usually the A drive) followed by your user ID (A:\mst3k), as shown in Exhibit 6.[1] Append the ".pfx" file extension if you like; if not, it will be added on export. If you do not specify a path for the file (A:\mst3k), it will be saved to your desktop. Click Next to continue.[1]

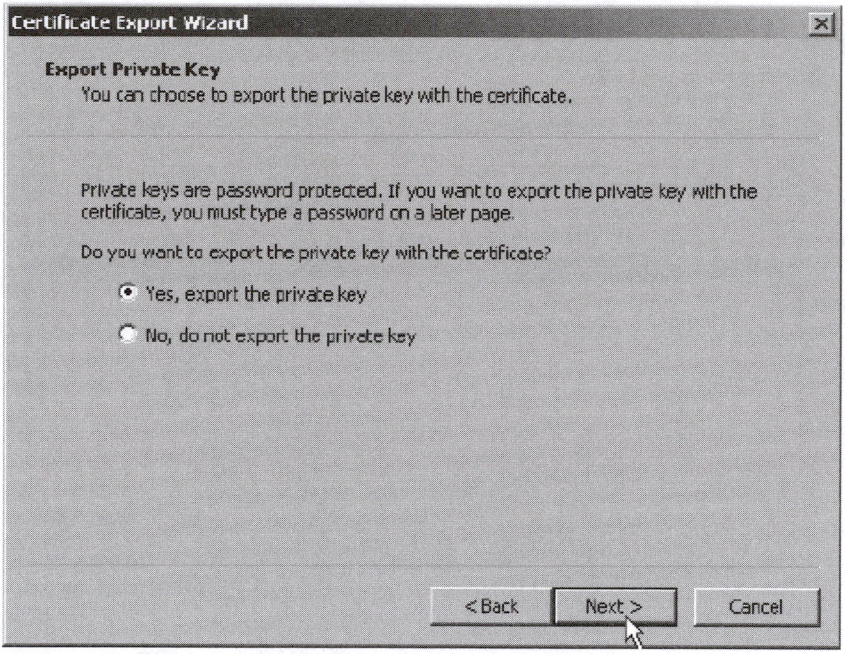

Exhibit 3 Certificate Export Wizard

Importing Certificates

The following recommendations should be adhered to in importing certificates:

- Obtain one personal digital certificate and export/import it.
- Store your certificate only on computers:
- To which you have exclusive use
- That you share under the following conditions:
- Computer is configured for multiple users
- Each person has a unique account
- Other users are individuals whom you trust
- Do not import your private key/certificate to "general-use" computers.
- Do not obtain a separate certificate for each computer you use.

Why Not Have Multiple Certificates?

Suppose you have a work computer and a home computer. If you obtain a personal certificate for your work computer and another for

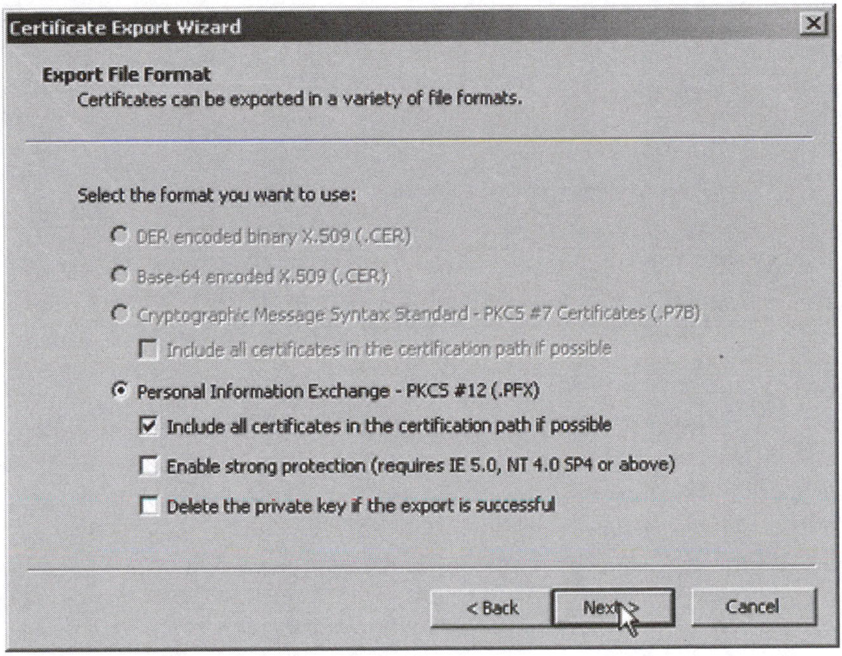

Exhibit 4 Certificate Export Wizard: Export File Format

your home computer, only one of them can be chosen for the LDAP directory, which will eventually publish the public key for your chosen certificate. If you have obtained multiple certificates, you will be asked to specify which one you want to be your preferred certificate. In the future, this key can be used by others to send you secure e-mail — encrypted by your public key. To view such e-mail, you must decrypt it using the corresponding private key, regardless of whether you are at work or home. If you had multiple certificates (one at work and another at home), you would have to have both private keys in each place in order to decrypt the e-mail at both locations.

Importing the Certificate

You can import certificates into browsers and other applications. The two primary browsers, Netscape and Internet Explorer, store certificates differently, and the procedures for importing and exporting are not alike. Choose from the following by platform and browser:[1]

- Windows: Internet Explorer
- Windows: Netscape 4.x
- Windows: Netscape 7.x

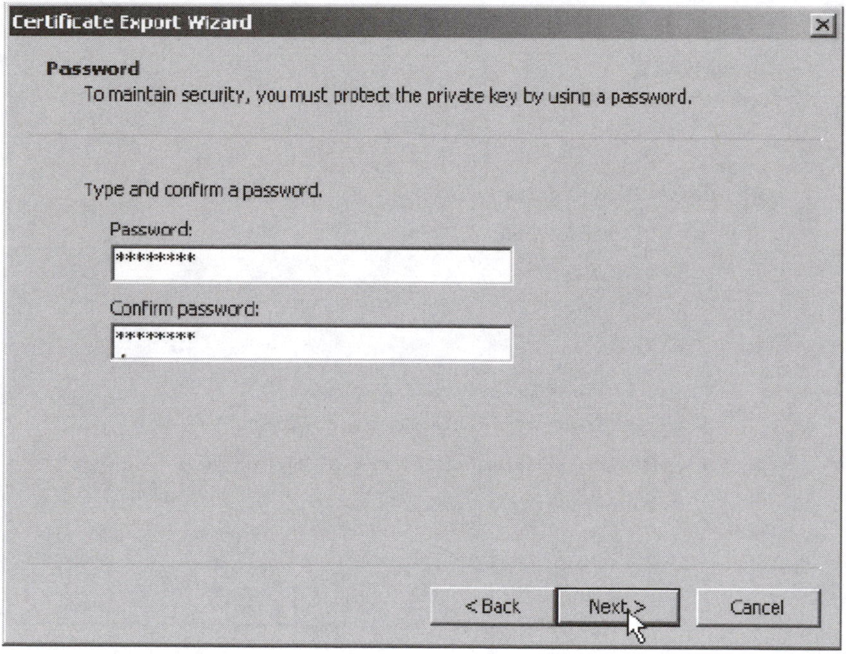

Exhibit 5   Certificate Export Wizard: Password

- Macintosh: Internet Explorer
- Macintosh: Netscape 4.x
- Macintosh: Netscape 6/7.x

Note: Cookies are enabled by default in most browsers. If you experience problems downloading, see sidebar on "How To Enable Cookies" to rule this out as the source.

How to Enable Cookies

The following are instructions for enabling cookies in the primary Web browsers. Follow the instructions given for your Web browser. After you have received your certificates, and you want to disable cookies again, just repeat the procedure to locate the setting. You should only disable cookies instead though.

Internet Explorer: Version 5.5

Follow the menus to allow first-party cookies:

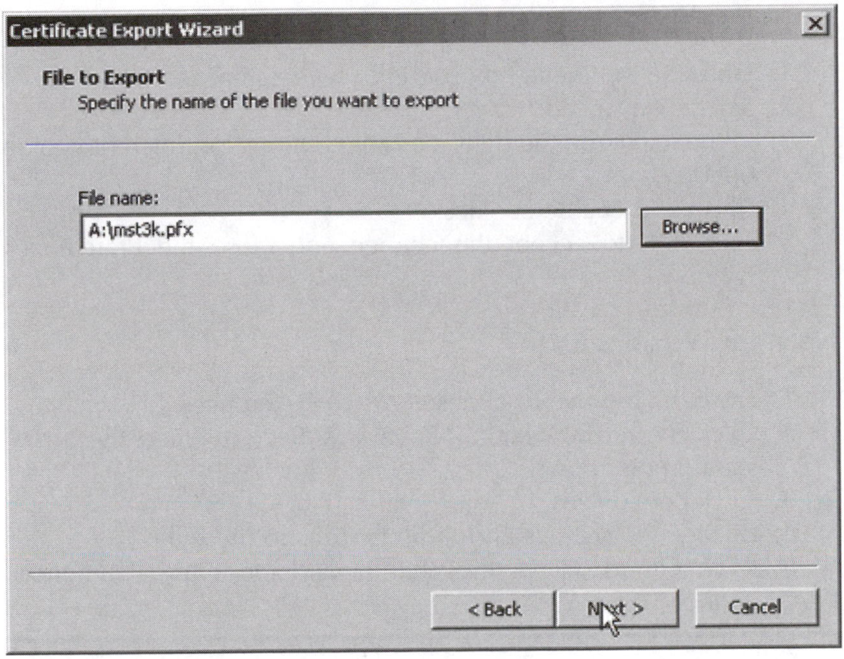

Certificate Export Wizard ☒

File to Export
Specify the name of the file you want to export

File name:

A:\mst3k.pfx   [Browse...]

[< Back] [Next >] [Cancel]

Exhibit 6   Certificate Export Wizard: File to Export

1. Tools -> Internet Options, choose the Security tab.
2. Unless you have modified things, every site will show up in "Local Internet."
3. Click on "Local Internet," then click on custom level.
4. Settings used appear in detail, including cookies.
5. Once set, click OK in each window to close and accept the changes.

Internet Explorer: Version 6

Follow the menus to make the following changes:

1. Tools -> Internet Options, choose the Privacy tab.
2. Notice that the vertical slide bar moves between less and more private.
3. The meaning of each setting appears to the right of the bar.
4. Click the "Advanced" button.
5. Choose "Override automatic cookie handling."
6. Click to "Accept" under First Party Cookies.
7. Click OK in the Advanced and again in the Internet Options windows to close them.

Netscape: Versions 4.7x

1. From the top menu, choose Edit -> Preferences.
2. Select "Advanced."
3. In the region on the right are radio buttons for different cookie options.
4. Choose to enable cookies.
5. Click OK to accept the change and close the Preferences window.

Netscape: Versions 6.x[1]

1. From the top menu, choose Edit -> Preferences.
2. Click the arrow next to "Privacy & Security" and the arrow should point down.
3. Click on Cookies.
4. Change the settings and radio buttons to the right.
5. Click OK to accept the change and close the Preferences window.

Obtain a Root Certificate

If you are Netscape users, refer to the separate instructions for your browser later in the chapter under "Certificates Via Netscape," for obtaining both root and personal certificates. If you are Internet Explorer users and asked to accept a root certificate, click Yes.

Obtain a Personal Certificate

To obtain a personal certificate, you need to look at the following security issues:[1]

- ■ Your computer should be set up to use Multiple Login mode so that each user has a different set of configuration files.
- ■ Use Internet Explorer to download certificates.
- ■ Install your personal certificate on one computer only, until you are more familiar with how certificates, keys, etc.... work.

Now, click on the following link to begin:

https://standard.pki.virginia.edu/ca/eecert/

Two new windows will open. The front window (see Exhibit 7) shows the agreement you must accept to be given a personal certificate.[1] Click

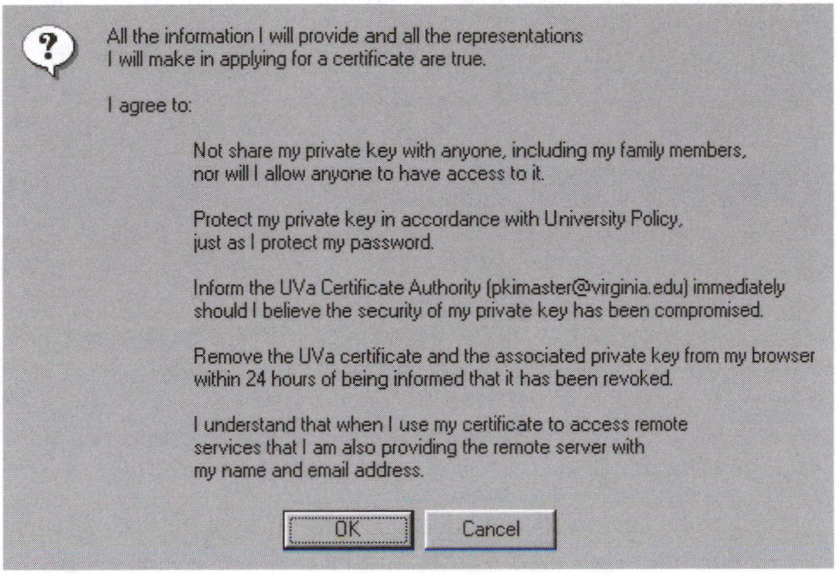

Exhibit 7   The Agreement You Must Accept to Be Given a Personal Certificate

"OK" to accept or "Cancel" to abort the process. Upon agreement, you will receive a copy through e-mail.

The second window contains a form as shown in Exhibit 8.[1] Enter the requested information and click "Submit information." A summary of the information appears, along with a client driver (the default is "Microsoft Enhanced Cryptographic Provider v1.0"). Click "Submit Request." A response page will show that your certificate has been downloaded successfully.

You must set your browser to accept cookies or you will be unable to complete the certification process. These instructions will remain open for your reference. For example, two separate windows (actually the same two windows: Exhibits 7 and 8) will open when you go to the UVa's Certificate Authority Web site at the following URL:

https://standard.pki.virginia.edu/ca/eecert/

If You Must Remove Certificates

Removing a certificate should only be necessary for beta-testers who have had "Pretend" certificates during the development phase of the project. To manage certificates in Internet Explorer, go to Tools -> Internet Options. Select the "Content" tab and click the "Certificates" button in the second blocked region. To remove a root certificate:[1]

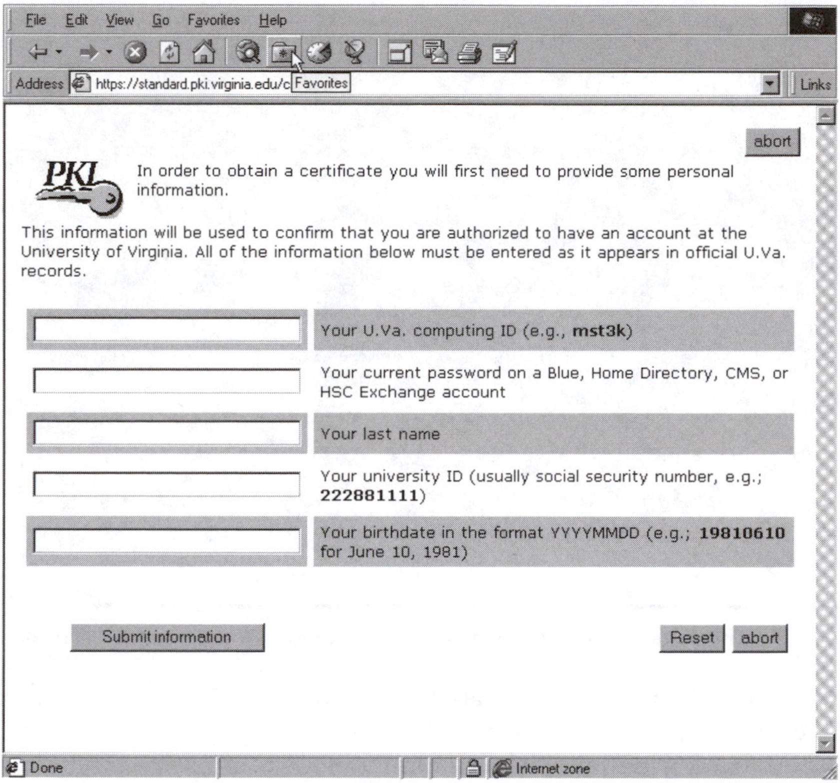

Exhibit 8   The Form Must Be Filled Out to Obtain a Personal Certificate

1. Choose the "Trusted Root Certification Authorities" tab.
2. Scroll down until you see "Pretend CREN Root Certificate;" click the entry to highlight it and then click the Remove button.

To remove your personal certificate:[1]

1. Choose the "Personal" tab to list your certificates.
2. Click on the entry or entries you want to remove, and then click Remove.

CERTIFICATES VIA NETSCAPE

The interface for the installation procedure is determined by the type of browser and its version number. This part of the chapter includes exhibits of the GUIs for Netscape Navigator 4.7x. If you use a different version of the browser, in particular Netscape 6.x or 7.x, the windows may differ

Exhibit 9   New Certificate Authority Instructions

from those shown, but the procedure and manner of storing the certificates remain the same.

Note: If you must remove any certificate(s) you have been issued, please refer to the procedure for removing certificates at the end of this chapter. Certificates are stored differently in Netscape and Internet Explorer, and the removal procedures are specific to each browser.

The procedures outlined here are accurate. Refer to the previous information on Certificate Management to see how to deal with both multiple certificates (which are discouraged) and importing certificates into Netscape from Internet Explorer (recommended). This part of the chapter is provided for those who insist on obtaining their certificates using the Netscape browser interface.

Obtain a Root Certificate

You should first set your browser to accept cookies or you will be unable to complete the certification process. These instructions will remain open for your reference. Take a moment to look at Exhibits 9 through 15 for this root certificate procedure.[1]

If you have obtained a root certificate at some prior time, the browser will send the following message: "The certificate that you are trying to

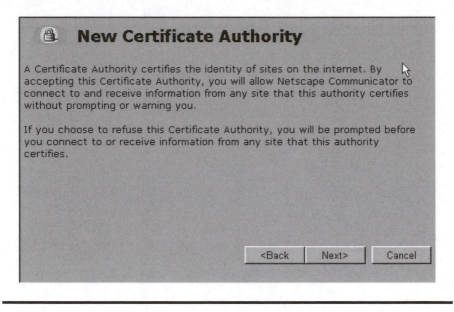

Exhibit 10 New Certificate Authority Instructions (continued)

download already exists in your database," and you will be unable to go farther with this step. Jump to the instructions to "Obtain a Personal Certificate" later in the chapter.

For example, when asked to name this certificate, use "UVa Root Certificate" for easy identification. Ready? Click the link below to proceed.

https://standard.pki.virginia.edu/pki/site.crt

Three windows (Exhibits 9 through 11), each with the heading "New Certificate Authority," appear in succession. You should move along by clicking "Next" in each case. The fourth window is similar to the one shown in Exhibit 12, and you must check at least one of the boxes. You should check this one first: "Accept this Certificate Authority for Certifying network sites."

You should then click Next. You are now given an opportunity to request a Warning before sending information to sites so certified (optional). As shown in Exhibit 13, click Next after making your decision.

In the next window (see Exhibit 14), you will name your certificate. Please enter the name "UVa Root Certificate" to make it easy to locate. Choose Finish to complete the "root" certificate process.

Note: The UVa Root Certificate appears in the list under the name you specified earlier.

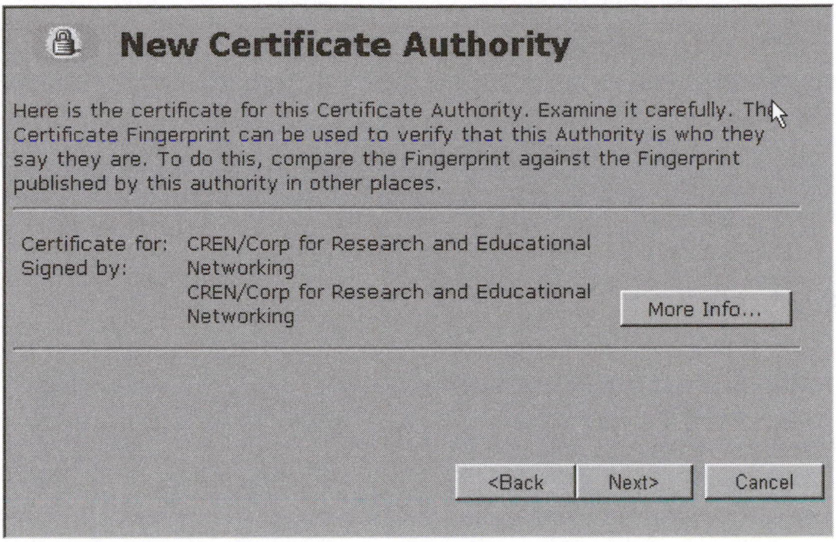

🔒 New Certificate Authority

Here is the certificate for this Certificate Authority. Examine it carefully. The Certificate Fingerprint can be used to verify that this Authority is who they say they are. To do this, compare the Fingerprint against the Fingerprint published by this authority in other places.

Certificate for: CREN/Corp for Research and Educational
Signed by: Networking
CREN/Corp for Research and Educational
Networking

More Info...

<Back | Next> | Cancel

Exhibit 11   The Certificate for This Certificate Authority

🔒 New Certificate Authority

Are you willing to accept this Certificate Authority for the purposes of certifying other internet sites, email users, or software developers?

☐ Accept this Certificate Authority for Certifying network sites
☐ Accept this Certificate Authority for Certifying e-mail users
☐ Accept this Certificate Authority for Certifying software developers

<Back | Next> | Cancel

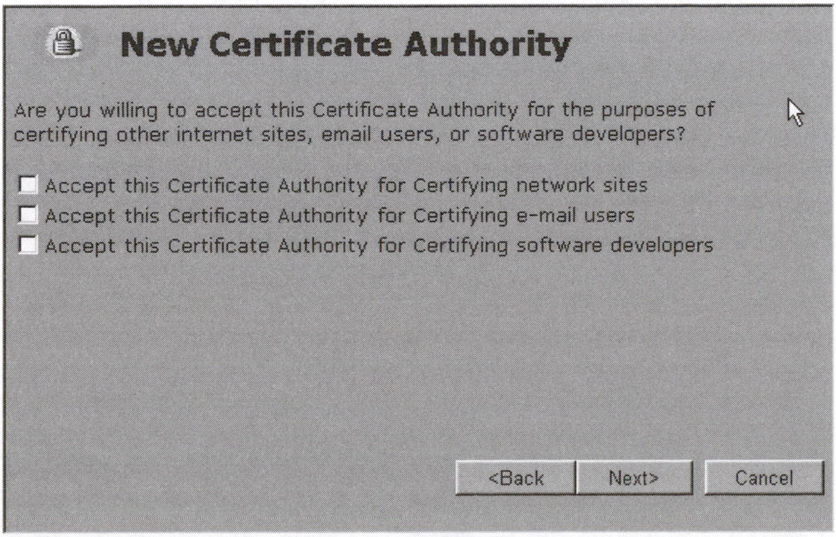

Exhibit 12   Accepting the Certificate Authority

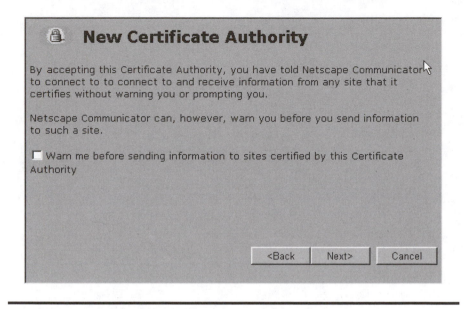

Exhibit 13   Connect to and Receive Information from Any Site Using Netscape Communicator

Exhibit 14   Accepting the CA

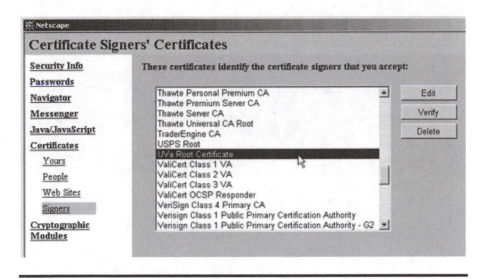

Exhibit 15   Certificate Signers' Certificates

Obtain a Personal Certificate

Now click on the link in Exhibit 15, and a couple of new windows open. The first window summarizes the agreement you must accept to be given a certificate for personal use, as shown in Exhibit 16:[1]

https://standard.pki.virginia.edu/ca/eecert/

Next, choose OK to continue, and enter the requested information about yourself. This time, the password must be yours on one of these systems: blue.unix, the Central Mail Server, HSC mail.

When all information has been entered, click OK. You are given a chance to select a specific client driver — just accept the default, "1024 (High Grade)." Next, click "Submit your certificate request," and a window entitled "Generate A Private Key" opens as shown in Exhibit 17.[1] The "More Info…" button provides details. Click OK to proceed.

Caution: Your password cannot be recovered. If you forget it, you will lose all of your certificates. Enter a password to protect this private key as shown in Exhibit 18.[1] Use something other than your e-mail password. To change your security preferences, including your password, select "Security Info" from the "Tools" menu.

Test Your Certificate

Once your personal certificate has been installed, you can click the "Test your digital certificate" button. If asked, select the certificate you want to

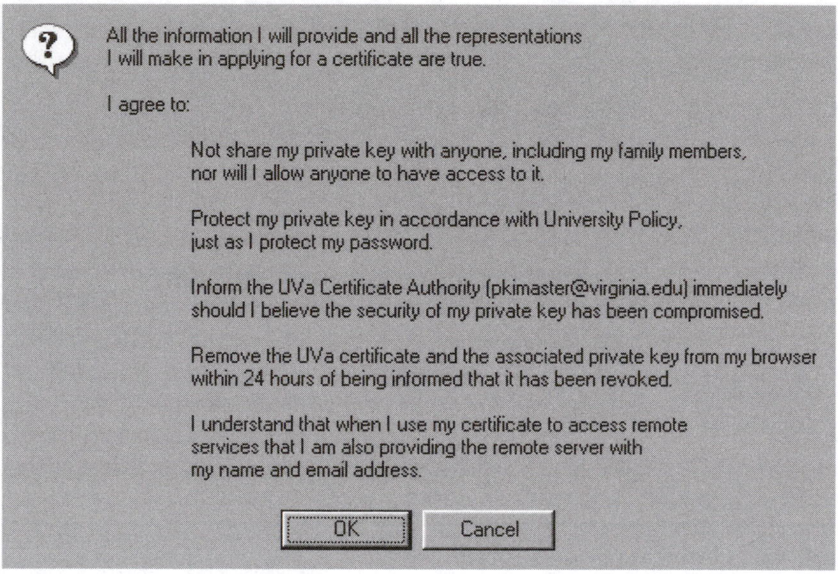

All the information I will provide and all the representations
I will make in applying for a certificate are true.

I agree to:

Not share my private key with anyone, including my family members,
nor will I allow anyone to have access to it.

Protect my private key in accordance with University Policy,
just as I protect my password.

Inform the UVa Certificate Authority (pkimaster@virginia.edu) immediately
should I believe the security of my private key has been compromised.

Remove the UVa certificate and the associated private key from my browser
within 24 hours of being informed that it has been revoked.

I understand that when I use my certificate to access remote
services that I am also providing the remote server with
my name and email address.

[OK]   [Cancel]

Exhibit 16   Summarizes the Agreement

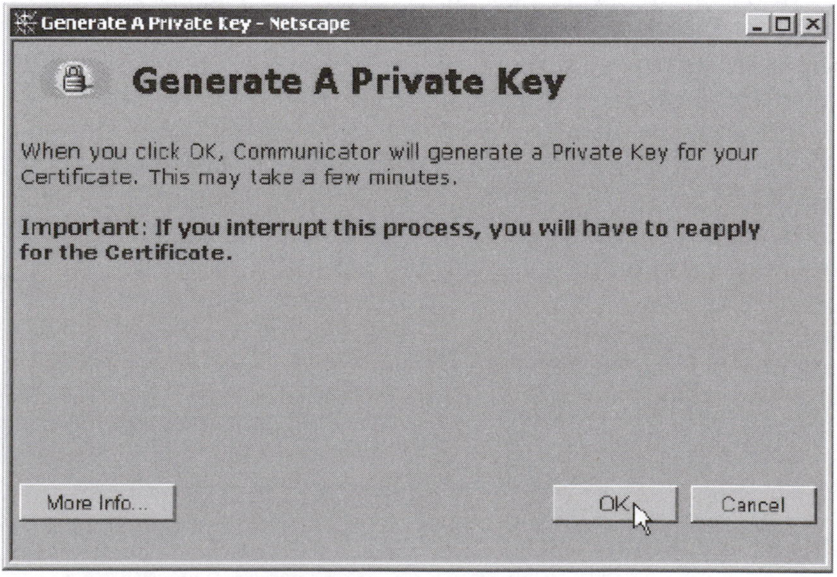

Generate A Private Key – Netscape

Generate A Private Key

When you click OK, Communicator will generate a Private Key for your
Certificate. This may take a few minutes.

**Important: If you interrupt this process, you will have to reapply
for the Certificate.**

[More Info...]   [OK]   [Cancel]

Exhibit 17   Generate a Private Key

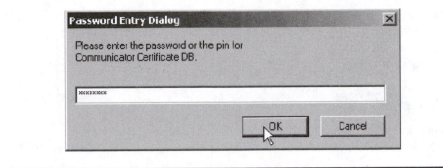

Exhibit 18 Password Entry Dialog

test. If the test is successful, you will receive the message "Your digital certificate appears to be OK. It contains the following identifying information:…," where the information appears in a formatted list in the same window. Close the pop-up window by clicking the button provided.

If the test fails, check on your desktop or in My Downloads folder to see if you saved the root certificate instead of running it from its download location. If so, request a root certificate.

If the Process Fails

Lots of things can happen to interrupt the process of setting up your certificates: power outage, personal interruption that is long enough to timeout, keying in incorrect information, etc. If this occurs, you may need to remove the certificate that was generated because it may have become corrupted.

In Netscape, if the certificate creation process was interrupted while you were obtaining a "root" or "personal" certificate, you can remedy the situation in one of at least two ways: File method and GUI method.

File Method

The file method will reset the browser's information about your certificates completely. Netscape stores its certificate information in files when run in a Windows environment. Some certificates "come with the package" and should not concern you. Other certificates (in particular, ones that are personal to you) are stored under your user ID. Perform the following steps if you are using the file method:[1]

1. Using Windows Explorer, go to C:\Program Files\Netscape\Users and click on your user ID. This should be the one you use when you log in to Windows (mst3k).

2. Of the files and folders displayed in the right-hand window of Explorer, move those that end in ".db" to the Recycle Bin.
3. Exit Netscape and open it anew to start over at the step for obtaining a root certificate.

GUI Method

Finally, the GUI method is useful when you only need to remove specific certificates. Perform the following steps if you are using the GUI method:[1]

1. Click on the Communicator menu at the top of the browser window. Go to "Tools" and select "Security Info" from the list. A large "Security Info" window opens.
2. If the process failed when you were obtaining a root certificate, then look under "Certificates… Signers." Scroll down until you locate "UVa Root Certificate," select it, and then click Delete. Exit Netscape and re-open to get a new root certificate.
3. If you want to remove your personal certificate, then select "Certificates… Yours," select the name assigned to the certificate, and then click Delete. Exit Netscape and re-open to obtain a new personal certificate.

SUMMARY

Certification is granted through a Standard Assurance Certification Authority. When you request a certificate, you will be asked to supply pertinent information about yourself, information that is verified by comparison with a database. Once authorized, you will be given a public/private key-pair and certification of identity. The certificate can then be used at local Web sites that require that you be affiliated with the issuing authority. This is a function heretofore carried out through the Proxy Server. Finally, certificates should simplify access to these sites.

REFERENCES

1. "Public Key Infrastructure," © 1996-2003 by the Rector and Visitors of the University of Virginia, Board of Visitors Office, NW Wing, The Rotunda, P.O. Box 400222, University of Virginia, Charlottesville, VA 22904-4222, 2003.

23

TEN RISKS OF PKI: WHAT YOU ARE NOT BEING TOLD ABOUT PUBLIC KEY INFRASTRUCTURE

Carl Ellison and Bruce Schneier

Computer security has been a victim of the "year of the…" syndrome. First it was firewalls, then intrusion detection systems, then VPNs, and now certification authorities (CAs) and public key infrastructure (PKI). "If you only buy X," the sales pitch goes, "then you will be secure." But reality is never that simple, and that is especially true with PKI.

Certificates provide an attractive business model. They cost almost nothing to make; and if you can convince someone to buy a certificate each year for $5, that times the population of the Internet is a big yearly income. If you can convince someone to purchase a private CA and pay you a fee for every certificate he issues, you are also in good shape. It is no wonder so many companies are trying to cash in on this potential market. With that much money at stake, it is also no wonder that PKI vendors produce almost all the literature and lobbying on the subject. And this literature leaves some pretty basic questions unanswered: What good are certificates anyway? Are they secure? For what? In this chapter, we hope to explore some of those questions.

Security is a chain; it is only as strong as the weakest link. The security of any CA-based system is based on many links, and they are not all cryptographic. People are involved.

Does the system aid those people, confuse them, or just ignore them? Does it rely inappropriately on the honesty or thoroughness of people? Computer systems are involved. Are those systems secure? These all work together in an overall process. Is the process designed to maximize security or just profit? Each of these questions can indicate security risks that need to be addressed.

Before we start, do we even need a PKI for E-commerce? Open any article on PKI in the popular or technical press and you are likely to find the statement that a PKI is desperately needed for E-commerce to flourish. This statement is patently false. E-commerce is already flourishing, and there is no such PKI. Web sites are happy to take your order, whether or not you have a certificate. Still, as with many other false statements, there is a related true statement: commercial PKI desperately needs E-commerce in order to flourish. In other words, PKI start-ups need the claim of being essential to E-commerce in order to get investors.

There are risks in believing this popular falsehood. The immediate risk is on the part of investors. The security risks are borne by anyone who decides to actually use the product of a commercial PKI.

RISK 1: WHO DO WE TRUST, AND FOR WHAT?

> There is a risk from an imprecise use of the word "trust. "A CA is often defined as "trusted."

In the cryptographic literature, this only means that it handles its own private keys well. This does not mean you can necessarily trust a certificate from that CA for a particular purpose: making a micropayment or signing a million-dollar purchase order.

Who gave the CA the authority to grant such authorizations? Who made it trusted?

A CA can do a superb job of writing a detailed Certificate Practice Statement (CPS) — all the ones we have read disclaim all liability and any meaning to the certificate — and then do a great job following that CPS, but that does not mean you can trust a certificate for your application. Many CAs sidestep the question of having no authority to delegate authorizations by issuing ID certificates. Anyone can assign names. We each do that all the time. This leaves the risk in the hands of the verifier of the certificate, if he uses an ID certificate as if it implied some kind of authorization.

There are those who even try to induce a PKI customer to do just that. Their logic goes: (1) you have an ID certificate, (2) that gives you the key holder's name, (3) that means you know who the key holder is, and (4) that is what you needed to know. Of course, that is not what you needed to know. In addition, the logical links from 1 to 2, 2 to 3, and 3 to 4 are individually flawed. (We leave finding those as an exercise for the reader.)

RISK 2: WHO IS USING MY KEY?

One of the biggest risks in any CA-based system is with your own private signing key. How do you protect it? You almost certainly do not own a secure computing system with physical access controls, TEMPEST shielding, "air wall" network security, and other protections; you store your private key on a conventional computer. There, it is subject to attack by viruses and other malicious programs. Even if your private key is safe on your computer, is your computer in a locked room, with video surveillance, so that you know no one but you ever uses it? If it is protected by a password, how difficult is it to guess that password? If your key is stored on a smart card, how attack-resistant is the card? (Most are very weak.) If it is stored in a truly attack-resistant device, can an infected driving computer get the trustworthy device to sign something you did not intend to sign?

This matters mostly because of the term "non-repudiation." Like "trusted," this term is taken from the literature of academic cryptography. There, it means something very specific: that the digital signature algorithm is not breakable, so a third party cannot forge your signature. PKI vendors have latched onto the term and used it in a legal sense, lobbying for laws to the effect that if someone uses your private signing key, then you are not allowed to repudiate the signature. In other words, under some digital signature laws (e.g., in Utah and Washington), if your signing key has been certified by an approved CA, then you are responsible for whatever that private key does. It does not matter who was at the computer keyboard or what virus did the signing; you are legally responsible.

Contrast this with the practice regarding credit cards. Under mail-order/telephone-order (MOTO) rules, if you object to a line item on your credit card bill, you have the right to repudiate it — to say you did not buy that item — and the merchant is required to prove that you did.

RISK 3: HOW SECURE IS THE VERIFYING COMPUTER?

The previous section showed that the computer holding or driving the private key needs to be secure. Long keys do not make up for an insecure system because total security is weaker than the weakest component in the system.

The same applies to the verifying computer — the one that uses the certificate. Certificate verification does not use a secret key, only public keys. Therefore, there are no secrets to protect. However, it does use one or more "root" public keys. If the attacker can add his own public key to that list, then he can issue his own certificates, which will be treated exactly like the legitimate certificates. They can even match legitimate certificates in every other field except that they would contain a public key of the attacker instead of the correct one.

It does not help to hold these root keys in "root certificates." Such a certificate is self-signed and offers no increased security. The only answer is to do all certificate verification on a computer system that is invulnerable to penetration by hostile code or to physical tampering.

RISK 4: WHICH JOHN ROBINSON IS HE?

Certificates generally associate a public key with a name, but few people talk about how useful that association is. Imagine that you receive the certificate of John Robinson. You may know only one John Robinson personally, but how many does the CA know? How do you find out if the particular John Robinson certificate you received is your friend's certificate? You could have received his public key in person or verified it in person (PGP allows this), but more likely you received a certificate in e-mail and are simply trusting that it is the correct John Robinson. The certificate's Common Name will probably be extended with some other information, in order to make it unique among names issued by that one CA.

Do you know that other information about your friend? Do you know what CA his certificate should come from?

When Diffie and Hellman introduced public key cryptography, they proposed a modified telephone directory in which you could find public keys. Instead of name, address, and phone number, it would have name, address, and public key. If you wanted to find John Robinson's public key, you would look him up in the directory, get his public key, and send him a message for his eyes only using that public key. This might have worked with the Stanford Computer Science Department phone directory in 1976, but how many John Robinsons are in the New York City phone book, much less in a hypothetical phone book for the global Internet?

We grow up in small families where names work as identifiers. By the time we are five years old, we know that lesson. Names work. That is false in the bigger world, but things we learn as toddlers we never forget. In this case, we need to think carefully about names and not blindly accept their value by the five-year-old's lessons locked into our memories.

RISK 5: IS THE CA AN AUTHORITY?

The CA may be an authority on making certificates, but is it an authority on what the certificate contains? For example, an SSL server certificate contains two pieces of data of potential security interest: the name of the key holder (usually a corporate name) and the DNS name for the server. There are authorities on DNS name assignments, but none of the SSL CAs listed in the popular browsers is such an authority. That means that the DNS name in the certificate is not an authoritative statement. There are authorities on corporate names. These names must be registered when one gets a business license. However, none of the SSL CAs listed in the browsers is such an authority. In addition, when some server holds an SSL server certificate, it has permission to do SSL. Who granted the authority to an SSL CA to control that permission? Is the control of that permission even necessary? It serves an economic purpose (generating an income stream for CAs), but does it serve a security purpose? What harm is done if an uncertified server were allowed to use encryption? None.

RISK 6: IS THE USER PART OF THE SECURITY DESIGN?

Does the application using certificates take the user into account, or does it concern itself only with cryptography?

For example, a normal user makes a decision on whether or not to shop with a given SSL-protected Web page based on what is displayed on that page. The certificate is not displayed and does not necessarily have a relation to what is displayed. SSL security does not have the ability to control or even react to the content of the Web page, only its DNS address. The corporate name is not compared to anything the user sees, and there are some Web pages whose certificate is for a company that does Web hosting, not for the company whose logo appears on the displayed page. Users cannot, and cannot be expected to, sort this all out.

RISK 7: WAS IT ONE CA OR A CA PLUS A REGISTRATION AUTHORITY?

Some CAs, in response to the fact that they are not authorities on the certificate contents, have created a two-part certification structure: a registration authority (RA), run by the authority on the contents, in secure communication with the CA that just issues certificates. Other vendors sell CA machinery directly to the content authority.

The RA+CA model is categorically less secure than a system with a CA at the authority's desk. The RA+CA model allows some entity (the CA) that is not an authority on the contents to forge a certificate with that content. Of course, the CA would sign a contract promising not to do so, but that does not remove the capability. Meanwhile, because the security of a chain is weaker than the weakest link, the RA+CA is less secure than either the RA or the CA, no matter how strong the CA or how good the contract with the CA. Of course, the model with a CA at the authority's desk (not at the vendor's site) violates some PKI vendors' business models. It is more difficult to charge for certificates when you sell someone the CA code (or they get it for free, as Open Source).

RISK 8: HOW DID THE CA IDENTIFY THE CERTIFICATE HOLDER?

Whether a certificate holds just an identifier or some specific authorization, the CA needs to identify the applicant before issuing the certificate.

There was a credit bureau that thought they would get into the CA business. After all, they had a vast database on people, so the thinking ran that they should be able to establish someone's identity online with ease. If you want to establish identity online, you can do that provided you have a shared secret with the subject and a secure channel over which to reveal that secret. SSL provides the secure channel.

The trouble with a credit bureau serving this role is that in its vast database there is not one secret shared with the subject. This is because credit bureaus are in the business of selling their information to people other than the subject. Worse, because credit bureaus do such a good job of collecting and selling facts about people, others who might have information about a subject are probably hard-pressed to find any data shared with the subject that is not already available through some credit bureau. This puts at risk commercial CAs that use credit bureau information to verify identity online; the model just does not work.

Meanwhile, having identified the applicant somehow, how did the CA verify that the applicant really controlled the private key corresponding to the public key being certified? Some CAs do not even consider that to be part of the application process. Others might demand that the applicant sign some challenge right there on the spot, while the CA watches.

RISK 9: HOW SECURE ARE THE CERTIFICATE PRACTICES?

Certificates are not like some magic security elixir, where you can just add a drop to your system and it will become secure. Certificates must be used properly if you want security. Are these practices designed with solid security reasons, or are they just rituals or imitations of the behavior of someone else? Many such practices and even parts of some standards are just imitations that, when carefully traced back, started out as arbitrary choices by people who did not try to get a real answer.

How is key lifetime computed? Does the vendor use one year, just because that is common? A key has a cryptographic lifetime. It also has a theft lifetime, as a function of the vulnerability of the subsystem storing it, the rate of physical and network exposure, attractiveness of the key to an attacker, etc. From these, one can compute the probability of the loss of the key as a function of time and usage. Does the vendor do that computation? What probability threshold is used to consider a key invalid?

Does the vendor support certificate or key revocation? Certificate revocation lists (CRLs) are built into some certificate standards, but many implementations avoid them because they seem to be archaic remnants of the newsprint booklets of bad checking account numbers one used to find at the supermarket checkout stand. Like those booklets, CRLs are seen as too big and too outdated to be relevant. However, if CRLs are not used, how is revocation handled?

If revocation is handled, how is compromise of a key detected in order to trigger that revocation? Can revocation be retroactive? That is, can a certificate holder deny having made some signature in the past? If so, are signatures dated so that one knows good signatures from suspect ones? Is that dating done by a secure timestamp service?

How long are the generated public keys, and why was that length chosen? Does the vendor support 512-bit RSA keys just because they are fast, or 2,048-bit keys because someone over there in the corner said he thought it was secure?

Does the proper use of these certificates require user actions? Do users perform those actions? For example, when you establish an SSL connection with your browser, there is a visual indication that the SSL protocol worked and the link is encrypted. But who are you talking securely with? Unless you take the time to read the certificate that you received, you do not know.

Even then, you may not know (cf., Risk 4 above). But if you do not even look, it is much like going into a private room with the lights off: you might know that someone else is there and your conversation is private, but until you know who that other person is, you should not reveal any secret information.

RISK 10: WHY ARE WE USING THE CA PROCESS, ANYWAY?

One PKI vendor employee confided in us a few years ago that they had great success selling their PKI solution, but that customers were still unhappy. After the CA was installed and all employees had been issued certificates, the customer turned to the PKI vendor and asked, "OK, how do we do single sign-on?" The answer was, "You don't. That requires a massive change in the underlying system software."

Single sign-on (SSO) might be the killer app of PKI. Under SSO, you come into work in the morning, plug in your smart card, enter the PIN that activates it, and for the rest of the day, you do not have to do any more log-ins. All of that is handled for you by the SSO mechanism.

Attractive isn't it? Of course, it is attractive. Authentication is a pain. Anything we can do to avoid it, we will jump at.

Unfortunately, the security value of authentication is all but completely defeated by SSO. Authentication is supposed to prove that the user is present at the controlling computer, at the time of the test. Under SSO, when the user has to rush to the washroom, any passing person can walk up to that user's computer and sign on someplace via the SSO mechanism.

So, why are so many jumping at the CA process with such fervor? Do they use certificates out of empty ritual, just because the other guy does and it is the thing to do this year? Do they do it in order to pass the liability buck: to be able to blame the PKI experts if any insecurity sneaks through?

We are not that cynical. Our assessment is that security is very difficult — both to understand and to implement. Busy system administrators and IT managers do not have the time to really understand security. They read the trade press. The trade press, influenced by PKI vendors, sings the praises of PKIs. And PKI vendors know what busy people need: a minimal-impact solution. "Here, buy this one thing and it will make you secure." So that is what they offer. Reality falls far short of this promise; but then, this is a business and the prominent voices are those with something to sell. *Caveat emptor.*

24

USING A CERTIFICATE

Although digital certificates have been discussed at length in previous chapters, how to use them specifically has not. The information in this chapter covers some of the more common things you might want to do with your personal digital certificate and, more specifically, how to use it.

DIGITALLY SIGNING E-MAIL MESSAGES

The first step to securing your e-mail messages is to sign them using your personal digital certificate. Your digital signature enables recipients to verify that you actually sent the message and that the message was not altered during transmission.

Note: You must have a personal digital certificate to digitally sign messages.

Digitally signing a message does not affect the contents of the message in any way or protect the message from being intercepted and read by someone other than the intended recipient. To ensure that only intended recipients can read the message, you must also encrypt the message. Recipients of a signed message who are not using an S/MIME-enabled e-mail package (such as Netscape Messenger), will still be able to read digitally signed messages. Your digital signature simply shows up as an attachment.

The signed icon indicates that a message has been signed. When you receive a signed message, the signed icon is displayed when you view it in Netscape Messenger. Messenger also automatically stores the sender's personal digital certificate, enabling future messages sent to that person to be encrypted.

0-8493-0822-4/04/$0.00+$1.50
© 2004 by CRC Press LLC

Automatically Signing All Outgoing Messages

Netscape Messenger can be configured to automatically digitally sign all outgoing messages with a personal digital certificate installed in the Personal Security manager. To configure Netscape Messenger to automatically sign all outgoing e-mail with your personal digital certificate, consult the procedure for Automatically Signing E-Mail Messages with Netscape Messenger.

PROCEDURES FOR USING A PERSONAL DIGITAL CERTIFICATE

To secure communications, authentication is crucial. Users must be able to verify the identity of others, and must also be able to prove their identity to those with whom they communicate. Because the communicating parties do not physically meet as they communicate, authentication of identity on a network is complex. This can allow an unethical person to impersonate another person or entity, or to intercept messages. Therefore, within the communication process, a method must be worked out to maintain the necessary level of trust.

As explained in previous chapters, the digital certificate is a common credential that provides a means to verify identity. A certificate is a set of data that identifies an entity. A trusted organization assigns a certificate to an entity or an individual that associates a public key with the individual. The subject of that certificate is the individual or entity to which a certificate is issued. The trusted organization that issues the certificate is a certification authority (CA) and is known as the certificate's issuer. Only after verifying the identity of the certificate's subject will a trustworthy CA issue a certificate.

When dealing with personal or financial transactions on the Internet, you can protect your security by using personal digital certificates. Why? Because personal digital certificates bind the identity of the certificate owner to a pair (public and private) of electronic keys that can be used to encrypt and sign information digitally. These electronic credentials ensure that the keys actually belong to the person or organization specified. So, if you are using an Internet Explorer or Netscape browser, you can protect your privacy and security using a personal digital certificate. For example, if you are using Internet Explorer (Internet Explorer will be used throughout the remainder of this chapter as an example), you can install personal digital certificates and configure certificate settings using the following methods:

First of all, to install personal digital certificates within the browser itself, you can use the Internet Explorer Certificate Manager. In the Internet

Options dialog box, you can also configure advanced security options for certificates on the Advanced tab.

Second, for your user groups, you can use the Internet Explorer Customization Wizard to create custom packages of Internet Explorer that include preconfigured lists of trusted personal digital certificates, publishers, and CAs. You can also lock down these settings to prevent users from changing them — if you are a corporate administrator.

Third, you can use the IEAK Profile Manager to manage personal digital certificate settings through the automatic browser configuration feature of Internet Explorer, after deploying the browser. To enable you to manage security policy dynamically across all computers on the network, you can automatically push the updated information to each user's desktop computer.

The options for configuring personal digital certificates are the same. These options allow you to gain access to them from the IEAK Profile Manager, Internet Explorer 6 or higher, or the Internet Explorer Customization Wizard.

Note: Microsoft Outlook® Express also includes personal digital certificates, called *digital IDs,* which can be configured separately within the e-mail program.

Removing and Installing Trusted Personal Digital Certificates

You can install and remove trusted personal digital certificates for clients and CAs using the Internet Explorer Certificate Manager. Many CAs have their root personal digital certificates already installed in Internet Explorer. You can select any of these installed personal digital certificates as trusted CAs for client authentication, secure e-mail, or other certificate purposes, such as code signing and timestamping. You can import the root personal digital certificate if a CA does not have it in Internet Explorer. Instructions that describe how to obtain the root personal digital certificate are contained on each CA's Web site. You may also want to install client personal digital certificates. These personal digital certificates are used to authenticate users' computers as clients for secure Web communications. Now let us look at the following five steps that are required to remove and install CAs and Clients from the list of trusted personal digital certificates:

1. Click on Internet Options on the Tools menu, and then click on the Content tab.
2. Click on Certificates.
3. Click on one of the following tabbed categories for the type of certificates you want to remove or install:

- *Personal.* Certificates in the Personal category have an associated private key. Information signed using personal certificates is identified by the user's private key data. By default, Internet Explorer places all certificates that will identify the user (with a private key) in the Personal category.
- *Other People.* Certificates in the Other People category use public key cryptography to authenticate identity, based on a matching private key that is used to sign the information. By default, this category includes all certificates that are not in the Personal category (the user does not have a private key) and are not from CAs.
- *Intermediate Certification Authorities.* This category contains all certificates for CAs that are not root certificates.
- *Trusted Root Certification Authorities.* This category includes only self-signed certificates in the root store. When a CA's root certificate is listed in this category, you are trusting content from sites, people, and publishers with credentials issued by the CA.
- *Trusted Publishers.* This category contains only certificates from trusted publishers whose content can be downloaded without user intervention (unless downloading active content is disabled in the settings for a specific security zone).

4. Select, in the Intended Purpose box, the filter for the types of certificates that you want to be displayed in the list.
5. Use one of the following methods to work with particular certificates:
   - Click on Import to add other certificates to the list. The Certificate Manager Import Wizard steps you through the process of adding a certificate.
   - Click on Export to export certificates from the list. The Certificate Manager Export Wizard steps you through the process of exporting a certificate.
   - Click on Advanced to specify the default drag-and-drop export file format (when the user drags a certificate from the Certificate Manager and drops it into a folder).
   - Click on Remove to delete an existing certificate from the list of trusted certificates.
   - Click on View to display the properties for a selected certificate, including the issuer of the certificate and its valid dates.

Trusted Publisher Designation

You should use the Security Warning dialog box that appears when you attempt to download software from that publisher, in order to designate a trusted publisher for Internet Explorer. Unless you have disabled the downloading of active content in the settings for a specific security zone, active content that is digitally signed by trusted publishers with a valid personal digital certificate will download without user intervention. Now, if you want to add a trusted publisher, you should perform the following three steps:

1. To download signed active content from the publisher, you should use Internet Explorer.
2. Select the "Always trust content from" trusted publisher checkbox when the Security Warning dialog box appears.
3. Click on Yes to download the software and control, and add the publisher to the list of trusted publishers.

Advanced Security Options Configuration for Authentication and Personal Digital Certificate Features

Finally, you can easily configure options for certificate and authentication features that your users may need. Therefore, to configure advanced security options for personal digital certificates, you need to perform the following four steps:

1. Click on Internet Options on the Tools menu.
2. Next, click on the Advanced tab.
3. Review the selected options in the Security area.
4. Select or clear the appropriate checkboxes, depending on the needs of your organization and its users.

SUMMARY

In today's enterprises, electronic communication is a central part of the everyday flow of information, and privacy is a top priority. Whether your enterprise conducts sales over the Internet or hosts an enterprise-specific network, you want to know that your communications are safe from unauthorized interference.

Finally, for information exchange between servers and client browsers and server-to-server, load balancing devices and personal digital certificates have become recognized as the bottom line in security. Personal digital certificates protect enterprises against site spoofing, data corruption, and repudiation of agreements. They assure customers that it is safe to submit personal information, and provide colleagues with the trust they need to share sensitive enterprise information.

25

CERTIFICATE REVOCATION WITH VERISIGN MANAGED PKI: FLEXIBLE, OPEN REVOCATION SOLUTIONS FOR TODAY'S ENTERPRISE PKI NEEDS

VeriSign, Inc.

In a public key infrastructure (PKI), digital certificates, signed by certification authorities (CAs), are the means of distributing public keys accurately and reliably to users needing to encrypt messages or verify digital signatures. A certificate has a fixed lifetime, typically one year. However, a certificate may need to be revoked by a CA if a user private key is compromised or the CA is no longer willing to support the certification (for example, because the holder of the private key terminated employment with the enterprise). The PKI needs to provide applications that use certificates with the ability to check, at the time of usage, that the certificate is still valid.

VeriSign Managed PKI is VeriSign's unique integrated PKI platform.[1] Managed PKI combines enterprise-controlled and operated PKI software/hardware, an open PKI architecture giving compatibility with all popular applications, and the certificate processing services and infrastructure of a high-availability, high-security *PKI backbone*. The result is the most fully featured, cost-effective, high-availability, and high-security PKI solution for the enterprise available in the world today.

Easy-to-use, readily deployable certificate revocation is an important enterprise PKI requirement, and VeriSign has built into Managed PKI the best in revocation technology. Revocation, however, depends as much on the application software product as it does on the infrastructure. Today's PKI-enabled products include varying degrees of support for certificate revocation.

Most of the application vendors participating in the Open PKI initiative[2] are responding rapidly to customer revocation/status-checking requirements that are emerging as PKI is being progressively deployed in mainstream business applications. As these applications expand their revocation/status-checking feature sets, VeriSign provides complementary functions on the infrastructure side.

This chapter describes today's revocation needs, available techniques for revocation/status-checking, and VeriSign's current products/services and strategic directions relating to this aspect of PKI.

In today's fast-moving network security marketplace, it is important to ensure that today's PKI procurement decision will not become obsolete tomorrow. The breadth and depth of VeriSign's varied customer base and technical partners provides our enterprise customers with the utmost confidence that their PKI investment will grow as their needs grow.

TODAY'S NEEDS

Drawing on input gathered from more than 120 VeriSign Managed PKI enterprise customers; plus prospective customers, affiliates, channel partners, and software vendor partners; and from the operational experience gained from issuing and managing millions of consumer and Web site certificates, VeriSign has assembled a clear picture of revocation requirements in enterprise PKI today.

Revocation in enterprise PKI falls into two categories:

1. *Server-side revocation checking.* A web server supporting SSL needs to check that a client certificate presented in an SSL handshake is valid, prior to granting access to resources on the basis of that certificate.
2. *Client-side revocation checking.* A client using a certificate presented by a server or another client needs to check the validity of that certificate (e.g., for e-mail security purposes).

In the short term, server-side revocation checking is considered most important, and often indispensable, in order to close off access to Web resources from credentials reported lost or compromised by customers or employees. Client-side revocation checking is also rapidly becoming an important requirement for some applications. Subsidiary requirements are:

- Revocation checking *must* work with native-mode client software; that is, it must not depend on the installation of special client-side software. For example, server-side revocation checking must work with native browsers from the major browser vendors.
- It must be possible to revoke a certificate either manually by an administrator or automatically from enterprise administration systems or databases: for example, automatically revoke an employee's certificate when the human resources database is updated to indicate that the employee has terminated employment with the enterprise.
- While many applications can operate with latency of up to a day in a reported revocation becoming effective, other applications require much shorter latency and some require real-time status checking.
- As a foundation for non-repudiation, records of revocation requests and notification postings must be retained securely under rigidly audited controls, and must be independently verifiable in the event of dispute resolution.
- Tools must be available to allow revocation status checking to be integrated into any application in accordance with the principles of *Open PKI* (vendor independence).

VeriSign is committed to satisfying all of these requirements, in conjunction with its market-leading application partners. These requirements cannot be met with the stand-alone PKI software approach to building an enterprise PKI.

REVOCATION FUNCTIONS IN VERISIGN MANAGED PKI

Revoking a Certificate

The VeriSign Managed PKI customer is always in control of the enterprise PKI. The Managed PKI Control Center provides an easy-to-use interface with which an administrator can:

- Revoke a subscriber's certificate
- Query the status of current certificates
- Manually download a CRL, produced nightly

End users can also revoke their own certificates and query the current status of issued certificates.

In addition, the Automated Administration option of Managed PKI allows an enterprise to interface Managed PKI to a local administration system and revoke certificates automatically. For example, if Managed PKI is interfaced to the enterprise human resources database, an employee's certificate can be automatically revoked when the database is updated to indicate that the employee is about to terminate employment.

Enterprise PKI must support various revocation requirements of different applications. VeriSign generates CRLs daily or hourly for all enterprise customers. OCSP will also be supported for OCSP-enabled clients. In contrast, stand-alone PKI software vendors support only CRLs, usually only in conjunction with their proprietary client software.

CRLs

CRLs are generated daily by the VeriSign data center and made available for fetching by the enterprise. An option for hourly CRL issuance is also available with OnSite 4.0.

Managed PKI Validation Module for Web Servers

This Managed PKI module satisfies the requirement for server-side revocation checking. It features:

- A validation engine plug-in for Microsoft and Netscape Web Servers (IIS 4.0 and ES 3.5.1 or above, respectively) that enforces access control certificate revocation
- Full configurability of CRL and CA certificate locations
- An API providing application-level access to the validation engine's CRL maintenance, checking, and automated retrieval functions
- Automatic download of the Managed PKI daily or hourly CRLs

VeriSign's Managed PKI Validation Module provides turnkey revocation status checking for enterprise Web servers that can operate with standard Web browsers. In contrast, stand-alone PKI software vendors only implement revocation in conjunction with their proprietary client software products.

Online Status (OCSP)

VeriSign pioneered the development of real-time, automated status checking (OCSP). In the interests of industry-wide interoperability, VeriSign initiated and led the effort with the Internet Engineering Task Force (IETF) to establish OCSP as an industry standard. It was the first vendor to demonstrate OCSP operation in the 1998 National Automated Clearinghouse Association (NACHA) PKI trials and will provide OCSP support in conjunction with Netscape Communications Corporation's implementation of this protocol (as announced by Netscape in August 1998).

Client-Side Revocation Checking

Client-side revocation checking functions largely depend on the implementation choice of the client software vendor. VeriSign supports all the revocation mechanisms implemented by major vendors. For example, Microsoft has foreshadowed support for CRLs in forthcoming client product releases, and Netscape has foreshadowed support for OCSP in its forthcoming releases. VeriSign Managed PKI will work with both as shipped — there is no need for troublesome proprietary client plug-ins as needed with PKI offerings of stand-alone PKI software vendors.

Furthermore, VeriSign supplies an application PKI-enablement toolkit that allows application implementers to easily incorporate CRL-based revocation checking into their applications.

AVAILABLE REVOCATION MECHANISMS

Discussions between VeriSign and its leading partners and major customers have conclusively established that no single mechanism for certificate revocation will meet all needs. Risk management policy, trust models, timeliness requirements, population size, and relationships between subscribers and relying parties create a variety of complementary mechanisms. Let us explain the mechanism options.

Certificate Revocation Lists (CRLs)

A certificate revocation list (CRL) is a digitally signed, timestamped *blacklist* of revoked but unexpired certificates, issued by a CA periodically (e.g., daily). CRLs have the attractions of having a widely recognized standard format (defined in the X.509 standard) and of being suitable for caching and use in non-online environments (e.g., when processing secure e-mail in a client that is not currently network-connected). They have limitations, in that the CRL on hand may not be considered sufficiently fresh and they may grow to an unacceptably large size.

Partitioned CRLs

To counter the problems of CRLs growing too large, there are various mechanisms of partitioning a CRL into smaller pieces. The CRL distribution point (CDP) mechanism defined in the X.509 standard provides for the population of users of a CA to be partitioned into fixed groups, with each group having its own CRL. A pointer in the certificate indicates the CRL partition (group) appropriate for that certificate. Application software follows this link to acquire the correct CRL partition. The group or link name is also included in the CRL and is used to confirm that this is the correct CRL for the certificate in question.

For greater flexibility in partitioning CRLs, VeriSign developed the *Open CDP* (OCDP) mechanism.[3] Open CDP provides for CRL partitioning without fixed pointers in certificates.

Another mechanism defined in X.509 to help keep CRL sizes down is the *delta CRL* mechanism; a delta CRL contains only the latest revocation updates since a prior CRL was issued.

Online Certificate Status Protocol (OCSP)

Some applications — such as high value funds transfer — require immediate online checking of a certificate's status, rather than tolerating any latency as is inherent in all CRL-based mechanisms. An online mechanism is also ideally suited to integration of business processes that are inherently transaction oriented, automated clearing-house (ACH) transactions being a prime example. For such applications, the Internet Engineering Task Force (IETF) Public-Key Infrastructure X.509 (PKIX) Working Group developed the Online Certificate Status Protocol (OCSP) standard. OCSP specifies a transaction whereby a certificate-using application can obtain from a CA a digitally signed indication of the current status of any certificate. While OCSP has excellent timeliness characteristics, it may present performance problems in comparison with CRLs, and is therefore not suitable for all applications.

Trusted Directories

For an intranet application, one approach to revoking certificates is to simply delete them from the enterprise directory. Such can be the case, for example, when an employee leaves a company — the employee's account is deleted from the system, including any digital certificates. To the extent that applications are designed to check for certificates in the directory prior to relying on them, this enables an expedient solution to the revocation requirement. This approach has its cost, however: the directory now becomes a prime target of attack and must be protected with comprehensive security controls. Furthermore, with inter-enterprise PKI, it may not be practical to make the trusted directory available to external relying parties to acquire the necessary account information for privacy reasons. Therefore, the trusted directory approach is of limited utility.

SUMMARY

Open PKI — Best-of-Breed Applications

VeriSign's strategy has been to partner with leading software vendors such as Microsoft, Netscape, or Cisco in producing PKI-enabled applications.

This allows VeriSign to focus on establishing and servicing the infrastructure that transforms commercial PKI into an integral component of everyday business processes. The software vendors — and others — are moving swiftly to expand their PKI offerings to address the concerns of their leading customers. Revocation is high on the list of "must-haves." The VeriSign customer has the widest possible set of deployment options, using industry leading PKI-enabled applications.

More Options

Some options — such as the trusted directory approach — are only useful in well-defined scenarios. CRLs, with or without the various CRL-partitioning mechanisms, show the most promise for interoperability. Finally, there will exist high-value, mission-critical applications that demand the immediate responsiveness and trust model flexibility that CRLs cannot provide. OCSP meets this need.

Lowest Total Cost

The VeriSign customer buys much more than software. VeriSign's integrated PKI platform solution represents an investment in physical structures, high-availability systems, off-site disaster recovery facilities, and key management hardware and software that are benchmarks for the rest of the industry. VeriSign pioneered, developed, and refined the commercialization of key management principles and processes that were previously only known to a select few within the defense community. More important, however, are the skilled and knowledgeable staff members who are required to operate these types of facilities and execute these highly trusted processes. These costs — frequently overlooked in *software-only* comparisons of PKI offerings — can make a massive difference for an enterprise considering a large, full-service operation.

Real-World Non-Repudiation

VeriSign Managed PKI supports non-repudiation in ways that are unattainable with fully enterprise-operated, stand-alone PKI products. With Managed PKI, while the enterprise has full control over the issuance and revocation of digital certificates, complete records of the issuance and lifecycle management of certificates are maintained by VeriSign in a high-security, independently audited data center. Disaster recovery services operate around-the-clock at a geographically separated backup site. VeriSign's secure records are a readily available source of independent evidence that is available, if necessary, to facilitate speedy dispute resolution.

Exhibit 1   Revocation Features: VeriSign versus Entrust

Feature	VeriSign Managed PKI	Entrust
CRLs issued regularly	Yes	Yes
Server-side revocation checking, working with standard browsers	Yes	No
Automated revocation from enterprise administration system	Yes	No
Independently secured and verifiable revocation records to achieve non-repudiation	Yes	No
Disaster recovery	Yes	No
Online Certificate Status Protocol (OCSP)	Yes	No
Open PKI toolkit for enabling revocation in applications	Yes	No

COMPARATIVE FEATURE SUPPORT: VERISIGN-ENTRUST

VeriSign's features compare favorably with those of stand-alone PKI software product vendors. For example, Exhibit 1 compares the VeriSign revocation features with those of Entrust.

NOTES

1. For further details, see "Public-Key Infrastructure — The VeriSign Difference," VeriSign Strategy White Paper #98-01, 1998.
2. See White Paper #98-01 for further details on Open PKI. Application vendors working on Open PKI initiatives with VeriSign include Microsoft, Netscape, and Lotus.
3. So named because this mechanism was developed originally as a free, "open" substitute for CDPs. The holder of the patent on CDPs was attempting, at the time, to levy license fees across the PKI industry for the use of CDPs. Two days after the publication of VeriSign's "Open CDP," the demands for license fees on CDP usage were withdrawn.

26

SUMMARY, CONCLUSIONS, AND RECOMMENDATIONS

M. Benantar

Public key security holds a great deal of promise for Internet-based applications and services. Public key security provides critical security services — including authentication, integrity, and confidentiality — in highly distributed systems, making it ideal for Internet applications. Therefore, it seems inevitable that some form of public key security will become the preferred security system for important Internet applications. Indeed, public key security has become the foundation for important Internet security standards, including the Transport Layer Security standard (formerly known as SSL) for authenticating Web servers and the Secure Multipurpose Internet Mail Extensions (S/MIME) standard for secure messaging.

SUMMARY

It is important to distinguish between public key security and the public key infrastructure (PKI) necessary to manage it. PKI adds layers of security to public key systems by supporting X.509 digital certificates and the facilities for managing both encryption keys and certificates. In short, PKI adds many useful features and functions to public key systems. But, as is the case with any technology, those features and functions come at the price of additional complexity. Today, then, there are many outstanding issues related to PKI.

First and foremost, it is important to remember that PKI is not a complete security solution on its own. PKI will serve the enterprise best when it is part of a comprehensive security architecture that includes general-purpose directory and authorization services. In addition, it is important to understand that PKI is not just technology. It involves people, process, policy, and law. The industry has yet to sort out many issues, including complexity, manageability, and legal precedent, so caution is warranted.

For these reasons, the "I" in PKI is only just emerging. The industry has made a great deal of progress in creating PKI standards in the past four years, and vendors are providing increasingly robust products. But many standards are immature; and as is the case in any market, customer needs (and products) are evolving faster than the standards. Today, interoperability, manageability, liability, and policy remain significant issues.

Yet there are reasons to deploy PKI and to seriously consider plans for deploying PKI in the future. This is especially true for enterprises. As previously mentioned, public key security is poised to play a strategic role in Internet applications. Consequently, enterprises that intend to use the Internet to conduct business must prepare themselves for the inevitable. And enterprises that want to shape PKI policy within their community must get involved early in order to influence that community.

Today, there are several standards efforts and community enterprises working to address the deployment barriers that prevent wider PKI adoption. The Internet2, Educause, and CREN have collaborated to create the Higher Ed Bridge Certificate Authority, which just completed a successful round of testing with the Federal Bridge Certificate Authority. The Organization for the Advancement of Structured Information Standards (OASIS) has technical committees developing the Security Assertions Markup Language (SAML) and XML Key Management Services (XKMS), which will have potentially significant impact on an enterprise's plans to deploy PKI. In addition, Internet2 has made great strides with the Shibboleth project and is working closely with the SAML community to bring viable cross-security domain identity sharing to reality. While complexity, interoperability, application integration, and cost issues are barriers to immediate PKI deployment, enterprises must prepare for PKI by first planning and then deploying PKI applications with clear scopes (limitations) and goals (solving a real problem). Simply put, an enterprise should be planning its PKI strategies and policies, viewing those efforts as an essential part of creating an E-business infrastructure. Whenever possible, the enterprise should strive to create general-purpose security infrastructure that many applications can leverage, integrating that infrastructure with directory and authorization services.

Only then can an enterprise meet its goals of inter-institutional information sharing, cross-institutional curriculum enrollment, and secure electronic grant submissions in a scalable, secure, and manageable form. And, by getting actively involved now, an enterprise can influence the evolution of PKI policy and law as well as interoperability improvements in the higher education community at large.

Digital signature requirements vary widely across applications. For example, applying digital signatures to grade submissions can be very different from signing grant requests to be submitted to the National Institutes of Health (NIH). A key aspect of this problem is the degree to which an enterprise will go to validate the identity of individuals that digital certificates are issued to and the assurance level assigned to those certificates.

Validating the identity of digital certificate recipients will be a formidable challenge that will become manageable if an enterprise outlines a clear and simple policy outlining certificate assurance levels. Once policy is determined, an enterprise can decide what mechanisms and processes to employ to satisfy certificate policy guidelines. The enterprise must clearly analyze the objectives of all efforts to issue digital certificates to the various constituencies it deals with to ensure project success.

Finally, in addition to the technical level investigation of PKI that an enterprise will undertake, an enterprise must also prepare for the training and awareness necessary to educate users who will be issued digital certificates. Today, most computer users are not aware of what digital certificates are, how to properly handle or store them, or what to do when something goes wrong. Application developers do not have an abundance of easy-to-use programming tools to incorporate PKI into applications and systems. Furthermore, system administrators will have new system components to manage and maintain to ensure adequate availability.

CONCLUSIONS

Long before the advent of electronic systems, different methods of information scrambling were used. Early attempts at data security in electronic computers employed some of the same transformations. Modern secret key cryptography brought much greater security, but eventually proved vulnerable to brute-force attacks. Public key cryptography has now emerged as the core technology for modern computing security systems. By associating a public key with a private key, many of the key distribution problems of earlier systems are avoided. The Internet public key infrastructure provides the secure digital certification required to establish a network of trust for public commerce. This part of the chapter explores some concluding details of PKI.

Public key cryptography has emerged as a core technology and has been adopted in many modern computing security systems. The concept of related private and public key-pairs is probably its most appealing aspect. The notion that one cryptographic operation (encryption) can be performed using one key from the pair, while the reverse transformation can only be computed using the other key in the pair, is indeed a giant step toward solving the secret key distribution problem. The proliferation of public cryptographic keys, on the other hand, needs to be achieved in a controlled fashion to ensure that public keys are securely bound to legitimate entities. The Internet public key infrastructure defines secure digital certification for public keys. This part of the chapter explores some concluding details of this infrastructure. Let us begin with an overview of secret key cryptography; and then introduce the secret key distribution problem and explain how public key cryptography contributes to its resolution. Subsequently, let us discuss the foundations of the Internet public key certification, the reasons it is needed, and its defining components.

Secret Key Cryptography

"Data confidentiality" is defined here as an attempt to confine knowledge of the represented information within a particular set of entities, either human or programmable. Secrecy is achieved by scrambling the plaintext form of the data into a representation that perhaps has no syntax, and certainly should have no semantics.

Long before the advent of electronic systems, different methods of data-scrambling transformations, known in contemporary terms as the science of cryptography, have been used. A cryptographic transformation of data is a deterministic procedure by which data, in its plaintext form, is disguised to result in a ciphertext representation that does not reveal the original data. Similarly, the ciphertext can be reverse-transformed in a deterministic fashion by the target recipient so that the original data can be recovered.

Early cryptographic algorithms manipulated the plaintext input, character by character, using the methods of substitution and transposition. A substitution operation replaces a character in the input stream by another character from the alphabet set of the target ciphertext. On the other hand, a transposition, also referred to as a permutation, replaces a character from the input stream by another character of that same input and thus results in shuffling character positions and preserving all characters of the plaintext in the final ciphertext. An example of a substitution is the famous "Caesar cipher," which is said to have been used by Julius Caesar to communicate with his army. This cipher replaces each character of the input text by the third character to its right in the alphabet. Formally, this transformation consists of adding 3 to the position of the input character (modulo 26) to yield the substituting character. Exhibit 1 shows how this simple transformation is applied.[1]

Exhibit 1   A Simple Substitution Cipher

Plain Message:	RETURN TO BASE
Enciphered Message:	UHWXUQ WR EDVH

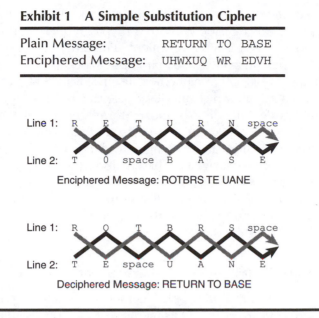

Enciphered Message: ROTBRS TE UANE

Deciphered Message: RETURN TO BASE

Exhibit 2   A Character Transposition Enciphering/Deciphering Example

A transposition cipher, generally, consists of breaking the plaintext into separate blocks; a deterministic procedure is then applied to shuffle characters across the different blocks. Exhibit 2 illustrates a character transposition example in which the secret message "RETURN TO BASE" is first split into two blocks consisting of "RETURN" and "TO BASE," then characters are shuffled across the two blocks in a cyclic fashion to result in the ciphertext "ROTBRS TE UANE."[1]

Although it employs a very basic algorithm, the substitution example points to the concept of the secret key (the number of positions to shift right, 3). Keeping the key secret while divulging the algorithm will, in this case, permit the plaintext to be recovered only by exhaustively processing the key space, which simply consists of the set of integers {1, 2, 3, 4, ..., 26}. The strength of the methods used in this era rested on the secrecy of the encryption algorithm itself.

With the advent of electronic computers, early modern cryptography carried on these same concepts, employing transposition and substitution transformations. The primary difference is that these transformations are now applied at the bit level, rather than the character level, of the binary representation of data. Strength of the encryption method no longer rests in the secrecy of its algorithm, but rather in the secrecy of the key used by that algorithm. This development gave rise to modern secret key cryptography, best known through the Data Encryption Standard (DES) algorithm.

DES, a symmetric cipher in which the same key is used for encryption and decryption, was developed by IBM cryptographers in the early 1970s and was adopted as a U.S. Government standard in 1976. The algorithm is a block cipher, in which a 64-bit input block is transformed into a corresponding 64-bit output ciphertext. It employs a 56-bit key expressed as a 64-bit quantity in which the least relevant bit in each byte is used for parity checking. DES, in its standard form, iterates over 16 rounds, in each of which data is manipulated using a combination of permutation and substitution transformations along with standard arithmetic and logical operations, such as exclusive-OR, based upon the key. For many years, the DES algorithm withstood attacks, but in recent years and mostly due to the increased speed of computing systems, DES has come under brute-force attack on several occasions, thus demonstrating its vulnerability to exhaustive search of the key space.

The Secret Key Distribution and Management Problem

Assume that a group of n people decides to establish a cryptographic communications channel among its members based on a symmetric cipher. Different scenarios for secret key distribution can arise within the group. In the first, all the group members decide to share a single secret key and use it to encrypt and decrypt any exchanged messages. In this basic scenario, the shared secret key requires n distributions, and each user needs to manage a single key. A breach in secrecy of the key results in all communications among the group members being compromised.

In a second scenario, each group member decides to maintain a separate secret key and therefore needs to communicate it to each of the other members of the group. Here $n(n - 1)$ key distributions are required, and n keys need to be stored and managed by each user. Compromising one key results in exposing all the communications destined to that key owner.

In the second scenario, the secret key of each user is divulged to the rest of the group members. One user might masquerade under another user's identity — a potential security threat. To resolve this problem, each pair of users can resort to a separate key for their communications. In a scenario where every two members of the community require a communications channel, the group must distribute $n(n - 1)/2$, whereas each member must manage $n - 1$ keys. Exhibit 3 illustrates three variations in the communication patterns that can take place within a group of seven users. Each member of the group is represented by a node on a graph, with the edge adjacency in the graph representing two-way communication links among the members. Assuming that each pair of users maintains a distinct secret key, the total number of key distributions in each scenario

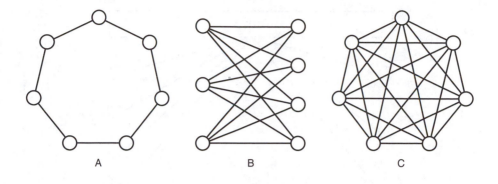

A   B   C

Exhibit 3   Number of Secret Key Distributions Is Directly Related to the Underlying Communication Pattern

will be equal to the number of edges on the corresponding graph. Therefore, as shown in Exhibit 3, in (A) 7 key distributions are required; in (B), where users are partitioned along a bipartite graph, 12 key distributions are required; and, in the case of complete graph (C), in which each user needs to communicate with the rest of the group, a total of 21 key distributions are needed.

These scenarios point out the fact that the number of secret key distributions among a population of users is increasingly proportionate to the number of communication links among the group. Upon renewal of a secret key, the key distribution process takes place all over again. Naturally, the more often a secret key is distributed, the more likely it is to become compromised. A compromise can occur when the key is in transmission or while it is on a storage medium. Distribution of long-term secret keys goes against the core premise of symmetric key cryptography, for which the strength lies in the secrecy of the key.

Advances in software systems have mitigated the problem posed by secret key distribution and management by adopting a central repository of keys, managed by a single server, and the key distribution center (KDC). Each of the communicating entities divulges its secret key to the KDC only, resulting in n key distributions, where n is the size of the community involved. The mere presence of a KDC, however, is not sufficient to disseminate the secret keys across the community of users. A security protocol is also needed, to introduce the communicating parties to one another. For example, the Needham-Schroeder scheme presents a novel method for achieving such a secure introduction of entities. Authenticity and confidentiality of a communication are achieved through a temporary secret key, generated by the KDC. This key applies only to the active session and is shared between the two communicating entities. Advancement in this area came in a variant of the Needham-Schroeder scheme

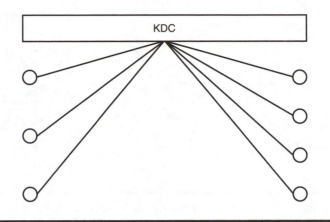

Exhibit 4　A Centralized Key Distribution Scheme

known as the Kerberos protocol, which has proven to be one of the best third-party authentication protocols ever devised. Exhibit 4 illustrates the concept of the trusted third-party KDC; the number of secret key distributions necessary is always equal to the size of the community involved.[1]

Kerberos has been integrated into a number of operating systems and has become an Internet standard. With all its protocol elegance and security, it still has a few shortcomings in today's pervasive paradigm of computing over the Internet. For one thing, the use of the third-party KDC server requires its availability to the communicating parties for the introduction step. Additionally, the KDC, in maintaining all the secret keys, becomes a single point of a catastrophic failure once it is compromised.

The problem with secret key distribution is not so much the number of distributions needed to propagate the keys; rather, it is the need to find a secure channel for their distribution. Due to the recursive nature of this problem, secret key cryptographic systems alone cannot resolve the key distribution issue.

Now take a look at public key cryptography, which deals with the key distribution problem.

Foundations of Public Key Cryptography

Public key cryptography emerged in the mid-1970s with the work published by Whitfield Diffie and Martin Hellman and separately by Ralph Merkle. The concept is simple and elegant, yet it has had far-reaching effects on the science of cryptography and its applications. Public key cryptography is based on the notion that encryption keys come in related pairs — private and public. The private key remains concealed by the key owner, while the public key is freely disseminated. The premise is that it is computationally infeasible to compute the private key by knowing the public key — data encrypted using the public key can only be decrypted using the associated private key. The elegance and strength of public key cryptography are derived from its reliance on purely mathematical foundations that are based on the one-way "trapdoor" functions that exist in the abstractions of number theory. Encryption is the easy direction; decryption is hard. With knowledge of the trapdoor, or private key, decryption can be as easy as encryption.

Two of these currently known one-way functions form the basis of modern public key cryptography. These functions are discussed later in the chapter.

The Problem of Factoring Large Numbers

The first of these one-way functions is based on the ease of multiplying two large prime numbers. The reverse process, of factoring a very large number, is far more complex. Factoring an integer n means finding a series of prime factors such that their product yields n. A prime number is one that has only two irreducible factors, itself and 1. Factoring large numbers (more than 1024 bits) is known to be computationally infeasible with today's computers; with modular arithmetic, the multiplication of such numbers is far easier.

Public Key Cryptography and Digital Signatures

Public key cryptography combined with one-way hash functions gave rise to documents with digital signatures that can withstand repudiation. A one-way hash function, $H(p)$, maps or "digests" its input p onto a fixed-length hash h.

To digitally sign a document using a public key cryptographic algorithm, a hashing function is applied to the document, and then the hash is encrypted using the private key of a public key-pair. The premise is that the signature can only be verified using the public key corresponding to the private key used during signing. Thus, with the assumption that the private key remains confined to the secrecy of the owner, and furthermore by preventing users from obtaining direct access to their own private keys, a digital signature prevents a user from denying the signing of a document. This property is referred to as non-repudiation of the signing action. Preventing direct access to the private key precludes someone from intentionally disclosing his or her own private key and later denying the signing process. Commonly used digital signature algorithms are RSA and DSA. Exhibit 5 illustrates the process of computing and validating a signature using a public key cryptographic algorithm.[1]

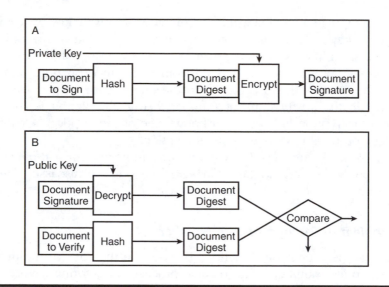

Exhibit 5   (A) Generating and (B) Validating a Digital Signature Using a Public Key Encryption Algorithm Such as RSA

By definition, verifying a digital signature automatically proves the authenticity of the signer. With its inherent support for data origin authentication and non-repudiation, public key cryptography has taken computer security to a new level. However, there is still a weak point in binding the publicly available key to the legitimate owner of the associated private key. Further details are provided next.

Trusting a Public Key

From the outset, public key cryptography elegantly solved the key distribution and management problem introduced by secret key cryptography. Anyone can use the public key to encrypt data, but only the owner of the private key can decrypt it. The community of users in the earlier example can now adopt a public key cryptographic system for securing its communications, dispelling concerns over key distribution and simply sharing a repository that maintains the public keys of its members. Consider a scenario in which Elyes and Aicha, two members of this community, wish to communicate with each other. Elyes looks up the public key of Aicha from the repository of keys, then uses it to encrypt and send a message to Aicha. A third person, Alice, wants to listen in on this communication channel, mounting the attack illustrated in Exhibit 6.[1] Before any communication takes place, in step 1, Alice replaces the public key of Aicha in the key repository with her own public key. In step 2, while Elyes thinks he retrieved the public key of Aicha, he in fact now

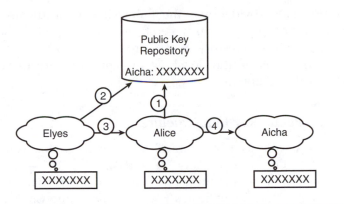

Exhibit 6   Compromising a Public Key

has the public key of Alice. In step 3, Elyes uses the key he retrieved in step 2, encrypts a message, and sends it to Aicha. In step 4, Alice intercepts the message, uses her private key to successfully decrypt it, reads the message, then re-encrypts it using the public key of Aicha, and forwards the message. Finally, Aicha receives the message and decrypts it using her private key, unaware of the eavesdropping.

This illustrates the weakness in using a public key without securely verifying that it indeed belongs to the designated party. It raises the fundamental question of how a secure binding can be achieved between a publicly available key and its holder so that a user of a public key, referred to as a reliant party, can securely verify the binding prior to using the key.

One promising answer lies in the certification process that a public key infrastructure (PKI) can provide. At the heart of a PKI is the digital signature technology that was introduced earlier. Parties reliant on public keys place their trust in a single entity, known as the certificate authority (CA). Before a user's public key is disseminated to a public repository, the underlying high-assurance CA uses its own private key to digitally sign it. A reliant party securely installs the public key of the trusted CA and uses it to verify the signature of each user's public key. Only upon a successful verification of the signature does a reliant party initiate a communications channel. This simple method of certification thwarts an attacker who does not have a public key signed by the same CA as that of the two communicating parties, but fails to do so when the attacker is also in possession of a key signed by the same CA.

To provide reliable assurance, a comprehensive public key certification process requires more security elements than simply a signed encryption key. These elements are embedded in the data construct to be certified. For the Internet, this construct is an X.509 certificate, and the secure infrastructure that provides it is the public key infrastructure for X.509 (PKIX); the repository in which certificates are kept is based on the standard Lightweight Directory Access Protocol (LDAP) service.

Now let us focus on the details of this infrastructure throughout the remainder of this chapter.

The Internet Public Key Infrastructure

The issuing CA name is a hierarchical X.500 name — for example, CN = SecureWay CA, OU = SecureWay, O = IBM, C = US — that uniquely identifies the certification authority within the naming space. The issuing name is common to all certificates issued by the same CA. Similarly, the subject name is a hierarchical X.500 name, such as CN = Elyes, OU = SecureWay, O = IBM, C = US, that uniquely identifies the subject of the certificate within the naming space.

Note: The DN representation is based on RFC 148517 and represents distinguished names in a user-oriented manner. As a good security practice, it is generally mandated that certificate holders within a particular enterprise be assigned distinct X.500 names.

It is the role of the CA to ensure that a particular subject name is not issued multiple certificates that differ only in the public key value. Multiple certificates can be issued for functionally meaningful reasons (one key for signing documents and another for enciphering data). In the absence of functionally differentiating factors, such as those defined by Certificate Policy 18 rules, a comprehensive PKIX should require that an old certificate for a subject be revoked before issuing a new one. The key to enforcing the uniqueness rule is the requirement that the CA maintain a repository of all the certificates it issues during its entire time of operation. The CA repository, or Issued Certificates List (ICL), along with a registration procedure enforced by the enterprise PKI, provides control over granting certificates.

Note: A reliable PKIX is one in which certificates are always issued in a controllable way, analogous to the practice of creating users in a legacy authentication registry.

The validity period of a certificate is the time interval during which the certificate maintains its validity of use, provided it has not been explicitly revoked. It is defined by beginning and end dates. Time is represented according to an international standard and is computed with respect to Greenwich Mean Time (GMT), ensuring independence from the physical location of applications using PKIX.

The subject public key field contains the bit string representing the public key material that is being certified. The extensions field represents an interesting aspect of the extendibility of an X.509 certificate. It may contain zero or more extensions, each of which adds specific information about the certificate, such as the intended usage of the underlying public key. A number of these extensions have been defined by the IETF body. Private extensions can also be exploited within a particular enterprise.

Finally, the signature value field contains the CA digital signature computed over the Distinguished Encoding Rules (DERs) of the X.509 data type as represented by Abstract Syntax Notation One (ASN.1), an International Telecommunication Union (ITU) standard syntax for data transfer.

Note: The CA signature certifies the entire content of a certificate and not just the public key portion of it.

One other fundamental element that builds trust in an enterprise PKIX is the ability to certify a public key for an end-user entity without requiring that the corresponding private key be communicated online or offline to the certification authority or any other entity. In most practical cases, the public and private key-pair is generated at the end-user side of the infrastructure, with the private key remaining securely stored in the user's local environment. The underlying storage mechanism can be chosen appropriately, based upon the exploiting applications. An example of such a mechanism would be a smart card token.

The protocol underlying certification management allows for proof of possession, known as POP, of the private key to be communicated through secure cryptographic means, such as a signature, and verified by the serving CA. An enterprise-level PKIX should support the proof of private key possession in ways appropriate to the type of key usage specified by the requesting entity. For example, when the key to be certified is intended for enciphering data, the CA should use the public key to encrypt a specific data item and challenge the entity to decrypt it using the private key.

The Infrastructure Topology

As shown in Exhibit 7, a PKIX has three main components: the end entity (EE) representing the user side, the registration authority (RA) in the middle, and finally the certifying authority (CA).[1] The RA, an optional but integral component of the CA, represents an intermediary point of trust through which an EE request is channeled to the CA. It performs a number of functions, most notably the registration of candidate certificate requesters and their authentication, in a secure fashion. The RA may also perform

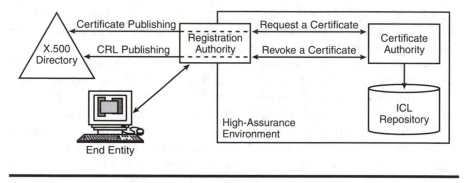

Exhibit 7   The Main PKIX Participating Components

some processing on the EE request, such as the verification of the POP calculated using the EE private key, or the validation of certain requested certificate extensions in accordance with a policy implemented by the enterprise. The RA also represents the access point for the infrastructure's administrator to perform interactive tasks, such as registration and approval or denial of requests.

Additionally, a directory service such as LDAP is generally made available to the infrastructure for the publication of certificates and CRLs. In an enterprise PKIX, the CA interactions should be limited to the RA, the one entity with which it has established trust. The directory service should connect to the RA that performs certificate and CRL publication in response to CA notifications. Communications between the EE, RA, and CA are driven by the standard Certificate Management Protocol (CMP), which is in turn based on the syntax defined by the Certificate Request Message Format (CRMF).

Note: Although not widely adopted, certificate management over CMS (CMC) is also a proposed IETF draft standard for a certificate life-cycle management protocol. Cryptographic Message Syntax (CMS) is the IETF standard for a cryptographic enveloping technique for protecting messages.

CMP is a secure protocol that carries a data protection field of its own and thus does not rely on an underlying secure transport for the security of its messages. It consists of a relatively large set of message types and is independent of the transport layer of the underlying communications system. Common implementations have been written mainly over direct Transmission Control Protocol (TCP), with some others over the Hypertext Transfer Protocol (HTTP). Additionally, the industry *de facto* standards commonly known as Public Key Cryptographic Standards, or PKCS #10

Exhibit 8   Core Content of an X.509 CRL

```
version number:                      v2
signature algorithm:                 xxxxxxx
issuer name:                         xxxxxxxxxx
this update:                         xxxx
next update:                         xxxx
revoked certificates {
    certificate serial number:       xxxxxx
    revocation date:                 xxxxx

    ...
}

extensions:                          xxxxxxxxxx
signature algorithm:                 xxxxxxx
signature value:                     xxxxxxxxxx
```

and PKCS #7, are also widely adopted messaging formats for certificate enrollment. CMP has been widely implemented by PKIX vendors, including IBM and Lotus, and has lately been the subject of interoperation testing.

Certificate Revocation

A certificate may cease to be valid for two explicit reasons: first, when the current date is not within the validity period stated in the certificate (the certificate has expired or has not yet entered use); and second, when the certificate subject is no longer entitled to the certificate. In the latter case, the certificate is revoked by the issuing CA. The breakup of the binding represented in a certificate is announced by a certification authority, through a CRL. The CA periodically issues and signs CRLs, updating them with recently revoked certificates. A typical X.509 CRL contains the data illustrated in Exhibit 8.[1]

A CRL shares five data types with a certificate: a version number, a signature algorithm identifier, the issuing CA name, zero or more extensions, and a signature value. The signature is computed over the flattened DER encoding of the CRL content. Each revoked certificate is identified by its serial number. Because certificate serial numbers are unique with respect to the issuing CA, a reliable PKIX revokes certificates through the same CA entity that issued them. The first timestamp encountered in a CRL indicates its date of issuance; the second one is the date for the next CRL update. The most notable component of the extensions field is the issuing distribution point name, a standard extension that indicates the location where the CRL is to be published.

Next, let us discuss CRL distribution points in further detail.

CRL Distribution Points

Reliable applications that use X.509 certificates are required to actively verify the validity of a certificate at the time of its use, including whether or not the certificate has been explicitly revoked. Conceptually, this verification step is a simple one; it consists of determining whether or not the certificate has become a member of any applicable CRL. Such a simple yet time-sensitive task requires a number of cooperating elements. First, where is the applicable CRL? With the globalization of today's Internet computing, interacting applications are not necessarily tightly coupled within an enterprise-specific environment.

The CRL distribution points extension is an X.509 certificate extension that indicates the location of the revocation information. Distribution points, therefore, represent a bridge between the certificate and its controlling CRL. CRL distribution points also address the issue of scale that might be introduced in an enterprise that could revoke large numbers of certificates. By distributing CRLs across multiple locations, applications are able to offload smaller portions of CRLs while performing validation. The format of a CRL distribution point name is generalized enough to allow a variety of CRL hosting services, for example, an X.500 directory name, a remote uniform resource identifier (URI) such as an LDAP uniform resource locator (URL), or some other server based on the Internet HTTP.

CRL distribution points also allow redundant CRL locations, so that certificate validation is not affected by a CRL hosting server that becomes unavailable. CRLs can be stored in an LDAP server as attributes of the issuing CA. Exhibit 9 illustrates three CRLs located at three distribution points in the form of a directory name: CN = CRL DP0, OU = SecureWay, O = IBM, C = US, CN = CRL DP1, OU = SecureWay, O = IBM, C = US, and CN = CRL DP2, OU = SecureWay, O = IBM, C = US.[1]

All CRLs located at these points are issued by a CA with name CN = SecureWay CA, OU = SecureWay, O = IBM, C = US. In this example, the CRLs are physically stored at their respective directory names as indicated by the distribution points under the attribute certificateRevocationList, defined by the standard PKIX LDAP schema.

Cross-Domain Certification

The proliferation of public key infrastructures ultimately leads to their extension across the boundaries of certification domains. Such domains

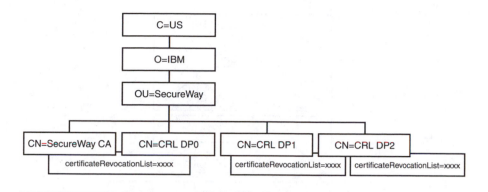

Exhibit 9   An Example of Three CRLs Stored at Distribution Points, All of Which Are in the Form of a Directory Name

may consist of multiple enterprises, or departments within a single enterprise, or multiple independent enterprises. Bridging multiple domains can be driven by the need to maintain the benefits of PKI-based security in applications that support interactions across enterprises. The basic issue is to join independently deployed public key infrastructures with minimal disruption and the greatest transparency possible, allowing each certification authority to remain the sole authority for its own domain of operations.

PKIX provides two methods for achieving cross-domain certification. The first is through hierarchical certification authorities; the second is through a peer-to-peer relationship in which a CA from one domain is cross certified with a CA of another domain. Exhibit 10 (A) illustrates a hierarchical relationship between two domains served by CA1 and CA2.[1] The hierarchy implies that CA1 and CA2 are not in possession of self-signed certificates (one in which the issuer and the subject names are the same). Instead, both of these certificates are issued by the root CA bridging the two domains.

Note: The depth of a hierarchy is not limited to a single level as shown in Exhibit 10.

Validating a user certificate in the domain served by CA1 or CA2 is a recursive process that applies to the chain of certificates extending from the root CA to the user. Additionally, a certificate issued within the domain of CA1 can be validated by an application running within the domain of CA2 by similarly finding a validation path starting at the high-assurance root CA.

Cross certification is a peer-to-peer joining of two disparate infrastructures. As illustrated in Exhibit 10 (B), CA1 issues a cross certificate for CA2 to indicate that user certificates issued by CA2 for its population are

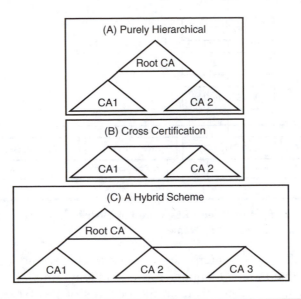

Exhibit 10   Some Scenarios of Cross-Domain Relationships: (A) Purely Hierarchical, (B) Cross Certification, and (C) A Hybrid Scheme

now trusted for use within the domain served by CA1, provided of course that they pass the standard test of validity. A cross certificate is simply an X.509 CA certificate that is signed by another authority. A reliant party in the domain of CA1 (such as an application server) that receives a service request with a certificate attached to it from a client in the domain of CA2 will perform the following steps:[1]

1. Determine that CA2, the issuer of the requester's certificate, is cross certified by CA1. This could be done by looking up the crossCertificatePair attribute in the CA2 entry of the requester's directory server.
2. Validate the requester's certificate using the public key of CA2.
3. Validate the cross certificate using the public key of CA1 and hence establish trust in the client certificate.

Similarly, CA2 can also cross certify CA1, and thus certificates issued by both certification authorities can be interchangeably consumed by applications across the two domains. Essentially, the two domains then become fully bridged.

Note: Each of the certification authorities remains the root CA for its own domain and each is still known through its self-signed certificate.

In the hierarchical case, each of the subordinate certificate authorities maintains a certificate issued by a higher CA. This certificate validation path spans an entire branch of the tree, starting from the root down to the leaf user entity. This process is applied each time a certificate is used. In the cross-certification scenario, however, validating a certificate from an application running in the same domain does not require use of any CA cross certificates.

The hierarchical scheme establishes the cross-domain trust via a single third-party certification authority. A higher assurance in the infrastructure can, therefore, be maintained by strongly securing one entity, the root certificate authority. Prior knowledge of the legitimate validation path by an application leads to the detection of any compromise of a subordinate authority. In the cross-certification case, the same high level of assurance is required in all of the certificate authorities in order to avoid a compromise. Leaving any of the certification authorities exposed may lead to the compromise in using certificates across domains.

Note: A hybrid method that combines hierarchies and horizontal cross certification can also be used to join disparate infrastructures. Exhibit 10 (C) illustrates a hybrid cross-domain topology that includes four certification authorities in which CA1 and CA2 are subordinate to a common root, while CA2 and CA3 participate in a horizontal cross-certification relationship. CA hierarchies are generally recommended when joining multiple domains that require a high level of assurance.

Note: The trust relationship in the case of horizontal cross certification is not a transitive one (CA1 cross certifying CA2 and CA2), in turn, cross certifying CA3 does not imply that CA1 has cross certified CA3. Certification here is not implied; it must be explicitly designated. In the hierarchical case, however, the relationship is transitive upwards.

Certificate Validation

While a certificate explicitly carries a time period that can be checked for validity with respect to the time of use, it can also become completely invalid for other reasons. A certificate may be revoked by its CA through a CRL issuance. A certificate may also be compromised by replacing it with a masquerading certificate that is issued by the same or a different authority. Certificate validation, therefore, should precede every use of the public key it certifies. Such a procedure consists of a number of validity checks, some of which are summarized here.

Validate the Trust Chain

Determine a trust path from the root CA to the end entity. The path can span a hybrid scheme in which both horizontal and hierarchical cross-domain certification can be in use. In a purely hierarchical trust topology, the highly assured public key of the root CA is first used to verify the integrity and authenticity of the immediate subordinate CA certificate. This is used to extract the certified public key of the immediate subordinate CA, which now inherits the highly assured trust property. The process is then recursively applied down the tree until the end entity certificate is reached. In the horizontal cross-certificate case, the certificate of the cross-certified CA is verified using the assured key of the certifying peer CA. The verified CA key is then extracted and used to verify the integrity of possibly a subordinate CA certificate or the underlying end entity certificate.

Determine the Certificate Revocation Status

Compute a Boolean decision on the membership of the underlying certificate within an appropriate CRL. The certificate here is uniquely defined through its serial number relative to the issuing certificate authority. The verification process should check for these two elements in the set of revoked certificates represented by the CRL. Due to the reliance of this computation on the most up-to-date CRLs, which are generally stored at a central network location such as an LDAP repository, this task is gradually shifting to a specialized server. This server is known as the Online Certificate Status Protocol (OCSP) responder, which specializes in computing the Boolean decision of a particular certificate membership in the published CRLs.

Determine the Certificate Usage

Validate the use of the certificate against any applicable policy. An example would be to compare the cryptographic function for which the public key is about to be used, against the key usage extension found in the certificate.

Managing the Private Key

While a public key infrastructure provides a reliable solution to the key distribution problem, a PKI user remains in control of his or her private key material. A breach in the private key eventually leads to the total compromise in security of any communication channel that is governed by the certificate associated with the private key. The process of managing

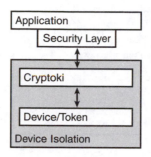

Exhibit 11   Isolating the Manipulation of a Private Key

the private key generally centers around the method by which the key material is stored in some encrypted form. Perhaps the simplest of such methods is the wrapping provided by the PKCS #8 *de facto* standard, where the private key is encrypted using a master key derived from a user password, which is never maintained in any stored form. A more thorough solution that is similar in concept is provided by the PKCS #12 standard, which has become widely used as an offline means of transporting the PKI credentials of a user, including certificates and private keys. The wrapping of private keys that is employed here can also be based on secret key encryption where the encryption key is derived from a password.

One method that brings a higher level of assurance and reliability to PKI-based applications is embodied in the *de facto* standards of PKCS #11 and PKCS #15 for managing and manipulating private keys. The main concept adopted is the isolation of any manipulation of the private key by a security layer of an application to within the confines of a single component (usually in the form of a shared dynamic library). The component provides a set of cryptographic operations and interacts directly with a storage medium called a credentials token, widely implemented as a hardware device. Software implementations of the token are also available.

Existing Internet browsers are good examples of applications that provide software implementations of the PKCS #11 tokens. As illustrated in Exhibit 11, the PKCS #11 library, commonly known as cryptoki (short for cryptographic token interface), provides for a common logical view of the cryptographic token,[1] When invoked by a security layer of an application, through a standard set of interfaces, the PKCS #11 library interacts with the device driver of the token for cryptographic services based upon the user's public and private keys. PKCS #11 seeks not only to maintain secure storage of a private key through a secret personal identification number (PIN) access, but equally important, it also provides

```
version number:        v1, v2
holder:                xxxxxxxxx
issuer:                xxxxxxxxx
signature algorithm:   xxxxxxx
serial number:         xxxxxxxx
validity period:       xxxxxxx
authz attributes:      xxxxxxxxxxxxxx
extensions:            xxxxxxxxxxxx
signature algorithm:   xxxxxxx
signature value:       xxxxxxxxxx
```

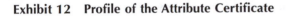

X.509 PKC

X.509 AC

Exhibit 12   Profile of the Attribute Certificate

a portable security layer that isolates users from the details of the hardware tokens in which public key credentials reside.

Attribute Certificates: The Next Evolution of PKIX

A public key certificate (PKC) serves as the basis for the authentication of the subject it identifies. Provided a user's certificate is validated with respect to a trusted root authority, a simple method, such as a verifiable digital signature, leads to proof of possessing the underlying identity, otherwise known as authentication. Secure identification is the key precondition for granting access to controllable resources. A resource manager will attempt to enforce an access control policy only after a successful authentication.

The X.509 attribute certificate (AC), of which an X.509 certificate is a fundamental part, seeks to certify or securely bind a set of authorization capabilities to a subject, in the same way that an X.509 PKC binds a public key to its subject. The distinction between these two types of certificates is dictated by the dynamic nature of authorization roles that a particular entity can assume over time, while possessing the same public key certificate. Exhibit 12 shows how a trust path is established in an AC by tracing back the holder to the associated X.509 PKC.[1]

Note: The authority issuing an AC uses the public key certified by its PKC in order to sign it. Thus, the validation path of an AC ultimately requires the presence of the holder's PKC and the PKC of the issuer of the AC, as well as a valid trust chain to the root signing authority for each of the public key certificates. The set of authorization privileges that an AC certifies are defined by an ASN.1 Attribute type, which is a sequence of (key, value) pairs identifying access right types and their associated values. For example, a clearance is identified through an ASN.1 object identifier {of 2 5 1 5 5 5}, whereas its value may carry a security labeling based on a multilevel security policy.

Finally, public key cryptography is rapidly transforming the technical aspects surrounding systems and network security. The concept is based on mathematical foundations and is computationally reliable, simple, and elegant. The ramifications are far-reaching. The Internet public key infrastructure for X.509 certificates is an attempt to remedy the lack of assurance in the public key. The underlying PKIX technologies providing the solution are robust and promising. Internet-based E-business applications are quickly adopting PKIX as the cornerstone of their security solutions. While PKIX attribute certificates for authorization credentials are evolving, enterprises will largely rely on mappings between X.509 public key certificates and local identities, so that legacy access control systems can remain in effect.

RECOMMENDATIONS

PKI can help anywhere strong authentication is needed — in business-to-business transactions, in bank exchanges, and in communications involving human resources data. These types of transactions are usually encrypted using digital keys, and PKI comprises the policies and equipment to manage those keys.

In recent history, PKI has taken its place alongside firewalls and VPNs as a security must-have for a growing number of enterprise networks. However, PKI design remains something of a black art, forcing network professionals to wade through a thicket of acronyms and algorithms. It is little wonder many enterprises opt to outsource the entire process. Others, mistrustful of delegating too much security, muddle through rolling out their own.

For network managers opting to build their own PKI, the biggest risk is compromised certificates resulting from network, physical, or personnel security that is not up to a specification. Outsourcers are usually strong in these areas, but any enterprise going with a commercial certificate authority provider must see to it that the provider keeps the enterprise's data private.

Deciding whether to build or buy is probably the most important step in any PKI implementation. Neither route is easy, and both pose serious security risks if poorly implemented.

Designing Issues

For build and buy decisions, network executives will need to understand the various PKI components, the elements of PKI design, and the ways in which PKI interacts with existing applications and network infrastructure. By mixing and matching the basic building blocks, network designers can put together the PKI for a department, an enterprise, many enterprises, or many individuals. The design phase is where PKI gets tricky.

In the most basic case, all users request certificates from one certificate authority. This design is simple but also unrealistic in most enterprise settings because it may not scale to encompass multiple offices or large numbers of users.

A more common type of PKI design involves a hierarchy of certificate authorities with a "root" certificate authority at the top of a tree. A hierarchical design is relatively simple; but on the downside, it does not provide for direct any-to-any connectivity among certificate authorities.

Using this model, any PKI-enabled application must first verify the authenticity of a certificate before using it. This involves the certificate application walking the tree of certificate authorities and thereby establishing a so-called certification path. In a hierarchical design like this, all certification paths must begin at the root certificate authority as a design restriction — in this case, the root certificate authority is the one vouching for all the certificate authorities below it. The deeper the hierarchy, the more complex the certification paths become.

An alternate design employs a mesh topology, with all or most certificate authorities directly connected to each other. Here, certification paths may begin at any point. Accordingly, the certification paths are more varied than in the hierarchical model, but they may actually be simpler for the certificate user. The benefits of a shorter certification path are that authentication may happen more quickly and management traffic is reduced.

Unfortunately, most certificates do not offer clues as to whether they belong in a hierarchy or mesh, or at which point along the certification path they should begin to make a query to the originating certificate authority. For security, it probably will not be apparent to end users exactly who is doing the certifying. For performance, longer look-up paths take more time to traverse. Some implementations build a "certificate cache" in PKI-enabled applications (a store of all previously used certificate paths) to speed future attempts at certificate path construction.

Note: These are design and not product issues. Any commercial certificate authority product will work in either design.

The PKI market includes software and equipment vendors and outsourced service bureaus. Software and equipment vendors offer tools such as certificate authorities, smart cards, and encryption algorithms. Major vendors in this area include Baltimore Technologies, Entrust, RSA Security, and VeriSign. Service bureaus such as Electronic Data Systems, IBM, the Big 5 consulting firms, and numerous ISPs offer the same tools as equipment vendors, along with value-adds such as integration.

From the Buy Side

Service bureaus will integrate PKI into just about anything — be it an enterprise application, a router, a set of VPN gateways, or a wireless infrastructure. Service bureaus also manage the certificate authority and handle the issues surrounding certificate management, such as obtaining a certificate (called "enrollment" in PKI-speak) and keeping certificate revocation lists current. Outsourcing also moves the responsibility for securing the certificate authority away from the enterprise.

Many enterprises find it more convenient to hand over these tasks than to manage their own certificate authorities. It remains difficult to do enrollment and revocation, partially because the protocols are difficult and partly because they are not implemented in a neat, tidy way.

Another plus for service bureaus is they set up and manage public certificate authorities, an important consideration for E-commerce applications. Public certificate authorities give customers a ready means of mutual authentication without the need to expose an enterprise's internal network.

One last consideration in favor of service bureaus is that PKI standards are still a moving target. Going with a service bureau could relieve an enterprise of having to keep current with the alphabet soup of PKI protocols and the politics that surround them.

Consider the two competing proposals for "certificate life-cycle" issues — enrollment, revocation, and expiration. Entrust and Baltimore Technologies back a specification called certificate management protocol, while VeriSign, Cisco, and Microsoft support a competing specification called certificate management protocol using cryptographic message syntax. The two protocols differ in the extensions and cryptography standards they support. Enterprises without an abiding interest in these topics may find it more worthwhile to pay someone else to sort it out.

The biggest downside for buying a managed PKI service is the farming out of trust. Some enterprises will not outsource any security function because they are not comfortable delegating security to outsiders.

Builder's Choice

With the preceding in mind, it does not mean that outsourcing is automatically the best choice. Arguments for rolling out your own PKI include project scope and a desire to control all aspects of key management.

A project involving one certificate authority, a small set of users, and a simple security policy may not justify bringing in a service bureau. For more complex situations, the buy/build decision may be a question of deciding whose time is more valuable — the internal staff or the outsourcer.

Internal certificate authorities are recommended here, regardless of project size.

People always say internal certificate authorities are difficult to do, but they are really not any more difficult than outsourcing. When you look at all the procedures you end up going through with service bureaus, it ends up about the same.

The notion that outsourcing enables cross certification of multiple enterprises' certificate authorities is rejected here. Cross certification is a trust leakage mechanism.

While building one's own PKI has its advantages, the learning curve is definitely steeper. Network executives will need to learn PKI protocols and design issues that can make even the most complex lower-layer network design look like child's play.

Certified, But Safe?

Regardless of which way you go with the buy/build decision, there are serious issues of trust management that must be addressed in any PKI design. These issues include the security of the certificates and certificate authorities; the authority of the certificate authority; the uniqueness of certificates; and the degree to which integration of other systems into PKI might compromise the system.

Certificates are assumed to be secure because they are issued by an authority and signed with a user's private key. However, the vast majority of users store certificates on conventional computers or smart cards, both of which are prone to attack. As in any system design, security is only as strong as the weakest component. If the storage medium is vulnerable to viruses, other malicious code, or even physical attacks, the certificate is also vulnerable.

In some states, the holder of a key certified by an approved certificate authority is responsible for whatever that key does. The problem with this is that it does not matter who was at the keyboard or what virus may have done the signing.

PKI vendors generally consider non-repudiation (the inability of a certificate holder to deny that a transaction took place) to be a benefit. However, non-repudiation is not a valid practice in all cases. For example, with regard to credit cards, users can repudiate unauthorized charges. There is not yet a similar mechanism in most PKI designs.

Of course, securing the certificate authority is also a major issue in the case of buying or building. A compromise of the certificate authority's private key would be a disaster in security terms because it means the attacker could issue bogus certificates.

However, attackers can compromise the certificate authority's authority even without compromising the certificate authority. Recently, in an alarmingly high-profile case, attackers posing as Microsoft employees successfully extracted bogus certificates from a certificate authority run by VeriSign. Microsoft was forced to issue a security bulletin stating that the vulnerability could affect "all customers using Microsoft products." VeriSign determined the breach occurred because humans did insufficient checking on the validity of the attacker's request.

Although the bogus certificates apparently were never used, they could have been used for anything — and that raises the issue of certificate legitimacy. For example, your assistant could pose as you and tell your bank to "withdraw all my money" or tell your doctor to "send all my medical records to XYZ address."

Microsoft asks users to decide whether they trust Microsoft content when they download bug fixes. Few users actually inspect the digital signature to verify its content, making it just as easy to accept forged certificates as legitimate certificates.

Furthermore, looking at an even more pervasive example — the Secure Sockets Layer encryption that is used to secure Web transactions — there are Web pages whose certificate is for the Web hosting enterprise, not for the enterprise whose logo appears on the pages. In such situations, it is not clear with whom the end user is having a "secure" conversation. Worse, most end users cannot or will not be bothered to find out.

Yet another generic problem with certificates is that they may not be unique. For example, let us look at a certificate for someone named Russ Weidle. Even if a user knows only one person named Russ Weidle, the certificate authority may know dozens. The X.509 format allows the use of many other attributes besides the "Common Name" for identifying a certificate holder, but this practice assumes the certificate user also knows to use those other means when looking for the correct Russ Weidle.

A final issue is that of integrating PKI with existing applications, especially authentication schemes. Consider single sign-on (SSO) authentication mechanisms. It is possible to integrate a certificate-issuing smart card into an SSO system, so that a user only has to authenticate once a day to reach all the computing resources in the enterprise.

Caution: While it sounds convenient, it also defeats the PKI's intent of validating every transaction at the time of the transaction. For an office clerk, it may not be a big deal if someone "borrows" the computer while he or she is at lunch. In the boiler room of a brokerage-trading floor, the stakes could be different.

Finally, properly implemented, PKI can deliver a powerful means of making any transaction so secure it is virtually immune to attack. It can also pose some of the thorniest security challenges network designers have ever faced. Getting it done right is difficult and requires taking the time to understand and implement the various pieces of the PKI in a truly secure way.

NOTES

1. Benantar, M., "The Internet public key infrastructure," *IBM Systems Journal,* 40(3), 2001, © 2001, International Business Machines Corporation, Corporate Offices, International Business Machines Corporation, New Orchard Road, Armonk, NY 10504, 2003.

V

APPENDICES

Appendix A

CONTRIBUTORS OF PKI SOFTWARE SOLUTIONS

The market for PKI solutions remains in a state of anticipation; and as vendors await the explosion of demand that has been expected for several years now, they are jockeying for position with a variety of acquisitions and partnerships. The three leading contributors or vendors of PKI software solutions are VeriSign, Entrust, and Baltimore Technologies. They provide several types of PKI solutions, including outsourced solutions in which the vendor manages the infrastructure and issues the certificates, in-house solutions in which the customer issues the certificates, and merchant certificates used mainly for business-to-consumer (B2C) transactions. While the three leading vendors have historically emphasized different types of solutions, they have started to converge in terms of their offerings. In addition, they have been busy rectifying perceived weaknesses, expanding geographically, and experimenting with new types of integration. While revenues for all three are still low (less than $400 million), they are enjoying rapid growth. Meanwhile, several other vendors also want to play in this space, and some of them are quite competitive. Let us first take a look at the leading three.

ENTRUST

Based in Canada, Entrust (http://www.entrust.com/) has added many features and enhancements to its basic PKI product, making it very useful for supporting a variety of needs. Entrust has traditionally emphasized in-house solutions, but it recently forged a partnership with First Data Corporation to provide a co-branded outsourced solution. It also acquired

0-8493-0822-4/04/$0.00+$1.50
© 2004 by CRC Press LLC

enCommerce, which helped Entrust marry its authentication capabilities with the authorization capabilities that allow PKI to realize its potential. Entrust is also challenging VeriSign in the area of direct certificate issuance, having sold 50,000 certificates in the second quarter of 2003, which is quite a bit less than VeriSign's total of 104,000, but nevertheless a huge leap from the previous year. A key strength of Entrust's solution has been its well-developed client-side software, including software that provides protection for the private key. To some extent, the heavy load on the client has also been a liability, making it less suitable for customers that want to include extranet partners in their PKIs. But Entrust has recently addressed this issue by offering TruePass, a server-based option that only requires a small Java applet on the client.

BALTIMORE TECHNOLOGIES

Based in Ireland, Baltimore Technologies (http://www.baltimore.ie/) has a strong presence in international markets, especially Europe and Australia. Like Entrust, Baltimore has emphasized in-house PKI solutions. Recently, however, it acquired the fourth largest PKI vendor, GTE CyberTrust, to help the company provide outsourced solutions and to increase its strength in the United States and Japanese markets. More recently, Baltimore has made important moves in other directions as well. The company announced a partnership with Securant to improve the authorization link to applications. Then it acquired Content Technologies, placing a bold bet that content filtering and PKI capabilities are a natural fit. Baltimore's solution does not have all of the business-oriented features of Entrust, but it is well-suited for customers that need to share credentials across corporate boundaries. Baltimore has a toolkit that allows customers to build protection for private keys.

VERISIGN

Based in California, VeriSign (https://www.verisign.com/) has traditionally emphasized outsourced solutions but has always had in-house solutions as well. A weakness of VeriSign's corporate PKI solution is that it relies on the certificate control features built into browsers to protect the private key. In the area of merchant certificates, it has had almost a monopoly, receiving about a third of its revenue from these sales. That monopoly was strengthened by the acquisition of its main challenger, Thawte Certificates, but other vendors are also moving into this area. VeriSign hopes to stay one step ahead by offering new merchants a one-stop shop for enabling Web commerce, and it acquired Network Solutions to provide domain-name registration.

OTHER VENDORS

Although the top three vendors dominate the market, several other vendors listed next are attempting to push into the market as well.

RSA Security

RSA Security is a well-known name in security, and it is now leveraging its expertise and reputation to offer a full-fledged PKI in its Keon line of products. As a relative latecomer, it must challenge the more established players in the market, and PKI is not its main business (less than a quarter of its total revenues). However, the fact that it has developed its product in a more mature standards environment also means that it has achieved greater interoperability with other PKI solutions.

Xcert

Xcert has been selling PKI solutions for several years now; and like RSA Security, it has the potential to become a serious challenger to the big three. It also emphasizes interoperability with other PKI solutions and related applications, and frequently gets good marks from reviewers.

Certicom

For several years now, Certicom has focused on wireless PKI solutions based on elliptic curve cryptography, a technology designed for low-power devices. With its acquisition of Trustpoint, the company has provided general PKI solutions, but initiatives like MobileTrust managed certificate service continue to leverage its strength in wireless.

Microsoft

Windows XP comes with a complete, although basic, PKI solution. It is an inexpensive alternative, but it lacks the full set of features offered by other vendors. Also, it is most appropriate for a homogenous Windows environment, offering less streamlined integration with other applications and platforms. Entrust and Microsoft have a close working relationship, although it may be some time before Entrust's PKI integrates fully with Windows XP.

Netscape, Digital Signature Trust, and Interclear

Like the PKI in Windows XP, Netscape's solution makes it more difficult to build the type of complete solution that a PKI vendor can offer.

U.S.-based Digital Signature Trust provides in-house solutions and is now selling merchant certificates. Interclear, a newcomer based in the United Kingdom, is differentiating itself from the big three by offering an outsourced solution in which the customer still retains control of the policies, responsibilities, and liabilities that govern the operation of the PKI.

Appendix B

PKI PRODUCTS: IMPLEMENTATIONS, TOOLKITS, AND VENDORS

1. SECUDE (http://www.secude.de/)
2. NCSA httpd (http://hoohoo.ncsa.uiuc.edu/docs/PEMPGP.html): Using PGP/PEM encryption
3. SESAME (https://www.cosic.esat.kuleuven.ac.be/sesame/): Cryptographic applications (secure site)
4. Baltimore Technologies: UniCERT (http://www.baltimore.com/unicert/index.asp) Certification Authority System
5. Cryptlib (http://www.cs.auckland.ac.nz/~pgut001/cryptlib/): freely available Encryption Toolkit (Peter Gutmann)
6. Apache-SSL (http://www.apache-ssl.org/): Secure Webserver (Ben Laurie)
7. Java Security Toolkit (TU Graz): (http://jce.iaik.tugraz.at/)
8. Tools from Diversinet Corp. (http://www.dvnet.com/)
9. Jonah PKIX (http://web.mit.edu/pfl//): a freeware PKIX (see below) reference implementation (IBM)
10. Jonah PKIX (http://www.foobar.com/jonah/): same as above but internationally available! (note: site seems to be dead!)
11. J/CA Certification Toolkit (Phaos Corp.): (http://www.phaos.com/home.html)
12. Entrust Technologies (http://www.entrust.com/products/index.htm)
13. Entegrity Solutions Corp. (http://www.entegrity.com/)
14. Structured Arts Computing Corp. (http://www.structuredarts.com/)
15. The OpenCA Project (http://www.openca.org/)

0-8493-0822-4/04/$0.00+$1.50
© 2004 by CRC Press LLC

16. PyCA (http://www.pyca.de/): Software for running a certificate authority
17. JCSI (http://www.wedgetail.com/jcsi/): DSTC's Java Crypto and Security Implementation
18. SmartTrust (http://www.smarttrust.com/)
19. Radicchio (http://www.radicchio.org/)
20. Alphaworks/IBM: KeyMan (http://www.alphaworks.ibm.com/tech/keyman/) PKI client side management tool
21. R&L GmbH: safeX (http://www.rl-pl.de/en/main_tech_safex.html)
22. M2Crypto (http://mars.post1.com/home/ngps/m2/) Cryptography, SSL and S/MIMEv2 for Python
23. NSS + PSM (http://www.mozilla.org/projects/security/pki/src/download.html) Open Source PKI projects on Mozilla
24. Safelayer Secure Communications S. A. (http://www.safelayer.com/)
25. Conclusive Logic, Inc. (http://www.conclusive.com/home.jsp)
26. Kyberpass Corporation (http://www.kyberpass.com/)
27. PHAOS Technology (http://www.kyberpass.com/)
28. Capslock (http://www.capslock.fi/)
29. Valimo Wireless Oy (http://www.valimo.com/)
30. Awanim (http://www.awanim.com/)
31. CrypTool (http://www.cryptool.de/)
32. IDX-PKI (http://idx-pki.idealx.org/)
33. Biodata Systems GmbH (http://www.biodata-systems.info/index_e.html)
34. Certicom Corp. (http://www.certicom.com/)
35. ValiCert (http://www.valicert.com/)
36. .pkicomplete (http://www.labcal.com/pkicomplete.php3)
37. Java Certification Path API (http://jcp.org/en/jsr/detail?id=055)
38. trustsuite.de (http://www.trustsuite.de/) (note: German language)
39. timeproof (http://www.timeproof.de/)
40. e-Security, Inc. (http://www.esecurityinc.com/)
41. Hush Communications (https://www.hushmail.com/?PHPSESSID=59ff401ff6b4a28f13efe9da522e9aa5)
42. PKI Group Test (http://www.nss.co.uk/download_form.htm): (The NSS Group)
43. db-order (http://www.cib.db.com/gtf/trs/risk_services/db-order.htm): (note: German language!)
44. upki (http://www.wedgetail.com/usec/eol.html)
45. CertPath APIs (http://java.sun.com/j2se/1.4/): (as part of J2SE 1.4)
46. Project Ägypten (http://www.gnupg.org/aegypten/index.html): Free Software SPHINX Clients
47. EJBCA (http://ejbca.sourceforge.net/): J2EE Certificate Authority

48. AET Europe BV (http://www.aeteurope.com/): (Advanced Encryption Technology)
49. Utimaco Safeware (http://www.utimaco.de/eng/indexmain.html)
50. HYPERTRUST (http://www.hypertrust.com/new/index.html)
51. FlexiProvider (http://www.flexiprovider.de/)
52. RSA Keon (http://www.rsasecurity.com/products/keon/index.html)
53. ArticSoft (http://www.articsoft.com/index.htm)
54. SECUonline AG (http://www.secu-online.com/)
55. Baltimore Keytools (http://www.baltimore.com/keytools/)
56. gpkcs11 (http://gpkcs11.sourceforge.net/)
57. ValiCert ASN.1 Parser (http://www.valicert.com/developers/)
58. CryptoEx (http://www.cryptoex.com/)
59. Tekki (http://www.tekki.se/)
60. pki.ssh.com (http://www.ssh.com/support/testzone/pki.html)
61. C&A (http://www.com-and.com/)
62. nCipher (http://www.ncipher.com/)
63. KSIGN Co. Ltd. (http://www.ksign.co.kr/english/about/about.html): (Korea)
64. Dreamsecurity Co. Ltd. (http://www.dreamsecurity.co.kr/): (Korea)
65. INITECH Co. Ltd. (http://www.initech.com/english/index.html): (Korea)
66. OnePKI (http://www.finallysoftware.com/onenet/onepki.htm)
67. GUIdumpASN (http://www.geminisecurity.com/guidumpasn.html)
68. CPKtec (http://www.cpktec.com/)
69. BCQRE (http://www.bcqre.com/eng/index_en.asp): (note: Korean language!)
70. Glück & Kanja Technology AG (http://redirect.glueckkanja.com/index.htm)
71. CSP: Certificate Service Provider (http://devel.it.su.se/projects/CSP/)
72. e-CryptIt Engine 7.0 (http://www.einhugur.com/Html/eCrypt/index.html)
73. SimpleCA (http://users.skynet.be/ballet/joris/SimpleCA/)
74. Evidian (http://www.evidian.com/)
75. NewPKI (http://www.newpki.org/)
76. Chrysalis-ITS (http://www.chrysalis-its.com/)
77. Fortrus WebPKI (http://www.e-witness.ca/products_fortrus_pki.phtml)
78. Guardeonic (http://www.guardeonic.com/index.php)
79. Evincible (http://www.evincible.com/)
80. Libgcrypt (http://www.gnu.org/directory/security/libgcrypt.html)
81. Ascertia Corp. (http://www.ascertia.com/)
82. Globus Simple CA Package (http://www.globus.org/security/simple-ca.html)

83. Rainbow CryptoSwift (http://www.rainbow.com/cryptoswifthsm/index.html)
84. AEP SureWare Keyper (http://www.aepsystems.com/products_sure_keyper.htm)
85. Oasis Digital Signature Services (http://www.infomosaic.net/DSS.htm)
86. Teraview (http://www.teraview.ca/ereg/ereg_security.html)
87. DigiStamp (http://www.digistamp.com/)
88. Signature Perfect KG (http://www.signature-perfect.com/uk/index_uk.html)
89. XCA (http://www.hohnstaedt.de/xca.html)

Appendix C

COMPREHENSIVE LIST OF CERTIFICATE AUTHORITIES (CAS)

1. DFN — PCA (The PCA for the German Research Network): http://www.dfn-pca.de/
2. IPRA: Internet PCA Registration Authority (MIT): http://bs.mit.edu:8001/ipra.html
3. CREN (U.S. Corporation for Research and Educational Networking) CA: http://www.cren.net/ca/index.html
4. VeriSign, Inc. (http://www.verisign.com/) and its Certificate Practice Statement (CPS): http://www.verisign.com/repository/CPS/
5. Sun (http://wwws.sun.com/software/security/product/ca.html) Certificate Authorities
6. Thawte Certification Division: http://www.thawte.com/
7. Free certificates by Entrust Technologies: http://www.entrust.com/freecerts/
8. Spyrus (http://www.spyrus.com.au/) Certification Authorities (Australia)
9. Net.Registry (IBM): http://www-3.ibm.com/software/
10. SoftForum CA: http://www.softforum.com/english/
11. EuroTrust: (http://www.baltimore.com/securityapplications/index.asp) EU Research contract for TTP/CA infrastructure
12. Government of Canada Public Key Infrastructure: http://www.cio-dpi.gc.ca/pki-icp/gocpki/gocpki_e.asp
13. Internet Publishing Services (IPS): http://www.ips.es/(note: Spanish language)

0-8493-0822-4/04/$0.00+$1.50
© 2004 by CRC Press LLC

14. KeyPOST (Australia Post): http://www.auspost.com.au/ IXP/0%2C%2CCH2183%25257EMO19%2C00.html
15. Columbia CA: http://www.columbia.edu/acis/rad/columbiaca/
16. KAIST network CA (note: Korean language!): http://camis.kaist.ac.kr/kaist-ca/
17. PVT CA (note: Czech language!): http://www.ica.cz/ica0.html
18. Telecom Italia Net CA (note: Italian language!): http://tin.virgilio.it/
19. World Wide Wedlin CA: http://www.wedlin.pp.se/ca/index.html
20. Australian Government Public Key Authority: http://www.noie.gov. au/projects/confidence/Securing/Gatekeeper.htm
21. SSB — SpA CA (note: Italian language!): http://www.ssb.it/SSBOnline.nsf
22. University of Torino (note: Italian language!): http://ca.unito.it/
23. The USERTRUST Network: http://www.usertrust.com/
24. GlobalSign: http://www.globalsign.net/
25. Netrust: http://www.netrust.com.sg/
26. CrossCert (Korean Electronic Certification Authority): http://www.crosscert.com/
27. Equifax Secure: http://www.equifax.com/DigitalCertificates/
28. KMDs certificeringscenter (note: Danish language): http://www.kmd-ca.dk/index.htm
29. Security Domain Pty Limited: http://www.secdom.com.au/
30. Certificates Australia Pty Limited: http://www.certificates-australia. com.au/
31. a-sign (note: German language!): http://www.a-trust.at/
32. WIS@key: http://www.eto.ch/pages/home.htm
33. Tele Danmark certificeringscenter (note: Danish language): http://www1.certifikat.dk/producer/vis_side.pl?id=145&tmpl=23
34. AlphaTrust: http://alphatrust.com/
35. ACES (http://www.gsa.gov/Portal/content/offerings_content. jsp?contentOID=121109&contentType=1004&P=1&S=1): Access Certificates for Electronic Services (U.S. General Services Administration)
36. WildID LLC: http://www.wildid.com/
37. EuroPKI: http://www.europki.org/
38. SURFnet PCA (note: Dutch language): http://pki.surfnet.nl/
39. Väestörekisterikeskus (http://www.fineid.fi/Default.asp?todo= setlang&lang=uk): The Finnish Population Register Centre's CA (note: mostly Finnish language)
40. Powszechne Centrum Certyfikacji (note: Polish language): http://www.certum.pl/en/eng/index.html
41. Acepta.com (Autoridad Certificadora) (note: Spanish language): http://www.acepta.com/

42. E-certify Corporation: http://www.e-certify.com/
43. ACES (http://aces.orc.com/): Access Certificates for Electronic Services
44. ORC's DoD IECA (http://eca.orc.com/): Interim External Certification Authority
45. freecerts.com (http://www.freecerts.com/): free WAP test certificates
46. beTRUSTed: http://betrusted.com/
47. TC TrustCenter: http://www.trustcenter.de/
48. The Bridge-CA: http://www.bridge-ca.org/
49. Certall Finland Oy: https://www.radiolinja.fi/go?section=ratkaisut/palveluntarjoajille/varmennepalvelut&page=varmennepalvelut&lang=fi&side=2
50. DoD PKI (DoD PKI External CAs): http://jitc.fhu.disa.mil/pki/
51. a-trust (note: German language): http://www.a-trust.at/
52. Health eSignature Authority Pty Ltd: http://www.hesa.com.au/
53. IG tOP (http://www.igtop.ch/): Trägerschaft öffentliche PKI Schweiz (note: German language)
54. QuoVadis Limited (http://www.quovadis.bm/): Bermuda Digital CA
55. Certipor (http://www.certipor.com/): Sociedade Portuguesa de Certificados Digitais, S.A.
56. Identrus: http://www.identrus.com/
57. E-Commerce PKI CA: http://www.ecommercepki.com/
58. Certeca (Offshore CA): http://www.certeca.com/
59. Digital Signature Trust Company: http://www.digsigtrust.com/home.html
60. BCA (http://www.anassoc.com/BCA.html): US DoD Bridge Certification Authority Technology Demonstration
61. DecidirCA: http://www.baltimore-decidir.com/
62. MEDePass, Inc.: http://www.medepass.com/
63. euSign S.A.: http://www.eusign.com/
64. TrustCenter berlin.de (note: German language): http://www.Berlin.de/trustcenter/index.html
65. Ezitrust: http://www.ezitrust.com/
66. Keystorm: http://www.wedgetail.com/keystorm/eol.html
67. Geotrust: http://www.geotrust.com/index_default.htm
68. SignGATE (Korea Information CA, Inc.): http://www.signgate.co.kr/eng/index.htm
69. YESSIGN (note: Korean language!): http://www.yessign.or.kr/
70. Korea Certification Authority Central: http://www.rootca.or.kr/eng/index_en.html
71. NCASign (note: Korean language): http://sign.nca.or.kr/index.html
72. The Federal Bridge-CA (NIST): http://csrc.nist.gov/pki/fbca/
73. Belgacom E-Trust: http://www.e-trust.be/en/

74. SafeWeb (note: Portuguese language): http://www.safeweb.com. br/empresa/

75. PKI — Infraestructura de Firma Digital para el Sector Publico — Argentina (note: Spanish language): http://www.pki.gov.ar/

76. OpenCerts: http://www.opencerts.com/

77. SwUPKI (http://www.swupki.su.se/): PKI for Universities and University Colleges in Sweden

78. SIGEN-CA (Slovenia): http://www.sigen-ca.si/eng/index.htm

79. SIGOV-CA (Slovenia): http://www.sigov-ca.gov.si/index-en.htm

80. Gatekeeper (Australia): http://www.noie.gov.au/projects/ confidence/Securing/Gatekeeper.htm

81. WISeCert: http://www.wisecert.com/

82. Portas: http://www.portas.ca/

83. Cacert: http://www.cacert.org/

84. SwisSsign: http://www.swisssign.com/

85. SSLpartner: http://www.sslpartner.com/

86. Scandtrust: http://www.scandtrust.se/

87. InstantSSL (Comodo Group): http://www.instantssl.com/

Appendix D

INFORMATION SECURITY MANAGEMENT ISSUE STANDARDS

Security is a subjective term. It can be defined as all acceptable balance of threats against safeguards for a particular circumstance. It is important to bear in mind that the implementation of specific information security measures should be guided by an overall security policy. The major areas for consideration in developing such a policy are:

- Activities
- Evaluation criteria for information security systems
- Safeguards
- Threats
- Trusted third parties

ACTIVITIES

It is important to appreciate the different activities related to the management and planning of information security; as well as the associated roles and responsibilities within an enterprise. The main security management activities include:

- Determining enterprise information security requirements and developing a security awareness program
- Determining security objectives, strategies, and policies
- Developing plans for incident handling
- Identifying and analyzing security threats to information assets

0-8493-0822-4/04/$0.00+$1.50
© 2004 by CRC Press LLC

- Identifying and planning the implementation of adequate safeguards to the threats
- Managing information security risks based on evaluating criteria to determine the importance of those risks
- Managing trusted third parties (TTPs)
- Planning follow-up programs for monitoring, reviewing, and maintenance of security services

EVALUATION CRITERIA FOR INFORMATION SECURITY SYSTEMS

To provide a method to measure the capability of an (to be) installed system of trust or information security products is the main objective of common security evaluation criteria. This is generally based on specifications for information products and systems, defining the general concepts and principles, presenting a general model, and then expressing functional security and assurance requirements. This produces a protection profile that allows creation of generalized, reusable sets of security requirements against specific products or systems to be evaluated — the security target. Therefore, it is necessary to establish a set of components for expressing the functional security requirements in a standard way in order to create this profile. See the following standards and specifications:

- BS 7799:1999 Part I: Code of practice for information security management; and Part 2: Specification for information security management systems and ISO/IEC 17799:2000 (equivalent to BS 7799:1999 Part 1)
- Common Criteria for Information Technology Security Evaluation, part of the Mutual Recognition Agreement signed in 2000 by a number of nations
- Common Data Security Architecture (CDSA) Version 2.0 from The Open Group
- FIPS PUB 140-1 Security Requirements for Cryptographic Modules from the U.S. Department of Defense
- ISO/IEC 15408:1999 Evaluation Criteria for IT Security. (Part 1: Introduction and general model; Part 2: Security functional requirements; Part 3: Security assurance requirements)
- ISO/IEC CD DTR 15947: Information Technology (Security techniques) IT Intrusion Detection Framework
- ISO/IEC TR 13335 Guidelines for the Management of IT Security. (Part 1: Concepts and models for IT Security; Part 2: Managing and planning IT Security; Part 3: Techniques for the management of IT Security; Part 4: Selection of safeguards)

SAFEGUARDS

To achieve appropriate levels of protection against the threats identified, specific safeguards can be selected. Additionally, to meet the enterprise's needs, enterprisewide minimum security requirements can be implemented. Guidelines containing baseline safeguards are often useful, in order to provide help for the safeguard selection to support the management and maintenance of the site, particularly those connected to any external networks (and specifically the Internet). The guidance typically includes the selection and use of safeguards. Safeguards range from enterprise policy and operational statements to more physical examples such as firewalls and tamper-proof devices.

THREATS

It is necessary to identify the minimum requirements to be addressed in managing information security for strategic risk management. The development and implementation of an IT security plan to address these risks need to be identified, as well as risk management techniques. In security terms, these risks are known as *threats*. The following are some examples of threats:

- *Authentication:* impersonation of the messaging system, false acknowledgment of receipt, and false origination of the message.
- *Confidentiality:* loss of confidentiality (content revealed to third party), loss of anonymity (identities revealed to second or third party), and traffic analysis (deductions from message flow/times).
- *Data integrity:* data incomplete, unreasonable, and inconsistent.
- *Message integrity:* message modification, addition, destruction, replay, preplay, reordering within a sequence, delay, and routing corruption.
- *Non-repudiation:* denial by originator/recipient of origin/content, lack of acknowledgment authentication.
- *Other issues:* no originator clearance (access control), misrouting through insecure channels, denial of communications, channel flooding, and refusal to complete a transaction.

TRUSTED THIRD PARTIES

Trusted third parties (TTPs) typically have a prominent role in a secure system. It is, therefore, essential to ensure that TTPs are respected and trusted. This means that business users, system managers, developers, and operators of TTPs conform to certain responsibilities and that the services they offer are fully understood.

Appendix E

INFORMATION SECURITY TECHNICAL ELEMENTS STANDARDS

The main technical elements of information security are:

- Certificates
- Digital signatures
- Encryption
- Keys
- Hash functions

The preceding technical elements are interrelated.

CERTIFICATES

A certificate is an electronic record that lists a public key, together with the name of the certificate subscriber (its principal function is irrefutably binding a [public] key with a particular holder). It may also confirm that the prospective subscriber signer identified in the certificate holds the corresponding private key.

To verify that the digital signature was created with the corresponding private key, a recipient of the certificate can use the public key listed in the certificate. If such certification is successful, assurance is provided that the holder of the public key created the digital signature named in the certificate, and that the corresponding message had not been modified since it was digitally signed.

0-8493-0822-4/04/$0.00+$1.50
© 2004 by CRC Press LLC

Certificates are generally issued by certification authorities, which in turn are often part of a physical key infrastructure involving certification authorities, registration authorities, and directory service agents. To ensure the authenticity of the certificate with respect to both its contents and its source, the certification authority also digitally signs it. The issuing certification authority's digital signature on the certificate can be verified by using the public key of the certification authority listed in another certificate issued by another certification authority. Then that other certificate can, in turn, be authenticated by the public key listed in yet another certificate, and so on until the entity relying on the digital signature is adequately assured of its veracity.

Known as X.509 v3, the format of certificates that is most widely accepted is that defined by ISO/IEC JTCI SC21. It provides support for a wide range of applications and is generally considered to support a flexible trust model corresponding to user requirements. X.509 v3 is widely adopted as "the" general-purpose public key certificate format. There is also a development in progress of a so-called simple public key certificate.

It is not possible to predict the way that certificate usage will grow. Factors such as user acceptability, pubic policy, and vendor support will all be significant. It also seems likely that there will be a proliferation of certificate types conforming to the X.509 v3 standard and there are steps to initiate action, such as the registration of certificate variants, to minimize the varieties of certificates and make interoperability easier.

To assist the writers of certificate policies or Certification Practice Statements with their task (but not to define particular certificate policies), a framework that identifies the elements for formulating a certificate policy is highly useful. The main elements of this framework include:

- Authorities
- Authorities and certification
- Community definition and applicability
- Certificate and Certificate Revocation List profiles
- Identification and authentication policy for subjects, registration
- Key management policy
- Legal and business provisions
- Nontechnical security policy
- Operational requirements
- Policy administration
- Technical security policy

The degree to which a certificate user can trust the binding of a certificate (the binding between a name and a public key) depends on such factors as the certification authority policy, the procedures for authentication of end entities, the procedures and security controls, and the policy and procedures of the end entity for handling private keys. The liability assumed by certificate issuers and end entities also plays a role in the degree of trust. A certificate policy allows the users of a certificate to decide how much trust to place in the certificate. A key certificate itself generally provides:

- Alternative names for a certificate subject, a certificate issuer, or a certificate revocation list issuer, and additional attribute information about a certificate subject
- Constraint specifications to be included in Certification Authority certificates (certificates for CAs issued by other CAs) to facilitate the automated processing of certification paths when multiple certificate policies are involved (when policies vary for different applications in an environment or when interoperation with external environments occurs)
- Information about the keys involved, including key identifiers for subject and issuer keys, indicators of intended or restricted key usage, and indicators of certificate policy

To provide these features, specifications and profiles must be available for the format and semantics of certificates. This then allows community- or organization-specific certificate profiles while ensuring interoperability of the different types of certificate. Some communities will need to supplement, or possibly replace, this profile to meet the requirements of specialized application domains or environments with additional authorization, assurance, or operational requirements. Implementations are not required to use any particular cryptographic algorithms.

An alternate to a "full certificate" is that of a simple public key infrastructure certificate (SPKI — ["a simple certificate"]). This grants a specific authority to a public key rather than binding an "identity" (such as a person's name) to that key. For example, one SPKI certificate might grant permission for a given public key to authenticate logins over a specific network on a given host for a period of time.

One of the (perceived) problems of X.509 certificates is that it uses a (technical) abstract syntax notation (ASN.1) to define its data structures. This is in contrast to SPKI certificates, which have a text-based structure. The main driving force behind SPKI is the desire to keep down overheads arising from use of an ASN. 1-based certificate and an infrastructure supporting a global directory, the search for an efficient implementation, and freedom and flexibility to develop structures for a growing number of applications.

The main purpose of an SPKI certificate is to authorize some action, give permission, grant a capability, etc. The first requirement for an SPKI certificate is then to bind a meaningful or useful attribute to a public key (and therefore to the key holder of the corresponding private key). In many cases, the attribute would not involve any recognizable name. The definition of attributes or authorizations in a certificate is up to the author of the application code that uses the certificate. The creation of new authorizations should not require interaction with any other person or organization, but rather be under the total control of the author of the code using the certificate. See the following list of standards and specifications for certificates:

- ANSI X9.5 Extensions to Public Key Certificates and CRLs
- ANSI X9.57 Certificate Management for Financial Services
- European Electronic Signature Standardization Initiative under the auspices of ICTSB
- FIPS 102 Guidelines for Computer Security Certification and Accreditation
- ISO/IEC 9594-8:1995 Information Technology (Open Systems Interconnection) The Directory: Authentication Framework. (ITU-T Recommendation X.509.) Definition of the X509 certificate format for public keys
- ISO/IEC 14888 Digital signatures with appendix; Part 3 defines certificate-based mechanisms
- ISO 15782 Banking — Certificate Management, which describes certification techniques relevant to banking messages
- ISO/IEC 8824-1: 1998 Information technology — Abstract Syntax Notation One (ASN.1): Specification of basic notation
- PKCS #6, which describes a format for extended certificates (Note: PKCS #6 is being phased out in favor of Version 3 of X.509)
- RFC 2459 Internet X.509 Public Key Infrastructure Certificate and CRL Profile
- RFC 2510 Internet X.509 Public Key Infrastructure Certificate Management Protocols
- RFC 2511 Internet X.509 Certificate Request Message Format
- RFC 2527 Internet X.509 Public Key Infrastructure Certificate Policy and Certification Practices Framework

DIGITAL SIGNATURES

From a legal point of view, the concept of "signature" means any mark made with the intention of authenticating the marked document. In an electronic environment, today's broad concept of signature may well include markings such as digitized images of paper signatures, typed notations such as "s/John Smith," or even electronic organizational e-mail headers.

From an information security viewpoint, these "electronic signatures" are entirely different from "digital signatures," although the term "digital signature" is still used colloquially, but incorrectly, tò mean any form of computer-based signature. Digital signatures are irrefutably derived from documents, while electronic signatures simply infer the source of documents through placement of signature.

For transformation using digital signatures, two different electronic keys are generally used: one for creating a digital signature or transforming data into a seemingly unintelligible form, and another key for verifying a digital signature or returning the message to its original form.

A digital signature is a digitally signed hash result of a delimited "block of data" — the message. Typically, it is attached to its message and stored or transmitted with its message. However, it may also be sent or stored as a separate element, as long as it maintains a reliable association with its message. Because a digital signature is unique to its message, it is useless if permanently disassociated from its message. Digital signatures principally allow the verification of the originator or the integrity of a block of data. Following is a list of standards and specifications for digital signatures:

- CEN ENV 12388 Medical Informatics — RSA Algorithm for Digital Signature Services
- Digital Signature Standard/Digital Signature Algorithm (DSS/DSA) from NIST
- European Electronic Signature Standardization Initiative under the auspices of ICTSB
- ISO/IEC 14888 Digital signatures with appendix; Part I defines the general principles
- ISO/IEC 9796 Digital signature scheme giving message recovery
- PKCS #1 Rivest-Shamir-Adelman (RSA) signature; digital signature scheme giving message recovery
- XML Digital Signatures (XMLDSIG) from IETF/W3C

ENCRYPTION

Encryption is generally related either to the encryption of the content or the production of a unique digital signature based on the content. In the former, it is the content that is secured, while the latter secures the authentication (source, timestamp) of the information. See the following standards and specifications for encryption:

- Advanced Encryption Standard (AES) from the U.S. Department of Commerce and NIST
- Data Encryption Standard (DES) from the U.S. Department of Commerce and NIST
- ISO 9735: 1999 EDIFACT (Application level syntax rules) Part 7: Security rules for batch EDI (confidentiality)
- ISO/IEC 10181: 1996 Information Technology (Open Systems Interconnection) Security frameworks for open systems (Part 5: Confidentiality framework)
- RFCs 1968 and 1969 — PPP Encryption
- XML Encryption (XMLENC) from W3C

The W3C has set up a Working Group to develop a process for encrypting/decrypting digital content (including XML documents and portions thereof) and an XML syntax used to represent the (1) encrypted content and (2) information that enables an intended recipient to decrypt it.

KEYS

Keys are very large numeric values that, when applied to an input data stream, produce (via an algorithmic function) an output that is generally an encrypted, unique "summary" of the input — its digital signature — and a confidential output — an encrypted message. Keys are assigned to identified entities (consumers, businesses). Generally, each key belongs to only one entity, although in so-called symmetric cryptosystems, the same key may belong to more than one party (usually two). However, one entity may own multiple keys either through a key-pair arrangement or because the different nature of transactions warrant different keys for the individual arrangements. Keys, digital signatures, and encrypted information are created and verified by means of cryptography, the branch of applied mathematics concerned with transforming information into complex, seemingly unintelligible forms and back again.

The keys used to generate digital signatures and encrypted messages are most commonly generated through algorithms based upon an important feature of large prime numbers: once they are multiplied together to produce a new number, it is virtually impossible to determine which numbers created that new, larger number.

A "symmetric cryptosystem" is one where a single key is used and "owned" by the originating and receiving parties. This has the advantage of being simpler to manage, but the major disadvantage of the inability to prove which of the two parties originated or was involved with the transaction at a precise moment in time. Such a system depends on the parties involved trusting each other not to reveal the key to any other party.

In an "asymmetric cryptosystem," there are two keys — the key-pair. The private key is known only to the signer and is used to create the digital signature. The public key is more widely known and is used to verify the digital signature. A recipient must have the corresponding public key in order to verify that a digital signature is that of the signer. If many people need to verify the signer's digital signatures, the public key must be distributed to all of them, perhaps by publication in an online repository or directory where they can easily obtain it.

Although keys of the pair are mathematically related, it is computationally unfeasible (or at least exceedingly improbable) to derive one key from the other, if the asymmetric cryptosystem has been designed and implemented securely for digital signatures. Although many people will know the public key of a given signer and use it to verify that signer's signature, they cannot discover that signer's private key and use it to forge digital signatures. Refer to the following standards and specifications for keys:

- ISO/IEC 11770 Information Technology (Security techniques) Key Management
- PKCS#8 Private-Key Information Syntax Standard RFC 1422 Privacy Enhancement for Internet Electronic Mail: Part II: Certificate-Based Key Management
- RFC 2408 Internet Security Association and Key Management Protocol (ISAKMP)
- RFC 2409 The Internet Key Exchange (IKE)
- RFC 2528 Representation of Key Exchange Algorithm (KEA) Keys in Internet X.509 Public Key Infrastructure Certificates
- RFC 2631 Diffie-Hellman Key Agreement Method
- XML Key Management (XKMS) from W3C

HASH FUNCTION

A "hash function" is used in both creating and verifying digital signatures. A hash function creates, in effect, a digital freeze frame of the information, by presenting a "code" usually much smaller than the message, but nevertheless is unique to it. This compressed form of the message is often referred to as a "message digest," or fingerprint of the message, in the form of a hash value or hash result and has a standard length. It is virtually impossible to derive the original message from knowledge of the hash value. Hash functions therefore enable the software for creating digital signatures to operate on smaller and predictable amounts of data, while still providing robust evidentiary correlation to the original content, thereby efficiently providing assurance that there has been no modification of the message since it was digitally signed.

If the message changes, the hash result of the message will invariably be different. See the following standards and specifications for the hash function:

- ISO/IEC 10118: Information Technology (Security Techniques) Hash-Functions
- PKCS #1 Rivest-Shamir-Adelman (RSA) signature based on ISO/IEC 9796-2. Digital signature scheme giving message recovery — Mechanisms using a hash-function
- PKCS #5 Password Based Encryption. How to derive a symmetric key from a password using a hash function
- RFC 1319 MD2 Message-Digest Algorithm RFC 1320 MD4 Message-Digest Algorithm RFC 1321 MD5 Message-Digest Algorithm
- Secure Hash System/Secure Hash Algorithm (SHS/SHA)

Appendix F

BASIC CERTIFICATES FOR WEB ADMINISTRATION

Trust used to be all about a handshake — and nothing has changed. Although the Internet has shifted the goalposts, offering an exciting new business platform and a wealth of opportunities, the traditional elements of trust and security remain essential to the success of any enterprise.

SSL WEB SERVER CERTIFICATE ADMINISTRATION

With a Secure Sockets Layer (SSL) Web Server Certificate on your Web site, any information sent to your Web server is encrypted or scrambled, making it impossible to intercept or steal. It also displays the identity of the Web site owner and the name of the independent authority that verified that identity. The Web Server Certificate connects at 128 bit, 56 bit, or 40 bit, depending on the client's browser capability. A SSL Web Server Certificate enables your customers to view the following information:

- *The domain for which the certificate was issued.* This allows them to check that the SSL Web Server Certificate was issued for your domain (URL).
- *The owner of the certificate.* This acts as further reassurance because customers are able to see with whom they are doing business.
- *The physical location of the owner.* Once again, this reassures customers that they are dealing with the actual entity.
- *The validity dates of the certificate.* This is extremely important because it shows users that your SSL Web Server Certificate is current.

0-8493-0822-4/04/$0.00+$1.50
© 2004 by CRC Press LLC

WHY YOU NEED AN SSL WEB SERVER CERTIFICATE

Many online transactions fail at the last minute when consumers consider the potential risks of entering their credit card and other personal information, or when it is not clear whether it is safe to download code from your site. Utilizing a digital SSL "handshake," based on the leading security protocol on the Internet, you and your customers can rest assured that all online communications are secure while the information is being transmitted.

Securing the transmission of information to your enterprise holds obvious benefits, as does signifying that you are a trustworthy online organization. The tried-and-tested technology of SSL Web Server Certificates protects against password and information interception, ensuring that your online relationship with your customers will be one that is based on trust.

WHAT'S IN IT FOR YOU

Again, it is all about trust. By utilizing an SSL Web Server Certificate, you are sending a clear signal to your customers. They know that the information they submit will not be intercepted while in transit, and that you are a verified, real-world organization.

Appendix G

GLOSSARY

Access control: A mechanism for limiting use of some resource (system) to authorized users.

Access control certificate: ADI in the form of a security certificate.

Access control decision function (ADF): A specialized function that makes access control decisions by applying access control policy rules to a requested action, ACI (of initiators, targets, actions, or that retained from prior actions), and the context in which the request is made.

Access control decision information (ADI): The portion (possibly all) of the ACI made available to the ADF in making a particular access control decision.

Access control enforcement function (AEF): A specialized function that is part of the access path between an initiator and a target on each access that enforces the decisions made by the ADF.

Access control information (ACI): Any information used for access control purposes, including contextual information.

Access control list (ACL): A list associated with a resource (system) that specifies the authorized users.

Access control policy: The set of rules that define the conditions under which an access can take place.

Accountability: The property that ensures that the actions of an entity can be traced to that entity.

ACI: Access control information.

ACL: Access control list.

Action: The operations and operands that form part of an attempted access.

Action ADI: Action decision information associated with the action.

Active threat: The threat of a deliberate unauthorized change to the state of the system.

Administrative security information: Persistent information associated with entities; it is conceptually stored in the Security Management Information Base. Examples are security attributes associated with users and set up on user account installation, which is used to configure the user's identity and privileges within the system information configuring a secure interaction policy between one entity and another entity, which is used as the basis for the establishment of operational associations between those two entities.

AEF: Access control enforcement function.

Alarm collector function: A function that collects the security alarm messages, translates them into security alarm records, and writes them to the security alarm log.

Alarm examiner function: A function that interfaces with a security alarm administrator.

API: Application Programming Interface. The interface between the application software and the application platform, across which all services are provided. The application programming interface is primarily in support of application portability, but system and application interoperability are also supported by a communication API.

Assertion: Explicit statement in a system security policy that security measures in one security domain constitute an adequate basis for security measures (or lack of them) in another.

Association-security-state: The collection of information that is relevant to the control of communications security for a particular application-association.

Asymmetric cryptosystem: This is an information system utilizing an algorithm or series of algorithms that provide a cryptographic key-pair consisting of a private key and a corresponding public key. The keys of the pair have the properties that (1) the public key can verify a digital signature that the private key creates, and (2) it is computationally infeasible to discover or derive the private key from the public key. The public key can therefore be disclosed without significantly risking disclosure of the private key. This can be used for confidentiality as well as for authentication.

Audit authority: The manager responsible for defining those aspects of a security policy applicable to maintaining a security audit.

Audit event detector function: A function that detects the occurrence of security-relevant events. This function is normally an inherent part of the functionality implementing the event.

Audit recorder function: A function that records the security-relevant messages in a security audit trail.

Audit trail analyzer function: A function that checks a security audit trail in order to produce, if appropriate, security alarm messages.

Audit trail archiver function: A function that archives a part of the security audit trail.

Audit trail collector function: A function that collects individual audit trail records into a security audit trail.

Audit trail examiner function: A function that builds security reports out of one or more security audit trails.

Audit trail provider function: A function that provides security audit trails according to some criteria.

Authenticated identity: An identity of a principal that has been assured through authentication.

Authentication: This is a function for establishing the validity of a claimed identity of a user, device, or another entity in an information or communication system.

Authentication certificate: Authentication information in the form of a security certificate that may be used to assure the identity of an entity guaranteed by an authentication authority.

Authentication exchange: A sequence of one or more transfers of exchange authentication information (AI) for the purposes of performing an authentication.

Authentication information (AI): Information used to establish the validity of a claimed identity.

Authentication initiator: The entity that starts an authentication exchange.

Authentication method: Method for demonstrating knowledge of a secret. The quality of the authentication method, its strength is determined by the cryptographic basis of the key Architecture for Public-Key Infrastructure (APKI) Draft distribution service on which it is based. A symmetric key-based method, in which both entities share common authentication information, is considered to be a weaker method than an asymmetric key-based method, in which not all the authentication information is shared by both entities.

Authorization: The granting of rights, which includes the granting of access based on access rights.

Authorization policy: A set of rules, part of an access control policy, by which access by security subjects to security objects is granted or denied. An authorization policy can be defined in terms of access control lists, capabilities, or attributes assigned to security subjects, security objects, or both.

Availability: The property of being accessible and usable upon demand by an authorized entity.

Capability: A token used as an identifier for a resource such that possession of the token confers access rights for the resource.

Certificate: A set of information that at least identifies the certification authority issuing the certificate, unambiguously names or identifies its owner, contains the owner's public key, and is digitally signed by the certification authority issuing it.

Certification: This means independently verifying certain information about transactions in the electronic environment.

Certification authority (CA): Someone or something trusted to sign and issue public key certificates.

Certification authority: A certification authority provides to users a digital certificate that links the public key with some assertion about the user, such as identity, credit payment card number, etc. Certification authorities may offer other services such as timestamping, key management services, and certificate revocation services. It can also be defined as an independent trusted source that attests to some factual element of information for the purposes of certifying information in the electronic environment.

Certification Practices Statement (CPS): A statement of the certification authorities' practices with respect to a wide range of technical, business, and legal issues that may be used as a basis for the certification authority's contract with the entity to whom the certificate was issued.

Ciphertext: A message that is encrypted.

Claim authentication information: Information used by a claimant to generate exchange AI needed to authenticate a principal.

Claimant: An entity that is or represents a principal for the purposes of authentication. A claimant includes the functions necessary for engaging in authentication exchanges on behalf of a principal.

Cleartext: A message that is not encrypted.

Client/server: These operations occur between a pair of communicating independent peer processes. The peer process initiating a service request is termed the client. The peer process responding to a service request is termed the server. A process can act as both client and server in the context of a set of transactions.

Closed network/closed user group: These are systems that generally represent those in which certificates are used within a bounded context, such as within a payment system. A contract or series of contracts identify and define the rights and responsibilities of all parties to a particular transaction.

Confidentiality: The property that data or information is not made available or disclosed to unauthorized individuals, entities, or processes.

Contextual information: Information derived from the context in which an access is made (for example, time of day).

Corporate security policy: The set of laws, rules and practices that regulate how assets including sensitive information are managed, protected, and distributed within a user organization.

Countermeasure: The deployment of a set of security services to protect against a security threat.

Credentials: Data that is transferred to establish the claimed identity of an entity.

Cross certification: Practice of mutual recognition of another certification authority is *certificates* to an agreed level of confidence. Usually evidenced in contract.

Cryptanalysis: The analysis of a cryptographic system and its inputs and outputs to derive confidential variables or sensitive data, including cleartext.

Cryptography: The discipline that embodies principles, means, and methods for the transformation of data in order to hide its information content, establish its authenticity, prevent its undetected modification, prevent its repudiation, or prevent its unauthorized use.

Cryptographic algorithm: A method of performing a cryptographic transformation (see cryptography) on a data unit. Cryptographic algorithms can be based on symmetric key methods (the same key is used for both encipher and decipher transformations) or on asymmetric keys (different keys are used for encipher and decipher transformations).

Cryptographic checkvalue: Information that is derived by performing a cryptographic transformation on a data unit.

Cryptographic key: A parameter used with a cryptographic algorithm to transform, validate, authenticate, encrypt, or decrypt data.

Data integrity: The property that data has not been altered or destroyed in an unauthorized manner.

Data origin authentication: The corroboration that the entity responsible for the creation of a set of data is the one claimed.

Decipherment: The reversal of a corresponding reversible encipherment.

Decrypt: To undo the encryption process.

Denial-of-Service: The unauthorized prevention of authorized access to resources or the delaying of time-critical operations.

Digital fingerprint: A characteristic of a data item, such as a cryptographic checkvalue or the result of performing a one-way hash function on the data, that is sufficiently peculiar to the data item that it is computationally infeasible to find another data item that possesses the same characteristics.

Digital signature: Data appended to a message that allows a recipient of the message to prove the source and integrity of the message.

Directory service: A service provided on a computer network that allows one to look up addresses (and perhaps other information such as public key certificates) based upon user-names.

Discretionary access control: A discretionary authorization scheme is one under which any principal using the domain services can be authorized to assign or modify ACI such that he may modify the authorizations of other principals under the scheme. A typical example is an ACL scheme that is often referred to as Discretionary Access Control (DAC).

Distinguishing identifier: Data that unambiguously distinguishes an entity in the authentication process. Such an identifier shall be unambiguous at least within a security domain.

Distributed application: A set of information processing resources distributed over one or more open systems and which provides a well-defined set of functionality to (human) users, to assist a given (office) task.

Electronic commerce: Is a broad concept that covers any trade or commercial transaction that is effected via electronic means; this would include such means as facsimile, telex, EDI, Internet, and the telephone. For the purpose of this book, the term is limited to those commercial transactions involving computer-to-computer communications, whether utilizing an open or closed network.

Electronic data interchange (EDI): A system allowing for inter-corporate commerce by the automated electronic exchange of structured business information.

Electronic signature: Any symbol or method executed or adopted by a party with the present intention to be bound by or to authenticate a record accomplished by electronic means.

Encapsulated subsystem: A collection of procedures and data objects that is protected in a domain of its own so that the internal structure of a data object is accessible only to the procedures of the encapsulated subsystem and that those procedures may be called only at designated domain entry points. Encapsulated subsystem, protected subsystem, and protected mechanisms of the TCB are terms that can be used interchangeably.

Encipherment: The cryptographic transformation of data (see cryptography) to produce ciphertext.

Encrypt: To scramble information so that only someone knowing the appropriate secret can obtain the original information (through decryption).

Encryption: The transformation of data by the use of cryptography to produce unintelligible data (encrypted data) to ensure its confidentiality.

End-to-end encipherment: Encipherment of data within or at the source end system, with the corresponding decipherment occurring only within or at the destination end system.

Exchange authentication information: Information exchanged between a claimant and a verifier during the process of authenticating a principal.

Hash function/hashing: A hash function is a mathematical process based on an algorithm that creates a digital representation or compressed form of the message. It is often referred to as the message digest in the form of a hash value or hash result of a standard length which is usually much smaller than the message, but nevertheless substantially unique to it.

Identification: The assignment of a name by which an entity can be referenced. The entity can be high level (such as a user) or low level (such as a process or communication channel).

Identity-based security policy: A security policy based on the identities or attributes of users, a group of users, or entities acting on behalf of the users and the resources or targets being accessed.

Initiator: An entity (e.g., human user or computer-based entity) that attempts to access other entities.

Initiator access control decision information: ADI associated with the initiator.

Initiator access control information: Access control information relating to the initiator.

Integrity: The property that data or information has not been modified or altered in an unauthorized manner.

Key: A quantity (number) used in cryptography to encrypt or decrypt information.

Key management: The generation, storage, distribution, deletion, archiving, and application of keys in accordance with a security policy.

Masquerade: The unauthorized pretence by an entity to be a different entity.

Messaging application: An application based on a store-and-forward paradigm; it requires an appropriate security context to be bound with the message itself.

Non-discretionary access control: A non-discretionary authorization scheme is one under which only the recognized security authority of the security domain can assign or modify the ACI for the authorization scheme such that the authorizations of principals under the scheme are modified.

Non-repudiation: A property achieved through cryptographic methods that prevents an individual or entity from denying having performed a particular action related to data (such as mechanisms for non-rejection or authority [origin]; for proof of obligation, intent, or commitment; or for proof of ownership).

Offline authentication certificate: A particular form of authentication information binding an entity to a cryptographic key, certified by a trusted authority, which can be used for authentication without directly interacting with the authority.

Online authentication certificate: A particular form of authentication information, certified by a trusted authority, that can be used for authentication following direct interaction with the authority.

Open network/system: Network or system in which, at the extremes, unknown parties, possibly in a different state or national jurisdictions, will exchange or trade data. To do this will require an overarching framework that will engender trust and certainty. A user of online services might go through a single authentication process with a trusted third party, receive certification of their public key, and then be able to enter into electronic transactions/data exchanges with merchants, governments, banks, etc., using the certificate so provided for multiple purposes.

Operational security information: Transient information related to a single operation or set of operations within the context of an operational association (e.g., a user session). Operational security information represents the current security context of the operations and can be passed as parameters to the operational primitives or retrieved from the operations environment as defaults.

Organizational security policy: The set of laws, rules, and practices that regulates how an organization manages, protects, and distributes sensitive information.

Password: Confidential authentication information, usually composed of a string of characters.

Peer-entity authentication: The corroboration that a peer entity in an association is the one claimed.

Physical security: The measures used to provide physical protection of resources against deliberate and accidental threats.

Platform domain: A security domain encompassing the operating system, the entities and operations it supports, and its security policy.

Primary service: An independent category of service such as operating system services, communication services, and data management services. Each primary service provides a discrete set of functionality. Each primary service inherently includes generic qualities such as usability, manageability, and security. Security services are therefore not primary services but are invoked as part of the provision of primary services by the primary service provider.

Principal: An entity whose identity can be authenticated.

Privacy: The right of individuals to control or influence what information related to them can be collected and stored, and by whom and to whom that information can be disclosed.

Private key: The private or secret key of a key-pair that must be kept confidential and is used to decrypt messages encrypted with the public key, or to digitally sign messages that can then be validated with the public key.

Public key: A key whose value can be published widely without compromising encryption or digital signature processes. Typically, a public key can be used to encrypt but not decrypt, or to validate a signature but not to sign.

Public key cryptography: An asymmetric cryptosystem where the encrypting and decrypting keys are different and it is computationally infeasible to calculate one from the other, given the encrypting algorithm. In public key cryptography, the encrypting key is made public but the decrypting key is kept secret.

Public key infrastructure (PKI): Supporting infrastructure, including nontechnical aspects, for the management of public keys.

Relying third party: The entity, such as a merchant, offering goods or services online that will receive a certificate as part of a process of completing a transaction with the user.

Repudiation: Denying that you did something, or sent some message.

Secret key cryptography: A cryptographic system where encryption and decryption are performed using the same key.

Sign a message: To use your private key to generate a digital signature as a means of proving you generated, or to certify, some message.

Signature (digital): A quantity (number) associated with a message that only someone with knowledge of your private key could have generated, but which can be verified through knowledge of your public key.

Signature Dynamics: A form of electronic signatures that involves the biometric recording of the pen dynamics used in signing the document.

Timestamping: An electronic equivalent of mail franking.

Trading partner agreement: This is a contractual arrangement that specifies the legal terms and conditions under which parties operate when conducting transactions by the use of EDI. It may cover such things as validity and formation of contract; admissibility in evidence of EDI messages; processing and acknowledgment of receipt of EDI messages; security; confidentiality, and protection of personal data; recording and storage of EDI messages; operational requirements for EDI message standards, codes, transaction and operations logs; technical specifications and requirements; liability, including use of intermediaries and third-party service providers; dispute resolution; and applicable law.

Trusted third party (TTP): An entity trusted by other entities with respect to security-related services and activities, such as a certification authority.

User/subscriber: An individual procuring goods or services online who obtains a certificate from a certification authority. Because both consumers and merchants can have digital certificates that are used to conclude a transaction, they may both be subscribers in certain circumstances. This person may also be referred to as the signer of a digital signature or the sender of a data message signed with a digital signature.

Verify: To determine accurately that (1) the digital signature was created by the private key corresponding to the public key; and (2) the message has not been altered since its digital signature was created.

Verify a signature: Perform a cryptographic calculation using a message, a signature for the message, and a public key to determine whether the signature was generated by someone knowing the corresponding private key.

X.509: A standard that is part of the X.500 specifications and defines the format of a public key certificate.

INDEX

INDEX